# ANNE BOLEYN

The daughter of a British diplomat, Marie Louise Bruce was born in Rio de Janeiro and spent some months at an American school in Panama. She took an honours degree at Oxford University where she part-owned and edited *Cherwell* magazine. *Anne Boleyn* is her first book. She is married to historian, writer and journalist, George Bruce. They live in the Thames Valley with their three children and one dog.

D1100581

Marie Louise Bruce

# ANNE BOLEYN

Pan Books Ltd  London and Sydney

First published 1972 by William Collins Sons & Co Ltd
This edition published 1975 by
Pan Books Ltd, Cavaye Place, London SW10 9PG
ISBN 0 330 24348 9
© Marie Louise Bruce 1972
Printed in Great Britain by
Richard Clay (The Chaucer Press) Ltd, Bungay, Suffolk

# CONTENTS

# ACKNOWLEDGEMENTS

Among the many people who have helped me in different ways, I am grateful to Lord Astor for valuable information and for his kindness in showing me round Hever Castle. I should also like to thank the following: the Rev. J. B. Collins for information on the graves of Anne Boleyn's brothers in the churches of Hever and Penshurst; Dr Neville Williams for greatly facilitating my researches in the Public Record Office; Dr J. Gledhill Russell, lecturer in History at St Hugh's College, Oxford, for assistance on the subject of Lutheran ritual in Germany; Mr John P. Brooke-Little, Richmond Herald, for his analysis of coats-of-arms; Miss Elizabeth M. Walter of Collins for her constructive criticism; and Mr R. Black for his translation of the indictments read at Queen Anne's trial. No acknowledgement of help would be complete without mention of my husband's constant encouragement and professional advice. I should also like to thank the staffs of the National Portrait Gallery, British Museum, Ashmolean Museum, London Library, Bodleian Library and Reading Public Library for their assistance; as well as Mrs Elizabeth Webb and Mrs Pearl Brennan for their prompt and painstaking typing.

# ILLUSTRATIONS

# Chapter 1

# THE YOUNGEST BOLEYN

THE new baby was remarkable for three things: the opaqueness of her eyes that could never become anything but darkest brown, a large black mole on her neck and a small deformity of the right hand, where a tiny second nail grew out of one of her fingers. Later when she had grown into a woman, it was to be magnified into a sixth finger by enemies anxious to depict her physically as well as spiritually a monster. But as she lay swaddled in her solid oak cradle beside a curtained and canopied bed in a room heavy with the odours of confinement and the scent of sweet herbs, Anne Boleyn's prospects were as good as gold.

No parish records were then kept, so Anne's birth was unrecorded, but the scholar, historian and antiquary William Camden, in his *History of Queen Elizabeth*, published in 1615, sets it as 1507, a date which fits in with other clues we have and which is positively confirmed in a life of Jane Dormer, Duchess of Feria. The Duchess, a friend of Queen Mary I of England, was born in 1538, and her biographer, Henry Clifford, was for many years a member of her household, so is a trustworthy source. Like her date of birth, the place where Anne first opened her huge dark eyes has been the subject of argument and speculation, both Blickling Hall near Aylsham and Rochford Hall in Essex laying claim to the honour. It was, however, much more likely to have been Hever Castle, ornamenting with its façade, then painted in brilliant colours, the pleasant water meadows of Kent and set in a fork of the sparkling little River Eden.

Hever Castle is a misleading name, for this is no bristling fortress, but an attractive manor house first built by a prosperous Norfolk merchant, Sir Geoffrey Boleyn - Mayor from 1457 to 1458 of the city of London - within already old fortified walls and a broad moat. Half a century later it was here that his grandson, Thomas Boleyn, an ambitious courtier in his twenties, brought his wife Elizabeth across the creaking draw-bridge and the dark waters of the moat, beneath the menacing portcullises and thence, suddenly, into a most unmilitary small cobbled courtyard, where leaded windows adorned timbered walls and rose-red many-sided chimneys pointed at the passing clouds.

In the dangerous unstable life of the King's Court, Thomas Boleyn had not at the turn of the fifteenth century made much headway. Required by King Henry VII to be in attendance on certain ceremonial occasions, in 1501 he was present at the marriage of the fifteen-year-olds, Prince Arthur, heir to the English throne, and Catherine of Aragon; and in 1503 he attended on Princess Margaret in her progress to Scotland as bride of King James IV.

But Boleyn had no official appointment at Court and, in the early years of his marriage before Anne was born, only fifty pounds a year with which to clothe himself in the customary velvets, satins and jewels and to provide for his house in the country, his family and his servants. With the provisions from the home farm as well as the game from the park, without which no large Tudor residence was viable, the Boleyn house-hold made ends meet; although Elizabeth was almost embar-rassingly fruitful. 'She brought me every year a child,' Boleyn was to write years later in shuddering reminiscence, for the memory of that genteel poverty was to haunt him all his life.

Infant mortality was at the time, however, high, and two of these children who so strained Boleyn's slender financial re-sources, Henry and Thomas, died early, to be commemorated by two small brass crosses which can still be seen on the stone floors of the neighbouring churches of Hever and of Penshurst. Three children survived, George, born about 1503, Mary about 1504, and Anne, the youngest.

Hard up though they were when first married, fortunately for the Boleyns they were also related to two powerful families, both of which claimed descent from King Edward I. Through her mother Elizabeth, Anne was granddaughter of the Earl of Surrey, High Treasurer of England, who was to become in

1514 Duke of Norfolk, head of the Howards. Though temporarily also short of money through having found themselves
on the Plantagenet side at the end of the Wars of the Roses, the
Howards had soon regained their influence at Court. Through
her father, Anne was the great-granddaughter of the rich Earl
of Ormond, possessor of the major areas of Tipperary and
Kilkenny as well as seventy-two manors in England. Ormond
would live until 1515 but his son-in-law William was less
lucky. He died in 1505, leaving Thomas Boleyn eight manors.

So by Anne's birth date two years later, the shadow of
genteel poverty had already lifted from the stone towers and
raftered rooms of Hever Castle. And by the time Anne was
toddling about the rush-strewn floors of her nursery and
reaching up to the scented herbs on the window-sills, Thomas's
career had taken a dramatic step forward too. The ageing King
Henry VII had appointed him to that much-coveted position
among the lesser courtiers, Esquire to the Body, a position
which had the clear advantage of giving access to the monarch
in days when he was the chief source of wealth and power, of
preferment and perquisites.

Thomas Boleyn, as one of Henry's six Esquires, slept on a
pallet within call, personally dressed the King in the royal
Bed Chamber, with garments handed to him on the threshold
by a groom who was forbidden to enter, and who, in his turn,
had received the sacred garment from the Yeoman of the
Wardrobe at the door of the Privy Chamber.

When in 1509 the old King Henry VII died, to be replaced by
his athletic, seventeen-year-old son as Henry VIII, Boleyn at the
age of thirty-two somehow hung on to his position in the royal
household. It's new master, who before Prince Arthur's death
had been intended for the Church, and spent his childhood
secluded from the world, living in apartments whose only door
opened out of his father's rooms, forbidden to speak to any but
specially selected people and allowed to walk only in the royal
park, now emerged from this cocoon-like existence into the
sudden brilliance and freedom of life as a King, He was suggest-
ible and easily flattered. Boleyn made profitable use of these fail-
ings in the monarch's character.

The young Henry, reacting against his upbringing, ushered

in his spectacular reign by executing his father's two tax-collectors, Empson and Dudley, then squandering the carefully hoarded money. He turned the sober Court of his parsimonious father into a gorgeous display of colour and gaiety and music; he masked and danced to the sound of lute, fife and tabor; built great tiltyards, adorned them with stands and tiny towers for the audience, and himself thundered down the lists where, emblazoned with some cryptic message of love, he jousted for his lady's favour like the knights in the old romances.

Boleyn forced himself to take part in these simple entertainments, to dress up in the exotic disguise of a Moor or a Muscovite and revel in the palace banqueting rooms, to risk being swept from his horse in the tiltyard by the lance and superior weight of the King, six feet two inches tall with massive shoulders and limbs and an aggressive spirit to match. Boleyn was a man with ambition, few scruples, more than average intelligence and the foresight to become a fluent speaker of French, a rare attainment among his contemporaries at Court.

Henry was quick to recognize the usefulness of such a servant. As Anne grew from toddler to little girl, dressed in the clothes of a miniature adult – consisting of a smock or 'shirt', the only undergarment worn, stockings with garters, petticoats and long gown, her father rose steadily in the royal favour. He was created Knight of the Bath at the coronation; Keeper of the Exchange at Calais and of the Foreign Exchange in England three months later. In 1511 he became sheriff of Kent; in 1512 joint constable of Norwich Castle. That same year he was appointed Ambassador to the Emperor, Maximilian, and the following year, Ambassador to Margaret of Savoy, Archduchess of Austria and Regent of the Netherlands. Boleyn's embassy to Margaret was to have important repercussions on the lives of both Anne and her elder sister Mary.

By this time her father was well able to afford a larger household than Hever. But a larger household meant more servants, more beef, mutton and ale, more costly hangings and tapestries for the walls, more expense. Boleyn, like Henry VII, did not enjoy expense. And so at Hever the family remained, moving to another manor only when it was strictly necessary to have the house cleaned for fear of the plague, that dreaded summer visitor known in England because of its most obvious symptom as 'the sweat'.

From what we know of Anne in later life we can imagine her at the age of six a black-haired, black-eyed child with a terrible temper, a gift for wild infectious gaiety and a corresponding moodiness. Like all children of her class, she would have been cared for mainly by servants, her mother, Lady Elizabeth Boleyn, being too busy managing the household and farm to give her much attention. Nevertheless, an affectionate warm relationship did grow up between Anne and her mother.

Elizabeth Boleyn, eldest daughter of the Earl of Surrey by his first marriage, is a somewhat shadowy woman about whom history tells us far too little. She must have possessed some of the sexual magnetism and gaiety of her daughters, for her sole claim to personal notice rests on a scandalous tale about her relationship with the young King Henry VIII - a scandal that became current years later, repeated by Catholic writers in the hope of discrediting Anne: she was Henry's daughter by her mother. It was an implausible tale, which Henry furiously denied. Apart from this one unhappy venture into the limelight of history Elizabeth retires once more into oblivion, never again achieving notice or position on her own account at Court. Often there in later years, she is rarely mentioned. Alone among the Boleyn family she is responsible neither for explosively provocative comments nor for love dramas, an apparently gentle, self-effacing woman whose influence on her children paled beside her husband's. And despite Anne's affection for her mother, it was her father's ambitious thrusting nature that was to drive her throughout her life.

Anne's father's character is plain for all to see in the coloured drawing by Holbein. In the expensive but tasteless clothes, the huge slashed sleeves, the fashionable velvet cap aslant his bobbed hair, Boleyn is an impressive figure: broad-shouldered, bull-necked, with strong features, dark hair and reddish beard - a handsome man. There is yet a terrible neurotic fixation about Boleyn's face, a flatness of the blue eyes, a lack of warmth in the unsmiling mouth. Boleyn's dominant emotion was avarice, a characteristic he was to hand down to his most famous descendant, the future Queen Elizabeth. His love for his children was closely involved with their chances of worldly success for which he laid careful plans, paying particular attention to the education of his daughters.

Girls and boys of royal birth in the sixteenth century were given the same rigorous intellectual education, but the lowlier daughters of the English aristocracy, like Anne, were taught little beyond basic reading, writing and the social accomplishments of the day. To learn these a girl was normally sent away at the age of about seven to live in the house of some great noblewoman, where she would learn to ride side-saddle, to hawk and to hunt, chasing hares with her own hound, shooting deer with a bow and arrow while standing on a specially made platform in the deer park; she would learn to sing, dance and play the lute, and most important of all, to conform to the laws of courtesy, that mixture of etiquette, good manners and chivalry that was considered the cornerstone of a sixteenth-century noblewoman's upbringing.

This included how to kneel when speaking to royalty, and how to conduct herself at the complicated ceremony of dinner, the main meal of the day, which took place at mid-morning in the great hall, where the whole household gathered – the lord and his guests sitting at a table on the dais looking down on those of humbler degree. The daily ritual involved many points of deportment. The young girl would be taught how to sit up straight at a trestle table on a wooden form (for chairs were reserved only for most important people); how to wash her hands in a ewer before and after the meal; how to cope at a sitting with twenty different dishes, which in a nobleman's household was the average number and consisted of a much wider variety of meat and fish than is eaten today, anything from peacocks or swans to porpoise and peas. Many different dishes were served at a course, each course being announced by a fanfare of trumpets and brought in in solemn procession by the household officials. She would learn how to eat delicately and efficiently with knife and fingers – for forks were not generally used in England until the reign of James I; how to take salt with her knife instead of dipping her food in the big communal salt-cellar as the common people did. And she would herself take her turn carving for and waiting on the noble-woman in whose care she had been placed.

All these things Anne and Mary had of course to learn. But they must learn more. Boleyn sought for them not so much an intellectual education as that extra polish and breadth that would attract attention at Court and help them to make advantageous marriages; for though most of these were ar-ranged there was still a small leeway for attraction. A daughter who married well could benefit her father by providing useful connections; and the fortunes of the Boleyns – only three generations ago an obscure Norfolk family – were virtually founded on a succession of brilliant marriages.

Anne's great-grandfather, Geoffrey Boleyn, the silk and wool merchant who rose to be Mayor of London, had also contrived to marry the heiress daughter of Lord Hoo; Anne's grand-father William Boleyn married Margaret, younger daughter of the Earl of Ormond; and Anne's father had continued the family tradition by marrying a member of the illustrious Howard family. Boleyn ambitiously decided to have his daughters educated, not in the horsy, hearty atmosphere of some large country manor, but at Court; not in England, but abroad, where new forms of art, new ideas, were more quickly accepted and the Renaissance was already in full bloom.

Thomas Boleyn's embassy of 1513 brought him the acquain-tance of Margaret, Archduchess of Austria, Regent of the Netherlands. The Archduchess accepted his proposal that his elder daughter should come to her as Maid of Honour. And Mary, a pretty, engaging, precocious little girl, was duly packed off to the Court at Brussels, where Margaret was delighted with her. Enthusiastically she wrote:

I have received your letter by the Esquire Bouton, who presented to me your daughter, who was very welcome to me, and I hope to treat her in such a fashion that you will have reason to be content with it; at least be sure that until your return there need be no other intermediary between you and me than she; and I find her of such good address and so pleasing in her youthful age that I am more beholden to you for having sent her to me than you are to me.

Encouraging indeed was the success of Boleyn's first attempt at launching a daughter into a foreign Court. It tempted him to be even more ambitious. If Mary was such a success at ten, why not Anne at seven? And why should they not both be brought up in fashionable France?

In 1514 the betrothal of Henry VIII's sister, the gay and beautiful eighteen-year-old Princess Mary, to the old and ailing Louis XII of France, gave Boleyn the opportunity he wanted. He despatched an escort to Brussels with a letter for the Archduchess:

'My very dear and renowned lady, I recommend myself as humbly as possible to your good graces.' He went on to say that the King's sister, Princess Mary, had requested the company of his daughter on her approaching trip to France and to ask Margaret, very humbly again, to release her. This the Archduchess did, and Mary became one of the Queen's women in the distinguished company of the two sisters of the Marquis of Dorset, the sister of Lord Grey and the daughter of Lord Dacre – a group of young girls, all under the supervision of Lady Guildford. Boleyn arranged for Anne to accompany them, although she was too young to have any official position.

In the stormy autumn of 1514, seven-year-old Anne, a miniature lady on horseback, with her father and her elder sister, joined the gorgeous cavalcade that rode in damasks and satins, in velvets and gold chains from the Court to Dover. Led by the King and his short, smiling, visibly pregnant Spanish Queen, all the chief courtiers travelled down to see the Princess safely launched on the grey seas for France. It was probably Anne's first sight of the King, now twenty-three and, according to Piero Pasqualigo, the Ambassador Extraordinary from Venice, a paragon of manly beauty and accomplishment.

His Majesty is the handsomest potentate I ever set eyes upon: above the usual height, with an extremely fine calf to his leg, his complexion very fair and bright, with auburn hair combed straight and short in the French fashion, and a round face so very beautiful that it would become a pretty woman, his throat being rather long and thick . . . He speaks French, English and Latin, and a little Italian, plays well on the lute and harpsichord, sings from the book at sight, draws the bow with greater strength than any man in England, and jousts marvellously.

To the Boleyn children, whose father's career depended on him, this young Henry VIII must have been a dazzling figure indeed. But in the sixteenth century even so splendid and powerful a creature as the King of England had to defer to wind and weather when it came to crossing the Channel.

On reaching Dover they found the sea so wild they had to wait several days in the castle before it was safe to load the Princess's horses, dowry and wardrobe on board, for the Princess and her numerous escort, including Boleyn, to embark, and for the little fleet to cast anchor.

In the small hours of the morning of 2 October 1514, vaguely resplendent in the flickering torchlight, the young King came gallantly down to the harbour to kiss his favourite sister and wish her godspeed. At four o'clock the dark water was calm; the ships set sail. But before they had gone a quarter of the way, the wind suddenly rose again and scattered the vessels, some ships making for Flanders, some for Calais and the Princess's for Boulogne, where the Captain ran aground before they reached harbour and the terrified passengers had to take to the boats. Sir Christopher Garnish, a gentleman of great presence of mind – and considerable strength – gallantly ran into the water, picked up the Princess and carried her in his arms to dry land.

But lesser ladies, and the Boleyn children, had to rely on tiny French row-boats to convey them to shore, where the official reception awaited. In Boulogne the royal company rested to recover from their experience before riding on by easy stages to Abbeville, where seven-year-old Anne had a foretaste of the pomp and triumph of a royal wedding.

Through the gates in the ramparts of this ancient town Princess Mary, future Queen of France, made a magnificent ceremonial entry. The graceful Princess, in cloth of silver, rode a horse caparisoned in gold, and was followed by a train of thirty-six ladies, which almost certainly included the two Boleyn children. The ladies rode palfreys caparisoned in embroidered crimson velvet, a colour that would have contrasted well with Anne's dark hair and eyes. They were followed by three chariots, one covered in cloth of tissue, the second in cloth of gold, and the third in crimson velvet, embroidered with the arms of the French King and the English Princess and 'full of roses'. After those came companies of archers, then wagons laden with plate, jewels, money, apparel and wall-hangings.

The next day in the high vaulted space and rainbow light of the newly-built church, Anne saw the impressive mediæval service of the King's marriage to the Princess, both clothed all in gold, heard the chanting of the choristers, the sonorous Latin plainsong. But immediately after the wedding the prematurely senile, jealous Louis rudely dismissed all his wife's more experienced ladies, including Lady Guildford, leaving the Princess with no one to attend on her but a group of young girls, among whom were Mary and Anne.

It was a doleful situation but not one to last long. Princess Mary plunged the Court into an orgy of gaiety, feasts and dances that wrought havoc with King Louis's already failing health. Less than three months after the wedding in the great church of Abbeville, King Louis died, leaving the widowed Queen to be closely confined according to custom for six weeks in the Hôtel de Cluny - a measure at least as practical as it was sentimental since six weeks would show whether or not a posthumous heir to the throne was on the way. None was.

The mourning period over, the King of England sent the Duke of Suffolk to bring his sister home again. It was the beginning of a love drama as exciting as any in Malory's recently printed *Morte D'Arthur*, the popular literature of the day.


Henry Brandon, Duke of Suffolk, short-sighted and in his thirties, had risen to power largely through physical attributes. The son of Henry VII's standard-bearer, he was a man of no particular intelligence but superb looks; as tall and almost as broad as the King, with dense black hair and beard, a marvellous strength and vitality, he was a huge hearty extrovert and just the companion the King needed for his rumbustious revels and athletic pursuits. He had received his dukedom in 1514 and had been christened the King's *alter ego* by a Venetian ambassador. He was also irresistible to women. Princess Mary had set her heart on him before her wedding to Louis and had extracted from her brother Henry a promise: if Louis should die she might be allowed to choose her own next husband. But Mary Tudor knew her brother too well to trust him to keep it. Loath to become the victim of another dynastic marriage, Princess Mary, with a Tudor determination that belied her roselike appearance, forced the nervous Suffolk to marry her secretly in France, before returning to face her brother's wrath in England and eventually to receive his forgiveness. Mary Tudor's example was to give Anne altogether the wrong idea about King Henry's clemency in matters of love.

That Princess Mary - or the French Queen as she was henceforth known - had returned to England, did not distract Boleyn from his purpose.

In France the Boleyn children remained. Exactly where is uncertain. Anne, according to one theory, stayed for some time in the household of a nobleman friend of her father's near Paris in the tiny village of Briis-sous-Forges, while Boleyn persisted doggedly in his determined efforts to find a new place for his daughters at the French Court. He managed to find one for Mary. Finally, he wrote triumphantly to tell Anne that he had been successful in placing her too. She was to become one of the select group of girls under the patronage of Claude, Queen of King Louis's twenty-year-old successor, the elegant, long-nosed, sensual, witty King Francis I.

Sternly, Boleyn wrote telling Anne of her good fortune, advising her to study hard at speaking and writing French, on pain of forfeiting his goodwill to advance her interests. It was no idle threat; Boleyn was never to have any patience with members of his family who failed to use their chances. We still have Anne's letter of reply. Dictated in French by her governess called Semmonet, full of phrases and misspelt words the child could not understand, it still shows the hold her ambitious father exercised over her and her conscientious desire to please him:

Sir,

I understand by your letter that you wish that I shall be
of all virtuous repute when I come to the Court and you
inform me that the Queen will take the trouble to converse
with me, which rejoices me greatly to think of talking with a
person so wise and virtuous. This will make me have greater
desire to continue to speak French well and also spell,
especially because you have so recommended me to do so,
and with my own hand I inform you that I will observe it
the best I can. Sir, I beg you to excuse me if my letter is
badly written, for I assure you that the spelling is from my
own understanding alone, whereas the others were only
written by my hand, and Semmonet tells me the letter will
wait unless I do it myself, for fear that it shall not be known
unless I write to you, and I pray you that in the light of
what you see you will not feel free to part from the will
which you say you have to help me. For it seems that you
are sure where you can, if you please, make me a declaration
of your word, and on my part be certain that there shall be
neither [ ? ?] nor ingratitude which might check or efface my
affection, which is determined to [ ?] as much unless it shall
please you to order me, and I promise you that my love is
based on such great firmness that it will never grow less,
and I will make an end to my [ ?] after having commended
myself right humbly to your good grace. Written at five
o'clock by

Your very humble and obedient daughter

*Anna de Boullan*

Boleyn was pleased with his daughter's letter, for he kept it
carefully; and Anne joined Queen Claude's group of young
girls at the French Court.

There, in the palaces of Les Tournelles in Paris and many-
pinnacled Amboise near the swift-flowing Loire, at the heart of
sophisticated and corrupt Renaissance France, Anne Boleyn
was to spend all the formative years of her childhood and
adolescence.

*Chapter 2*

# A FRENCH EDUCATION

ANNE BOLEYN'S education in France was influenced by two opposing attitudes in the King's Court; a devout, almost monastic religious piety; and a rampant eroticism disguised by the gallant conventions of 'courtly love'. Both were to have a profound influence on Anne's character and future life.

Anne's patroness, the small, square, kindly Queen Claude, seemed to Thomas Boleyn the perfect choice to supervise his daughter's upbringing. Famed for her moral excellence – after her death it was suggested that she should be canonized – it seemed her ambition to impart this to the daughters of all the noble families of France, for she kept as many as three hundred girls at a time under her wing, inculcating morality and devout thoughts as if they were destined for the nunnery. Like the rest of these *demoiselles*, Mary and Anne Boleyn were kept bent over their religious texts or plying their needles hour after hour, while being forbidden the society of men.

Claude's household, however, was a small beleaguered island of piety surrounded by the ever-encroaching sea of the Court, a flood of sensuousness, inspired by her husband King Francis I. From his victorious campaign in Italy, that flamboyant young monarch had returned in 1516 himself conquered by the beauty of the new Italian art, a collection of fine paintings by Raphael carefully stowed away in his baggage, and most important of all, that great genius Leonardo da Vinci among his retinue. The Italian was to stay and paint for the King in France until his death in 1519.

Anne's visual sensibility could not fail to be stimulated by what she saw in France, to which we must attribute the elegance of dress for which she was later famed, her love of fine furnishings and buildings. While over the Channel in England

King Henry and his nobles still happily added courtyards and windows and ponderous gatehouses at random to their already rambling manors, in France it was a different story. Among her green plains and forests Renaissance châteaux sprang up, examples of the new symmetry; Azay-le-Rideau, a miracle of lightness and grace, Chenonceaux, and Francis's own fairytale folly of Chambord.

But Francis not only encouraged artists and architects. He was a patron of everything beautiful; including women.

The richly-hung rooms of his palaces, with ceilings patterned in intricate designs of rare woods, were a-whisper with romantic intrigues. And the youthful Francis, long-legged and slant-eyed, boldly set the moral tone himself, parading his favourite mistress, madonna-faced Françoise de Foix, at the same Court functions as the Queen. Francis openly encouraged his courtiers to have affairs, writes the Seigneur de Brantôme, relating what his grandmother, lady-in-waiting to the King's sister Marguerite, had told him. 'The King wished none of the gentlemen of his Court to be without mistresses, and thought they were strutting fops if they had none.'

Often he would ask one courtier or another his mistress's name and would then promise to be her servant and to speak well of her . . . Often too, when he saw a gentleman having an argument with his mistress, he would accost him and ask what was the great talk he was having with her; and if he found the gentleman ill-disposed, would correct him and teach him better manners. . . He was very curious to know of the loves of this one and that; especially he liked descriptions of amorous combats, with details of the lady's expression when being ridden, of her position and movements and utterances. How he would laugh over these, often throwing back his head and roaring. But afterwards he would forbid the publication as scandalous, saying that honour decreed secrecy.

Though ribaldry sometimes broke through his own gallant attitude to the fair sex, King Francis insisted on a more constant politeness among his courtiers. On one occasion he carried this attitude to extremes. Hearing that a gentleman waiter had made a ribald joke at the expense of a group of ladies he was serving at dinner, he ordered him to be taken out and hanged immediately; fortunately for the gentleman in question he was given time to escape.

To this morally loose atmosphere at Court, Francis's Queen imposed her own pious influence in vain. She could not guard her girls for long. Claude herself was almost continuously pregnant and sickly; her society was worthy but dull. The gentlemen of the Court from the King to the Cardinal of Lorraine, according to Brantôme's gossiping grandmother, were on the lookout for new beauties; the maturing girls were eager for sensation. Her pathetic little island of sobriety in the midst of the whirlpool of Court gaiety was bound to become engulfed.

At the age of at most fifteen, probably younger, Anne's sister Mary Boleyn escaped from the island to become first the mistress of the King and then of one courtier after another. Francis ungallantly christened her his English mare in reference to the number of times he had 'ridden' her, and was to refer to her years later as '*una grandissima ribalda, et infame sopra tutte*' (a great prostitute and infamous above all).

Warm-hearted and ductile, Mary Boleyn made the mistake of scattering her favours too widely and making her affairs too public. It was one thing to be the King's mistress; quite another to be known to be at everyone's disposal. Even at the lascivious French Court there was a code of discretion; Mary had offended it. She was either sent or withdrawn hastily to England.

The lesson of Mary's disgrace was not to be wasted on her little sister. It is doubtless at this time that Thomas and Elizabeth Boleyn's disapproval of their elder daughter was born. Her father and even her gentle mother developed feelings of dislike; her sister Anne alone retained an affection for her, demonstrated in her protective attitude towards Mary in later life. Mary added to the unforgivable errors of her ways in her family's eyes by marrying in February 1520, presumably for love, young William Carey, Esquire to the Body at the English Court, a man from a good but not a noble Devonshire family.

It was a sorry match for a Boleyn but Mary had spoiled her chances of a good one. Significantly, her father did not attend the wedding. It took place while he was on embassy in France.

To Anne it was a cautionary lesson that may have helped to teach her a deep fear of sex, which prevented her fulfilling what her manner promised, and which led her to tantalize her suitors. This in a society where chastity was rare was to be a vital ingredient in the spell she cast over men.

By the summer of 1520 Anne had lived in France for six years. She was thirteen, growing tall, with a small, pale, rather sallow-complexioned oval face, dominated by long, large, expressive black eyes; already she had learnt to flirt with them. A poet who saw her at the Court has left us his impression of her in an anonymous French poem written in 1536. She spoke the language fluently, he says, and was so 'full of graces . . . you would never have thought her English . . .'

> She knew how to sing and dance well and talk wisely, to play the lute and other instruments to distract her hearers from sad thoughts. Besides . . . she was pretty and of an elegant figure. But most attractive of her features were her eyes, which she well knew how to use, holding them sometimes still, at others, making them send a message, carrying from her heart the secret witness. And in truth such was their power that many a man paid his allegiance.

Other qualities we know Anne possessed – her gift for light-hearted repartee and the fashionable art of punning, coupled with her high-spirited gaiety – would no doubt have enabled her to remain a virgin despite her melting eyes.

But it was not only in sexual matters that the French Court set its mark on Anne. It was dominated, like its master, by women, by Louise, King Francis's mother, and above all by his sister Marguerite, the outrageous, adored, intellectual Duchess of Alençon, author of that classic collection of bawdy tales, the *Heptameron*, and of passionate love poems to her own brother. So well recognized was her influence over her brother that ambassadors, having made their bow to the King, would pass on and lay their actual business before her, states Brantôme. One day Anne, in the very different masculine atmosphere of the English Court, would try to emulate Marguerite, for whom she felt a lively affection and admiration.

Francis was indulgent to all women. When he discovered Françoise de Foix to be unfaithful to him, she suffered no worse fate than exile from his Court. But he was especially indulgent to his sister Marguerite, particularly in the delicate question of her religious orthodoxy.

It was while Anne was growing up in France that a young monk called Martin Luther committed an act that shook the foundations of the Roman Catholic Church. In 1517 Luther had nailed his ninety-five theses against the doctrine and sale of indulgences to the church door of the castle in the university town of Wittenberg. Luther's Protestant ideas and those of his rival reformers, Zwingli and Calvin, would send increasing repercussions through Europe as the century wore on. Monarchs of Catholic countries would display their zeal for the orthodox faith by making public bonfires of heretics. King Francis was himself to give the royal approval to these holocausts by attending them in person while in his own Court he let Marguerite openly question Church doctrines. Did the soul leave the body at the moment of death? Marguerite watched for the soul carefully while one of her maidens died and decided it did not. If Francis sought heretics to burn, scandal said, the greatest was at his own Court. Marguerite at heart probably never considered herself other than a good Catholic, but she provided a climate of thought in which the seeds of Lutheranism could flourish and some of them took root in Anne.

She was encouraged as well to have confidence in and voice her own judgements on subjects which, at the English Court, were usually reserved for men only. The details of Anne's education are impossible now to determine, but we can be reasonably sure that while it included all the social graces and accomplishments it had little to do with any real mental training. Anne's later intellectual arrogance was based on a sharp and sometimes uncannily accurate instinct, a quick but entirely illogical mind. Her judgement on superficial matters of taste, court lyrics, dress, was acute; her assessment of politics haphazard and subjective. She could compose long letters in French as well as in her native tongue - as could few of her English contemporaries – but her letters, like her speech, lack logical development. When talking, she jumped jerkily from subject to subject and expressed herself in hyperboles – an idiosyncrasy which merely made the future Court butterfly yet more pleasing. Added to her wit, her frequent, pretty laugh and elegant appearance, it helped to create the peculiar charm which hid her vanity and egotism from her male admirers.

Such was the woman Anne was growing up to be when she saw King Henry VIII again in June 1520 at the Field of Cloth of Gold.

As attendant on Queen Claude, Anne lodged with the French Court and nobility in a city of silken tents and pavilions in all the colours of the heraldic rainbow outside the town of Ardres. (It had been battered by English cannon only a few years before.) The English Court lodged at Guines. Four days later a storm broke up the French encampment, soaked the gay fringed satins, plastered blue velvet and cloth of gold in a sodden mess to the ground and toppled the life-size statue of St Michael from the top of King Francis's tall tent. Anne and her companions sought cramped and crowded accommodation in the little town: but to an aspiring Court lady aged thirteen such discomfort and inconvenience can have weighed nothing beside the excitement of seeing King Henry again.

Queen Claude and her entourage were not present on that first hot June evening. So Anne did not witness the dramatic encounter of those traditional enemies, the Kings of England and France. Glittering and sweating in cloth-of-gold and silver, the black plumes of their black velvet caps motionless in the still air, Henry and Francis sat their horses for a moment and eyed each other haughtily across the little valley which had been specially made for the occasion. Then in the words of the chronicler, Edward Hall, 'up blew the trumpets, "sagbuttes", clarions and all other minstrels on both sides, and the Kings descended down toward the bottom of the valley . . .'

But though Anne did not see the two tall Kings meet and embrace, then, vying in prearranged courtesy, enter the pavilion of cloth of gold, she had many chances to admire King Henry during the seventeen days of jousting, banqueting and athletic contests that followed. Henry was twenty-eight.

He was massive without yet being gross, and still of very fine appearance by contemporary standards.

'His Majesty is . . . extremely handsome,' had reported the Venetian ambassador, Sebastian Giustinian, in October of the previous year to his senate. 'Nature could not have done more for him . . . very fair, and his whole frame admirably proportioned . . . He is affable, gracious . . .'

Another Venetian who was present at the Field of Cloth of Gold described Henry as the most jovial prince he had ever beheld. The one moment when Anne might have seen a less attractive side, when Francis threw him in a wrestling match, causing Henry's fair skin to flush with anger and his small mouth to set with fury, was quickly glossed over by tactful officials, and conveniently forgotten by the English chronicler Edward Hall.

Anne saw Henry courteous, ebullient: dressed as the most magnificent of princes; or masking as Hercules, garlanded in green, clad in a silver shirt and gold lionskin with buskins of gold, dancing tirelessly, leaping like a stag with the lady of his choice.

On the first Sunday when Henry came to banquet with Queen Claude and Marguerite at Ardres, Anne quite probably danced with him herself. And the massive, ever-smiling, effusive King of England may even have seemed to her a little naïve beside the thin, sophisticated Francis, in whose Court she felt at home. But by the time the gallant caperings of the Field of Cloth of Gold came to an end, when on 20 June 1520 King Henry with tears in his eyes parted from his 'good brother' Francis, the events were already in train which would end Anne's stay in France also.


At thirteen, by sixteenth-century standards, she was of marriageable age, a pawn that could be deployed according to the unsentimental notions of the day by her elders to solve their own personal problems. At the time Anne reached this useful age a feud had long been smouldering between the Boleyns and their relations in Ireland. It was a quarrel that not only ruffled the smooth surface of the life of the nobility, which the King

liked to preserve, but which, far worse, threatened the success
of his policies in Ireland.

The feud had begun five years before, and since it was to
play such an important part in Anne's life, some account of its
origin must be given.

On 3 August 1515, Anne's maternal great-grandfather, the
Earl of Ormond, had died, leaving behind, besides his ancient
title, enormous estates in Ireland, which his two daughters,
Margaret Boleyn and Anne St Leger and their families confidently expected to inherit. But before the candles had failed
round the dead Earl's bier, before the monks had finished
chanting the requiem for his soul, his second cousin, the
red-haired Sir Piers Butler, had laid claim to both title and
land.

Sir Piers was well placed to make good his claim. The Earls
of Ormond preferred to live in the orderly peace of England
rather than in an Ireland ravaged by tribal wars (where,
according to one of the ubiquitous Venetians, the chiefs were
as savage as their country, with barefoot, ferocious followers
in saffron mantles). They had been in the habit of making some
other member of their family deputy administrator of their
Irish lands. To secure this position, in 1497, Sir Piers had already
murdered an illegitimate cousin, known as the Black Butler.
As the family chronicler puts it admiringly: 'Piers . . . did
forestall him in the way and with a courageous charge gored
the bastard through with his spear' - since when he had been
happily enjoying the fruits of his enterprise.

The Earl of Ormond had generously recompensed Sir Piers
for his services, granting in 1505 to Sir Piers Butler and the
heirs male of his body all the Ormond lands, rents, services and
manors in Ireland, reserving to himself and his heirs a fourth
part of the profits yearly as well as the 'Seignory, name and
dignity of Ormond'. He hoped and expected to bequeath these
things to his daughters and their families, including his
favourite grandson, Thomas Boleyn, to whom he had already
given a treasured family relic, the ivory drinking-horn of St
Thomas Becket.

But three-quarters of the rent was not enough for the
violent Sir Piers when there was a chance of getting more. He

claimed the earldom by right of being the nearest descendant in the male line. The earldom, he maintained, had been entailed specifically to heirs male and not, as Boleyns and St Legers believed, to heirs general. Not surprisingly, considering the power of his position, he found plenty of witnesses to prove his claim by hearsay, but he had no written evidence.

The original fourteenth-century charter had been conveniently lost. Instigated by Sir Thomas, Margaret Boleyn and Anne St Leger at once protested to King Henry himself, who clearly believed in the justice of their case; as did the Lord Deputy, the Earl of Kildare, in Ireland. Realizing this, Sir Piers stiffly refused to come to the hearing. He pleaded that he was too busy with the 'King's wars' and placed Henry in an awkward dilemma. Ireland was on the verge of rebellion; Sir Piers, one of King Henry's few loyal supporters, had just built up a strong federation of Irish chiefs, useful for or against the King. It was not the moment to offend him. So the Lord Deputy merely ordered that the profits and rents of the Ormond lands should remain in the hands of the 'farmers', the dispute was left unsettled and the situation was thoroughly unsatisfactory for all concerned. While Boleyn fulminated vainly in England, Sir Piers continued to use the family title and administer without profit the Ormond lands.

Then in 1520 Sir Piers found an ally in Anne Boleyn's uncle, the small, spare, dark Earl of Surrey, who had taken Kildare's place as Lord Deputy. Surrey, though conservative by inclination, was a pragmatist in most of his acts, a basic contradiction that accounts perhaps for the harsh misery of his countenance as depicted in Holbein's famous drawing. To the Earl, Ireland was a headache, and Sir Piers an ally so useful that he must be pleased at all costs. 'He sheweth himself ever, with his good advice and strength, to bring the King's intended purpose to good effect,' Surrey wrote home to England. 'Undoubtedly he is not only a wise man, and hath a true English heart, but also he is the man of most experience of the feats of war of this country of whom I have at all times the best counsel, of any of this land.'

In September 1520 Surrey finally wrote to Henry VIII proposing a solution to the Boleyn-Butler feud, a scheme that was characteristic of this unsentimental, authoritarian man who had little love for his kin. Anne Boleyn should marry James, son of Sir Piers Butler. The King, glad of such an easy answer to his problem, wrote back enthusiastically. Surrey, he ordered, should propose the match to Sir Piers, and let the King know his reactions as soon as possible. In the meantime Henry himself would 'advance the said matter' with Boleyn, 'and certify you how we shall find him inclined thereunto'. In those days of arranged marriages it never occurred to the King to see how Anne was 'inclined thereunto'; he naturally presumed she would instantly acquiesce in her father's wishes.

Not content with enlisting the aid of the King of England to further this marriage of convenience between his niece and the son of Sir Piers, Surrey and the Council of Ireland had meanwhile also written to Cardinal Wolsey, the Ipswich butcher's son who had risen, by his vigorous ability and genius at delighting the King with wonderful entertainments, to be the second, some said the first, most powerful man in the king- dom. Through Wolsey's capable hands most of the nation's business passed, while the still immature Henry preferred to spend his days shooting, running at the ring, hunting and jousting; and his nights in dancing and revelling. Would the mighty Cardinal, Surrey begged, lend his weight to the match? 'We think if your Grace caused that to be done and also a final end to be made between them for the title of lands . . . it should cause the said Earl to be the better willed to see this land [Ireland] brought to good order.'

Typical of their day, neither Boleyn nor Butler worried about condemning their children to a loveless match, if the terms were right. But the haggling was complicated, a year passed without any final settlement, by which time Surrey had been recalled and Sir Piers himself become Lord Deputy of Ireland. But the more King Henry and Cardinal Wolsey thought about the match, the better they liked it. James was, at the time, still living at the English Court, and Sir Piers requested that as his gouty foot made even riding impossible, James should be allowed to return home to help him keep the peace. King Henry passed on the request to Cardinal Wolsey, then on embassy in France, who advised him with ruthless

cynicism. Sir Piers's request was very reasonable, the Cardinal
wrote in November 1521:

> The towardness of his son considered, who is right active,
> discreet and wise, I suppose he, being with his father in that
> land, should do unto your Grace right acceptable service.
> Howbeit, Sir, good shall it be to prove how the said Sir
> Piers Butler shall acquit himself in the authority by your
> Grace lately to him committed, not doubting but his said
> son being within your realm, he will do far the better;
> trusting thereby the rather to get him home. And I shall, at
> my return to your presence, devise with your Grace how the
> marriage betwixt him and Sir Thomas Boleyn's daughter
> may be brought to pass, which shall be a reasonable cause
> to 'tracte' the time for sending his said son over unto him;
> for the perfecting of which marriage I shall endeavour
> myself, at my said return, with all effect.

When Wolsey put his mind to something it was as good as
done. But he had not yet finally arranged the marriage when
urgent events precipitated Anne's return to England. Less than
two years after the Field of Cloth of Gold, the King of England
was about to declare war on his 'good brother' Francis and join
forces with his enemy, the Emperor.

English foreign policy during Anne's lifetime was largely
a question of England's shifting relations with these two great
rival giants of Europe – France, and the dominions of the
Emperor Charles V, which included Spain, Sicily, Naples, the
Netherlands and what we now call Germany. In 1520 King
Francis and Charles V had each sought King Henry's help
against the other. For over a year England had sat on the fence
while Henry and Wolsey negotiated with both sides at once.

Germany was England's traditional ally and trading partner,
but the election of its new Emperor, Charles V, who was also
King of Spain, by joining these two nations under one ruler,
threatened to upset the balance of power in Europe. To restore
it, Cardinal Wolsey now favoured a French alliance. Henry,
while equally reluctant to make Charles V too powerful, had
grandiose dreams of inheriting the mantle of Henry V and
sitting on the French throne. The whole situation was further

complicated by alliances with the states of Italy where the two great powers competed for domination. While England dithered undecided, the torch of war was lit along the French borders. In the summer of 1521 rebellion broke out in Spain. Francis seized the opportunity to attack. Boleyn and Butler haggled over Anne's dowry while French armies with heraldic banners marched into Navarre to the sound of fife, trumpet and drum and the heavy boom of primitive artillery. As Anne learned the newest dances and songs with the lute at the French Court, the Imperial armies struck back. Soon, not only Navarre but also the Low Countries and Italy echoed to the clash of armour.

Henry finally made up his mind to join in the fray. In August of 1521 he sent Cardinal Wolsey to Calais, ostensibly to negotiate peace, but the outcome was the secret Treaty of Bruges with the Emperor. England still pretended amity to France, but secretly mustered her troops and recalled her nationals – the scholars from Paris, and Anne Boleyn from the French King's Court.

King Francis himself, that arch-admirer of female attractions, even in the middle of grave worries – everywhere his forces were being beaten by the Emperor, and now he guessed he had lost the English alliance as well – still found time to note her departure. He trusted, Francis wrote, in a letter intended for Henry's eyes, that his suspicions were unfounded, but he considered his 'good brother's' actions curious if he intended to maintain his fraternal love and alliance.

I think it very strange that this Treaty of Bruges was concealed from me, and also the powder and balls that are going to Antwerp; that his subjects go and take the Emperor's pay; that the English scholars of Paris have returned home, and also the daughter of Mr Boullan . . .

The deliberate interpolation of Anne's name suggests that she had become someone of importance in the knowing eyes of King Francis. Now, aged nearly fifteen, and French in all her ways, Anne at last set sail for England and the marriage that had been arranged for her there.

# Chapter 3

# AT COURT

MISTRESS ANNE BOLEYN sailed from France in January 1522 and a few weeks later arrived at the Court of King Henry VIII, where her husband-to-be, James Butler, awaited her.

In the sixteenth century this Court, like the other Courts of Europe, migrated frequently from palace to palace. So overcrowded was it with great nobles and officials, their wives, relatives, retainers and servants, a large number of whom were entitled to live there – as well as the multitudinous members of the households of the King and the Queen – that it had to keep moving for health reasons.

At the royal command all the carts, wagons and horses in the neighbourhood were appropriated; long processions of courtiers, cooks, liveried servants and yeomen of the guard set out by road or river, laden with beds, chests, stools, cushions, wall-hangings and locks for the King's doors. In motley procession the Court moved from the ancient stone fortress of Windsor to the turreted domes of Richmond, built by Henry VII on the site of the ruined manor of Sheen.

Approaching this riverside palace on a blustery day, the Court could hear high sweet sounds from vanes bearing the King's arms in azure-and-gold as they turned in the wind. Restlessly, the Court shifted from Baynard's Castle in London, battlemented towers rising precipitously from the Thames, to Bridewell across the narrow River Fleet, a residence built specially for the visit of the Emperor in 1522. From Woodstock to Eltham to Beaulieu, and a host of lesser manors, the Court trotted in varying succession. And during its absence the vacated palace rooms could be 'sweetened', the 'jakes' [lavatories] emptied, the rushes on the floors renewed, the slops cleaned from courtyards and the dreaded plague averted.

That February and March of 1522 the Court had made

Greenwich, on the bank of the Thames, its temporary abode.

So it was in the pale light of winter that, on her return from France, Anne first saw the palace where most of the momentous events of her life were to take place. In the leafless landscape, the rambling building, shaped like a vast letter T, and divided by courtyards, was clearly etched; church spire and hall lantern, the twin towers of Henry's new armoury by the tiltyard and the battlements of the river façade stood out against the sky. From the red brick walls shone the great windows with which King Henry loved to embellish his palaces and through which he could watch the stately galleys which he had had built in the neighbouring yard of Deptford sail slowly down the Thames, firing thunderous salvoes in salute as they passed.

If Anne arrived on horseback she would have ridden across a wide lawn before clattering through the first of the courtyards to her lodging, but she may just as likely have come by river in her father's painted barge; for once past the rapids of London bridge, the Thames was a smoother thoroughfare than the pot-holed and often flooded roads. Arrived at Greenwich, Anne must almost immediately have set her perceptive black eyes on James Butler, whom the King had decided she was to marry.

An arranged marriage was one of the occupational hazards of being well born, and Mistress Anne was more fortunate than many of her contemporaries. James Butler was at least young; that much we know even if his exact date of birth is lost. He was, according to Wolsey, 'right active, discreet and wise' and, for an Irishman of his day, comparatively civilized. He had been brought up at the English Court, whose pastimes he had grown to like so well that he was reluctant to return to Ireland.

Anne, however, was not grateful for her luck. As soon as she met James she seems to have made up her mind she would not have him. The attractions of his person could not compensate for the life, far from the delights of Court, that she would face in Ireland with its everlasting feuds and savage barefoot peasants. No record exists of whether she at once told her family of her decision; to judge by the reckless courage and impulsiveness which were among her dominant characteristics she may well have informed her father, but if so, that careful man did not see fit to send word of the girl's defiance to King and Cardinal. That his daughter at less than fifteen was determined to stand out against a match that had become a cornerstone of the King's Irish policy was a piece of news it was for the time being politic to keep to himself. It is possible that, having been Esquire to the Body and knowing most of the King's secrets, including his taste for young girls, Boleyn realized, now his accomplished daughter was at Court, that she had a chance of contracting a relationship which, though illicit, would be potentially much more profitable to himself than marriage with a mere Butler.

Meanwhile Anne had decided to pick her own husband from the wide field that was open to a girl of her exceptional prospects and attractions.

During Anne's years in France her family's status, no less than its finances, had been transfigured like the sky at dawn. When first she set foot in the spacious galleries of Greenwich Palace with their painted and gilded ceilings, it was no longer as the daughter of an impecunious branch of the Howard clan. Her father, though still a commoner, was richer than many a peer, having gained control through his pliant mother in 1515 of half the Earl of Ormond's English estates, which numbered no less than thirty-six manors and included Newhall in Essex, a copy of a palace of the ancient Kings of Ulster.

This was a dwelling so grand and delightful that the King himself had bought it for the then magnificent sum of £1000, added a ponderous gatehouse, romantically rechristened it Beaulieu, and turned it into one of his favourite residences.

Boleyn was himself also now a very important Court official: since 1520 Controller of the Household, with one of the best chambers at Court, ranking only just below the Treasurer who, in his turn, ranked next to the Lord Steward, the courtier in charge of all the below-stairs departments. Together with the Cofferer and the clerks, these three met in the counting-house round a green baize-covered table to plan dinners and feasts, check accounts, discipline servants and tradesmen, and generally oversee the many different kitchen departments - 'spicery', 'saucery', 'wafery', 'pastry', 'poultry' and 'acatary' - where the gargantuan meals were cooked.

Anne's father was not the only member of her family whose position gave her importance at Court in 1522. The palace was honeycombed with the apartments of her relations, and whether the occasion was public or private, one of them was sure to be near the King or the Queen. One of the Gentlemen of the King's Privy Chamber was her cousin, Sir Francis Brian, a rakish poet nicknamed the Vicar of Hell; the Lord High Treasurer of England was Anne's grandfather, the aged Duke of Norfolk; her uncle and aunt, Sir Edward and Lady Anne Boleyn, were members respectively of both the King's and the Queen's households; Anne's brother-in-law, William Carey, was Esquire to the Body. There was also Anne's sister, Mary Carey, on whom the King's small blue lecherous eyes had probably already been fixed.

Anne herself, without any regular duties, seems to have been attached to the household of the Queen, who had, like the King, her own suite of rooms, including Bed Chamber, Privy Chamber and Presence Chamber, as well as her own household officers, ladies-of-honour, cooks, maids and other servants. Catherine of Aragon, five years older than her husband, was now thirty-six, her small figure thickened by frequent pregnancies, so that in the top-heavy, jewel-encrusted head-dresses and Spanish farthingales to which she clung as obstinately as she kept her Spanish accent, she had appeared 'deformed' to Francis I at the Field of Cloth of Gold.

Like Anne's former mistress, Queen Claude, she was deeply religious, wearing the habit of the Third Order of St Francis beneath her opulent gowns, fasting on Fridays and Saturdays, spending much of her day in the royal chapel, where she prayed on her knees on the cold stone floor without the customary cushions. Catherine was, however, a more formidable person than Claude, with a lively intellect and a cheerful dignity that had won the hearts of the forthright citizens of London.

As daughter of the Controller, Anne enjoyed the life and amusements of a Court lady: watching cock fights, bear- or bull-baiting in the 'inner palace courtyard'; smiling encouragingly at her favourite 'knight' as he jousted for her favour in the palace tiltyard; hunting and hawking in the parks; entertaining the gentlemen in the Queen's chamber, where they gathered to flirt, watching the ladies dance or listening to them singing to the lute the newest love lyric, all accomplishments at which Anne excelled.

Observing her, polished and vivacious, a star among the dull, semi-literate girls brought up in the narrow barbarity of English country houses, Boleyn must have congratulated himself on her education. And her French manners, French expressions and French clothes – which included the pretty French hood so much more flattering than the gable head-dress worn by the Queen – lent her added elegance. England might be about to declare war on France; but French still remained the language of gallantry, of love letters and Court revels; the King himself might cherish a deep animus against France; he still had his hair cut in the French way, and though at the instigation of the Privy Council in 1518 he banished from his presence those boon companions too prone to French fashions, he soon reinstated them in his favour. The fact that Anne was more French than English undoubtedly helped to attract her to his notice.

In the brief time Anne was to remain at Court that year of 1522 she created a sensation. One of her admirers was the youthful poet Thomas Wyatt. His thunderstruck reactions were described by his grandson, George Wyatt, in his life of Anne Boleyn written at the end of the century:

The knight in the beginning coming to behold the sudden appearance of this new beauty came to be holden and surprised somewhat with the sight thereof, after much more with her witty and graceful speech, his ear also had him chained unto her, so as finally his heart seemed to say, 'I could gladly yield to be tied for ever with the knot of her love.'

Unfortunately for Thomas, although only nineteen years old, he was already tied legally in marriage to someone else, Elizabeth Brooke, daughter of Lord Cobham, a neighbour of the Boleyns in Kent; and had had a son by her in 1521. But at Henry VIII's Court a wife was no impediment to adventures, so long as these did not upset the *status quo*. George Wyatt has

left us a haunting picture of 'the rare and admirable beauty of
the fresh and young . . . Anne Boleyn' as she first appeared at
fifteen to the 'eye of the Court' and the susceptible Thomas:

> In this noble imp the graces of nature graced by gracious
> education, seemed even at the first to have promised bliss unto
> her aftertimes. She was taken at that time to have a beauty
> not so whitely as clear and fresh above all we may esteem,
> which appeared much more excellent by her favour, passing
> sweet and cheerful; and these, both also increased by her
> noble presence of shape and fashion, representing both mild-
> ness and majesty more than can be expressed.
>
> There was found, indeed, upon the side of her nail upon
> one of her fingers, some little show of a nail, which yet was
> so small, by the report of those that have seen her, as the
> workmaster seemed to leave it an occasion of greater grace
> to her hand, which, with the tip of one of her other fingers,
> might be and was usually by her hidden without any least
> blemish to it. Likewise there were said to be upon some
> parts of her body certain small moles incident to the clearest
> complexions.

Against this glowing description of Anne must be set that
of the rabidly hostile Catholic writer, Nicholas Sanders, in his
book on the Reformation, published in 1585:

> Anne Boleyn was rather tall of stature, with black hair and
> an oval face of a sallowish complexion, as if troubled with
> jaundice. She had a projecting tooth under the upper lip,
> and on her right hand six fingers. There was a large wen
> under her chin, and therefore to hide its ugliness, she wore a
> high dress covering her throat . . . She was handsome to
> look at, with a pretty mouth, amusing in her ways, playing
> well on the lute, and was a good dancer.

Neither writer was Anne's contemporary, Nicholas Sanders
being born in 1527. Both were prejudiced by the violent
religious passions Anne was to arouse. But Sanders's prejudice
is so blatant that his denigrations cannot be taken seriously.
He may be forgiven the confusion between two sisters, both in
France at the same time, which led him to state that it was

Anne rather than Mary who was guilty of gross immorality there. But he was not content with that one baseless scandal. Sanders was the chief propagator of the story that Anne was the King's own daughter, conceived during Boleyn's absence on embassy abroad, a tale so manifestly impossible that it robs his other statements of credibility. Anne, he added for good measure, had also had intercourse with one of her father's household officials before she even went to France. Since Anne must at that time have been no more than seven years old, Nicholas Sanders can be judged no better than a scandal-monger.

George Wyatt, on the other hand, although born later than Sanders, got his facts from the testimony of two people who knew Anne well, his grandfather and her maid-of-honour, Lady Anne Gainsford. Their testimony that the mole on her throat was not prominent is borne out by the official portrait of Anne which shows her in a low and not, as Sanders says, in a high-necked gown, as well as by the excited stir she created among the young men at Court. Anne's physical shortcomings must have been slight and easily hidden, her general appearance beguilingly attractive, for her to be surrounded by so many admirers. Their number was about to include the King.

On 4 March 1522, Anne was given a part in a revel with Henry VIII.

The revels or 'disguisings' were among the King's favourite pastimes, fulfilling his love of spectacle and of music, but above all his passion for showing off. In the middle of a banquet the King and his boon companions would disappear and in their place would enter an exotic procession of, for instance, Turks, Russians and Prussians, surrounded by torch-bearers, faces blackened to resemble Moors.

On one famous occasion Cardinal Wolsey gave a banquet in his riverside mansion of York Place. The King mysteriously was not present. Suddenly to a volley of small cannon from the river, followed by the warble of fifes and the beat of drums, there erupted into Wolsey's splendid room a band of shepherds from a foreign land - rather exceptional shepherds; their gar-

ments were of cloth of gold and crimson satin, their beards
and wigs of gold and silver wire and black silk. After a while
the King and his companions unmasked and the dancing
began.

Since the beginning of Henry's reign the revels had grown
more and more elaborate; there was often an allegorical script,
a mock battle, a large set-piece of grove or castle and a mixed
cast of male and female players. The Master of the Revels was
an important Court official and no grand banquet was complete without one of his productions.

On 2 March 1522 the Emperor's ambassadors arrived in
England on their way to Spain. Since Henry and Charles were
now allies, his ambassadors were royally entertained. There was
jousting on March 2 in the new tiltyard – the King competing
on a horse caparisoned in silver, with a wounded heart and a
motto in black-and-gold, '*Elle mon cœur a navera*' (She has
wounded my heart). On March 4 the ambassadors were treated
to a banquet given by Cardinal Wolsey at York Place, followed
by an allegory of love, called the Château Vert. The cast of this
revel included both the King and Anne Boleyn, and it is worth
noticing in detail since this must have been their first close
encounter.

The auditorium, arras-hung, bright with a myriad candles
in branched candlesticks of silver or gold, was embellished with
everything to delight and astonish the senses. Across the room
stretched a huge, shiny green castle adorned with banners
and towers from which floated the sweet sounds of minstrels
playing and the high, pure voices of the children of my Lord
Wolsey's chapel. Eight fair ladies graced the battlements in
gold-embroidered white satin gowns, their bonnets flashing
with jewels. At the foot of the green castle, to contrast with
the angelic figures above, were eight more ladies, dressed as
Indian women with black velvet bonnets. The name of each
lady was on her bonnet – the white-and-gold ladies: 'Beauty,
Honour, Perseverance, Kindness, Constancy, Bounty, Mercy
and Pity'; the Indian ladies: 'Danger, Disdain, Jealousy, Unkindness, Scorn, Malebouche [sic] and Strangeness'. A gentle
scene, it was soon to be disrupted, because a castle in the revels –
as in real life – was there to be attacked.

Eight gallant knights entered, in cloaks of blue satin, blue velvet buskins and coats of cloth of gold – 'Amorous, Nobleness, Youth, Attendance, Loyalty, Pleasure, Gentleness and Liberty'. They were led by a crimson-clad figure called 'Ardent Desire', most probably the King. Persuaded by his honey-tongued words, the white-and-gold ladies were quite ready to surrender the castle, but the Indian ladies resisted, and to the thunder of cannon outside the palace, the pretty mock battle began.

As the knights ran at the castle its defenders pelted them with sugar-plums and rose-water. The knights retaliated with oranges and dates, until the Indian ladies were driven off and the gold-and-white ladies taken prisoner, when everyone unmasked and danced together.

Dancing the fashionable galliard with its flamboyant leaps and capers for men gave Henry a chance to show off the fine calf of his leg and his incredible animal energy – and his disguise freed him from the isolation of royalty and enabled him to indulge in one of his favourite pastimes, 'sporting with ladies'.

It was by her sparkling performance in the revels that Henry's best-known mistress to date, Elizabeth Blount, maid of honour to Queen Catherine, had, according to the chronicler Edward Hall, 'won the King's heart', a 'damsel' who 'in singing, dancing and in all goodly pastimes exceeded all other'. Her first revel with the King took place in the company of Thomas and George Boleyn, when she was aged at most thirteen, her last, four years later in October 1518. Shortly after this festive occasion Wolsey arranged for her to retire to the Priory of St Lawrence where a boy, Henry Fitzroy, was born about June 1519, and proudly acknowledged by the King to be his son; since when she had not returned to Court.

Anne's talents were at least equal to Elizabeth's. Henry's reactions to her are easy to guess. With his penchant for youth, he could not fail to be fascinated by the black-haired, volatile, outspoken girl, with a temper as proud and independent as his own. Her long black eyes beckoned and laughed at him, her wit flashed and tantalized, leaving him, thirty and a King, floundering in pursuit.

Anne's encounter with Henry had almost immediate repercussions. In April, just over a month after the revel, Anne's father Sir Thomas Boleyn was promoted from Controller to be Treasurer of the Household, a position he had first made suit for seven years before.

It has been argued that this promotion was due to the King's feeling for Mary Boleyn; but Mary had already been at Court two years. It was Anne who had just arrived. Both the contemporary writer Cavendish, and George Wyatt writing in Elizabeth's reign, imply that she immediately attracted the King's attention. Henry wanted to impress this mocking girl with a proper sense of the royal power. Significantly also, it is very soon after Anne's arrival at Court that Wolsey married off Henry's discarded mistress Elizabeth Blount to a Sir Gilbert Tailbois and, to salve the King's conscience she was invested by act of parliament with a life estate in her father-in-law's considerable lands and manors.

But just as 'the handsomest potentate' showed interest in Anne, she herself fell heavily in love with someone else.

# Chapter 4

# FIRST LOVE

ANNE BOLEYN's first love was gentle Lord Henry Percy, twenty-year-old eldest son of the 'magnificent' Earl of Northumberland. This gorgeous personage Anne had seen at the Field of Cloth of Gold with a retinue of no less than five hundred liveried retainers. Head of the ancient and powerful Percy family, he ruled over huge estates and numerous castles in the northern border counties and Yorkshire, as well as a liberal scattering of lands and manors further south.

The heir to all this was a splendid match even for a Boleyn, a consideration that must have invested him with special glamour in the eyes of a girl like Anne, conditioned by family ambition and a society which held noble birth a virtue. Though that does not make her feeling for Percy the less genuine.

Percy was a gawky, tactless, timid youth, delicate in health; he does not seem to us a romantic figure. But as well as his high degree, Percy had qualities rare for his day, and these, strangely enough, appealed to Anne. Percy's still surviving letters reveal that, in a ruthless, grasping world, he was generous and affectionate, with feelings of mercy and justice in advance of his time. To Anne he could give the emotional warmth of which, during her childhood away from her family, she had been starved.

As for Percy, brought up in his father's bleak Yorkshire castles of Wressel and Leconfield, used to the company of barely educated, unfinished daughters of the backwoods nobility, Anne's fashionable airs must have gone to his head like strong wine.

Anne and Lord Henry Percy saw each other every Sunday morning in the spring of 1522. On this day the mighty Cardinal Wolsey had a regular appointment with the King, and among his attendants as he floated down river from his London mansion of York Place to Greenwich Palace was young Percy.

During Anne's brief stay at Court in the early months of 1522, he was completing his education in the Cardinal's household, along with a number of other young lords and gentlemen. Wolsey, among all his cares of state, found time to keep a paternal eye on these boys. They ate in the Cardinal's dining chamber, the lords at a separate table from the gentlemen who, in turn, ate separately from the officers of the household; while the mighty, corpulent Cardinal dined hugely at a vast loaded table alone, under a canopy – a 'cloth of estate' – like the King.

Living in Wolsey's household was probably the best way to find out how the government of England was ordered. When Wolsey made his magnificent way to Westminster Hall to preside over the courts, in scarlet hat, gloves and gown, astride a scarlet-trapped mule, surrounded by four footmen with gilt poleaxes, Lord Henry Percy, attending on him, could observe how justice was administered. Serving or bringing the Cardinal water to wash his hands at a banquet, the future Earl would learn the elaborate rituals and ceremonies that were so important a part of Court life; and he would meet and mingle with his fellow peers, with whom, by virtue of his high birth, he would one day play a leading part in his country's affairs.

The spectacle that would have met Anne's eyes, if she watched the river on Sunday mornings from one of the great bay windows of the palace, was superb. For the Cardinal delighted in pomp. Round the wide double bend of the Thames, through the flat, marshy green fields, the great gilded, painted state barge would glide into view. Gowned in scarlet satin, silk or taffeta, a priest's round hat on his head, the Archbishop of York, Chancellor of England and papal legate, sat under an awning a-flutter with banners, surrounded by his richly dressed retinue; tall yeomen in scarlet coats, trimmed with black velvet, balanced on the bulwarks.

Oars flashed in the sunshine, the water sparkled, the barge floated slowly in to the palace landing-stage. Ponderously, Wolsey ascended the steps, heralded as always by his symbols of office: his Cardinal's red hat, his two silver pillars and two silver crosses, and the great seal of England. He was received by the Treasurer, the Controller (Anne's father) and other chief officers of the household, with their gold chains and white staffs, then ceremoniously ushered through the gates, up the stairs to the first floor and to the King in his Privy Chamber.

And while King and Cardinal arranged the country's affairs between them, Lord Henry Percy was free to make his way to the Queen's suite of rooms, adjoining the King's, where Anne eagerly awaited him. Here in Catherine of Aragon's Presence Chamber, sitting close together on the bright cushions, velvet-covered stools or carved chests that even in the royal rooms did service for chairs, they could 'fall in dalliance' together, their shadows merging in the sunlight on the silken wall-hangings behind them. And here their feeling for each other grew with each meeting until attraction ripened into love. But it went unnoticed in the flirtatious atmosphere of the Court, where ladies and gentlemen kissed each other in greeting and leave-taking and a code of artificial courtship flourished, a code described by a Venetian ambassador who attended the banquet given for the Emperor Charles V, on 28 May 1520. The trestle tables, he reported, were surrounded by youths, each of whom pretended to be passionately enamoured of the lady nearest to him, a gallant device in the ambassador's opinion. Under these conditions Anne's and Percy's genuine love escaped detection for some time. Although Percy was no more free than Anne to follow the inclinations of his heart, since for him too a marriage had been arranged.

Six years before, Percy's father had gone on pilgrimage, for the improvement of his soul, to the jewel-encrusted tomb of St Thomas Becket at Canterbury. He and a fellow peer had whiled away the long jogging hours in the saddle with discussion of more worldly matters, a promise by the Earl of Northumberland of his eldest son to the Earl of Shrewsbury's daughter, Lady Mary Talbot. It was a sensible, no-romantic-nonsense marriage between the children of two men of similar rank and interests. It would relate young Percy to Shrewsbury's other son-in-law, Lord Thomas Dacre, Warden of the East and Middle Marches, who was responsible for governing the north and protecting the borders against the Scots, a task in which Percy according to family tradition would be expected to play a leading part. Such a match could not fail to appeal both to the King and Wolsey. Like Anne's match, it formed part of a network of national policy.

Only two people as naïve as young Percy and Anne could believe they would be allowed to escape. But this – according to the life of Wolsey written by his gentleman usher, George Cavendish – is what they did believe. Had not Mary Tudor braved her royal brother's wrath to marry the Duke of Suffolk and been forgiven, even though the Duke's enemies recommended Henry to behead him for his insolence? The thought must have passed through Anne's head and, since hers was the dominant personality, the decision to resist authority, one suspects, was hers also, rather than Percy's.

Alas, disillusion was inevitable. The blow fell one Sunday morning, after Anne and Percy's passionate tête-à-tête. According to Cavendish, word of the unauthorized romance was brought to the King, whose temper, usually sunny at this date, deserted him. He was, to use the chronicler's understatement, 'much offended'. But ever careful of his regal status, Henry left the hatchet work to someone else: Cardinal Wolsey, his unfailing servant, whose wealth and position being entirely dependent on the King, was ready to obey his least whim in however delicate a matter. And what more easily torn asunder than young love?

Wolsey's words to Anne (if he even condescended to speak to her on the subject at all) have long since vanished from human memory. But miraculously and completely preserved, like a fly in amber, in the pages of George Cavendish's narrative about his master, is Wolsey's bullying reprimand of Percy.

During the return trip up river, the Cardinal said nothing to the young man until his gilded barge was securely moored back at York Place. Then, sitting at the end of his tapestried gallery, he sent for him and at Percy's approach the Cardinal's round thyroid eyes, set in pouched yellow flesh, bulged further with anger. It was an intimidating sight. Wolsey in wrath was as vigorous as in his other activities, and his vengefulness was memorable: merely for saying in a letter to a friend that Wolsey was tyrannical, the learned Polydore Vergil had languished for months in the Tower. Diffident young Percy must have been shaken even before the Cardinal spoke.

I marvel not a little [Wolsey began, working himself up into one of his famous rages] of thy peevish folly, that thou wouldest tangle and insure thyself with a foolish girl yonder in the Court, I mean Anne Boleyn. Dost thou not consider the estate that God hath called thee unto in this world? For after the death of thy noble father thou art most like to inherit and possess one of the most worthiest earldoms of this realm. Therefore it had been most meet and convenient for thee to have sued for the consent of thy father in that behalf and to have also made the King's highness privy thereto, requiring then his princely favour, submitting all thy whole proceeding in such matters unto his highness; who would not only accept thankfully your submission, but would, I assure thee, provide so for your purpose therein that he would advance you much more nobly and have matched you according to your estate and honour. Whereby you might have grown so by your wisdom and honourable behaviour into the King's high estimation that it would have been much to your increase of honour.

It was an onslaught designed to crush at once the love-lorn young noble. There was worse to come. Short of breath though not of eloquence, Wolsey blustered on:

But now behold what ye have done through your wilfulness. Ye have not only offended your natural father but also your most gracious sovereign lord, and matched yourself with one such as neither the King ne [nor] yet your father will be agreeable with the matter. And thereof I put you out of doubt that I will send for your father, and at his coming he shall either break this unadvised contract or disinherit thee for ever. The King's majesty himself will complain to thy father on thee and require no less at his hands than I have said; whose highness intended to have preferred her unto another person . . .

Tortured by the thought of his sweetheart marrying James Butler, dismayed by the furious torrent of his mentor's opposition, Lord Percy yet stood his ground courageously. The imputation that Anne was beneath him as a match he contra-

dicted, quoting her Howard blood, her father's descent from the
Earl of Ormond. 'Her descent,' he declared proudly, 'is equiva-
lent with mine, when I shall be in most dignity.' He lowered
his voice to a more tactful tone of supplication. 'I most humbly
require your grace of your especial favour herein; and also to
entreat the King's most royal majesty most lowly on my
behalf for his princely benevolence in this matter, the which,'
he ended with a burst of proud defiance, 'I cannot deny or
forsake.'

The Cardinal was not used to opposition. Was this stripling
of his household actually daring to resist his wishes? Wolsey
may well have been astonished. He turned with heavy sarcasm
to his gentleman usher, George Cavendish, and the eagerly
listening servants. 'Lo, sirs, ye may see what conformity of
wisdom is in this wilful boy's head . . .'

Percy squirmed under the lash. Blind opposition was obviously useless. He tried reason. He had pledged himself to Anne;
he could not now honourably withdraw. But honour was no
argument with which to persuade the unscrupulous Cardinal,
whose response was prompt and business-like. 'Why, thinkest
thou that the King and I know not what we have to do in as
weighty a matter as this? . . . I will send for your father out of
the north parts, and he and we shall take such order for the
avoiding of this thy hasty folly as shall be by the King thought
most expedient. And in the mean season, I charge thee, and in
the King's name command thee, that thou presume not once
to resort into her company, as thou intendest to ignore the
King's high indignation.'

Anne and Percy were not even to be allowed the courtesy
of taking leave of each other. The breaking of their romance is
a fact that does much to explain and exonerate Anne's behaviour
towards the Cardinal in years to come. And another fact that
should be remembered when judging her later conduct is the
disastrous effect the murdered romance had on the man she
loved. To begin with it ruined an already strained relationship
between Percy and his father.

At the sight of the sweating horse standing at his gate and
the contents of the missive held out to him by the Cardinal's

messenger, the Earl of Northumberland's worst fears were confirmed.

For a long time Northumberland had deferred sending his dangerously unpredictable son to Court, afraid that he might land himself and his family in trouble. The Earl wanted no repetition of the £10,000 fine imposed on him by Henry VII for disposing illegally but profitably of a wardship and marriage, or the imprisonment he had suffered in 1516 for being suspiciously friendly with the Duke of Buckingham, later executed for treason. For this new summons to London he would never forgive his heir.

The post-haste ride down the pot-holed roads of England all the way from his lands in the north did not help to sweeten his attitude to his son. Arrived at York Place, he had a long consultation with Wolsey in the gallery, and then, taking his leave of the Cardinal, he sat on a bench used by gentlemen and yeomen waiters at the head of the stairs and called his son to him. When the boy appeared, the Earl wasted no time on preliminaries.

'Son,' he greeted him, 'thou hast always been a proud, presumptuous, disdainful and very unthrift waster. And even so hast thou now declared thyself.' There followed a wordy drubbing which ended with a threat of disinheritance.

Under its terrible shadow, with the all-powerful combination of King and Cardinal against him, Percy could not but miserably submit, give up Anne and return to the north, where he was promptly appointed to office - in July, as a member of the Council of the North; in October, as Deputy Warden of the East Marches. The next year his marriage was finally arranged to Lady Mary Talbot - an ill-fated union that was to end with accusations of poisoning, and Lady Mary going home to her father. On Percy's sensitive nature, the effect of his disrupted relationship with Anne was disastrous. Tormented by a wife who hated him, by mysterious agues and swellings of the stomach, and most of all by Wolsey, who from this date was his unrelenting enemy, Percy became a wretched, broken man.

But Anne was made of a different metal, one that grew hard and bright in the fire of disappointment. With an openness that must have terrified her cautious father, she fumed against

Wolsey. Filled with sadness and frustration, reckless of any harm the powerful Cardinal might do her, she declared angrily that 'if it lay ever in her power, she would do the Cardinal as much displeasure'. At the time it seemed an empty threat.

One might have expected Anne's punishment, like Percy's, to include final condemnation to the marriage arranged for her. Significantly, this did not happen. Anne was banished from Court and sent home to her father's country house at Hever in Kent - a heavy enough punishment for a girl of her temperament and education. But James Butler's name is never again mentioned in the state papers as a prospective husband for Anne. The inference is clear. Tantalized by Anne's attractions, outraged by her proud defiance of his wishes, King Henry was eager to show her who was master, but not prepared to banish her for ever to Ireland and another man's arms. Consciously or not, already in 1522 Henry seemingly had other plans for her.

# Chapter 5

# EXILE

ANNE's banishment from Court was a forewarning, a taste of the all-powerful King's wrath which every courtier feared. 'The King's wrath is death' was a proverb they constantly and with truth repeated to one another. And while Henry would not go so far as to execute a subject who refused to marry as instructed, he might withdraw his favour. Anne was a member of a class considerably dependent on the King's monthly grants – a park keepership there, an import licence here, the odd manor confiscated from someone accused of treason.

Women as well as men could benefit from this regular hand-out of perquisites. Anne at fifteen, still being kept by her father, was not yet of an age to be concerned with these. But she was to suffer for her insubordination all the same, removed from the glittering society she had known all her life, with its swift round of banquets and revels, to the slow, dull pace of the country. Hers was no brief sentence of banishment. It was to be three years before she was recalled to Court.

For those three hidden years her name vanishes completely from the state papers of the period. The last glimpse we catch of her, through the pages of Cavendish, is riding home to Hever Castle, in the flat green meadows of Kent. We can only imagine her feelings of rebellion and despair as she crossed the wide drawbridge, entered the little timbered courtyard again and climbed a spiral stone staircase to her room. This pleasant moated manor house with its honey-coloured stone walls and spacious views of meadow, woodland and river, must have been for Anne a prison in which she had all too much time to dwell on her murdered romance.

The separation was final. There was no possible chance of another, clandestine beginning. For fear her messenger would be stopped and searched she could not even write to Percy. Looking back across four centuries at the ruthless destruction of Anne's and Percy's love, it is hard not to conclude that for her this was the point of no return. That from then onwards she knew the pursuit of happiness alone was impossible. A woman placed as she was in the society of her time needed, to enjoy any happiness, power as great as Wolsey's. To this adolescent period of her life can be traced Anne's vaulting ambition, an ambition that, at the time, she appeared unlikely ever to gratify.

King Henry's sexual desires were fleeting and inconstant. At Court the immature Anne Boleyn had dazzled his sight; now that she was out of it, she seems to have disappeared also from his mind. He turned instead to her elder sister. Mary was pretty and available. Enchanted once more by the glamour of royalty, she again became a King's mistress. While for Anne at Hever all was bleak and dark, Mary basked in the warmth of King Henry's amorous attentions, scintillating in the gorgeous apparel and jewels that were a sign of his affection for the current lady.

Henry managed his love-life more discreetly than did his 'good brother' Francis across the Channel. The servants of his Privy Chamber were discouraged from talking. In the Ordinances of the Royal Household of 1525 a special order was actually laid down that they were to keep secret everything 'done or said' in the Privy Chamber and were not to talk of the 'King's pastime, late or early going to bed or anything else done by his Grace'. Henry's mistress of the moment was never paraded in public; she was nevertheless accepted by the Court as part of the general atmosphere of 'gallantry', and by Queen Catherine as a cross she had to bear.

Catherine tolerated her husband's mistresses with patient, uncomplaining realism. She was secure in the knowledge that, despite Henry's huge flaunted codpieces and powerful frame, his passion usually grew tepid after the first passionate excitement of the chase and capture. So now, virtuously loving and loyal to her husband, she waited patiently for his affair with Mary to grow cool and end like the others. And warm-hearted Mary, grateful for Queen Catherine's politeness and forbearance, named her daughter after her. Her son (born about 1524) she named Henry. Mary's tact was rewarded. Alone among Henry's ladies to date – with the possible exception of Elizabeth Blount – she was to remain his mistress for a number of years. But they were years in which the relationship seems rapidly to have become of little importance to Henry.

No ridicule or shame attached to the husband or family of the King's mistress; indeed, it was a recognized source of promotion and perquisites. Young William Carey's perquisites were no greater than he might have expected anyway to enable him to keep up appearances as a gentleman of the Privy Chamber; he either did not know how or did not care to take advantage of the King's passion for his wife.

But Mary's father, Thomas Boleyn, was not so particular. His career went forward by leaps and bounds. Ambassador to the Emperor in Spain from October 1522 to May 1523, he was in the meantime, on 23 April 1523, created a Knight of the Garter. Numerous profitable grants of stewardships rained money into his coffers. In the same year, on June 18, he became a peer.

In the great hall of Bridewell Palace, hung with arras depicting the fall of Troy, he was led up an aisle between the chief notabilities of the land to where the King stood under his gold cloth of estate. The occasion chosen was a sign of the King's exceptional favour. Boleyn was proclaimed Viscount Rochford, to the sound of trumpets, just before the King created his own son, Elizabeth Blount's little boy, Duke of Richmond. So influential was Boleyn considered to be by now that his potential services were rewarded by the Emperor with a pension of a thousand crowns.

The sunshine of the royal favour even extended to Anne's brother George, who was singled out on 2 July 1524 for the grant of a manor in Norfolk. When her father and sister paid their brief triumphant visits to Hever, Anne must have felt herself to be the family Cinderella.

The pastimes available to a girl of her birth in the country, hunting and hawking with the neighbours, embroidery and sewing, helping her mother or her grandmother, now resident at Hever, with the administration of the household, must have

seemed to Mistress Anne most tiresomely tame. It is tempting
to believe that she spent some of her empty hours exploring
Lutheran ideas which were already gaining a footing in this
south-eastern corner of England whose ports traded with the
Netherlands. But if so, her interest, originally awakened in
France, was still superficial, a mere palliative for boredom.

That she spent all her time alone, however, is unlikely. Since
her brother had not yet acquired any regular appointment at
Court, it is a fair supposition that he was at least occasionally
in Anne's company.

George Boleyn, whose name would later be linked with his
sister's in the charge of incest, was at the time of her banishment from Court aged about nineteen. Rather indifferently
educated for a man who is supposed to have attended the
Oxford of his day (George could understand but not write
Latin and Italian), he made up for this ignorance by more
fashionable attainments. He was remarkable for his charm,
physical grace and good looks, his skill at composing ballads
and seducing women, both maidens and matrons. And like
other members of his family he spoke French fluently, a fact
that suggests he too may have spent some time in France,
perhaps living with his father when Boleyn was on embassy
there for a year, from 1519 to 1520.

Though the incest charge was almost certainly unfounded,
a strong mutual affection did exist between Anne and George,
who shared the same characteristics of wit, arrogance, and a
reckless, mocking, disrespectful sense of humour. There was
no one so great that they might not laugh at him. It was a
pastime safe enough while, far from the listening ears and
spying eyes of the Court, they rode together through the green
Kentish hills, along the banks of the little River Eden, or over
to the grey towers of Allington Castle.


Allington Castle was a fourteenth-century building on the
River Medway and the paternal home of Thomas Wyatt who,
already strongly attracted to Anne, was to follow in Percy's
footsteps and become the next victim of her eloquent black eyes
and personal magnetism.

The two families had known each other for years, though, according to George Cavendish, Anne had not met Thomas until her arrival at Court in 1522. George and Thomas shared the same interest in composing poetry and borrowed each other's books. Their fathers, Sir Henry Wyatt and Sir Thomas Boleyn, were old acquaintances. Simultaneously they had been created Knights of the Bath at Henry VIII's coronation, made Constables of Norwich Castle in 1511, and both were now officials on the financial side of the King's household. Sir Henry rejoiced in the title of Master of the King's Jewels. It was natural that Anne and young Thomas Wyatt should be thrown together socially both in the country and when she eventually returned to the English Court to become maid of honour to Queen Catherine.

Anne's return to Court is veiled in the mystery that obscures so much of her life, but we know that she was there again early in the year 1526 and it may be, as Shakespeare suggests in his play of *Henry VIII*, that she returned at the end of 1525. By that time Thomas himself had a regular position in the royal household as Clerk of the King's Jewels, a position he had held since 1524; and his domestic circumstances had changed. He had separated irrevocably from his wife.

Now he poured his feelings for Anne into elegant lyrics that were passed round the Court and sung to the lute:

> *What word is that that changeth not,*
> *Though it be turned and made in twain?*
> *It is mine answer, God it wot,*
> *And eke the causer of my pain.*
> *A love rewardeth with disdain,*
> *Yet is it love. What would ye more?*
> *It is my health eke and my sore.*

The answer to this poetic riddle, as any courtier of the day could guess, was 'Anna'. The disdainful mistress was part of the current poetic convention. That Anne did not at first treat young Wyatt with disdain but, on the contrary, flirted happily with him is pretty clear.

Wyatt was himself exceptionally attractive and talented, the epitome of the Renaissance ideal of the all-round man. Tall and athletic, with curly blond hair, large liquid eyes, aquiline nose and an expression both sensitive and firm, he was a brilliant poet, scholar and linguist, a charming and accomplished talker, who could also joust with courageous panache in the tiltyard. He had, besides, a depth of personality, a gift for friendship rare among his contemporaries.

That Anne enjoyed the admiration of such a delightful young man is beyond doubt, but that, in view of her earlier setback at Wolsey's hands over Percy, she enjoyed more than a casual flirtation with him is unlikely. Subsequent events indicate that already Anne had learned the lesson of realism, at least about the opposite sex, that her status demanded. She could not marry Wyatt since he was married already, and even had he been free it is doubtful if she would have wanted to, conditioned as she was by a degree-conscious society. Although their fathers' early careers had briefly run parallel, Anne was by this date of much higher rank than Thomas. She was the daughter of a viscount who might one day acquire his grandfather's earldom; her uncle was now the Duke of Norfolk. Thomas's father was still a mere knight – and Thomas himself would not be knighted until 1535.

The claim of Anne's enemies that she had an affair with Thomas Wyatt is based on very shaky foundations,* among them a scrawled message on a sixteenth-century manuscript of poems preserved now in the British Museum. The lyrics were written by and passed round among Anne's circle of friends at Court. Scrawled hastily across a page stained by dust and time are the words: 'I am yours, An.' A sudden impulsive message from Anne Boleyn to Wyatt? A brief glance at the writing of the alleged message, in large uneven letters and black ink, proves that this is not so; for it is not in Anne's distinctive, carefully elegant handwriting.

* The most telling argument against Anne and Wyatt is contained in two letters written in 1536 connected with his brief imprisonment then (*L & P* X, 1131, and *L & P* XI, 1492), letters that definitely refer to some serious misdemeanour. But in those dark suspicious spring days of 1536 there were, short of fornication, many misdemeanours Thomas Wyatt might have committed in regard to Anne that could have appeared to be vice in the eyes of the King.

Though Wyatt was the most persistent and sincere of Anne's suitors and the one she liked best, he makes it clear in his best-known lyric about her, the one beginning 'Whoso list to hunt . . .', that he was far from being the only one. Anne at the age of nineteen, newly returned to the pleasures of Court after more than three years of banishment, revelled in the attention. Wary after her bitter experience with Percy of getting herself too deeply involved, she flirted cruelly, her behaviour vain and giddy. The dark eyes which she had learned to use at the French Court 'holding them sometimes still, sometimes making them send a message, the secret witness of her heart', rarely told the truth. Love was a game to Anne. Wyatt compares her in his lyrics to the deer he hunted but could not catch, the wind he sought to hold in a net, the fire that burned him. Her flippant attitude remained the same when the King himself became one of her suitors.

The particular aura Anne had created about her was bound to attract a man as sexually romantic as Henry VIII. Anne's elusiveness suggested she would make an exciting quarry. And there was the delight of competition to be overcome. With the same exuberant enthusiasm with which he rivalled and excelled all others in running at the ring, shooting at the butts, dancing and jousting, King Henry flung himself into the fashionable chase of Mistress Anne Boleyn. Naturally, he was confident of success.

At the age of thirty-four Henry was still a magnificent-looking man, his girth still in proportion to his height; and his natural advantages were enhanced by the glories of the royal wardrobe on which he lavished a fifth of his entire expenditure. On each of the many holidays and saints' days the King would appear in a new outfit, of yellow silk or green velvet, crimson satin or cloth of gold, adorned with 'collars' (chains) of priceless gems. Although his auburn hair was thinning, Henry was still the furious rider who never hunted 'without tiring eight or ten horses, which he caused to be stationed beforehand along the line of country he may mean to take', the prince of many parts who excelled at 'shooting, singing, dancing, wrestling, casting of the bar, playing at the recorders, flute, virginals', and who had composed his own Mass.

While nothing like so accomplished a poet as Thomas Wyatt, the King could still turn a pretty ballad to please a lady's ear.

> *Green groweth the holly: so doth the ivy*
> *Though winter blasts blow neu [never] so high*
> *green groweth the holly*
> *As the holly groweth green and neu [never] changeth hue*
> *So I am ever hath been unto my lady true*
> *As the holly groweth green with ivy all alone*
> *When flowers cannot be seen: and greenwood leaves be gone*
> *Now unto my lady promise to her I make*
> *From all other only to her I me betake.*

All the songs from Henry's lute, however, his tender wooing, the flattery of his attentions, his usually irresistible charm, strangely enough made no headway with Mistress Anne Boleyn. The outraged King found himself used by this nineteen-year-old girl no better and no worse than the humble Thomas Wyatt.

Anne's reasons for this cavalier treatment obviously derive from the experience of her elder sister Mary, who had been – possibly still was – the King's mistress. Mary could bear witness to the pathologically cold streak in the King's nature that lurked beneath the surface charm and showed itself when his passion was spent. She was also the living proof that there was in 1526 small personal advantage to be gained from taking the King as a lover, for while Thomas Boleyn had grown considerably richer on the liaison, Mary herself had gained little in the way of property or goods. The King's generosity to his mistresses never lasted long.

Thus, even had Anne not been basically afraid of the sex act and willing to succeed her sister in a relationship smacking of incest, there were good reasons for keeping the King at arm's length.

Anne flirted with King Henry in the same light-hearted mocking way as she tantalized other men. She even played him off against Wyatt. Recklessly she bestowed tokens on both at the same time: to Henry she gave a ring which he proudly displayed on his little finger; to Wyatt she gave a small jewelled tablet on a lace, which he hung round his neck under his doublet. The King became furiously jealous, and the antagonism between Anne's two suitors came to a head in the middle of a game of bowls, a dramatic scene which has been recorded for us by the poet's grandson.

The King and Wyatt were on opposing sides in a game that included among other courtiers the Duke of Suffolk and Sir Francis Brian. Suddenly the King, in what appeared to be a fit of forgetfulness, claimed someone else's cast to be his.

When Wyatt's team, respectfully 'with his Grace's leave', disagreed, Henry fixed the poet with his small blue eyes, pointed his little finger at the bowl, insisted: 'Wyatt, I tell thee it is mine - I tell thee it is mine.'

Wyatt, recognizing Anne's ring but noting that the King was smiling, replied merrily, with who knows what vain hope in his heart: 'And if it may like your Majesty to give me leave to measure it, I hope it will be mine.' He took from his neck the lace with the little jewelled tablet, stooped and pretended to measure the cast.

At sight of Anne's token Henry's face darkened. Angrily he kicked aside the bowl. 'It may be so, but then I am deceived.' He strode away, breaking up the game.

Back in his own private royal apartments, Henry called Anne to him and demanded an explanation. Anne realized she had gone dangerously too far. Did not the King hold the fate of her whole family in his hand? Her brother George had his way yet to make at Court. Already the King had shown him favour in the matter of his marriage to Jane Parker, for when Jane's father, Henry Parker, Lord Morley, had been unable to provide the full £300 dowry demanded by the rapacious Thomas Boleyn, the King had generously made up the difference. Anne dared not endanger her beloved brother's chances.

The King proved unexpectedly easy to mollify. Thomas Wyatt, Anne told him, had taken and kept the token against her will. Henry as always chose to believe what he wanted to. He accepted this unlikely excuse and forgave Anne; while his more sceptical courtiers stored away in their memories this seed of scandal for future use.

Warned off, Wyatt did not remain long in England to watch his rival's triumph. In January 1527 his friend John Russell, on his way down the Thames, bound on embassy to the Pope, met Wyatt, who asked where he was going. 'To Italy, sent by the King,' said Russell. 'And I,' said Wyatt, 'if you please, will ask leave, get money, and go with you.'

*Chapter 6*

# A ROYAL PROMISE

ROUGHLY, capriciously, King Henry had ousted the poor poet
Thomas Wyatt. By the laws of the code of courtly love then in
vogue – inspired by the twelfth-century songs of the trouba-
dours – which placed the woman on a pedestal and made her
lover hers to command in all things, Henry had become Anne's
true knight, servant and accepted wooer. He had achieved no
more. For weeks after Wyatt's discomfiture Anne seems to have
kept Henry guessing as to her true feelings for him. The King,
whose pursuit had lasted for nearly a year, had by this time
fallen heavily in love with her – and in love, Henry who could
be so crudely callous was tenderly romantic. The summit of
his ambition was now a humble one: to obtain a firm declaration from Mistress Anne that she returned his passionate
affection.

It was a pleasure Anne dared not give him.

What were Anne's true feelings towards the King at the
beginning of 1527? That she was helplessly in love with him
it is plain from her behaviour she was not. How could she
forget the flaws in his character, of which she had learned
from Mary? It is equally unlikely that she could fail to be
fascinated by a man of Henry's charm and talent, a man
who was, moreover, her King and who excelled in all her favourite extrovert amusements – masking, hunting, singing
and dancing.

Anne's dilemma was great. Having hooked this royal fish
without any particular desire to catch him – 'I never wished
to choose the King in my heart,' she was to admit years afterwards – she did not know what to do with him. If she told him
she could never love him her family would undoubtedly suffer;
and George now had his foot on the ladder of promotion. On

26 February 1526 he was appointed 'to be one of the King's cup-bearers when he dineth out'. On the other hand, should she tell him she returned his passion she was more or less bound to embark on a love-affair with him, for which at this stage in their relationship she evidently had no desire at all.

So Anne Boleyn continued to prevaricate, to lead him on, then evade him at the last moment. With the help of her lightning wit, her ready laugh and the convention of courtly love, according to which the would-be lover must obey his lady's every whim, she avoided committing herself while driving the King into a frenzy of passion. Faced with the demand for an honest answer, she could always resort to the argument that virtue forbade her to entertain feelings of love for a married man. And when Henry became too persistent she simply retired to one of her father's mansions in the country.

Henry pursued her there with letters, in French and in English. Proudly, Anne preserved them. Later they were mysteriously stolen and conveyed out of England to the Vatican, where they are still to be seen today. These letters are a window through which we can watch Henry and Anne acting out the turbulent, catastrophic relationship that would lead eventually to the splitting asunder of Christendom.

Trusted messengers, able to support the King's suit with their own persuasive speeches, carried the King's letters to Anne.

'To my mistress,' Henry wrote in black ink and his own bold, flamboyant hand, in what may be the first of these undated letters, the words slanting optimistically upwards across the parchment.

Because it seems to me a very long time since I heard of your good health and of you, the great affection I have for you persuades me to send this messenger the better to ascertain your health and wishes; and because, since my leaving you, I have been informed that the opinion in which I left you has been wholly changed, and that you will not come to Court either with madam your mother or otherwise; which report, if true, I cannot enough marvel at, since I am sure that I have never committed any fault against you there, and it seems to me a very small return for the great love I bear you to be kept at a distance from the conversation and the person of the woman whom I most esteem in the world, and if you love me with such good affection as I hope, I am sure that the distance between our two selves must be a little wearisome to you, although at the same time this pertains not so much to the mistress as to the servant. Consider well, my mistress, that absence from you grieves me greatly, hoping that it is not by your will that it is so; but if I understood for certain that you indeed wished it I could do no other than lament my ill fortune while abating little by little my great folly; and thus, for lack of time, I make an end to my rude letter, begging you to believe what the bearer will say to you on my behalf.

Written by the hand of your entire servant.

*H Rex*

Anne's reply to this heartfelt plea, written in French, from H Rex has not survived. Like all her letters, it was destroyed by a monarch careful of the all-seeing eyes of his Court; (the letter that purports to be Anne's reply is apocryphal). But it is possible to deduce the contents of Anne's letters from Henry's answers. Writing back now, humbly respectful, full of gratitude for the King's interest, Anne seems merely to have said that she should really be his servant. To which impersonal note, Henry who had looked eagerly for expressions of affection, wrote back exasperated, again in French.

Though it does not become a gentleman to treat his lady as his servant, nevertheless in following your wishes, I willingly grant them if thereby you find yourself less unpleasantly settled in the place of your choice than in that given by me; at the same time thanking you very cordially if it please you still to have some remembrance of me.

*Henry Rex*

Thus cool and formal were Henry's letters, at the beginning; then abruptly they became much warmer. 'Darling', they began, or 'Mine own sweetheart'; for there had been a revolutionary change in their relationship. Anne had committed herself at last, declared she was in love with him. She had seen

a glittering prospect open before her, the chance to sit on the
throne beside Henry under her own golden cloth of estate. The
chance indeed to become Queen of England.

For several years Henry had been desperately concerned that
he had no male heir to succeed him. Of his six children by
Catherine, including at least three boys, the only survivor was
the delicate, auburn-haired Princess Mary, who was small and
slight for her age. Despite Catherine's fervent prayers and
pilgrimages, despite Henry's offer to God to go on a crusade if
He would give him an heir, all the other royal offspring had
died in the womb or within a few weeks of birth.

Not since 1518 had Catherine been pregnant and physicians
sent from Spain could not cure the affliction (described by
Henry as 'certain diseases') that prevented her conceiving. By
July 1525 Henry's ambassador stated openly in the Imperial
court that at thirty-nine she was 'past the age at which women
most commonly are wont to be fruitful and have children'. So
the future of the kingdom rested upon one frail girl.

Anne must soon have realized Henry's preoccupying anxiety,
if not from the King himself, from her own relations at Court.
Callous though Henry was of the welfare of individuals, he
was keenly concerned for the good of his kingdom and haunted
by the memory of the recent civil war between Yorkists and
Lancastrians. Could a woman ruler be strong enough to keep
the peace? The example of Matilda, the only previous Queen of
England in her own right, was not reassuring.

There was also the problem of marriage. When Mary was
two years old and Henry still expected sons, he had promised
her to the Dauphin. Now however the picture was changed.
Henry no longer expected sons by Catherine. Now if Mary took
a foreign prince for her husband as befitted her rank, this would
almost certainly lead, should she become Queen, to the domination of England by another country. In 1521 Henry had
arranged for Mary to wed the Emperor, a consort acceptable
to the English people because of trade links between the two
countries, but when, in 1525, the Emperor chose instead to
marry the wealthy Isabella of Portugal, Henry felt obliged to

resume negotiations for a French son-in-law. English people, he knew, would never stand a Frenchman's yoke. Although he was now again at peace with the French they remained England's traditional enemy. It had become essential to find an alternative heir.

Desperate with anxiety for the future of his kingdom, Henry sought for some solution. Briefly he toyed with the idea of marrying Mary to her half-brother, Elizabeth Blount's little son Henry Fitzroy. He also considered making this boy his heir. Creating him Duke of Richmond in 1525 at the age of six, he gave him Henry VII's title and a household larger than Princess Mary's; but besotted though Henry was by this proof of his manhood, this child whom he called his 'worldly jewel', he was aware that it would not be easy to make a bastard – even a royal one – the King.

By accident of fate it was at this critical moment that Anne became the object of Henry's passion; the two obsessions became intermingled and the sequel was inevitable. A delightful if daring solution to the problem of an heir occurred to him by which he could realize his two most pressing wishes at the same time: acquire Anne, who would not return his affection or sleep with him without marriage; and beget a son. He would divorce his plain, barren, obedient wife, Catherine, and marry again.

Was it Anne, as Cardinal Pole later claimed, who first put the idea of the divorce into Henry's mind, using as mouthpiece a sympathetic priest? Or did Henry himself think of it? Unfortunately we shall never know. What we can be reasonably sure of – remembering Henry's obedient conscience which raised no barriers to his wishes – is that the suggestion did not originally come, as the King claimed, from the Bishop of Tarbes (the French ambassador who visited England to negotiate Mary's marriage) and that the desire to be free of Catherine preceded his doubts about the validity of their union.

Divorce in the modern sense was then impossible; but a reason might be found for the marriage to be pronounced invalid, for the Pope had always been sympathetic to the marital problems of fellow princes. In the previous century Henry IV of Castile, having no children by his first wife, was

given a special dispensation to marry a second. Henry's sister
Margaret had been granted a divorce on the grounds that her
second husband, the Earl of Angus, had had a pre-contract with
another woman; and also that at the time of her marriage to
him her first husband, King James IV of Scotland, had still
been alive – a manifest impossibility, since James's body was
found on the field at Flodden. The Duke of Suffolk had been
married no less than three times. His first marriage, for which
he had had to get a Papal dispensation, since his wife was
related to him within the forbidden degrees of affinity, had
been declared null by an official of the Archdeacon of London
on the grounds that the dispensation was invalid. Suffolk had
then proceeded to marry a woman to whom he had earlier been
contracted and, after her death, he married Mary Tudor.

No less leniency would surely be accorded the King of
England, to whom the Pontiff himself had awarded the title
'Defender of the Faith' for his loyal services in writing a book
opposing Luther in 1521.

His own case for 'divorcing' Catherine – a parallel with
Suffolk's – seemed to Henry faultless, for Catherine had been
his brother's wife and was thus, according to canon law,
related to the King within the forbidden degrees. Although
Catherine had been the wife of fifteen-year-old Prince Arthur
for only four months before he died, when Henry, on acceding
to the throne, had decided to marry her, he had been obliged
to apply for a special dispensation. Pope Julius had granted it,
but the Archbishop of Canterbury and the Bishop of Winchester had still questioned the legality of the marriage. Had
they been right, Henry asked himself now. Could the dispensation overcome the edict in Leviticus: 'If a man shall take his
brother's wife, it is an impurity: he hath uncovered his
brother's nakedness; they shall be childless'?

Henry's decision, not surprisingly, was in the negative, his
conviction strengthened by memory of Catherine's long history
of miscarriages and still births. The finger of God was on his
children. God had shown the marriage was accursed. And now
that he felt his situation was about to be changed, now that he
felt himself no longer married to Catherine, he was free to offer

Anne the one bribe no sixteenth-century Court lady - and certainly not Anne - could resist.

For a King to marry a subject in the sixteenth century was, however, a most exceptional and risky step to take. Henry's rival monarchs, King Francis and the Emperor Charles V, both married to found dynasties and satisfied love and lust with affairs. The last King of England to marry a subject, Edward IV, had nearly lost his throne through the jealousy and dissatisfaction that resulted from his choice of Elizabeth Woodville. On consideration of such disturbing facts, Henry not unnaturally seems to have hesitated before making his final proposal to Anne. Could he not still perhaps find a way to enjoy her without risking both his popularity in his own country and dangerous repercussions abroad?

Anne was absent from Court when Henry wrote his final desperate plea; among the whole revealing collection the letter that shows most completely how Anne had enthralled the King. Coming from a man who had never before been forced to beg for anything, and translated here from the original French, it is curiously pathetic.

In debating with myself the content of your letters I have been put in a great agony; not knowing how to understand them, whether to my disadvantage as shown in some places, or to my advantage, as I understand them, in others [he began, warming to his subject].

Beseeching you now with all my heart to let me know definitely your whole intention touching the love between us two; for necessity constrains me to pester you for this reply, having been for more than a year struck by the dart of love, being uncertain either of failure or of finding a place in your heart and affection. Certainly the last point has kept me for some time from naming you my mistress, because if you love me with only an ordinary love this name is not appropriate to you, since it denotes a singular situation which is very remote from the ordinary; but if it pleases you to do the duty of a true, loyal mistress and friend, and to give yourself body and heart to me, who will be (and have been) your very loyal servant (if your strictness does not forbid

me), I promise you that not only the name will be due to
you, but also to take you for my sole mistress, rejecting all
others except yourself out of mind and affection, and to
serve you alone; begging you to make me a complete answer
to this my rude letter as to how far and in what I can trust;
and if it does not please you to make a reply in writing, to
give me some place where I can have it by word of mouth,
which place I will seek out with all my heart. No more for
fear of boring you. Written by the hand of him who would
willing remain your

                                                    HR

But as Anne very well knew, the position Henry appeared in
this letter to be offering her was one that did not really exist
in England. In France the royal concubine or *maîtresse en titre*
was publicly paraded even on official occasions; in England
Henry's sexual partners were always surrounded with some
secrecy. Anne had already for some time been enjoying the
mixed blessing of being Henry's mistress in the courtly love
sense, which did not necessarily imply a sexual relationship. In
the circumstances the King's offer was no incentive at all.
Clearly there was only one bribe Anne would listen to and,
shortly after he wrote this letter, Henry must have finally
offered to marry her.

Dazzled by the glittering prospect ahead, the summit of all
her ambitions, Anne at last resolved her doubts and committed
herself. Was this disloyal to Catherine? A snatch of writing,
'Spanish Kathryn', on a book of French poetry belonging to
George Boleyn in 1526 and scribbled over with the signatures
of Wyatt and Marc Smeton, groom of the Privy Chamber and
musician, suggests that Anne's friends helped her to make up
her mind that it was not. Anne could easily quiet her conscience. There was no disloyalty if the marriage had never
been legal. Henry had chapter and verse and learned opinion
to support his case.

Anne seized her opportunity and accepted Henry's proposal.
She declared she loved him with a love as rare as his, said she
looked forward to sleeping with him when they were married;
virtue would prevent her doing so before. And she sent him,

as a token of her love, a jewel representing a lady in a storm-tossed ship, symbol of herself and the dangers she was prepared to brave for his sake. Henry wrote back in jubilation and graceful French:

For a gift so beautiful that nothing could be more (considering it as a whole) I thank you very cordially, not only for the fine diamond and the ship in which the lonely damsel is tossed about, but chiefly for the beautiful interpretation and too humble submission for which your kindness has used it; thinking well that it would be very difficult for me to find cause to merit it if I were not aided by your great generosity and favour, which I have sought, seek, and will ever seek, by everything in my power; and to remain in which my hope has put its unchangeable intention, which says: *aut illic, aut nullibi* [there or nowhere]. The demonstrations of your affection are such, the beautiful words of the letter so cordially couched, they oblige me ever truly to honour, love and serve you, begging you to continue in the same firm and constant purpose, assuring you that so far from merely returning your affection, I will outdo you in loyalty of heart and in the desire to please, and you with no bitterness in yours can further that; praying also that if at any time I have offended you, you will give me the same absolution as you yourself demand; assuring you that henceforth my heart shall be dedicated to you alone, wishing strongly that my body could also be so dedicated, as God can do if he pleases. This I pray Him daily to do, hoping that finally my prayer will be heard, wishing the time brief and thinking it long until we two meet again. Written by the hand of the one who in heart, body and will is Your loyal and most assured servant,

H seeks AB no other R

Round the initials AB he drew a heart to prove his devotion. By May 1527 Anne was back at Court, in high favour for all to see with the King. On Sunday, May 5, the King gave a banquet and dance in honour of the French ambassadors who had come to negotiate the marriage between Henry's daughter

Mary and a French prince. The King astonished them by choosing on this official occasion to lead out Anne as his partner. Henry had probably danced with her many times before. Now, however, he chose to do so when the eyes of some of the shrewdest observers in Europe were upon him.

In the magnificent new banqueting house that looked out over the King's moonlit garden, the entertainment that had started in the afternoon was lavish with every kind of spectacle. There was 'tourneying at the barrier' inside the banqueting hall itself, and a series of masques in one of which the eleven-year-old bride-to-be, Princess Mary, was the star.

Around midnight the King, the Vicomte de Turenne, one of the ambassadors, and six other maskers appeared, dressed as Venetian noblemen. Henry gestured to Turenne to dance with the Princess and himself openly chose Anne as his partner. Although the festivities went on until the early hours of the morning, the ambassadors were not too dazed to remember the name of Mistress Anne Boleyn when they returned to France.

Twelve days later, on May 17, King Henry secretly took the first legal steps to obtain a divorce from the wife he had been married to for nearly eighteen years so that he could make Anne his Queen instead.

# Chapter 7

# 'THE KING'S SECRET MATTER'

WHEN Anne sent Henry a jewelled representation of herself as a lady in a storm-tossed ship, she was realistic as well as being romantic. She was reminding him of the mighty forces that would seek to destroy her as soon as the King's intention to marry her became known. It would immediately provoke the hostility of the most powerful ruler in Europe. Charles V, Emperor of Germany and King of Spain, was Catherine of Aragon's nephew; family honour would require him to oppose the divorce of his aunt. Many of King Henry's own subjects, moreover, would be bound to object strongly when they saw their King attempt to marry a lady who was not of royal blood.

Henry was confident at this stage that he could successfully negotiate all problems, priding himself on his cunning, which he used to the full in his first moves towards a 'divorce'. His chief minister, Wolsey, would be outraged at the thought of his King throwing himself away on a mere subject, but the Cardinal, Henry knew also, still had his heart set on a French alliance. So when Henry told Wolsey he wished to 'divorce' Catherine, he encouraged him to believe that he contemplated wedding a French princess. The cherished alliance dangling before him, Wolsey set to work.

On 17 May 1527 a little flotilla of boats and barges was tied up discreetly and without ceremony by the landing-stage at York Place. Out of them stepped the King, the Archbishop of Canterbury, and a number of lawyers. As though on an ordinary informal visit, they filed up the stairs into the riverside palace and into one of the great rooms. Here the proceedings suddenly became very formal indeed. Once inside, shut away from prying eyes, the new arrivals took their places in an ecclesiastical court. It was opened and presided over by Wolsey. Appointed assessor was William Warham, the same Archbishop of Canterbury who had originally opposed Henry's marriage to Catherine, and whose square jowls and haunted eyes stare back at us disturbingly across the centuries from Holbein's drawing at Windsor Castle. The part he was now compelled to play was an unenviable one. For Warham, if not always an entirely courageous man, was an honest one, and the trial was an elaborately contrived lie. The King, sitting at Wolsey's right hand, was charged with living illegally for eighteen years with his wife. Henry submitted graciously to have the case examined.

Wolsey seems to have hoped that in his capacity as papal legate he could himself give sentence of 'divorce' without reference to the Pope, and that Catherine and her nephew the Emperor would not hear about the proceedings until it was too late to take effective action.

The 'divorce' might have gone through and Anne become Queen almost overnight had a disastrous event in Italy not suddenly intervened and upset all Wolsey's plans. Italy was at that time a patchwork of dukedoms and principalities, the scene of rival territorial claims and recurring war between the French and Imperial forces. Since the summer of 1526 there had been fighting between the Emperor on one side and a league composed of the Pope, several Italian princes and Francis I on the other, partly supported by English money.

On 1 June 1527 a travel-stained exhausted courier rode through the palace gates, and with the rest of the astonished and horrified Court, Anne heard the news. Three weeks before, the troops of Charles V had taken and sacked Rome. They had behaved with hideous barbarity. They had violated nuns, murdered priests, stabled their horses in the churches. Pope Clement VII had fled to the Castle of St Angelo, where he was virtually a prisoner of Catherine's nephew. Now he was no longer a free agent. While previously he might without protest have allowed Wolsey in his capacity of papal legate to pronounce Catherine's marriage to Henry null, he would now almost certainly be forced to deny the Cardinal's right to pronounce such a sentence. Without the Pope's signed and sealed permission, it was no longer safe to try the case in England.

Wolsey changed his plans. In June he closed the secret ecclesiastical court at York Place and prepared to journey majestically into France. He meant to effect the liberation of the Pope by arranging a general peace if he could; if he couldn't, he would conclude a hostile alliance against the Emperor. He still intended to stage a trial of the King's cause, but only when he could be sure of bringing it to a successful conclusion.

Henry was still anxious to conceal his intentions. In messages to Wolsey he referred discreetly to the 'divorce' as the 'King's great matter' or 'secret matter'. But Henry's secret had already leaked out. The ecclesiastical court had been a bad blunder. On May 18, Don Inigo de Mendoza, the Imperial ambassador in London, wrote a report to his master:

> I have heard for certain that this good legate [Wolsey], as the finishing stroke to all his iniquities, is working to divorce the Queen. And she is so afraid that she has not dared to speak with me. They have told me that the King has advanced so far in this matter that he has assembled certain bishops and lawyers . . .

On 22 June 1527, unaware of Mendoza's report, Henry forced himself to perform the unpleasant necessity of informing Catherine. Perhaps he nourished the wild hope that, as meekly as she had obeyed him in most things, she would do so now in this. All the years of their marriage, he blurted out, they had been living in mortal sin. So numerous canonists and theologians had told him, and his conscience was greatly troubled. He had resolved no longer to live with her. She must choose a house to which to retire. Catherine's only reply, her apprehensions confirmed, was to burst out weeping.

All would be done for the best, Henry murmured in a clumsy attempt to console her, to stop the embarrassing tears, and meanwhile she must keep the matter secret. He strode hastily away.

The 'King's great matter', Anne must have reflected, had hardly got off to an auspicious beginning. She had one overriding anxiety. She could not feel easy at the thought that negotiations for the 'divorce' were in the hands of her enemy. Wolsey still believed her to be, like her predecessors, a mere concubine. But when he learned, as he soon must, that she and not some foreign princess was the object of Henry's new matrimonial schemes, then he would surely do all he could to unseat her. Encouraged by the Lords of the Privy Council who hated him, and who in Wolsey's absence abroad quickly discovered the truth, Anne resolved to do everything in her power to unseat him first.

On July 3 the Cardinal had left his palace at Westminster for France. Winding through the narrow streets of London, his sumptuous retinue extended three-quarters of a mile. First came the gentlemen in black velvet and gold chains, then the portly Cardinal all in scarlet, preceded by his crosses and pillars of silver, his Cardinal's hat, the great seal of England, and a gentleman carrying a vast scarlet bag, embroidered with cloth of gold, which contained the Cardinal's cloak. He was followed by yeomen and servants in French tawny livery coats, embroidered on the back and breast with the initials T.C., for Thomas Cardinalis, under a Cardinal's hat.

With this princely procession Wolsey was received like royalty in France, but the cause of all this magnificence quailed inside himself. The Cardinal had received an exceedingly troubling letter from the King. Henry had accused him of being half-hearted about the 'divorce', an accusation Wolsey hastily denied. But could he convince the King? Wolsey was aware that he had not reigned as the most powerful man in the kingdom for fourteen years without acquiring many enemies. Now Henry appeared to be listening to them.

Within a few weeks, as, ageing and overweight, he laboured through the heat of a French summer, Wolsey must have realized the unwelcome and incredible truth: Mistress Anne Boleyn was no transitory figure in the King's life, no Mary Boleyn or Elizabeth Blount. Henry actually intended to marry her.

In an attempt to avoid this information getting out, Anne had withdrawn to Hever Castle in July; it was too late. In a

Court crowded with those whose fortunes depended on interpreting the King's least smile, the facts could not be hidden. Anne's manner with men had changed; there was a new dignity about her, an unapproachableness, and her wardrobe was suddenly fabulous. She 'was the model and the mirror of those who were at Court', says Nicholas Sanders, 'for she was always well dressed, and every day made some change in the fashion of her garments.' As well as the gorgeous gowns which, courtiers knew, the miserly Boleyn would never have bought her, the jewels that suddenly glistened against her pale olive skin and in her black hair told their story.

Thomas Wyatt had returned from Italy in May. The gleam of a diamond necklace caught his eye, to become the central image of a poignant little lyric:

> Whoso list to hunt, I know where is an hind,
> But as for me, helas, I may no more:
> The vain travail hath wearied me so sore.
> I am of them that farthest cometh behind;
> Yet may I by no means my wearied mind
> Draw from the deer: but as she fleeth afore,
> Fainting I follow. I leave off therefore,
> Since in a net I seek to hold the wind.
> Who list her hunt, I put him out of doubt,
> As well as I may spend his time in vain:
> And, graven with diamonds, in letters plain
> There is written her fair neck round about:
> Noli me tangere, for Caesar's I am;
> And wild for to hold, though I seem tame.

Even in Anne's absence from Court, the royal favouritism shown to her family continued to feed the gossip. At the end of July the King was at Beaulieu 'merry and in good health' and hunting daily, keeping 'a very great and expensive house', which included the Dukes of Norfolk and Suffolk, the Marquis of Exeter, the Earls of Oxford, Essex and Rutland, Viscount Fitzwilliam and Anne's father, Thomas Boleyn, Viscount Rochford. Despite his comparatively low position in the hierarchy of guests, Anne's father was one of the select little group, with the Dukes of Norfolk and Suffolk, and the Marquis of

Exeter, which usually supped with the King in his Privy Chamber.

The news was conveyed to Wolsey, who wrote a terrified letter from France. He protested that the successful conclusion of the King's 'secret matter' was his daily study and most inward desire and said that every day deprived of the sight of the King's noble and royal person felt like a year. As for his own poor person, it was his daily and continual solicitude, and ever would be, to do that thing which was agreeable to his Grace's pleasure and the advancement of his virtuous desires. He ended his letter: 'Written with the rude and shaking hand of your most humble subject, servant and chaplain, T. Carlis Ebor.'

While Wolsey in France trembled for his future, in the lush green countryside of England Anne revelled in her new-found power.

Despite the pleasures of the hunt, the satisfaction of showing off his exceptional skill with the cross-bow when, according to the usual method of deer-hunting at this date, the beaters drove the deer beneath his stand, Henry's thoughts were constantly returning to Anne and the wonderful time to come when he would finally enjoy her. They found expression in a stream of gifts and love-letters.

'My mistress and friend,' he began in one, in which he hinted wistfully that perhaps she might a little relent her hard conditions that insisted he should wait until after marriage.

I and my heart put ourselves in your hands, begging you to recommend us to your good grace and not to let absence lessen your affection, for to increase their pain would be a great pity since absence does that sufficiently and more than I could ever have thought possible; reminding us of a point in astronomy, which is that the longer the days are the farther off is the sun and yet the hotter; so is it with our love, for although by absence we are parted it nevertheless keeps its fervour, at least on my part, hoping the like on yours; assuring you that for myself the pain of absence already is too great, and when I think of the increase in what I must of necessity suffer it would be almost intolerable were it not for my firm hope of your unchanging affection for me; and to remind you occasionally of this, and seeing that in person I cannot be with you, I send you now the thing most nearly pertaining to it that I can, that is to say, my picture set in a bracelet with the whole device which you already know; wishing myself in their place when it shall please you. This by the hand of

Your loyal servant and friend,

H Rex

Meanwhile Wolsey laboured to save himself from the precipice he could see before him by inventing a desperate scheme that would enable the King to satisfy his desire and so look with favour again on his most wretched minister. The scheme was grandiose if unrealistic, in line with Wolsey's cherished ambition one day to be elected Pope. He would set up during Clement's captivity a papal government-in-exile at Avignon presided over by himself with full powers. First, however, the Pope's consent must be obtained. Someone must contrive to get past the Pope's Imperial guards to visit him clandestinely in the Castle of St Angelo in Rome. For a man of Wolsey's wide-ranging talents, the last was a small matter, easily settled.

On 11 August 1527 Wolsey wrote to Henry to say he had arranged for three men, Girolamo Ghinucci (Italian absentee Bishop of Worcester), Uberto de Gambara, Bishop of Tortona, and Gregory Casale, the King's agent in Rome, to bribe their way past the Spanish guards. They would ask the Pope to sign and seal a commission to make Wolsey his vicar with full powers.

Anne and her family, however, had made good use of their enemy's absence abroad. Instead of the letter from the King approving his scheme that the Cardinal expected, he received another. Henry had chosen his own messenger to the Pope, a Dr William Knight (whom Wolsey knew to be both old and incompetent). He would meet Wolsey at Compiègne to receive his instructions. The message was a fraud, as the Cardinal discovered even before Knight's arrival. For hidden in Knight's baggage was a document he had been told to present for the

Pope's signature but on no account to reveal to Wolsey: nothing less than a measure that would allow Henry to commit bigamy.

Wolsey was appalled, not only by the King's attempt to deceive him, but also at the reckless stupidity of presenting such a document to the Pope. It would undermine Henry's whole case, founded as it was ostensibly on the King's troubled conscience and his need for an heir. Wolsey wrote begging him to withdraw the ill-advised document, and Henry meekly agreed; perhaps he realized the dispensation would hardly fulfil Anne's conditions. This narrowly averted blunder, however, was followed by one of even greater dimensions, which Wolsey was unable to prevent. After Knight left Wolsey yet another secret document was packed off to him in the saddle-bags of a messenger chosen and trusted by the Boleyns, John Barlow, chaplain to Anne's father and rector of the church at Hever, Kent. The document was to be delivered to Knight in Italy.

It was a dispensation for the King to marry Anne.

Among the King's many mistakes in the long history of the divorce this document was the most incredible. The only explanation is that Henry's judgement at the time was blinded by passion and that he had it drawn up to please Anne. For not only would it reveal to Pope Clement VII that Henry's wish for a 'divorce' from Catherine was prompted by his desire for another woman – but that that woman was a most unsuitable choice for Queen.

Though it did not mention Anne by name, the dispensation plainly referred to her. It would allow Henry to marry any woman, even one to whom he was related in the first degree of affinity. Through her sister Mary he was related in this way to Anne. And – a factor that could hardly recommend the justice of Henry's case for a divorce – it was in this way that he had also been related to Catherine through his brother. The only difference on which Henry could claim that the Pope could legally allow him to marry Anne but not Catherine was a semantic quibble: his relationship with Mary, unlike his brother's relationship with Catherine, had been illicit.

But the document Knight was to present for the Pope's

signature included other almost equally undiplomatic provisions.

Henry was also to be allowed to marry a woman who had
been contracted in marriage to someone else but without
having intercourse with him, which was a clear reference to
Anne's relationship with Percy, since their promise to marry
each other, even without the sanction of their elders, could
legally be considered to constitute a pre-contract. As though
this was not enough to discourage the Pope from setting his
seal to the dispensation, Henry also asked to be allowed to wed
someone with whom he himself had already had intercourse.
Ever hopeful that Anne would relax her conditions, he wished
to provide for all future contingencies.

Of this document, so the King wrote to Knight, 'no man
doth know but they which I am sure will never disclose it to
no man living for any craft the Cardinal or any other can find'.
And he instructed Knight diligently to solicit the Pope to set
his seal to it, adding fervently: 'For that is it which I above all
things do desire.'

As Dr William Knight, filled with self-importance as the
King's secret messenger, rode off from Compiègne on his way
to Rome diligently to solicit the Pope's signature on this
disastrous document, the Cardinal, deeply suspicious of
Knight's errand, anxious about the forces building up against
him in England, hurried home from France. He rode straight
to Richmond Palace, whither the Court had moved, and sent
to ask where the King would see him. Wolsey's messenger
found Anne with Henry.

It was the opportunity for which Anne must have longed in
those years of her banishment - for, according to George
Cavendish, she believed them to be entirely the Cardinal's
fault, unaware that he was merely implementing his master's
wishes. She took it upon herself to answer the messenger.

Knowing that Wolsey was accustomed to seeing the King
alone, she spoke up quickly and haughtily, head high on her
graceful neck: 'Where else but here, where the King is.' Clay
in the hands of his beloved, Henry meekly agreed.

As he entered the chamber Thomas Wolsey was aware that,
after fourteen years of governing the kingdom as Henry's

first minister, his star had been displaced by the arrogant, black-eyed Mistress Anne Boleyn, whom he had described to Percy as 'a foolish girl yonder in the Court'. And Anne, observing the fixed, nervous smile of greeting on her defeated rival's suddenly shrunken face, savoured the first sweetness of revenge.

Such open exhibitions of her influence over the King, however, must be few; for Henry still cheated himself he could keep their relationship secret. At the end of the summer of 1527 Anne found herself in an anomalous situation. Though everyone suspected she was to be the next Queen, on the surface she was still just plain Mistress Anne, maid of honour at Catherine's beck and call. Fortunately for her, the Queen's nature was unusual.

Catherine had taken vigorous action to protect herself against 'divorce'. She had sent a messenger to her nephew the Emperor in July, asking him to persuade the Pope to judge her case himself in Rome – and she had informed the King firmly that since she had never had sexual relations with Prince Arthur he had no grounds. In every other respect Catherine prided herself on being an obedient, submissive wife, modelling herself on Chaucer's Patient Griselda. And she treated Anne with exaggerated kindness, having her, so she told her ladies, 'in more estimation for the King's sake than she had before'.

The only hint Anne had of the Queen's deeply buried antagonism lay in her repeated invitations to play cards. Playing cards with her, Anne could not be alone with Henry. Even better, Henry would see the deformity on her right hand that normally she kept hidden; and see too that his wife's hands, by contrast, were small and perfect. Catherine was human. Once, as they played a game in which whoever dealt a king had the advantage, and the advantage fell to Anne, Catherine could not contain her feelings and allowed herself one bitter remark: 'Mistress Anne, you have good hap to stop at a king, but you are not like the others. You will have all, or none.'

The slights and veiled insults that Anne invited proceeded not from the Queen herself, but from her outraged friends and attendants: Henry's sister Mary, now Duchess of Suffolk; the Duchess of Norfolk (Anne's aunt); as well as her aunt and namesake, Lady Anne Boleyn. Catherine was loved and respected; Anne the type of woman, vain, egocentric, exhibitionist, too attractive to men, who would always be disliked by her own sex.

Anne seems to have made no attempt at this time to appease these important ladies. Instead she surveyed her enemies arrogantly, dressed with ever-increasing splendour, and continued to enjoy her exquisite sense of power. The King hung on her least word, spent endless energy and time drawing up alternate legal documents with which to bombard Clement VII, in the hope that one of them would meet with papal approval and allow him to marry his sweetheart. For Anne these first months of negotiation for the 'divorce' were a time of tension and excitement. They were a time of clandestine meetings with Henry, and a time of secret scheming. Anne and her family were at the heart of it. While the rest of the Court guessed and speculated, Henry discussed his plans with Thomas Boleyn and used Boleyn's chaplain John Barlow repeatedly as his messenger.

As autumn darkened towards winter and the courtiers came in from their outside pastimes to gather, drink wine and gamble round the great fires, Anne knew that in Italy the King's agents were risking their lives for her sake. They rode through snow, floods and bands of mutinous, starving soldiers. They secretly entered Rome, bribing their way into the Castle of St Angelo to see the Pope. Messengers were always at hand to bring the latest news back to England. At any moment a man might gallop into the palace courtyard with the papal seal on a document that would make her Queen.

The divorce negotiations began promisingly. Dr Knight's first letter came in December 1527, as the Court prepared for the Christmas revels at Greenwich. Undaunted by narrowly escaping death at the hands of bandits twelve miles outside Rome, he had gone on and secretly entered the papal city, where he had smuggled in to the imprisoned Pope a letter setting out King Henry's requirements and had received a favourable reply: if Knight would withdraw from Rome where his presence was known, the Pope would send unto him all the King's requests, 'in as ample form as they beth [be] desired'.

On December 20 came further encouraging news. The Pope, disguised as a merchant, had escaped from Rome and fled north to Orvieto, a shabby, plague-infested little hillside town where the best lodging available was the half-ruined palace of the local bishop, its walls 'all naked and unhanged', but at least outside the reach of the Emperor's priest-murdering soldiery. London and the King's Court rejoiced. *Te Deums* rang out in thanksgiving, in the King's chapel on New Year's Day, in St Paul's on January 5, and that night the sky was red with the light of celebration bonfires burning in the streets and in the palace courtyards.

Surprisingly quickly, on January 28, arrived the hoped-for missive from Knight. No doubt Henry hurried with it to Anne. The Pope, an illegitimate member of the Medici family, a timid man much given to sighs and tears, had granted the dispensation – though at first he had tried to avoid it. He had objected that the Emperor had instructed him not to facilitate the divorce, that even in Orvieto he was not safe from the Emperor's vengeance. He begged King Henry to do nothing about his 'great matter' for the time being, and he had made Cardinal Pucci do a little rewording here and there. But in the end he had granted Henry's request. The dispensation was triumphantly despatched and joyfully received in England.

But before Henry and Anne could celebrate their personal triumph, they discovered Clement VII had tricked them. The ingenious Cardinal Pucci had altered the clause that would have allowed Wolsey to pronounce final judgement in favour of the divorce in an ecclesiastical court in England and so the rest of the dispensation was worthless.

Furious with Dr Knight for his failure, Henry commanded him to stay in France, whence the old man wrote pathetically: 'It pierceth my stomach deeply that any charge committed unto me by your commandment should not be likewise by me performed accordingly unto your pleasure' and wished it were God's will that he were able to succeed in Henry's affairs 'though it were to the effusion of my blood'.

For Anne it was an ominous setback. The Pope, now in a

position to grant Henry his 'divorce' so that he could marry her, was obviously in no hurry to do so. The King had made her a promise, but unless Clement would implement it, she could never become Queen. Somehow she must find a way to put pressure upon the Pope.

# Chapter 8

# A TRIANGLE OF FRIENDSHIP

POPE CLEMENT VII was not an impressive figure. With hook nose, large deep-set eyes and cunning mouth, as portrayed by Titian, his face was entirely unspiritual, and he did not appear at his best in the shabby, half-ruined palace at Orvieto as he assembled around him the tattered remnants of his once splendid Court. The reports Henry received from his agents who saw him there portrayed Clement as weak and indecisive, given to wild gesticulations, terrified for his own personal safety and that of his temporal possessions. In January, anxious whatever the cost to keep friends with everyone, he had even made the desperate suggestion that Henry should go ahead and commit bigamy, marry Anne, and ask for a papal ratification afterwards. That such a man might fail to grant the dispensation for reasons other than self-interest did not occur seriously to Henry, who was in any case convinced of the justice of his cause. Clement would not help him because he was terrified of Charles V? The situation could soon be righted.

On 21 January 1528 an English herald at Burgos read out a declaration of war on the Emperor. Henry later pretended that this grave step had been taken without his authority, and certainly he had no intention of engaging in battle, for the English wool and cloth trade depended on Flemish and Spanish markets. He doubtless hoped, nevertheless, that fear of England openly entering the fray would persuade Charles V to withdraw from Italy. But even lacking English help, the French should be able to drive the Emperor out. Wrapped in fur-lined gowns against the cold of an English winter, Henry was still optimistic that he would soon be able to marry the entrancing Mistress Anne Boleyn.

When Clement realized that the French armies in Italy were advancing, when he understood the purity of Henry's motives and the excellence of Anne's character, both of which, Henry felt, had been maliciously misrepresented, he would at once enable him to get his 'divorce'. But if Clement should continue to vacillate, a few threats - Henry was a great believer in threats - added to gratitude for past and future services, would soon induce him to come to heel. Thus Henry persuaded himself.

Dr William Knight's failure, however, had been a lesson to Henry. To steer his 'great matter' through the complexities of canon law and the shoals of papal politics he realized he would need someone far more able. He needed Wolsey.

Though the Cardinal had so far accomplished very little in the matter of the 'divorce' - he had been unable to make a general peace or to persuade the other Cardinals to come to Avignon - he had, in fact, never stopped working for it. In January 1528 he took total command in the clear knowledge, for the first time, that the end of his labour was to raise to the throne a woman who hated him, and whose relations and friends were his enemies; for Anne's father, Viscount Rochford, and the Duke of Norfolk, as well as the Duke of Suffolk who had also attached himself to her, were the leaders of the anti-Wolsey party at Court. That he was desperately worried about making Mistress Anne Queen is apparent from the letters of the Spanish ambassador. But as the King's creature, Thomas Wolsey had to obey.

Anne had no choice either. If she wanted the crown she must forget her suspicions and trust her old enemy too. So Henry seems to have convinced her. The early months of 1528 saw a radical change in the relationship between the experienced Cardinal and the King's sweetheart. In place of enmity an uneasy alliance was born. Anne, aged twenty, and faced with a Gordian knot of legal complications, had to put her faith in somebody: Wolsey knew that his future depended on winning that faith and flung himself into the battle, exerting all his charm and brilliant ingenuity to succeed.

By the beginning of February 1528, Henry and Wolsey had chosen two new emissaries to the Pope, both younger men this time: King Henry's almoner, Dr Edward Fox, and Wolsey's own secretary, Dr Stephen Gardiner, the ambitious son of a clothmaker. Anne was away from Court at Hever Castle when they set out, and Henry, eager to show how active he was on her behalf, insisted the two envoys visit her on the ride to Dover. At this stage in her life Anne was greatly impressed by Gardiner, a clever and eloquent canon lawyer who by sheer force of personality had assumed leadership over his companion; as the two strode in their clerical gowns into one of the tapestried rooms of Hever, it was to Gardiner that Anne's gaze would have been principally drawn, to his thick brows, bold eyes and determined tread.

Anne failed to see the basic dishonesty of the man beneath the flood of words and allowed him to convince her that he was hostile to the Queen, totally committed to the King's 'great matter', a friend she could rely on. Fox and Gardiner brought with them a briskly confident letter from the King. To judge from it, Anne in her last letter to Henry had voiced frantic doubts. Would they ever be able to marry? Surely something more could be done to speed the 'divorce'! She desired him to become her husband desperately. King Henry wrote to set Anne's mind at rest, and to reassure her that this time, with these new envoys, all would be well.

Darling,
   These shall be only to advertise you that this bearer and his fellow be despatched with as many things to compass our matter and to bring it to pass as our will could imagine or devise; which brought to pass, as I trust by their diligence it shall be shortly, you and I shall have our desired end, which should be more to my heart's ease and more quietness to my mind than any other thing in this world; as with God's grace shortly I trust it shall be proved, but not so soon as I would it were; yet I will assure you there will be no time lost that may be won, and further cannot be done; for *ultra posse non est esse*; keep him not too long with you, but desire him for your sake to make the more speed; for the sooner we shall have word from him the sooner shall our matter come to pass; and thus upon trust of your short repair to

London, I make an end to my letter, mine own Sweetheart; written with the hand of him which desireth as much to be yours as you do to have him.

HR

As well as the King's letter, Fox and Gardiner carried with them instructions, drafted by Wolsey, which included a lyrical list of Anne's virtues. These they were to reel off to the Pope in order to convince him of Anne's worthiness to become Queen. It seems likely that before leaving Hever they read out this list to Anne, seizing their golden opportunity to please and flatter the woman whom the King had decided to marry. According to Wolsey, these were the qualities for which Henry had chosen her:

... the purity of her life, her constant virginity, her maidenly and womanly pudicity, her soberness, chasteness, meekness, humility, wisdom, descent of right noble and high thorough regal blood, education in all good and laudable [qualities] and manners, apparent aptness to procreation of children, with her other infinite good qualities ...

It was a list to warm Anne's heart towards the Cardinal who had drawn it up, and who was already doing all he could to placate her family.

On 18 February 1528 Wolsey finally settled her father's old feud with Sir Piers Butler. The victory was given to the Boleyns, and regardless of the usefulness of Sir Piers as one of the King's few loyal supporters in Ireland, the Butlers were to be allowed to keep only two manors, for a term of thirty years, and any lands they could wrest back from the 'wild Irish'; but for the Castle of Kilkenny and the rest of the lands belonging to the Earldom of Ormond, they must pay rents to the Boleyns. Butler was no longer to be allowed to use the ancient title 'Earl of Ormond' which he had assumed after the last Earl's death. This was now to be at the King's disposal and was, in fact, later bestowed on Anne's father, while Butler as consolation was made Earl of Ossory.

It was but one of the many proofs of Wolsey's goodwill that Anne received in the early months of 1528 and which persuaded her that he really was acting for her in good faith – an impression strongly reinforced by Henry. Had she formerly misjudged the Cardinal? With characteristic impulsiveness she decided she had, and in the elegant script learnt in France, she set down her new feelings. 'Daily of your goodness I do perceive by all my friends,' she wrote in a letter to him, 'and though that I had not knowledge of them, the daily proof of your deeds doth declare your words and writing toward me to be true.'

It was customary in the sixteenth century to recognize a service with a reward. Anne had, she wrote, nothing as yet to give the Cardinal except her goodwill, but when she became Queen, she promised, 'then look what thing in this world I can imagine to do you pleasure in, you shall find me the gladdest woman in the world to do it. And next unto the King's grace, of one thing I make you full promise ... and that is my hearty love unfeignedly through my life. And being fully determined, with God's grace, never to change this purpose; I make an end of this my rude and true meaning letter; praying our Lord to send you much increase of honour, with long life. Your humble and obedient servant, Anne Boleyn.'

Anne's emotional *volte face* in this year of 1528 from bitter enmity to sudden affection for the Cardinal has been interpreted as a sign of slyness and insincerity. On the contrary, it was typical of Anne's wild moods, her habit of flying from one emotional extreme to the other which was mirrored in her exaggerated mode of self-expression.

How far did she deceive herself? It is, after all, easy to imagine love for the one person in the world who can give you what you most desire. Anne was not the type to analyse her motives. However false the roots of her affection for the Cardinal, it seemed genuine enough to her at the time. For Anne, Wolsey in 1528 was no longer the enemy who had wrenched asunder her youthful romance. He was the ally who, as she wrote in her letter to him, was studying by his 'wisdom and great diligence how to bring to pass honourably the greatest wealth that is possible to come to any creature living' – marriage to a reigning monarch.

Not only was Wolsey making every possible effort to get the

papal consent to the 'divorce'. He was also lavishly entertaining her, staging ever more magnificent and excitingly contrived revels at his palaces of York Place and Hampton Court (the lease of which he had presented to the King in 1525 although he continued to live there himself). He 'prepared great banquets and solemn feasts to entertain them both at his own house', wrote Wolsey's gentleman usher George Cavendish, 'and thus the world began to grow into wonderful inventions, not heard of before in this realm.' Lingering over the culinary delicacies served from Wolsey's famous gold plate, masking and dancing in his sumptuous gold-and-silver tapestried rooms to the music of his minstrels, it was for a girl of twenty-one easy to forget old scores.

The three of them, Cardinal, King and Mistress Anne, formed a strange triangle of friendship, foregathering on Monday nights when the Court was in or near London. When it was not, Anne showered the absent Wolsey with gushing messages and tokens of affection. 'Mistress Anne . . . thinketh long till she speak with you,' wrote Thomas Henneage, a gentleman of the King's Bed Chamber, to the Cardinal from Greenwich. For Wolsey, Anne's friendship held that quality of flirtatiousness with which, indiscriminately, she seems to have treated all her male friends at Court. When Wolsey was too busy, or forgot, to send a message or token in return, she complained petulantly.

In March, we learn from another of Henneage's letters, she was at Windsor, chaperoned by her mother, and enjoying a country idyll with the King in circumstances likely to cradle their romance, though Henneage was too discreet to say so outright. 'There is none here,' he wrote, 'but Master Norris and I to give attendance upon the King's Highness when he goeth to make water in his Bed Chamber, nor any other to keep the pallet but only I: and his Grace, every afternoon, when the weather is . . . fair, doth ride forth . . . hawking, or walketh in the park, and cometh not in again till it be late in the evening.'

On March 3, when the King sent down one of his own specially cooked dishes for Anne's supper, she asked Henneage to share it with her. Anne knew that a message had that day

arrived from Wolsey to the King; and she complained to
Henneage, knowing the remark would be passed on, that the
Cardinal must have forgotten her, for he had sent her no token.
How she longed, she sighed, daintily wolfing the gourmet dish
from the King's kitchens, for some carp, shrimps or other fish
from the Cardinal's famous fisheries at Norham.

Whether Wolsey produced the dishes she so much craved we
do not know, but he certainly sent her a letter in reply, for on
March 16 she asked Henneage to thank the Cardinal for his
'kind and favourable writing unto her'. Hearing that Wolsey
had ill-treated one of her friends, Sir Thomas Cheyney, who
had somehow offended him, Anne sent Wolsey a comparatively
humble message. She merely asked Henneage to appeal on
Cheyney's behalf, adding with only a hint of tartness, a faint
echo of the old enmity, that she was 'marvellously sorry he
should be in the Cardinal's displeasure'.

Both of them proud, both arrogant, both fond of power,
sooner or later Mistress Anne and Cardinal Wolsey were bound
to quarrel, but Anne's momentary irritation in the spring of
1528 was forgotten in her anxiety about the progress of negotiations with the Pope and her gratitude for Wolsey's efforts.
Impatiently she waited for news.


It was a long time coming. Rough, impassable seas, flooded
rivers and generally foul weather had delayed Gardiner and
Fox on the way to Italy. When finally they rode into Orvieto
they had lost every garment except the mud-splashed ones they
were wearing; they had to hide in their rooms while present-
able clothes were hastily run up for them, so losing yet another
day. Their reports from Orvieto did not reach England until
April, but the news they brought was worth waiting for.

The Pope had invited them into his Bed Chamber, where
they noted, with the disgust of an age in which poverty was
treated with contempt, that the furniture was not worth
twenty nobles, bed and all.

Many hours they had spent wrangling with Clement, his
cardinals and the Dean of the Rota, until finally Clement VII
had admitted that the King's case was just, had promised to do

all he could to satisfy him and had said he would tell the Emperor, if he complained, that in administering justice he was bound to favour anyone as meritorious as King Henry. In view of this, Gardiner and Fox expected 'short expedition' of their mission.

It had two principal objects. The King still hoped to get the Pope's agreement to stage a 'trial' in England, but in case Wolsey might be considered too partial, Henry's agents were to arrange for a second papal legate to be sent from Italy to judge the divorce case with him. Proposed was Cardinal Lorenzo Campeggio, absentee Bishop of Salisbury, who had visited England before and was considered to be pro-English. Gardiner and Fox were also to try and obtain a decretal commission, a document on which the King and Wolsey placed great store. Wolsey feared that after he and Campeggio had given judgement for the 'divorce' the Pope might still revoke the case to the papal curia where, because of the proximity of the Emperor, sentence would probably be given against Henry. The decretal commission would obviate this danger by setting out the law according to which the two delegates could give final judgement.

Now it appeared both these objects were about to be achieved with no difficulty at all. The letter from Gardiner and Fox must have raised Anne's hopes to dizzy heights of anticipation. Soon the King would be able to fulfil his promise; the glittering crown and the power that went with it would be hers and she would be rescued from her intolerable position as one of Catherine's ladies, hated by most of the others.

When the promised news came from Henry's envoys Anne was residing at Greenwich, the King's favourite springtime palace. On the afternoon of Sunday, May 3, Fox arrived at the palace to see the King, having crossed from Calais the previous night and ridden that day post-haste from Sandwich. Henry sent him straight to Anne in her chamber off the gallery over the tiltyard, where he had recently moved her because his daughter Princess Mary and some of the Queen's ladies were ill with 'smallpox' (at this date often confused with measles). At five o'clock Anne saw the envoy standing in her doorway.

The King's grace, Fox told her, had insisted she must be the first to hear the good news. Mr Stephens (this was Gardiner's usual appellation at the time) had arranged everything. All was set in hand for the coming of the legate. And he praised Gardiner's brilliant tactics that had persuaded the Pope to grant the general commission – the document that gave permission for Wolsey and Campeggio to judge the case in England – without the alteration of a word. It had been a battle of wills, Fox said. His Holiness had objected strongly to a number of things, but Gardiner 'spake roundly unto him'; finally threatening that King Henry would withdraw his friendship and support, and the Holy See would fall apart. At this alarming prospect the Pope, tears in his eyes, had thrown up his arms and submitted, committing himself to Henry's protection; for the sending of this commission, he said, was a declaration against the Emperor.

In her excitement at finding herself suddenly so near being Queen, with a fortune at her disposal, Anne promised Gardiner a large reward and repeatedly confused him with his colleague as they talked, addressing Fox as 'Mr Stephens'.

Huge and beaming, the King burst into the middle of this joyful scene. Tactfully Anne withdrew from the chamber, while Henry read the letters brought from Gardiner and from the Pope and commanded Fox briefly 'to show him what was done in his cause'.

Fox explained that, although the Pope would not grant a decretal commission, they had his verbal promise that he would confirm the sentence given at the approaching trial by Wolsey and Campeggio and would not revoke the cause to Rome. At which Henry 'made marvellous demonstrations of joy and gladness' (so Fox reported to his colleague in a letter describing this whole interview with the King and Anne), then, calling in his beloved, told Fox to 'repeat the same thing again before her'.

That spring night in Greenwich Palace as they stood together in the chamber off the tiltyard, listening to Fox, showering him with questions while he relived the scenes of Gardiner's triumph over the distraught and tearful Pope, was perhaps the moment of purest hope Anne and Henry were to experience in the whole disaster-chequered history of the 'divorce'. Their joy was almost immediately overcast.

When the King finally gave Fox leave to go that evening, despite the lateness of the hour, he sent him straight to Wolsey at Durham House, the mansion on the Strand where he was living while the hall in his palace at Westminster was being repaired and redecorated. It was ten o'clock when Fox arrived and requested an audience, and the Cardinal had already retired for the night; but he got out of bed to consider the new situation. Was the general commission obtained by Gardiner and Fox enough? Would it allow the legates to make a final judgement of the case in England? Or was this another trick of Clement's – to procrastinate while seeming to grant Henry what he wanted? Could he legally still revoke the cause to the curia? This was the problem.

For a week the issue was earnestly and lengthily debated between the King, Wolsey, doctors of canon law and Anne's father, Viscount Rochford. At last it was agreed that, as an essential precaution, they must force the Pope to grant a decretal commission as well.

On Monday, May 11 Fox added a postscript to this effect to his letter to Gardiner. John Barlow, the Boleyns' chaplain, galloped off with it on the long journey to Italy, and again the King's agents tackled the Pope. Clement VII was extremely unwilling to grant a document that would virtually prejudge the case in Henry's favour. Only fear that a frustrated King of England might leave the Roman Catholic Church, as well as concern for Wolsey's safety, persuaded him.

Back in February the Cardinal had sent a heartfelt plea. If the Pope would not help, Wolsey wrote, his position, even his very life would be in danger. To save Wolsey and the Roman Catholic Church in England, on 11 June 1528, Clement VII promised – on the understanding that it was to be kept secret and seen only by the King and Wolsey – to send with Campeggio the document which they believed would enable them finally to achieve the 'divorce'.

Now, surely, nothing could go wrong. So Anne must have felt

as she enjoyed the pleasant summer pastimes at Greenwich, walking with Henry under the green oak and beech leaves of Greenwich park, watching him play tennis for wagers, his fair skin glowing through the fine embroidered shirt over which he would afterwards don one of his special tennis coats of blue or black velvet.

Early in June she had had a slight indisposition; by 6 June 1528 Henneage wrote to Wolsey that she was 'very well amended', but the summer sun that sparkled through the leaves also brought out something less agreeable. Two different diseases decimated the population of England in the sixteenth century. The first of these was bubonic plague. In palace as well as cottage, behind the gold and silver hangings, above the Italian frescoes and gilded woodwork of Henry's ceilings, in the timbers of Greenwich and Hampton Court, scuttled the ubiquitous black rats. The warm weather awoke from their winter hibernation the fleas that infested them and carried the infection to human beings. No less alarming was the mysterious disease, which also appeared in the summer months in England, called the 'sweat' or the 'sweating sickness', perhaps a particularly deadly form of influenza. It also was referred to confusingly in the sixteenth century as the plague and had a number of other grimly descriptive nicknames: 'Stoop knave and know thy master'; 'Stop gallant'; and 'New acquaintance'.

Jean du Bellay, Bishop of Bayonne, the French ambassador who was to become a friend of Anne, described this disease as 'the easiest thing in the world to die of. You have a bit of pain in the head or the heart. Suddenly you start sweating, and a doctor is useless . . . In four hours, sometimes two or three, you are despatched without languishing.'

The sweat was said especially to attack young people and those 'full of meat'. The only prevention was to restrict your diet; the only generally recognized cure to go to bed, cover up moderately and remain there till the crisis passed. To put on too many or too few covers was as fatal as it was to expose any part of the body. The general belief was: 'If a man only put his hand out of bed during twenty-four hours, it becomes as stiff as a pane of glass.' Out of seven people who dined

together, wrote John Stow in his *Survey of London*, six were
dead within thirteen hours.

It was ten years since there had been an epidemic in England;
but it was clear from the beginning that this summer there
was to be another. Within twenty-four hours of the arrival of
the pestilence in London two thousand had caught it, and the
priests were busier than the doctors, reported du Bellay, who
saw panic-stricken crowds, feeling or imagining themselves
taken ill, rush 'in hordes like flies' from the streets and shops
of London into their homes. English soldiers were renowned
for their bravery. But faced with this invisible enemy, the
disease that worked in a mysterious way no one then understood, that seemed to kill as suddenly and indiscriminately as a
thunderbolt, men were as terrified as women, even avoiding
riding any distance or going out in the sun for fear it might
make them perspire and bring on the sickness.

The 'sweat' arrived in London on 14 June 1528. Overnight it
crept down the river to Greenwich. On June 15 it struck at one
of Anne's maids.

That morning the Court was to remove to Waltham in
Essex, and Anne should have joined the motley procession of
courtiers, officials, servants, servants' servants, yeomen of the
guard and children of the pantry, who with carts and boats
overloaded with furniture were to set off by road or river. But
the rule was that a contact of anyone ill of the 'sweat' must
leave the Court, and beloved of the King though Anne was,
she was no exception; immediately she was packed off to her
father at Hever Castle. Henry sent her a loving anxious message
in French:

The uneasiness caused me by doubts about your health has
greatly disturbed and alarmed me, and I should have had no
peace without knowing the truth, but as you have not yet
felt anything I hope and believe that it will pass you by as I
hope it has with us: I think if you would leave the Surrey
side as we did, you would escape without danger; and also
another thing may comfort you, that it is true, as they say,
that few women or none have this malady, and moreover
none of our Court and few elsewhere have died of it.

Henry's letter was also concerned with setting at rest the fearful doubts that made wretched Anne's enforced stay at Hever. He wrote comfortingly:

I beg of you, my wholly beloved, to have no fear nor to be too uneasy at our absence; for wherever I may be I am yours . . . Comfort yourself and be brave, and avoid the evil as much as you can . . . I wish you between my arms that I might a little dispel your unreasonable thoughts. Written by the hand of him who is, and always will be, your

Un-H-Rex-changeable.

The clue to Anne's 'unreasonable thoughts' lies in that last word 'unchangeable'. Henry had never been faithful to one woman for long, not even to Catherine of Aragon in the early years of their marriage. Now Anne was afraid he would change towards her, be distracted by other bright eyes at Court, or return to Catherine waiting patiently by his side, ever ready to forgive and forget.

The pressures on Henry to give her up were enormous. For how long would he resist them? For her sake he was risking his own popularity and the welfare of his country. The war with the Emperor, she knew, had had a disastrous effect on the English economy, causing widespread hardship and poverty in a year when shortage of sheep and cattle made food prices exceptionally dear. In April, Anne's father had helped to put down the resulting riots in Kent. If the people would not tolerate war with the Emperor, would Henry dare to insist on divorce from the Emperor's aunt? To continue to ally himself to the Emperor's enemy, France, the country that was also traditionally England's enemy? Recent events must have made her realize that there was a limit to his love, for he had not been to visit her. Great as was his infatuation, his terror of the 'sweat' and his duty to his kingdom were greater. How slender was the thread on which hung her fate: the fancy of a King.

As she waited at Hever the thought haunted her. She was terrified of the plague. Who was not? But she was still more frightened of what would happen if King Henry discarded her. Who then would dare to marry her? What sort of existence would be left to her? She was too notorious ever to lead an ordinary life again.

Then suddenly Anne ceased to gaze anxiously into the years ahead, and was concerned only with the frightening present. Drenched in perspiration, she lay in a canopied four-poster, aware that she had contracted the sweat, that she was in danger of dying.

# Chapter 9

# THE COMING OF THE LEGATE

WHEN late that night the King received word of Anne's illness, he rose at once from his bed, sent orders for one of his own doctors to get ready to leave and sat down in the flickering candlelight to write an affectionate letter. This was, as usual, in French, and most elaborately phrased to please Anne's French taste for elegance. 'There came to me suddenly in the night the most afflicting news that could arrive,' Henry wrote,

and I must lament it for three reasons: the first being because I heard of the sickness of my mistress, whom I esteem more than all the world, and whose health I desire as much as my own and would willingly bear the half of your malady to have you cured; the second because of my fear of being again endlessly tortured by my enemy absence, who until now has caused me every possible annoyance, and so far as I can judge is like to do worse, I pray God to rid me of so importunate a rebel; the third, because the physician in whom I most trust is absent at a time when he could do me the greatest pleasure; for I hoped through him, and his skills, to obtain one of my chief joys in this world, that is to say, that my mistress should be cured. However, for lack of him I send you the second, and the only one left, praying God that soon he can make you well again, when I shall love him more than ever; praying you to be governed by his advice regarding your illness, by doing which I hope soon to see you again, which will be better medicine for me than all the precious stones in the world. Written by the secretary, who is, and ever will be

Your loyal and most assured servant

H AB R

Anne's initials were as usual enclosed in a heart.

With this royal letter and the instruments of his profession in his saddlebags - including perhaps one of the King's personally invented remedies for the sweat, compounded of herbs and leaves, mixed with white wine or treacle - Dr Butts, ordered summarily from his rest, was sent galloping off through the darkness to Hever Castle. Meanwhile Anne's illness was probably already approaching its rapid crisis, preceded by the customary progress of racking symptoms: pains in the back or shoulder, in the liver and stomach, then in the head, leading to delirium and palpitations. Dr Butts cannot have been hopeful when he first examined his patient, for it was, we are told, a particularly dangerous attack that Anne suffered 'by the turning in of the sweat before the time'.

Had Anne been a victim in June 1528, the history of England would have been radically different. But whether saved by her own sound constitution or the skill of Dr Butts, Anne recovered and lived, in the words of her once admirer, Thomas Wyatt, to 'set all England in a bruit'.

She did not at once return to Court, but remained convalescing at Hever, while the plague reached epidemic proportions and threatened to sweep from the stage everyone involved in the drama of the 'divorce'. June was a month of anxiety for Anne as for the whole of England. The sweat that summer seemed especially to haunt the homes of the rich and powerful. It came to the household of the Archbishop of Canterbury, where eighteen people died within four hours; it came to Wolsey's palace - what would happen to the 'divorce' if Wolsey died? - and it came to the Court, where it struck disastrously at Anne's own family.

Her brother George, recently promoted through Anne's influence one of the King's Gentlemen of the Privy Chamber, caught the disease a few days after Anne left Greenwich for Hever; her father, Lord Rochford, at the same time as Anne. Both recovered. But Anne's brother-in-law William Carey was not so lucky; he died on 22 June 1528. The King himself would be fortunate indeed if he escaped. One after the other his personal servants succumbed: Zouche, the special bearer Henry entrusted with his notes to Anne; Sir William Compton who, like Carey, died; until all but one of the Gentlemen of the Privy Chamber had had it. Should Henry die, Anne would be at the mercy of Catherine's friends, and even if he survived there was still another hazard: that in this atmosphere of imminent death the King might repent and turn again to Catherine.

Brave to the point of rashness at the joust, tilting on one occasion with his visor up, Henry was terrified of this mysterious disease. Leaving sick and dying behind, he fled before it from manor to manor, finally reaching Wolsey's house at Tittenhanger, where he spent long hours in a tower with his physician, having made his will, confessed his sins and heard numerous Masses, while fires were built in every room to purge the infection.

In due course the epidemic abated its vigour. Most of those who had contracted it at Court had recovered. Henry wrote, in English this time, buoyantly to Anne:

> Since your last letters, mine own darling, Walter Welche [Walshe], Master Browne, John Care [Carey], Yrion of Brearton [Brereton], John Coke the apothecary be fallen of the 'sweat' in this house; and thanked be God all well recovered; so that as yet the plague is not fully ceased here but I trust shortly it shall by his mercy of God; the rest of us yet be well and I trust shall pass it, or not to have it, or at the least as easily as the rest have done.

In justice to Henry's feelings for Anne, it should be noted that, even when in terror for his own life, he did not cease thinking of her and attempting to reassure her. He sent for her 'consolation' a copy of a letter from the French King in support of the 'divorce'. He could have sent her nothing more likely to fill her with joy, for this document was of the utmost significance to her ambition, assuring Henry as it did of alliance with one of the two great powers of Europe should he offend the other by divorcing Catherine. In the years to come, French support was to be an essential foundation of Anne's power in England. As well as this delightfully comforting communication, Henry sent her gifts and he begged her to rejoin him, but she refused. She was not yet fully recovered, she pleaded. Any day now Lorenzo Campeggio would set out from Italy on his way to England for the trial of the King's cause; her presence at Court, she knew, might prejudice his verdict on the 'divorce'.

It was important that Campeggio should believe the King's claim that his only reasons for wanting to annul his marriage with Catherine were an uneasy conscience and desire for an heir. Reluctantly, Henry accepted Anne's decision. 'As touching your abode at Hever,' the King wrote, 'do therein as best shall like you, for you know best what air doth best with you.' He could not resist ending his letter on a note of ardent impatience at this continued separation:

> . . . But I would it were come thereto (if it pleased God) that neither of us need care for that, for I assure you I think it long . . . written with the hand of votre seulle
>
> HR

In Anne's mind her would-be lover's sighs weighed little compared to the success of the trial. To stiffen her determination to resist the royal pleading and her own longing to be back at Court, she had before her the warning example of her sister, then in a sad predicament, a reminder of what could so easily happen to Anne if the King did not marry her soon. When Mary's husband, William Carey, had died on June 22, his offices – Steward of the Duchy of Lancaster, Constable of the Castle of Plashy and Keeper of two parks – immediately reverted 'in the King's gift'. The Court jackals gathered round and made suit. The King generously distributed these sources of Carey's income, and Mary, his widow, was left destitute.

Despite their relationship of several years, Henry felt no lingering affection, no obligation; he scarcely even remembered Mary. When he acted it was only because Anne begged him, and then only to tell the unwilling miserly Rochford to support her. Henry's callousness at the desperate plight of his gentle ex-mistress strikes a chill note, and Anne must have read his letter on the subject, palpitating with desire for *her*, with mixed feelings. 'The cause of my writing at this time (good sweetheart) is only,' he explained, for once in English, 'to understand of your good health and prosperity.'

> Whereof to know I would be as glad as in manner mine own; praying God [that and it be his pleasure] to send us shortly

together; for I promise you I long for it; howbeit trust it shall not be long so; and seeing my darling is absent I can not less do than to send her some flesh representing my name; which is hart flesh for Henry; prognosticating that hereafter God willing you must enjoy some of mine, which He pleased, I would were now; as touching your sister's matter I have caused Walter Weltze [Walshe] to write to my Lord mine own mind therein . . . for surely whatsoever is said it cannot so stand with his honour but that he must needs take her his natural daughter now in her extreme necessity; no more to you at this time, mine own darling, but that . . . I would we were together an evening; with the hand of yours

                                                                    HR

The same hand, Anne must have reflected uneasily, had once belonged to Mary, whom the King had now utterly erased from his mind. As though his letter had not been enough to prove this, he even went so far as to give the wardship of Mary's son, Henry, to Anne, as well as the custody of Carey's lands during the boy's minority - a gesture less a tribute to Anne's ability to bring the boy up well, than a way of giving her yet another present; for she would be able to charge a fee on the boy's marriage as well as enjoying the rents from his property during his minority. And in fact she seems to have shown little interest in young Henry, who was sent to live in a religious house instead of at Court.

By July Anne had a new cause for concern. Progress in the 'divorce' appeared to have come to a halt. Although the Pope had agreed, on 11 June 1528, to send Cardinal Campeggio to preside with Wolsey over a trial of the King's cause, by the end of the month he had not even set out. Instead of taking horse for France, Anne was horrified to hear, he had taken to his bed with gout.

It would have been natural for a woman of Anne's youth in the sixteenth century to wait with what patience she could muster while the whole delicate business was handled by others. But that was not Anne's temperament and it is part of her interest as a person that she refused to be a passenger of events, was always spurring on her champions to new efforts. She wrote repeatedly to Wolsey, letters gushing with goodwill, promising tangible proof of it when she should have the power, letters that reveal beneath the artificial elegance of her style, intense anxiety about the 'divorce', which could make or mar her whole future

But despite Anne's prayers and promises and obsequious gratitude, despite Wolsey's strenuous and genuine efforts to further his sovereign's cause, the legate could not be hurried.

Not even the brilliant Wolsey could persuade Campeggio to make light of the painful swelling of his old joints; and as Campeggio lay there the military situation in Italy was changing. The tide of battle had turned against England's ally, France. Anne realized all too easily that unless it turned again in France's favour, Clement would be bound to make peace with Charles; and that would be the end of the 'divorce'. It was imperative for Campeggio to come soon. Anne's destiny was caught up in the ever-changing pattern of peace and war between the three great powers.

By mid-July, when there was still no news from France of Campeggio's arrival there, she grovelled again in another obsequious letter to Wolsey.

There must, she felt, be something he could do. Her letter was almost identical with the first, except that, this time, she persuaded Henry to add a postscript. And in the flush of a brief reunion, probably at Ampthill where the Court resided at the end of July, he indulged her whim. Anne wrote:

My Lord,
    In my most humblest wise that my heart can think, I desire you to pardon me that I am so bold, to trouble you with my simple and rude writing; esteeming it to proceed from her, that is much desirous to know that your Grace does well, as I perceive by this bearer that you do. The which I pray God long to continue, as I am most bound to pray; for I do know the great pains and trouble that you have taken for me, both day and night, is never like to be re-compensed on my part, but only in loving you, next unto the King's Grace, above all creatures living. And I do not doubt,

but the daily proofs of my deeds shall manifestly declare and affirm my writing to be true; and I do trust you do think the same. My Lord I do assure you, I do long to hear from you news of the legate; for I do hope, and they come from you, they shall be very good; and I am sure you desire it as much as I, and more, and if it were possible, as I know it is not. And thus, remaining in a steadfast hope, I make an end of my letter, written with the hand of her that is most bound to be . . .

Here she tenderly coaxed Henry into sitting down and taking her quill. The King did not see that there was much to be gained by writing to Wolsey at this point and, briefly reunited with Anne again, he could probably think of better ways of spending his time. But Anne continued to plead with him until finally he gave in, a fact he fondly recorded:

The writer of this letter would not cease, till she had caused me likewise to set to my hand; desiring you, though it be short, to take it in good part. I ensure you, there is neither of us, but that greatly desireth to see you, and much more joyous to hear that you have scaped this plague so well; trusting the fury thereof to be passed, specially with them that keepeth good diet, as I trust you do. The not hearing of the legate's arrival in France, causeth us somewhat to muse; notwithstanding, we trust by your diligence and vigilance (with the assistance of Almighty God) shortly to be eased out of that trouble. No more to you at this time; but that I pray God to send you as good health and prosperity, as the writer would.

Henry signed himself 'By your loving sovereign and friend, Henry R', and Anne appended her signature below, 'Your humble servant, Anne Boleyn'.

This letter to Cardinal Wolsey from the King and Anne creates a touching picture of their three-sided friendship, but already its smooth surface was showing cracks. Anne was first favourite with the King and meant to enjoy the power this gave her, both because she enjoyed power for its own sake and because she wanted to help her friends. Wolsey who had for so long been first favourite could not bear to yield his position to the King's latest woman, especially one whose judgement was as poor as Anne's.

On 24 April 1528, the abbess of a convent had died where William Carey's sister, Dame Eleanor Carey, was one of the nuns. Impulsively, without enquiring into the woman's character, Anne promised to use her influence to obtain the vacancy for her. Meanwhile Wolsey had discovered that Eleanor Carey had a startling past. Examined before him, she confessed to having had two illegitimate children by two different priests and to have been involved in a recent scandal with another man. Wolsey, thinking, understandably, that she would not make the most suitable head of a religious house, decided to appoint a much older woman, Isabel Jordan, who was also the convent's own choice.

Anne's reaction was all too personal. She surely should have listened to the facts, swallowed her resentment, pleaded ignorance and accepted the appointment of the best qualified woman. Instead she reacted with that touchy, narrow egotism which was a dominant part of her character. When her friends succeeded either in unearthing or inventing some ancient scandal about Isabel Jordan, Anne, feeling her honour was at stake, used this as an excuse to press Henry to make Eleanor Carey abbess.

But she had not counted on the King's strong sense of duty to his subjects which set a limit to his indulgence. It would not allow him to appoint so unsuitable a person, and the best he could do for Anne was to try and save her from humiliation. 'I would not for all the gold in the world clog your conscience nor mine,' he wrote,

> to make her ruler of a house which is of so ungodly demeanour, nor I trust you would not that neither for brother nor for sister distayne mine honour nor conscience . . . yet notwithstanding, to do you pleasure, I have done that neither of them shall have it, but some other and well-disposed woman . . .

Wolsey, however, despite being informed of Henry's wishes, still appointed Isabel Jordan, a dangerously arrogant move, since it must make Henry appear ineffectual in Anne's eyes. Inevitably it provoked a grave rebuke from the King, based on the Latin text *Quem Diligo Castigo* (those I love I punish), and accusing Wolsey of having not done the duty of a trusty, loving servant and friend.

Wolsey hurriedly apologized: his servants had been ill, he himself in fear of catching the sweat when he made the appointment. His humble submission was graciously accepted by the King. In their faith that Wolsey was wholeheartedly on their side, would somehow persuade Campeggio both to come and to give a favourable verdict on the 'divorce', Henry and Anne were willing to overlook this piece of high-handed behaviour on the Cardinal's part. So the cracks in their friendship were once more smoothed over. Upon the arrival of the legate Henry's and Anne's happiness depended.

At last, on July 25, Campeggio took ship for Provence and began journeying to England by slow stages. His old hands and feet too swollen to bear the pressure of bridle or stirrup, he was carried mostly on a horse-drawn litter, jolting agonizingly north, while in Italy the French armies suffered defeat after defeat, their general died of the plague, the Pope became less and less willing to grant the divorce. To Anne, waiting impatiently in England, once more in self-imposed banishment at Hever in a naïve attempt to deceive Campeggio, his journey must have seemed endless; and her anxiety was ameliorated only by new evidence of the King's love.

Her fleeting visit to the Court at Ampthill in the last week of July Anne had cunningly used to good effect, apparently promising Henry that he could caress her more intimately than she had ever permitted before. It had the desired result of fanning his passion to white heat before she vanished yet again from his side.

A few days after her departure Henry galloped off to Hever, sending a messenger ahead bearing this note:

Mine own sweetheart,
    These shall be to advertise you of the great elengenes

[loneliness] that I find here since your departing, for I assure you methinketh the time longer since your departing now last than I was wont to do a whole fortnight; I think your kindness and my fervencies of love causeth it, for otherwise I would not have thought it possible . . . but now that I was coming toward you methinketh my pains been half relieved . . . wishing myself (especially of an evening) in my sweetheart's arms, whose pretty duckies [breasts] I trust shortly to kiss; written with the hand of him that was, is, and shall be yours by his will

HR

Henry's declarations sounded fine, but unless Campeggio hurried up and came soon they were unlikely to be fulfilled. Anne's banishment was nerve-racking and tedious. A quiet country life did not suit the liveliness of her temperament; at the end of August she again threw caution to the winds and arranged to join him in London. To draw her back to Court Henry had promised a complete change in her status. No longer would she belong to the Queen's household, enduring slights from Catherine's other ladies – her situation now was to be entirely different. And though she would attend the Court pastimes she was not to live there but in a separate establishment which Wolsey had arranged for her.

'As touching a lodging for you we have gotten one by my lord Cardinal's means,' wrote Henry, 'the like whereof could not have been found here about for all causes . . .' This 'lodging' was almost certainly the stately old Durham House, one of the row of mansions on the Strand with walled orchards and gardens sweeping down to the river, where the Cardinal himself had been living in May 1528.

Built in the reign of Henry III, Durham House with its vast marble-pillared hall had been the abode of Catherine of Aragon before her marriage to Henry nineteen years before, and so must have seemed to the ambitious Anne a richly symbolic choice. Battlemented walls flanked by high towers stood four square to the river on the south side. To the north it looked across a huddle of pitched roofs to the open fields and hills. Anne, careful always to be chaperoned by a member of her family, would stay here with her father, a brief trip by boat from Henry's palace of Bridewell on the junction of the rivers Fleet and Thames.

The arrangements were to be kept secret until Anne was actually in residence, for the last thing the King wanted was to provide food for gossip before she had even arrived. But in her pride and excitement at receiving a large important house of her own, Anne seems to have been unable to resist boasting about it; several of their letters were intercepted in mysterious circumstances (they were taken to France) and the news spread. The incident was typical of that reckless indiscretion which was to be one of Anne's leading characteristics all her life; but Henry forgave her. Merely pointing out gently in his next letter that 'lack of discreet handling must needs be the cause thereof', he went on to write longingly of their approaching meeting. This was, he said in polished poetic French:

> more desirable than any earthly thing; for what joy in this world can be so great as to have the company of her who is the most loved; knowing also that she herself feels likewise, the thought of which gives me great pleasure. Judge then what her presence itself will do, whose absence has given me the greater pain at heart than either tongue or pen can express . . .

Begging his mistress to pray my lord her father 'to hasten by two days the time appointed' for her arrival, Henry signed himself with a chivalric flourish,

Votre loyal et plus assure serviteur<br>H aultre A B ne cherse R

The usual heart encircled her initials.

So Anne returned triumphantly to Court, her bold laughter was heard again in the great rooms, her dark eyes flashed in the bright torch-light. But yet once more it was to be only a temporary stay, for the King so delighted in her regained company that, oblivious of the strong moral line he had adopted with the Pope, he caressed Anne openly in the presence of his lords and ladies and visiting ambassadors, to whom such acts were meat and drink.

'Mademoiselle Boleyn has returned to Court,' wrote Jean du Bellay drily on August 20, 'the King is so infatuated that none but God can cure him.' His behaviour made it abundantly clear to this shrewd French ambassador that the King's main reason for wanting a divorce was neither of those advanced by his envoys to the Pope: his troubled conscience and his need for an heir; both had paled now in the hot light of his desire for Anne.

At last Campeggio was approaching England. What impression would he receive of this King who claimed to be such a devoted husband yet fondled Anne on his knee before his Court and allowed himself to be ruled by her whims? Had she been merely a plaything, the legate was man of the world enough to wink at the situation, but Anne's own proud manner showed to observers that this was a much more dangerous relationship. It might well influence Campeggio's judgement in the trial, Henry's closest advisers told him. Anne had become a kind of shuttlecock. In the first week of September they persuaded him to send her back to the country. Pulled in one direction by statesmanship, in another by infatuation, Henry let her go with the utmost reluctance but also with renewed hope of attaining his end - an optimism with which he apparently inffected Anne. For on September 18 the Spanish ambassador, Don Inigo de Mendoza, reported to the Emperor that both the King and his lady looked upon their future marriage as certain, preparations were already being made for the wedding.

At about the same time as Catherine's friend Mendoza sent this gloomy message to the Emperor, Henry was writing joyously to Anne:

> . . . the legate which we most desired arrived at Paris on Sunday or Monday last past [14 September 1528] so that I trust by the next Monday to hear of his arrival at Calais, and then I trust within a while after to enjoy that which I have so long longed for to God's pleasure and our both comfort; no more to you at present mine own darling for lack of time, but that I would you were in my arms or I in

yours, for I think it long since I kissed you; written after the killing of an hart at 11 of the clock, minding with God's grace tomorrow mightily timely to kill another; by the hand of him which I trust shortly shall be yours.

Henry R

On September 29 in golden autumn weather Cardinal Lorenzo Campeggio landed at Dover. Anne's cousin, Sir Francis Brian, met him with a present from the King of a magnificent litter to speed him on his way, but Campeggio said he would continue by muleback as long as it remained fine. He arrived at Canterbury on October 1, at Dartford four days later. And on Wednesday, October 7, nearly two and a half months after he had begun his journey, the papal legate on whom Anne's hopes rested reached the suburbs of London.

# Chapter 10

# THE SPANISH BRIEF

THE moment for which Anne had waited impatiently throughout that long plague-stricken summer of 1528 was a sad anti-
climax. On the night of his arrival at the suburbs of London,
Cardinal Lorenzo Campeggio lodged in a house belonging to
the Duke of Suffolk. A ceremonial entry into the City had been
arranged for him the next day, and people crowded the streets
in expectation of a scene that would outshine the unforgettable
pageantry of Campeggio's former visit to England. In 1518
he had been sent by Pope Leo X to persuade Henry to join a
crusade of all Christendom against the Turk. A procession two
miles long had ridden through the gates: first the nobility in
velvets, satins and gold chains, then the Cardinal in his robe of
scarlet edged with ermine – preceded by the cross, pillars and
poleaxes, that were his symbols of office – then his servants in
red livery, followed by a triumphant clatter of horsemen in
armour. The streets had been lined with the craft guilds of
London in their colourful liveries and the clergy in copes of
cloth of gold, throwing incense up into the air, sprinkling holy
water on the Cardinal as he passed, while church bells pealed,
river forts fired a salute. This time the procession would be
even more splendid. For Wolsey was to join it. Two Cardinals,
both papal legates, together in England would be a rare
sight.

In vain the Londoners waited to crane their necks at this
gorgeous spectacle. The day passed and the evening; there was
still no sign of Campeggio. A fresh attack of gout, worsened
by the prospect of a task for which the ageing Cardinal had no
stomach, made him so ill that he could not stand even the
jolting of his litter. Campeggio spent that night again in the
Duke of Suffolk's house. The next morning, long after the

crowds had gone home, heralded by neither bells nor gun salutes, he slipped quietly into London by river in a barge and went straight to bed again in Bath Place, the house supplied for him near Bridewell Palace.

Anne's waiting began all over again. Miles away from London where the Court was now based, she was frustratingly incapable of doing anything to help herself. And she must depend on messages from the King for her news.

For a fortnight Campeggio lay in his riverside mansion racked by gout in his knee; but that was not the worst of it. Quite apart from his illness, it soon became apparent that Campeggio had no intention of opening the trial immediately, that indeed, he hoped to avoid it altogether and find some other solution to Henry's matrimonial problem.

When Wolsey thrust his way into the invalid's room, Campeggio suggested that together they should attempt to persuade the King to patch up his present marriage. Vigorously, Wolsey protested that the trial must go ahead; the affairs of the kingdom were at a standstill; the succession to the throne was in doubt; total ruin would come to the realm, to the Church in England, and to himself, unless the Pope did as the King wished. In that case, before making any move, Campeggio remarked, he would have to inform the Pope, a statement that sounded ominously in Wolsey's ears, since it suggested Campeggio had no mandate to give final judgement on the 'divorce' after all.

On 22 October 1528, Campeggio finally dragged his painful old body out of bed to attend an official reception and have an audience with the King. In torrential rain he was borne downriver to Bridewell Palace where such a huge press of people waited to see him that the Venetian embassy lost their shoes. From the water's edge, since he could neither ride nor walk, Campeggio had to be carried in a crimson velvet-covered chair by four men while Wolsey rode abreast on his mule; it was a travesty of the dignified procession originally planned, but the best that could be done. The King himself waited to greet him at the bottom of the palace stairs, and in the great chamber above there was an impressive reception committee of noblemen, prelates and all the ambassadors, except the Imperial Don Inigo de Mendoza who, for obvious reasons, had not been invited. The occasion was as unproductive as it was magnifi-cent. After four hours spent in speeches and compliments and receiving the Pope's polite letters, King Henry was forced to realize that the wretched Campeggio was really ill and must be allowed to return to his bed in Bath Place.

Here, after dinner the following day, the King came to plead his own cause and to receive an unwelcome answer. If Henry's conscience was troubled about the validity of his marriage to Catherine, the papal legate remarked, Pope Clement could be asked to grant another dispensation that would make all well. Miraculously keeping his volatile temper under control, Henry insisted his marriage was invalid, and launched vigorously into learned theological argument to prove it. 'And I believe,' Campeggio was to report despondently after this interview, 'if an angel descended from heaven he would not be able to persuade his Majesty to the contrary.' Campeggio altered his tactics, suggesting that there might be still another way to settle the matter without resorting to a trial. If the Queen could be persuaded to enter a nunnery he was empowered to dissolve the marriage. Henry pounced on this wonderful idea – which was based on a precedent in France where the first Queen of King Louis XII had entered a religious house so that her husband could remarry. If Catherine agreed to this, Henry promised largely, he would settle the succession on her daughter should Anne not give him a son. And Catherine could have anything she pleased.

Campeggio's suggestion did not imply any great sacrifice on Catherine's part, for there existed at the time nunneries whose rules were so lax that noblewomen sometimes retired to them to live a quiet but thoroughly comfortable life. With the funds she would be able to bestow on the religious house of her choice, Catherine could live a life there of discreet luxury.

It seemed to offer a happy solution for everyone: Catherine's honour would be saved and the Emperor spared the trouble of fighting for it; the Pope need no longer make any decision, so need risk offending no one; King Henry could possess Mistress Anne Boleyn.

The following day, a Saturday, the two legates went to-gether to see Catherine at Bridewell Palace. It was, Campeggio stressed, the Pope's wish that she should enter a nunnery. By doing so she would avoid scandal and enmity and preserve her temporal goods to use as she wished. She could name her own terms. And she would lose nothing but the body of the King, which she had not enjoyed anyway for two years.

Catherine did not reply directly. She wanted time to consider. She was, she said, alone in a strange land. She would ask the King for counsellors and after consulting with them would give her answer.

On Sunday Campeggio visited John Fisher, Bishop of Rochester, whom the Queen was expected to choose as one of these, and asked him to use his influence with Catherine; Fisher allowed him to think that he would and Campeggio left in a state of optimism, only to have it utterly dispelled a few days later when Catherine herself came to see him. Prince Arthur, she swore, had slept with her only seven nights, leaving her as he found her, a virgin, and she added resolutely that she intended 'to live and die in the state of matrimony to which God had called her'. She had made her decision. Neither the whole kingdom on the one hand, nor any great punishment on the other, although she might be torn limb from limb, should compel her to alter it; and, she added, if after death she should return to life, rather than change her decision, she would prefer to die over again. She repeated this many times. 'I am convinced she will act accordingly,' concluded Campeggio, wearily reporting the scene to Rome.

Anne was singularly unlucky in her opponent. Had Catherine agreed to enter a convent in the autumn of 1528 her troubles would have ended. Anne could have married Henry without too many passions being aroused. It was the way any reasonable, sensible woman would have taken, but in this situation Catherine was neither: in her veins ran the same fanatic blood that coursed through her mother Isabella of Spain, who had led an army against the Moors, and through her sister, Juana the Mad, who would not let them bury her adored husband. Catherine had decided what were her own and her daughter's rights, and in their defence she would, if necessary, sacrifice her life and all she held dear. No argument would ever make her change her mind: not Wolsey pleading with her on his knees, nor a deputation of learned prelates pointing out the error of her ways; not the possibility of rebellion against the husband she loved, nor the embarrassing position of the Papacy; not even the physical danger of her own daughter - nothing could shake her resolve.

All this time, while Campeggio attempted unsuccessfully to patch up the King's marriage or to persuade Catherine to enter a convent, Anne, in the country, was in a frenzy of impatience. After waiting all summer for the legate, now that he had at last arrived still no progress was being made, no preparations for the trial had even started. She had been so sure that Campeggio's arrival would herald her almost immediate marriage to King Henry. The pendulum of her moods swung from wild optimism to black despair and suspicion: the delay was a plot, Campeggio's gout put on; he was simply trying to procrastinate because he sympathized with Catherine and the Emperor. If that was not so, why had he failed to come and see her as Henry had promised? Was she not the future Queen? Paranoiac with anxiety, Anne picked a furious quarrel with Henry. Somehow in messages and letters Henry managed to calm her down. Anne could and did create scenes to make strong men tremble, and Henry's letter at the end of this quarrel is a big sigh of relief.

To inform you what joy it is to me to understand of your comformableness to reason, and of the suppressing of your inutile and vain thoughts and fantasies with the bridle of reason, I assure you all the good in this world could not counterparse for my satisfaction in the knowledge and certainty thereof, wherefore good sweetheart continue the same not only in this but in all your doing hereafter, for thereby shall come both to you and me the greatest quietness that may be in this world . . . the unfeigned sickness of this well-willing legate doth somewhat retard his access to your presence, but I trust verily when God shall send him health he will with diligence recompense his demur; for I know well where he hath said (lamenting the saying and bruit that he should be imperial) that it should be well known in this matter that he is not imperial; and thus for lack of time sweetheart farewell. Written with the hand which fain would be yours and so is the heart,

HR

Anne, as we now know, was not far wrong in her fears. Indiscreet and ill-judged though her actions often were, she also had flashes of acute feminine intuition. The letters in cipher that flowed ceaselessly between Campeggio and the Vatican, whose secret contents are now laid open for us to read, tell a curious story – of tortured indecision on the Pope's part and unwilling duplicity on Campeggio's. The wretched legate was forced to abuse his native honesty and play a double game; and his gout, which grew worse as his situation grew more difficult, may well have been psychosomatic. Campeggio was in a tight spot. For the Emperor's continued military success in Italy and an opportunity to make a universal peace beneficial to the Church had caused the Pope to change his mind and secretly send Campeggio fresh instructions. Although Clement had not wanted to grant the divorce when Campeggio had set out, he had been prepared to do so if there seemed to be no alternative solution, but now, having decided to make peace with Charles, he dared not jeopardize it by giving sentence in Henry's favour. On the other hand, neither did he want to lose Henry's friendship by giving sentence against him, and certainly not before the peace was actually concluded. So, wringing his hands and complaining of his lot, he sent Campeggio instructions that he was on no account to pronounce sentence but must find some way of putting off the trial altogether. 'If in satisfying his Majesty,' wrote Clement VII's chamberlain, Sanga, 'the Pope would incur merely personal danger, his love and obligations to the King are so great that he would content him unhesitatingly; but as this involves the certain ruin of the Apostolic See and the Church, owing to recent events, the Pope must beware of kindling an inextinguishable conflagration in Christendom . . . If so great an injury be done to the Emperor all hope is lost of the universal peace, and the Church cannot escape utter ruin, as it is entirely in the power of the Emperor's servants . . .'

Timid, well-meaning Clement, in his desperate attempts to avoid offending either side, gave Campeggio an impossible brief. He was instructed to 'protract the matter as long as possible', in the hope that 'haply God shall put into the King's heart some holy thought, so that he may not desire from his Holiness a thing which cannot be granted without injustice, peril and scandal'.

To Campeggio it was soon apparent that the chances were slim of any convenient holy thought popping into Henry's mind to divert him from his purpose. 'These people warmly insist on the affair being despatched with all celerity,' the agonized Campeggio wrote to inform Clement.

> It is necessary that the Pope should take some resolution and write what I am to do . . . so as to leave no burden on my shoulders; for I am unable, being here, to defend myself from their constant solicitations . . . This movement cannot be suspended without peril. Again I humbly implore that such a reply may be given me that I may be able to breathe freely. You may judge of my condition, when, in addition to bodily indisposition, I find myself in an infinite agitation of mind . . .

The unfortunate Campeggio was left to suffer in the damp English climate that was so bad for his gout and in a limbo of indecision. The Pope would take no definite action.

Luckily for Anne, considering her growing tendency to hysteria, although she suspected the truth she could not be certain of it. The King continued to believe in Campeggio's good faith. Meanwhile a new hazard had appeared, making delay doubly dangerous.

Rumours of the King's 'great matter' had got abroad as early as July of the previous year, in spite of Henry's precautions. The whole business, Inigo de Mendoza had reported to the Emperor on 13 July 1527, was as notorious as if proclaimed by the town crier. The people of England had learned of the

King's intention to 'divorce' their Queen with stunned in-
credulity that changed rapidly to malevolent indignation. By
the autumn of 1528 the country seethed with it. Divorce
Queen Catherine after all these years of marriage? The mother
of Princess Mary? The people, especially the Londoners, had
always loved Catherine who, with her dignity and cheerful
smile, her piety and virtue, represented their idea of a Queen.
And now the King had sent for a legate from the Pope to annul
the marriage. And all for the sake of Mistress Nan Boleyn,
who was no more than a black-eyed whore. Anne became the
focus of hatred. The women particularly were aroused. For
them the issue was a simple and familiar one, even if it did
concern the mightiest in the land: Anne was the epitome of all
young girls who lure husbands from the course of duty.

Why, if a man were allowed to exchange his respectable
middle-aged wife for a young girl whenever he wished, what
would become of the sacrament of marriage? Such was the
burden of their furious murmuring. So discontented were the
people, wrote Don Inigo de Mendoza, that they could easily be
stirred into revolt, had they a leader.

An angry crowd gathered round Bridewell Palace where the
King and Queen were in residence. Catching sight of Catherine
as she passed one day through the gallery over the river, they
cheered her, and shouted encouragement: 'Victory over your
enemies!' It was a bad omen for Anne's future. Her subjects
hated her before she had even been openly acknowledged as
their future Queen.

Henry was both furious and concerned. He ordered that
crowds no longer be allowed to gather round the palace,
then did what he could to boost his cause and damaged popularity.

On the afternoon of Sunday, November 8, he summoned the
Mayor and aldermen of London into the great chamber at
Bridewell and pretended to take them into his confidence. The
'divorce' was really for their benefit; that was the theme of his
speech. He had asked Campeggio to come to England, he
explained disarmingly, for the good of the kingdom. His
marriage had been called in question and he had asked Campeggio to decide on its validity, as he was anxious to secure the

succession to the throne and thus the peace and tranquillity of the realm. If his marriage was pronounced legal, there could, he insisted hypocritically, be nothing 'more pleasant nor more acceptable' to him in his life. For the Queen, he said, 'is a woman of most gentleness, of most humility and buxomness; yea and of all good qualities appertaining to nobility she is without comparison . . . If I were to marry again . . . I would surely choose her above all other women.'

Henry was a persuasive speaker, clever at assessing and playing on the mood of the people, but even the chronicler Edward Hall, biased as he is in the King's favour, admits that on this occasion not everyone was convinced.

For the benefit of these, whose hearts remained untouched by Henry's description of the great sacrifice he was prepared to make on their behalf, Henry wound up, according to du Bellay, who has also left us an account of this scene, on a warmer note.

Meanwhile, the King concluded, with a flash of characteristic brutality, 'if I find anyone - whoever he is - who speaks in unsuitable terms of his prince, there is no head so fine but I will make it fly.'

King Henry, however, had not yet acquired the network of spies that in later years would enable him to put his threat into practice; in London's alehouses, barbers' shops and cock-pits the murmurs of unrest continued. Perhaps they would die down, his councillors suggested, if he went to live outside London - a plan to which the King, longing for Anne's company, was quick to agree. He sent Catherine to Greenwich, gave instructions for cart-loads of baggage to follow him and happily galloped off, meaning to spend a prolonged and delightful exile in a house a convenient five miles from Anne's abode, but a disappointment awaited him. Anne's welcome was distinctly cool. She was appalled at the prospect of his settling down near by; without the King in London to urge things on, she felt, there was no chance at all of getting the 'divorce'. She forced him to turn round and go back. So reported the Spanish ambassador, adding - somewhat unnecessarily - that the King was so in love he could not see his way clearly. Meanwhile another grave reason had appeared for delaying the trial, and a matter this time that made King Henry himself willing to wait a while before putting his cause to the final test.


Catherine had lately shown herself strangely untroubled by her threatening situation, so much so that in October Jean du Bellay had described her as looking as cheerful as in her greatest triumphs. On this occasion her quiet inner strength had a substantial foundation, for hidden in her possession for the past six months had been a key document for her defence - nothing less than the copy of a papal dispensation for her to marry King Henry that Pope Julius had sent to her mother Queen Isabella on her death-bed. Discovered in Spain, it had been secretly given to Catherine by the Imperial ambassador Don Inigo de Mendoza, its existence unknown to anybody else in England until, suddenly, after Campeggio's arrival, she produced it: a bombshell exploding all Henry's plans. Since the wording was slightly different from the original dispensation to which the commission granted to the legates applied, it shattered the careful legal preparations for the trial. Faced with this new anxiety, Henry and Wolsey were themselves now content to put off the trial while they again sent agents riding across the Alps (Anne's cousin Sir Francis Brian, Peter Vannes, William Knight and William Benet), this time to try to find some way of proving that the Spanish brief was a forgery, and to wrest from the reluctant Pope a further set of documents - which in their legal intricacy were probably as confusing to Anne in 1528 as they are to us today.

They included an amplified commission to deal with the Spanish brief and a written promise, known as a 'pollicitation', that the Pope would not revoke the commission already given to the legates. Though Clement had drafted this document in July 1528 he had not yet sent it. King Henry also hoped to persuade Clement to let him use in the trial the secret decretal commission which Campeggio had shown to the King and Wolsey but insisted on keeping in his own possession; and which, unknown to Henry, had by this date probably already been burnt at the Pope's command.

There was no longer any point in Anne's continued isolation.

Eager to be back where she could observe what was going on, she again allowed Henry to persuade her to return to Court, but this time she extracted a price. Durham House had a suggestion about it of the royal courtesan, which was not what Anne intended to be. She decided to return with the pomp that befitted a future Queen. In the first week of December 1528 King Henry left Catherine alone at Greenwich and went to join Anne at Bridewell Palace in London – where she now occupied splendidly furnished apartments next to his own. Before installing her here in royal state, Henry had been compelled to take certain precautions against an armed uprising among the Londoners, so violent had their hatred become of Catherine's young supplanter. He had drastically reduced the number of her sympathizers by expelling some of the Emperor's subjects. 'It has been commanded that only ten shopkeepers of each nation shall be allowed to remain in London,' wrote du Bellay on 9 December 1528, 'which will take away at least 15000 Flemings. There has also been a search for hackbutts and cross-bows, and all that have been found in the town have been taken, so that no worse weapon remains than the tongue . . .'

Already by Christmas 1528, when far from having married the King and attained the throne, the 'divorce' was not even in sight, Anne was surrounded by menace.

# Chapter 11

# ANNE AND WOLSEY

CHRISTMAS at Greenwich that year of 1528 had a bizarre note added to its usual air of carnival. There were two Queens in the T-shaped palace, the reigning Queen Catherine and the shadow Queen Anne Boleyn impatient to take her place.

To prevent embarrassing scenes when they met, Henry housed Anne in a separate wing, where in semi-regal splendour, surrounded by the tapestries and wall-hangings Henry had lavished on her, she could give discreet entertainments for her courtiers and friends. And here they flocked to pay their respects to her, the office seekers who hoped to succeed through the influence of this rising star, the fashionable crowd drawn by her youth and gaiety. 'Greater court is now paid to her every day,' reported du Bellay, 'than has been paid to the Queen for a long time.' Frequently among her visitors, doubtless to the indignation of their wives who were staunch supporters of Catherine, were Anne's uncle, the Duke of Norfolk, and Henry's brother-in-law, the Duke of Suffolk, who had their own private object in flattering Anne. Thither too came Anne's brother George, now Master of the Buckhounds as well as Esquire to the Body, her father Viscount Rochford, and the King himself. It was the nucleus of a formidable and brilliant circle.

Christmas, however, was a season to point up to Anne the difference between the reality and the pretence, for expensive as were the entertainments Henry undoubtedly allowed her, the true royal festival was not to be found in Anne's apartments, but in Catherine's. It was Catherine who with the King kept Christmas 'with much solemnity and great plenty of viands', who sat in bejewelled splendour at his right hand under a cloth of estate while 'all comers of any honest behaviour' crowded into the great hall and helped themselves from tables groaning with succulent dishes, including the traditional boar's head. It was Catherine who, though less cheerful than usual, presided over the wild antics of the Lord of Misrule, the customary disguisings, jousts and revels. And after Christmas when the new Venetian embassy arrived at Greenwich Palace and Henry received them standing on the dais of his Presence Chamber, dressed in a doublet of cloth of gold and a gown of gold brocade lined with lynx fur, it was Catherine with whom he dined. For Henry, incredibly, still believed he could hoodwink the world into believing that the spur that drove him to seek the divorce was a scruple of conscience and not his infatuation for Anne. And on all official occasions Catherine appeared at his side as though they were living in perfect harmony.

Anne, hidden away in her wing of the palace, heard the triumphant blaring of trumpets as Catherine with her train of ladies accompanied the King to Mass; she heard the shouted orders and the clatter of hoofs as Catherine rode abroad with the King on some state occasion, heard too the distant cheers of her subjects. And she knew that though Henry had refrained from intercourse with Catherine for two or more years, he still sometimes shared her bed for the sake of appearances - from Anne's point of view a dangerous situation. Especially as she dared not sleep with Henry herself though, judging from a letter he wrote her at Hever, she had promised to do so on her return to Court:

> . . . the cause why this bearer tarrieth so long is the business that I have had to dress up gear for you, which I trust ere long to see you occupy, [wrote Henry] and then I trust to occupy yours.

It was a promise in view of the new delays in the 'divorce' trial that she could not fulfil for fear that Henry might become bored with her before he had obtained his 'divorce'. This was what Catherine was counting on, Anne knew, and the Pope, whose whole policy of procrastination was based on the belief that the King would tire of his latest infatuation and the problem now threatening Christendom simply vanish. So Anne continued to hold Henry at bay. He had failed in his promise to marry her; why should she keep hers to sleep with

him? It was a game they were to play over and over again in
succeeding years.

Campeggio, married and widowed before he entered the
Church, summed up the situation in January: 'The King,' he
wrote, 'caresses her openly and in public as if she were his wife.'

> Notwithstanding this, I do not think he has proceeded to any
> ultimate conjunction, but that he awaits the answer and
> decision of his Holiness, from whom he fully expects to
> obtain some remedy whereby to gratify his desire.

Anne kept Henry's passion on the boil by allowing him every
intimacy except the last. But though she might keep Henry's
interest for longer by not sleeping with him, even he, she knew,
must weary eventually of such a frustrating situation. That
their unlikely relationship endured for as long as it did is
explicable only in the light of Anne's basic fear of the sex act
and Henry's underlying nervousness of his own potency, which
must already by now have been failing. But this nervousness
was hardly something the King would confess to Anne,
certainly nothing she could depend on, and her peculiar relationship was only a very short-term solution, a temporary
shelter against the threatening storm. It was vitally urgent to
find a way of soon entering the secure haven of marriage.

How in these circumstances Anne came to feel an intense
hatred for her rival, the Queen, it is easy to see - any other
emotion Anne at twenty-one was too immature and too
passionate to experience. Catherine alone stood between her
and all she coveted. She alone was responsible for Anne's predicament. Not the Pope; he would have been relieved had
Catherine entered a convent. Still less the Emperor, who was
only stirred into opposition by his aunt's pleas. To Anne,
Catherine's resistance must have seemed obstinately selfish; for
she was at once obstructing the King's happiness, preventing
the birth of a legitimate male heir, and jeopardizing the safety
of the realm. And her resistance must have come as a shock.
That Queen Catherine would resist all the efforts the most
eminent men in the kingdom made to persuade her to submit
was something Anne could hardly have expected. In October
1528 the King told Catherine that the Pope had already decided

against her, that the trial would be pure formality. Catherine knew her husband's devious tactics too well to believe him. He sent a deputation led by the Archbishop of Canterbury, William Warham, to threaten her. There were rumours, these gentlemen hinted, that she had been involved in a plot against the King. And they remarked that if any attempt were made on his life she would naturally be held responsible. Her recent behaviour, the delegation said, had led the King to believe she hated him. She had kept secret the Spanish brief, and she did 'not show such love to his most noble grace, neither in ne [nor] yet out of bed . . . as a woman ought to do to her husband'. Also considering the gravity of the offence she had committed by living in adultery with the King for many years, she appeared unsuitably merry, showing herself too much to the cheering populace, encouraging them with nods and smiles. Even if she were totally innocent, they argued, her resistance made her a focus for the King's enemies. The King had been advised to withdraw himself from her company at bed and board lest her servants should poison him. And for the same reason he would not allow her to see her daughter.

Thick with menace, the audience left Catherine in no doubt that Henry would go to any length to achieve his purpose – he was even prepared to have her executed as a traitor. After twenty years of being treated with the courtesy due to England's Queen, suddenly she was in the position of a suspected criminal.

But such bullying did nothing to help Anne's cause; it served only to strengthen Catherine's resistance and gain her sympathy. For Anne, the Queen was the most maddening of adversaries. Her patient, cheerful, dignified bearing made her a saint-like figure, winning her among many of her servants and subjects that unquenchable loyalty that defies the threat of death. But at the same time, beneath her patient appearance and her obedience to the King in all the unimportant details of domestic life, she was in reality waging a vigorous and successful campaign in her own defence. Henry's agents in Rome assured the Pope that Catherine wanted the trial to go ahead in England. Meanwhile, he kept strict watch on Catherine, surrounded her with spies, refused to let her see the Imperial ambassador Mendoza.

Somehow Catherine contrived to smuggle out in January a letter to Clement explaining the true state of affairs and begging him to hold the trial in Rome. Henry forced Catherine to write to the Emperor imploring him to send to England the original of the Spanish brief. (Once in his hands Henry meant either to destroy it or 'prove' it a forgery.) The bearer of this letter, Thomas Abell, chosen in the belief that he would perform the King's will and despatched on 9 January 1529, no sooner arrived at the Emperor's Court than he became an outspoken advocate of Catherine's cause and strongly advised Charles V to keep the brief safe in Spain.

It was at this time, in the winter of 1528-9 when so many things were going wrong, that Anne suddenly learned that Cardinal Wolsey, her friend for the past year, had secretly tried to discredit her with the King. Basically, the affair was Anne's own fault. A few months back she had thoughtlessly handed him a weapon with which to destroy her, and given him good reason for wanting to. She had admitted that she subscribed to the heretical new religion of Lutheranism.

When we describe Anne as a Lutheran - and she was to be called so many times by the Imperial ambassador Eustache Chapuis - what do we mean? To understand her attitude to the faith it is necessary to take a look at the progress this revolutionary movement, begun in 1517, had made by the late 1520s. It was still very new. Not until 1530 would Luther's own beliefs crystallize into the Confession of Augsburg, and though he had written a Mass in the vernacular in 1526, he insisted it should not become compulsory, thus opening the way for most of the leading towns in the Protestant states of Germany to write their own Masses in succeeding years. But in England, ruled over by the mainly conservative Henry VIII, no Protestant form of worship would emerge until his death in 1547 and the accession of his son as Edward VI. Meantime English Protestants would continue to celebrate the Roman Catholic Mass in Latin and to make and take confession, whatever their private feelings might be as to the significance of these acts. Indeed, as early as 1528 the finer points of Lutheranism can have been known to few people in England, since reading and owning Lutheran books was illegal, a fact that had been colourfully underlined by a series of public bonfires of these heretical works in 1521 and 1526 by St Paul's Cross which stood in the churchyard of St Paul's. Tenets that were to become the backbone of the Lutheran religion and to be accepted by many English Protestants – grace through faith, not through works, consubstantiation rather than transubstantiation – had not yet won the acceptance even of Thomas Cranmer. If this was the case with this future Protestant martyr and middle-aged academic, we can presume that Anne at twenty-one had given scarcely any thought to these aspects of Lutheranism.

The new religion's appeal for Anne lay in its better-known facets. Her pride, impatience and dislike of any authority except her own would have made her receptive to the idea of a Church freed from the domination of Rome and to the concept of a relationship between the individual and his God unhampered by priestly interference. Her childhood in France, where a French translation of the Bible had been reprinted seven times between 1487 and 1521, must have inclined her in favour of an English translation; and her love of fashion, of novelty, of creating a stir, must have given the new faith an aura of glamour. Thus predisposed by temperament and experience to accept what she believed to be Lutheranism, its appeal for her doubled when in 1528 she found her ambition balked by the Pope. The sequel was obvious.

Although Anne was not deeply religious, at least until the end of her life, religion was still a necessary comfort and prop, an accepted fact of her existence, as it was for most of her contemporaries. So in 1528 she simply discarded the old religion for the new. And having done so, being a woman who did nothing by halves, she would protect it in its cruder aspects which she understood, with loyalty and enthusiasm. Her change of faith was echoed by her father, whose attitude appears to have been even more superficial than hers, and by her brother who, towards the end of his life, became a passionate believer. Anne herself was to win by her patronage of the new religion much valuable support, but by declaring the truth to such a pillar of the Roman Catholic Church as Wolsey, who was both Cardinal and papal legate, she was jeopardizing her whole future.

In the summer of 1528 she had written begging Wolsey to use his influence on behalf of Dr Robert Farman, the parson of Honey Lane. Farman was a known reformer who had already been in trouble for heretical beliefs. He was suspected of being one of the chain of people involved in the large-scale supplying of William Tyndale's New Testament and other illicit works from a certain bookshop in Whitefriars to the students at Oxford. As a penalty for having been himself found in possession of Lutheran books, Farman had been forbidden in April 1528 to say Mass or to preach. By asking help for this man Anne not only revealed to Wolsey where her sympathies lay but also made it clear that on becoming Queen she would be a danger both to him and to the Church he represented. It was an extraordinary piece of indiscretion and one that was bound to tempt Wolsey. An opportunity soon came.

By the autumn of 1528 Lutheran books, printed in Antwerp, Mechlin and Brussels and hidden in cargoes smuggled in from the Low Countries, were secretly and avidly being read at Court. Anne carelessly left her copy of William Tyndale's *Obedience of a Christian Man* lying about in the recess by one of her windows. Here it was seen and borrowed by the suitor of her lady-in-waiting, Anne Gainsford. Dr Sampson, the Dean of the King's Chapel, removed it from the young man and, doubtless with a look of horror, gave it to Wolsey, who took it to the King. King Henry, the Cardinal knew, equated heretics with rebels, and hated both equally.

It could have been a dangerous moment for Anne. Though heretics were not at this date being burnt, they were normally forced to recant and might find themselves in prison or carrying a faggot humiliatingly in public procession. Anne ran the serious risk of losing Henry's favour. But on hearing the news she was undismayed. Swearing vengefully: 'Well, it shall be the dearest book that ever the Dean or Cardinal took away,' Anne wisely went straight to the King and fell on her knees before him, whereupon Henry promptly forgave her and, at her earnest request, read the book himself.

Anne had escaped Wolsey's trap and avoided Henry's wrath, but she was left full of burning hatred for the Cardinal, a sentiment carefully reinforced by the Dukes of Norfolk and Suffolk and by her own father. Although Suffolk and Rochford had been ennobled only recently, both were of gentlemanly stock, unlike Wolsey; yet he was the most powerful subject in the land, occupying a position they felt should rightly be theirs. Norfolk in particular, representative of the old aristocratic families whom it had been the Cardinal's deliberate policy to humble, wished to see his fall. Now Anne again joined the anti-Wolsey movement which she had deserted at the King's instance early in 1528. The sly hypocrisy of which Anne is accused over this is unjustified; far from dissimulating, Anne showed Wolsey open enmity, a fact illustrated by an incident in January 1529.

Wolsey had dismissed Anne's protégé, Sir Thomas Cheyney, from the Court. The previous year, when Cheyney fell into his disfavour, Anne had sent the Cardinal a fairly polite message; but this time she did not bother to contact him. Instead she persuaded the King to command Cheyney to return and herself uttered an angry tirade against the Cardinal before a room full of courtiers.

That Anne reacted thus in January 1529 is not surprising. New obstacles to the 'divorce' kept on appearing. The Pope fell critically ill and refused to see Henry's agents, and all negotiations for the documents he needed to secure a successful outcome of the trial came to a standstill – just at a time when it was urgent for Henry to push his advantage. For Clement, re-established in the magnificence of his Roman palace, thanks to the peace he had made with the Emperor, was surrounded by Imperial agents pressing him to revoke the commission given to the papal legates to try the 'divorce' cause in England and insisting that the trial should be held in Rome.

From the papal city Henry's envoys, Sir Francis Brian and Stephen Gardiner, sent letters full of despondency and warning, but Henry refused to be daunted. He was confident the Pope would find a way of satisfying him, that Campeggio would give him the verdict he wanted. Briskly, he replied: Considering that they had not even spoken to the Pope, he didn't see why they should be so gloomy.

In the same packet as this bracing letter from the King went a note from Anne to Gardiner in answer to one from him. Suspicious now of Wolsey as well as Campeggio, Anne rested her entire faith in this eloquent new royal agent. Very different in style, however, is this note from the gushing epistles she had formerly written to Wolsey. This is the letter of a woman who has learnt to be wary of friendship, and is very conscious of superior status. It is stiff with the dignity of the Queen she fully intended to be – whether through the Pope or by some other means.

> Master Stephyns,
>
> I thank you for my letter, wherein I perceive the willing and faithful mind that you have to do me pleasure, not doubting, but as much as is possible for man's wit to imagine, you will do. I pray God to send you well to speed in all your matters, so that you would put me to the study, how to reward your high service: I do trust in God you shall not repent it, and that the end of this journey shall be more pleasant to me than your first, for that was but a rejoicing hope, which causing the like of it, does put me to the more pain, and they that are partakers with me, as you do know: and therefore I do trust that this hard beginning shall make the better ending.

She was sending him, she added, a present of some cramp rings. These rings, Anne hoped, blessed by the Sovereign on Good Friday and supposed to prevent cramp and epilepsy, might help to create goodwill for the King's cause, if wisely distributed by Gardiner and his two assistants, Gregory Casale and Peter Vannes. Anne concluded her letter with a request that Gardiner should 'have me kindly recommended to them both, as she, that you may assure them, will be glad to do them any pleasure which shall be in my power. And thus I make an end, praying God send you good health. Written at Grenwiche, the 4th day of April. By your assured friend, Anne Boleyn.'

Alas, neither Anne's cramp rings nor Henry's brisk encouragement could stop the run of misfortune. A few weeks later that long-awaited document, the pollicitation, arrived; it proved to be as inadequate as Clement's other legal documents. Back went the royal instructions to Rome. Gardiner must get Clement to re-word it. He was to say that the document had got wet on the journey and that he had re-written it according to the best of his recollection; incorporated in the new document that he would then ask the Pope to sign would be all the clauses Henry and Wolsey felt lacking in the original.

The ruse was immediately transparent to Clement, himself too skilled in double-dealing to be deceived by such a naïve attempt at fraud.

In mid-May letters arrived at the King's Court full of bad news. One from Gardiner said that the Pope, recovered from his illness, would grant none of the necessary legal documents for which Henry had asked. And now there was serious danger that Clement would agree to the Emperor's request that the commission he had already given to the legates be revoked and the cause tried in Rome. There was also a letter from Sir Francis Brian in answer to one from Henry expressing the King's belief that Campeggio would do what he wanted. The royal faith, Brian wrote, was misplaced. Campeggio spoke fair only because he hoped Henry would bestow on him the vacant bishopric of Durham as well as Salisbury which he already held; he had assured the Pope that he was not committed to the King by any special promises.

The royal ambassadors usually included in a packet for their monarch a missive also for Anne, informing her personally of the latest news on the 'divorce'. This time the cautious Brian sent her a letter containing only compliments. He explained his reason to the King:

I dare not write unto my cousin Anne the truth of this matter, because I do not know your Grace's pleasure whether I shall so do or no; wherefore, if she be angry with me, I most humbly desire your Grace to make mine excuse. I have referred to her in her letter all the news to your Grace, so your Grace may use her in this as ye shall think best.

Unfortunately we do not know what Henry thought best.

Sir Francis Brian's letter suggests that by May of 1529 Anne had already begun to find release from her tense and perilous situation in frenzied outbursts of temper and storms of hysterical tears; and that the King, confused and upset by these scenes, desperately anxious to keep in Anne's good graces, had got into the habit of giving her a carefully censored version of the negotiations at Rome, a policy that could not but add to Anne's suspicions and anxieties. Now at last, however, Anne was spared the frustration of further delay and inaction, for, under the threat of the cause being revoked to Rome, Henry and Wolsey decided to go ahead at once with the 'divorce' trial in England. It was a momentous decision. On the result of this trial would depend at once the destiny of Anne Boleyn and the future of the Church in England.

# Chapter 12

# QUEEN OR CONCUBINE

THE court whose verdict would enable Anne Boleyn to become Queen of England, or relegate her to the status of concubine, first sat on 31 May 1529. On a freezing cold morning, by road and by river, the bishops of England, the counsels for the King and Queen, the officers of the court and the scribes, converged on the Dominican Priory of Blackfriars on the banks of the little River Fleet to assemble in the great parliament hall. On a platform above, the two legates presided, enthroned grandly in chairs and cushions covered with cloth of gold behind a table 'all covered with carpets and tapestry'.

In scarlet robes and scarlet hats, their outward magnificence hid shrinking inner fears: Campeggio, still urged by the Pope to procrastinate, wondered anxiously how he was going to manage it; Wolsey knew that if he failed to push through a favourable final sentence, his career was over. Each for his own reasons was fearful of the trial's outcome.

The legates took the first formal step: they decreed that the Bishop of Lincoln and the Bishop of Bath and Wells should summon the King and Queen to appear before them on June 18, to answer the charge that they had lived in adultery for twenty years.

It was a fantastic sham. During the trial, Henry had decided, he and Catherine would reside at Bridewell Palace across the little river from the priory. But since he did not look forward to parting from Anne so soon again, he put off the moment for as long as possible, spending a night as nearly alone with her as decorum would allow. On June 14 he left Hampton Court, where he had been staying, sent the Queen on ahead to London to spend a couple of days at Baynard's Castle, and himself set off by river. At the steps of Durham House, Viscount Rochford's town residence, in the soft evening light the gilded barge halted and the King descended. There, with Anne and a small party of lords and ladies, he spent the hours of darkness until the tide changed. 'I much fear,' wrote the French Ambassador, Jean du Bellay, in prurient speculation, 'that for some time past the King has come very near Mademoiselle Anne, so you will not be surprised if they want to hasten things *car si le ventre croist, tout sera gasté*.' Anne, however, had no intention of taking such a risk, especially when she might be within mere weeks of realizing her ambition; no evidence suggests that when King Henry continued down to Greenwich the following morning he had achieved his long-felt desire to possess her.

But his abandonment of Catherine at this critical time had been a serious mistake. For it was while she was alone and unwanted at Baynard's Castle that Catherine took the one grave step that would make all Henry's trial preparations useless: on June 16 she wrote to Clement VII a formal request to revoke the cause to Rome.

Court proceedings on June 18 began quietly, the King appearing only by proxy, the Queen to everyone's surprise, in person. Accompanied by four bishops, she addressed the legates in their scarlet robes. Neither the place of the trial nor the judges, she complained, were impartial; she appealed against their jurisdiction to Rome. The next session which both the King and Queen must attend was fixed for Monday, June 21, between nine and ten o'clock.

On that Monday morning Anne was probably waiting at Durham House, where she could receive news of the momentous proceedings at once, where, impatiently, she could see the state barges float down-river to Blackfriars, see the converging wherries of the curious Londoners and hear across the water the shrill cheers of the mob of women when Catherine entered the priory.

Inside the hall, each in a 'rich' chair under a gold cloth of estate the eager King and the melancholy Queen faced each other across the court. Catherine's protest against their jurisdiction the legates dismissed, and the King opened the proceedings with a fulsome speech about his troubled conscience and how it had driven him to bring the matter to trial.

It was an absurdly shaky foundation upon which rested the complicated edifice of the King's case; nothing more than the argument that Catherine had consummated her marriage with Henry's brother Arthur. But this, Catherine had vehemently denied. Henry himself had often, she claimed, admitted when merry-making with his boon companions that she was a virgin on their wedding night.

Now, before the court, suddenly the unexpected happened. Henry had finished speaking. Catherine arose with great dignity, crossed the floor and humbly knelt before the husband who after twenty years was repudiating her. Catherine's speech, as reported by George Cavendish, is one of the most dramatic in human history, a fact that Shakespeare was quick to note, using it almost verbatim in his play *Henry VIII*.

Her Spanish-accented voice carried her emotion through the hall: 'For all the loves that hath been between us . . . let me have justice.' She was, she declared, a stranger in the King's dominions. His court was biased against her.

> 'I take all the world to witness that I have been to you a true, humble and obedient wife, ever comformable to your will and pleasure . . . I loved all those whom ye loved only for your sake, whether I had cause or no; and whether they were my friends or my enemies. This twenty years I have been your true wife . . . and by me ye have had divers children, although it hath pleased God to call them out of this world . . .'

Her voice grew louder as she came to the climax of her speech: 'And when ye met me at the first, I take God to be my judge, I was a true maid without touch of man. And whether it be true or not I put it to your conscience.'

Henry remained silent and apparently unmoved. Again Catherine pleaded for justice. There was no answer. She rose to her feet. 'If ye will not extend to me such indifferent favour,' she said bitterly, 'I commit my cause to God,' and making a low curtsey, she left the hall. In vain the court criers called after her: 'Catherine, Queen of England, come into the court.'

Leaning on the arm of her General Receiver, Master Griffith, she continued to walk on through the great doors. From Durham House Anne must have again heard the crowd of women's cheers as they caught sight of her. The Queen should not despair, all would yet be well, they shouted encouragingly. Catherine waved and smiled bravely and besought them to pray for her.

The English have always loved the underdog, and from now on these cheering female mobs would wait wherever there was a chance of seeing their heroine; this small but regal foreign princess knew how to attract their sympathy, just as she had known how to play on the feelings of the court. It was a talent that Anne with all her grace and beauty would not acquire until just before the end of her life.

But Catherine's absence was in itself no bad thing. Moving as had been her speech, her sudden departure enabled the trial to proceed more quickly. She was pronounced 'contumacious' and the court sessions hurried on without her.

Speed was Anne's ally, for Henry now hourly expected the Pope to revoke the legates' commission. His hope was that he could obtain a sentence giving him his 'divorce' before the revocation was published.

While in Rome the English agent, William Benet, tried to delude Clement into inaction by telling him the trial had not yet started, in England the King's witnesses were hurriedly called. So weak was his case that he was forced to include among them Anne's obviously prejudiced father and step-grandmother. Rochford's testimony was mere hearsay: he had heard from many people that, on the morning after his wedding to Catherine, Prince Arthur had staggered out of the bridal chamber and boasted that he had been 'in the midst of Spain'. The Dowager Duchess of Norfolk had seen young Catherine and Arthur bedded together on their wedding night . . .

Campeggio, afflicted again with a severe attack of gout in no less than seven places of his old body, had to be carried from his barge and up the stairs with, he grumbled in his letter home, 'God knows . . . what discomfort . . . and what danger.' Henry would grant him no respite; the sessions continued. Things were going so fast, Campeggio complained, he did not even have breathing space.

One man alone tried bravely to stem the tide of evidence against Catherine: John Fisher, Bishop of Rochester, emaciated, ancient, with deep-set eyes. The Queen's marriage was holy and good, he maintained beneath Henry's furious stare; he was willing to die in its defence.

To Anne and Henry the need for haste became more apparent every day, for the news that came from Italy was disastrous. On 21 June 1529 the French had suffered a decisive defeat at Landriano, where the Imperial forces had captured all their equipment and their guns. On June 29 Clement and Charles had signed a treaty at Barcelona and now all three powers were negotiating peace at Cambrai. It looked as though the Emperor would be able to dictate the terms.

In the sweltering heat that had succeeded the freezing cold of early June, Anne waited for her fate to be decided. Distrusting both the legates, she cannot have been confident of the trial's outcome, although Henry remained optimistic. Was it Anne's voice that persuaded the King again to attempt to make Catherine submit? It may well have been, for Anne could never wait patiently. Under a broiling afternoon sun Rochford came by river to York Place where Wolsey, feeling his fifty-odd years, was lying in 'naked' bed, trying to sleep off the morning session in court and a lengthy drubbing by the King. Wolsey must immediately go and fetch Campeggio, Rochford told him; the King required the legates to go to the Queen and urge her once more 'to surrender the whole matter into the King's hands . . . which,' they were to tell her, 'should be much better to her honour than to stand to the trial of law and to be condemned.'

Wolsey, displeased at being dragged out of bed, especially on such a fruitless errand, was unwise enough to grumble about the entire wretched business to Anne's father. His invaluable gentleman usher, George Cavendish, recorded his prophetic words:

Ye and other my lords of the Council, which be near unto the King, are not a little to blame and misadvised to put any such fantasies into his head, whereby ye are the causes of great trouble to all the realm. And at length get you but small thanks either of God or of the world.

Nevertheless, Wolsey obeyed the King's command, climbed

into his hot scarlet robe, entered his barge under the burning sun, and went down to Bath Place to collect Campeggio. The legates had the advantage over Catherine of surprise. When they arrived in her apartments at Bridewell she was sewing with her ladies and came out of her Privy Chamber to greet them with a skein of white thread round her neck. But when she heard what the cardinals had to say she remained adamant. Wolsey's most forceful eloquence accomplished nothing.

The fine summer days of July sped by, beautiful as never before, but filled for Anne with fearful excitement. Soon now, if all went well, the crown could be hers, 'the greatest wealth that is possible to come to any creature living'.

On July 23, the day judgement was to be given, the King sat in a gallery with the Duke of Suffolk above the door of the great hall, whence he could hear and view the proceedings. The King's council called for judgement.

Campeggio now spoke out: 'I will give no judgement herein until I have made relation to the Pope . . .' The allegations, he said, 'were too doubtful, the people concerned too high and notable' for him to give any hasty decision.

Campeggio, after all the months of delay, suffering and pretence, took the final defiant step bravely.

Regardless of the terrible stare from the King, who sat in the gallery opposite, he inwardly said goodbye to the coveted bishopric of Durham and spoke in a loud clear voice:

I will not for favour or displeasure of any high estate or mighty prince do that thing that should be against the law of God. I am an old man, both sick and impotent, looking daily for death. What should it then avail me to put my soul in the danger of God's displeasure, to my utter damnation, for the favour of any prince or high estate in this world.

His speech rambled on, then came at last to a dramatic conclusion: he would adjourn the court until October 1 according to the practice in Rome. Everyone in the great hall knew what that meant. The court would never re-open. The trial was over without any verdict having been given.

In the silence that followed, the Duke of Suffolk gave tongue to the King's feelings. With a great clap on the table with his hand he declared ominously, 'By the Mass, now I see that the old said saw is true, that there was never legate nor Cardinal that did good in England.' But the King had already left the hall.

Anne Boleyn had lost.

Two years after Henry had promised to marry her she was further from becoming Queen than she had been at the start. For on July 16 Clement VII had agreed to Queen Catherine's request.

Lamenting that he was placed between the hammer and the anvil and that he foresaw the general ruin of Christendom, he had finally cancelled the legates' commission and revoked the cause to Rome - where a trial, it was now a foregone conclusion, would result in a verdict against the King. It looked as though Henry might never succeed in fulfilling his promise to Anne.

In her terrible disappointment Anne turned on Wolsey, the man who, for the second time in her life, she believed, had deprived her of her ambition. Besides her broken romance with Percy, she remembered other old scores: Wolsey had once prevented her father becoming Treasurer to the Household after the King had promised him the appointment; Wolsey had also humiliated her in the matter of the Abbess of Wilton.

To those who worked in her interests, Anne was generous; remorseless to those who worked against her. Henceforward she would not rest until she had persuaded Henry to wreak vengeance upon the Cardinal. And though Henry, remembering Wolsey's long efficient service, had earlier in the year been inclined to disregard Anne's suspicions, after the disastrous end to the trial he too was ready enough to find a scapegoat.

It was Wolsey's turn to be banished from the Court. Anne's new champion, Stephen Gardiner, was installed as secretary to the King, and Wolsey's request to see him refused.

Burning with anger and frustration, Henry turned his back on London and the scene of his defeat; taking Anne, her father, and the Dukes of Norfolk and Suffolk with him, he set off on his customary summer progress through the flowering countryside.

Every summer in the stag-hunting season Henry left his palaces near London to ride in the excitement of the chase, going from deer park to deer park. He quartered himself and the most important members of his Court in the largest available house, while lesser officials found lodgings where they could.

But the summer progress was not solely in pursuit of pleasure, it also gave his subjects a chance to see their King. That was why he had to take Queen Catherine as well as Mistress Anne. He had no choice, for she was still his Queen, must still appear by his side to receive the greeting of the local dignitaries in the towns through which they passed. The rest of the time he could spend with Anne, dining in her apartments, slaughtering deer with her, or coursing after hares with hound and horn.

This year Henry moved from place to place at a furious rate. Between August 2 and September 10 they progressed from Greenwich to Waltham, to Barnett, Tittenhanger Holborn, Windsor, Reading, Haseley, Woodstock, Langley, Buckingham and Grafton, 'beside Stony Stratford' - while Henry's ambassadors in Rome made the best of a grave setback and tried to persuade the Pope to put off the trial there for as long as possible.

At Grafton, in Northamptonshire, the King finally allowed Wolsey to visit him again. Campeggio was coming to ask formal permission to leave the country. At his repeated requests Wolsey was allowed to accompany him on condition that he came with none of his former pomp. Arriving in September sunshine at the gates of the manor, the Cardinal seemed a poor shadow of the once mighty prince of the Church. No silver crosses glittered before him; he was accompanied by ten or twelve servants only, a mere fraction of the usual winding train of liveried retainers. Inside the house the courtiers, watching through mullioned windows the legates dismount from their mules, laid bets that the King would not even speak to him. And - perhaps with Anne's help - the Duke of Suffolk prepared a humiliating insult to underline his fall.

When the Court officials had led Campeggio to his apartment, Wolsey in his turn waited to be conducted to the custo-

mary splendid lodging, only to be told: there was no room for
him at Court; he would have to make his own arrangements.
And Wolsey would have had nowhere even to change out of his
riding clothes had not Sir Henry Norris, chief gentleman of
the King's Privy Chamber, kindly lent him his room. Meanwhile, Wolsey's faithful George Cavendish, to whom we are
indebted for this story, had to chase round the neighbourhood
looking for somewhere for him to spend the night.

However, Anne and her party were also due for a shock. The
King summoned the Cardinal to his Presence Chamber, and
when he fell on his knees before him, lifted him up with both
arms and withdrew with him into the great window, from
which the avidly listening and watching courtiers could hear
only snatches of conversation. The King appeared to accuse
Wolsey of treachery, Wolsey burst into long eloquent explanation, the King seemed satisfied. His voice rose: 'After dinner
I will resort to you again. We will commune further with
you.'

Anne's party was in disarray. The bad news was conveyed to
her in her apartments where, says Cavendish, she 'kept an
estate more like a Queen than a simple maid'. Another interview
for Wolsey with the King might result, she knew, in Henry
slipping back into the old dependent relationship, in which
event, she believed, she would never become Queen.

In assessing Anne's character it is often forgotten that she
was far from being unique in her belief in Wolsey's treachery,
for which she had seemingly good evidence. The Duke of
Suffolk, sent on embassy to France in May, had reported a
remark he claimed had been made by King Francis that could
not be ignored. Wolsey, the French King had allegedly told
him, 'had a marvellous intelligence with the Pope, and in
Rome, and also with the Cardinal Campeggius'. In view of the
conflicting loyalties implicit in Wolsey's position as both
papal legate and the King's chief minister, it was a credible
story. Even so honest a man as Sir Thomas More believed the
Cardinal had 'craftily', 'scabbedly' and 'untruly juggled with
the King'. And the majority of the English considered Wolsey
to be responsible for every unpopular policy in recent years.
Anne had come to agree with them.

On the day of Wolsey's arrival at Grafton, Anne was ideally placed to influence the King against his favourite minister; for Henry had promised to dine with her that morning. What use she made of her opportunity is recounted by Cavendish, who had the story straight from the gentlemen who served them at dinner. 'As far as she durst,' says Cavendish, Anne took Henry to task for his gentle treatment of Wolsey. She went on to remind Henry of the many crimes the Cardinal was generally supposed to have committed: in particular, Wolsey's raising of an enforced 'loan' to pay for Henry's last French war; a measure that had earned him the hatred of the people and left the King burdened with a massive debt to add to the always keenly felt problem of his shrinking finances. This vulnerable spot Anne now attacked.

'Sir,' said Anne, 'is it not a marvellous thing to consider what debt and danger the Cardinal hath brought you in with all your subjects?'

'How so, sweetheart?' said the King, indulgently.

'Forsooth,' said she, 'there is not a man within all your realm, worth five pounds, but he hath indebted you unto him.'

The King contradicted Anne patiently. 'Well, well,' said he, 'as for that there is in him no blame; for I know that matter better than you, or any other.'

Anne changed tack. 'Nay, sir, besides all that, what things hath he wrought within this realm to your great slander and dishonour. There is never a nobleman within this realm that if he had done but half so much as he hath done, but he were well worthy to lose his head. If my Lord of Norfolk, my Lord of Suffolk, my lord my father, or any other noble person within your realm had done much less than he, but they should have lost their heads or [before] this.'

'Why, then, I perceive,' replied the King, unwilling to argue in what he had hoped would be a pleasant interlude in the affairs of state, 'ye are not the Cardinal's friend.'

But Anne refused to take the hint; she would have the last word:

'Forsooth, sir, I have no cause, nor any other that loveth your grace, no more have your grace, if ye consider well his doings.'

The serving men put an end to the conversation by taking up the trestle table.

Anne soon had the mortification of hearing that her efforts had been useless. Taking Wolsey by the hand, Henry led him into his Privy Chamber and remained there talking alone with him for the whole of the afternoon until it grew dark, and before Wolsey left to ride by torchlight the three miles to his lodging the King commanded him to come back and finish their talk the following morning.

Anne's desperate anxiety at this turn of events was encouraged by Suffolk, Norfolk and Rochford. She alone could now save the situation; but how, when Henry would not listen to her arguments?

Anne went to him. She had devised a delightful expedition, she told him: a long ride through the autumn countryside together. They would visit a site Henry was considering for a new deer park and have a picnic lunch; she had got it all arranged - only they would have to make a very early start. Henry swallowed the bait, for by comparison with such a day as his sweetheart had planned, a conversation with Wolsey seemed utterly dreary. He was already dressed for riding in his black satin cap and short gown when Wolsey arrived for an audience the next morning; informing him briskly that he could not wait, the King clattered out of the courtyard. The legates, Anne knew, had to leave Grafton that day. It was easy to ensure that Henry did not get back until after they had gone. Wolsey was never to set eyes on King Henry again.

On 9 October 1529 he was brought down by the statute of praemunire, originally enacted in 1351 and 1393, on the grave charge of setting above the authority of the King that of a foreign power - in Wolsey's case, the Pope. The penalty was forfeiture of lands and goods. Hoping to stave off further punishment, Wolsey submitted to this ridiculous accusation, confessed to the crime and offered all his possessions to the King - before he could confiscate them. On October 17 the Dukes of Norfolk and Suffolk deprived him of the Chancellor's great seal, and on October 22 Wolsey left York Place, the luxurious palace on the Thames where he had reigned like a second King. To watch the hated Cardinal depart in his barge there had gathered no less than 'a thousand boats full of men and women of the city of London who hoped to see him taken to the Tower', but for the time being - while Henry and Anne argued over his fate - he was merely to be banished to Esher.

Two days later, on October 24, the King and Anne came up-river secretly, chaperoned by Anne's mother and a gentleman of Henry's Privy Chamber, to inspect the famous treasures the Cardinal had relinquished at York Place; to admire the gallery shining with silver and gold hangings and rich ecclesiastical copes, and to wander blissfully from chamber to chamber gazing at tables glittering with Wolsey's lost riches.

Wolsey had laid them out carefully on two tables to a room. In the gallery Anne saw rolls of stuffs, brilliant velvets and satins; in the Gilt Chamber, a cupboard laden with huge vessels, ewers, basins and pots of gold plate sparkling with jewels; in the Council Chamber, white plate and parcel gilt, the broken plate neatly stacked in baskets beneath. Walking with the King from room to dazzling room, Anne would have remembered that it was here her fallen enemy had lectured her first love Henry Percy, now the Earl of Northumberland, about that 'foolish girl yonder', and she must have reflected that although she was not yet crowned Queen, she had come a long way from those powerless days; at last her position as royal first favourite seemed secure. Henceforward her influence for good or ill over the King of England would be supreme. She meant to use it to achieve her ambition, and she would let nothing and no one prevent her.

# Chapter 13

# ANNE'S VENGEANCE

ANNE'S triumph over Wolsey in the winter of 1529 was shadowed by the unalterable fact that she was still part of a *ménage à trois*; whichever palace Anne and Henry visited, whether it was Richmond, Windsor, Hampton Court, Bridewell or Greenwich, Catherine had to come too. Only when they went to the Cardinal's confiscated York Place could they leave her behind with the excuse that here there were no apartments grand enough for the Queen. Not surprisingly, this mansion which Henry was already planning to expand into the grandest of his palaces, great Whitehall, became Anne's favourite residence. As she discussed Henry's schemes for extra galleries and tennis courts, a vast new park and the inevitable ponderous gatehouses, she could temporarily forget her rival and believe that one day she would reign here as the King's true wife.

In the other royal residences Catherine remained a dominant, awe-inspiring figure in possession of all the outward show of queenship, and a disturbingly considerable influence over King Henry. In these palaces Catherine still occupied the chambers that adjoined the King's. Henry had at last plucked up the courage to avoid her bed; but he still dined with her on public occasions and important festivals, still visited or sent her a message enclosing the gift of a jewel at least every three days. Henry tried to convince Anne that this uncomfortable set-up was only temporary; he would marry her, he had sworn, with or without the Pope; he had boasted in January 1529 that if Clement would not assist him in the 'divorce' he would throw off his allegiance to Rome. But such threats were mere bravado, as Anne must have known to her cost; and he had as yet no idea how to implement them. Meanwhile, now that the cause

had been revoked to Rome it was only a matter of time before
a court was opened there and sentence pronounced against the
'divorce'.

In the circumstances, as the days darkened and the end of still
another year approached, it is not surprising that Anne was
sometimes plunged into black despair. On the evening of St
Andrew's Day, when the King came to have supper with her,
Anne, noticing his downcast looks, demanded to know the
reason. The story comes to us through Eustache Chapuis the
Savoyard who had now replaced Don Inigo de Mendoza as
Imperial ambassador. The cynical middle-aged Chapuis, who
yet felt a passionate devotion to Catherine, soon built up his
own network of spies; their observations he reported in detail
to Charles V. One of these spies was present at the interview between Henry and Anne.

Catherine had angered him, King Henry told her. He had
dined with her that morning, and they had quarrelled.
Catherine had complained of his not sleeping with her, and
when he had pointed out that he was not her legal husband
she had contradicted him, swearing that for each doctor
of canon law he could persuade to decide in his favour, she
would 'find a thousand to declare that the marriage was good
and indissoluble'.

The story filled Anne with foreboding. If Henry allowed
Catherine to speak thus to him, how would he ever pluck up
courage to rid himself of her? Anne would exist in a kind of
limbo until eventually time robbed her of her looks and the
King's love. She was only twenty-two, but youth faded fast in
the sixteenth century, and when she was no longer pretty
Henry would abandon her. The thought sparked off her volatile
temper, so that in place of the tender consolation King Henry
had probably hoped for, she hurled bitter reproaches:

Did I not tell you that whenever you disputed with the
Queen she was sure to have the upper hand? I see that some
fine morning you will succumb to her reasoning, and that
you will cast me off. I have been waiting long, and might in
the meantime have contracted some advantageous marriage,
out of which I might have had issue, which is the greatest

consolation in this world; but alas! farewell to my time and youth spent to no purpose at all.

'Farewell to my time and youth spent to no purpose.' Anne's poetic phrase unerringly summed up the futility of all the King's efforts to date.

Henry did his best to console her. Before Christmas, in preparation for the next great step up in the hierarchy, he raised her rank. On 8 December 1529 trumpets blew to celebrate the creation of Anne's father as Earl of Wiltshire in England, Earl of Ormond in Ireland – in a final thundering victory over the Butlers who had claimed the Irish title in 1515. As a result every member of the Boleyn family gained a title: Mary became Lady Mary Rochford – oddly enough dropping her husband's surname – George, Lord Rochford, Anne, Lady Anne Rochford; and the following day, to celebrate this event, Henry gave a magnificent banquet at Whitehall, seating Anne at his right hand in the place never before occupied by anyone but the Queen. After the final course of succulent dishes had been removed and the notes of the last trumpet fanfare died, there was, says Eustache Chapuis, 'dancing and carousing'.

Some of the 'carousing' must have rung a trifle false since the noble guests, who dared not refuse the King's invitation, included two of Anne's most implacable enemies, the Duchess of Suffolk, whose maid of honour Anne had once been, and the Duchess of Norfolk, Anne's aunt by marriage. Both ladies were superior to Anne in rank, the Duchess of Suffolk being the King's sister, the Duchess of Norfolk being the daughter of the Duke of Buckingham (beheaded in 1521) and a direct descendant of King Edward III. By contrast, Anne was a parvenu.

For these leaders of society, the sight of this girl, but yesterday plain Mistress Anne, taking precedence over them, must have been painful indeed, a slight to their social position that added fuel to the fire of their hatred. Anne's manner was defiantly confident and loving towards Henry. 'It seemed,' wrote Eustache Chapuis, 'as if nothing were wanting except the priest to give away the nuptial ring and pronounce the blessing.'

King Henry treated Anne in some other respects too as

though they were already married, even paying for her under-wear, as his privy purse expenses reveal: £23 'for linen cloth for my lady Anne for shirts and other necessaries'. On 28 November 1529 he paid £217 9s 8d 'for certain stuff . . . prepared for Mistress Anne of divers persons'. Henry seems, in fact, to have paid for all her basic expenses, as well as incidentals. He paid for her bows and arrows and a shooting glove, and when her Breton greyhound, called Uryen, pulled down and killed a cow by mistake, he gave the owner 10s compensation. More luxurious gifts also are listed in the privy purse expenses for the twelve months succeeding Wolsey's fall: purple velvet and crimson satin for Anne's gowns; and furs to line them in winter, as well as the handsome sum of £110 given to her on New Year's Day 1530.

The King left no one in any doubt that his feelings for Lady Anne bordered on mania. Wrote the new Imperial ambassador on 9 December 1529: 'Such is the blind passion of the King for the Lady, that I fear one of these days some disorderly act will take place . . . It never crossed my mind that the King's blind-ness could be so great.' And a few days later he wrote in acid amazement: 'The King thinks of nothing else but accomplish-ing his purpose.'

Anne's hopes at this stage must have been pinned to her own family and friends who, now that Wolsey's bulk no longer loomed between them and the King, had taken over the positions of power. Anne's father, the Earl of Wiltshire, had become Lord Privy Seal; her uncle, the Duke of Norfolk, was chief of the Privy Council (Henry's private body of advisers), and the Duke of Suffolk his deputy. Mindful of the veneration in which Sir Thomas More, friend of Erasmus and author of *Utopia*, was held both in England and across the Channel, Henry made him Chancellor - such a man would lend an air of respectability to Henry's schemes. However, it was not More but Wiltshire, Norfolk and Suffolk who largely helped the King to run the affairs of the kingdom, who negotiated with the French and Imperial ambassadors and remained constantly ready to offer advice near the King's person. And when Henry himself wanted ambassadors to send to France his choice included Anne's brother George, now Lord Rochford.

Norfolk and Suffolk were both Catholics but, like many humbler people, wished to curb the power of the Church in England, so for the time being their interests coincided with those of the Lutheran Wiltshire. The immediate effect of Wolsey's fall and the rise to power of these three men was the passing of a number of anti-ecclesiastical measures in the parliament of November 1529. These included the abolition of mortuaries, which were the fees paid to the clergy on a person's death; and the restraint of pluralities, and the non-residence of priests.

They were acts to rejoice Anne's heart for reasons of religion as well as ambition, since they meant the King himself was moving away from the orthodox Catholic Church. Henry, on the other hand, probably believed that these measures might yet frighten the Pope into granting the 'divorce'. For they would make it clear to him that there was a real danger of losing this kingdom to the Protestant movement which had swept Germany and gained a dangerous hold in Switzerland and the Netherlands.

Some such exceptionally strong pressure was certainly needed by January 1530 if the Pope were to be persuaded to change his tune. Clement VII and Charles V, the best of friends, were residing at the same palace in the Italian city of Bologna. On February 29 the Pope placed upon Charles's head the crown of the Holy Roman Empire, thus reviving the mediaeval ideal of a united Europe, ruled by the heads of Church and state in harmony.

Henry had the incredibly optimistic idea that by sending an ambassador to Bologna he could kill two birds with one stone and persuade both Emperor and Pope simultaneously of the justice of his proposed divorce. For this difficult task the King chose Anne's father, the Earl of Wiltshire, because, he cynically observed, no one could be more interested in the outcome than the man whose daughter stood to benefit. As the King's prospective father-in-law, Wiltshire was given the princely sum of £1,743 8s for his expenses. But if Anne shared Henry's hopes for her father's success, she was in for a disappointment.

Wiltshire clumsily made things worse. Charles V cut short the ambassador's long, prepared speech. Since he was an interested party, Charles declared, his argument was not worth hearing. And then, adding injury to insult, Wiltshire's presence at Bologna was actually used to speed the hearing of the case in Rome. This had been delayed by the difficult necessity of serving a writ on the King to appear and defend his cause before the court. Now an usher called on Anne's father at his lodgings and, backed by a threatening guard of Spanish soldiers, served the writ on him as King Henry's representative.

In the same week occurred a further event to blight Anne's chances. On March 7 the Pope issued a papal brief. It was nailed for all to read on to the church doors of Rome. On appeal of Queen Catherine from the judgement of the legates, it declared in Latin, the Pope had committed the cause to Dr Paulo Capisucchi, with power to cite the King and others. The Queen, it said, had complained that the King boasted he would proceed to a second marriage. The brief forbade Henry to do so before publication of the sentence. Meanwhile, he must treat Catherine as his lawful wife, under penalty of excommunication and an interdict to be laid on the kingdom. Henry had lost his chance to follow the suggestion made by the Pope in January 1528 that he should go ahead and marry Anne and sort the matter out with Clement afterwards - a move that might well have proved successful.

Should Henry now marry Anne he risked plunging his kingdom once more into the darkness it had known when King John had been excommunicated in the thirteenth century. Not only would the King and every one of his subjects be denied the benefit of sacraments and Christian burial; it might also lead to the invasion of England by other Christian nations in a holy war. Spanish ships might come sailing up the Thames under the black and gold standard of the Imperial eagle; Charles could come to avenge his aunt's honour with the papal blessing and attract to himself Catherine's many adherents. Invasion would bring in its wake rebellion and civil war. And even if there were no invasion, Henry might be forced, as had King John, to make humiliating submission to the Pope, to surrender his kingdom and receive it back as a fief of the papacy on payment of yearly tribute. Romantic, self-indulgent and infatuated as Henry was, it was too great a risk for him to take, even for Anne. He would not destroy England for her sake. In the bleak month of March 1530 it looked as though Henry might have to endure the trial in Rome, and that Anne's fortunes were doomed.

From this time on a sword of Damocles hung over Anne's head, and it is under its ever-present shadow that her consequent behaviour must be seen: her hysterical quarrels with Henry and others which became increasingly frequent; her vindictive pursuit of Wolsey; Wolsey who, she believed, was responsible for her present situation and who, she knew, would treat her as cruelly if he had the power.

Through the early months of 1530 Anne was haunted by the spectre of the fallen Cardinal rising again. That Henry was tempted to reinstate him, she knew. The King, surrounded by the commonplace abilities of Norfolk, Suffolk and Wiltshire, missed greatly the Cardinal's superior qualities. But even if he did not reinstate him, King Henry certainly did not yet want Wolsey killed. He wished first to milk him of large sums of money, particularly the French pensions due to him. Lady Anne simply wanted to get rid of Wolsey at any price.

'It will cost me a good 20,000 crowns before I have entirely done with him,' she boasted and, remembering Grafton, she extracted a promise from the King that he would never give Wolsey a hearing. 'For should you do so,' she said, 'I know you could not help but pity him.'

The tug-of-war between Henry's inclination to mercy, purely out of motives of self-interest, and Anne's wish for revenge, tormented Wolsey with alternate hope and terror for over a year. On the very day he left York Place in November 1529 Henry had sent him a message of goodwill. No sooner had the Cardinal landed from his barge at Putney, been heaved by his footmen on to the waiting mule and started up the hill with his escort, than Sir Henry Norris came galloping towards them. He gave Wolsey a gold ring with a rich stone as a token from the King, and announced cryptically:

Although the King has dealt with you unkindly as you suppose, it is for no displeasure that he beareth you, but only to satisfy more the minds of some which he knoweth be not your friends than for any indignation.

Overcome by emotion at this sudden, unexpected reversal of fortune, Wolsey leapt off his mule like a young man, threw himself on his knees in the mire, raised his hands for joy, then snatched off the velvet cap from his head, breaking the laces in his enthusiasm. But Wolsey's joy was premature, for it was not the King's goodwill, it was Anne's vindictiveness that won. When Wolsey reached the palace of Esher, where he was to be allowed to spend the winter, a bleak sight awaited him.

The place was bare of even the most basic furniture. Wolsey, whose household had once boasted, for the use of guests alone, two hundred and forty-eight beds with silk sheets, found himself without any beds at all, without cups, plates and tablecloths. And although the King later restored some of his goods, the Cardinal's life at Esher was made a misery by petty acts of revenge – one day, a request for some of his prized tall yeomen; another, a command that the new gallery in which he took such pleasure should be dismantled and 'sent to the King's palace at Westminster'. Wolsey knew who was responsible.

To Thomas Cromwell, who had wisely deserted his service for that of the King, but still pretended loyalty to his old master, Wolsey wrote:

If the displeasure of my lady Anne be somewhat assuaged, as I pray God the same may be, then it should be devised that by some convenient mean she be further laboured, for this is the only help and remedy. All possible means must be used for attaining of her favour.

Wolsey also wrote to Anne herself, begging that she would promise to intercede for him with the King, a plea she refused though its pathetic tone so far penetrated the armour of her hatred as to persuade her to utter a few kind words. He bestowed an annuity of £200 on her beloved brother out of the lands of the bishopric of Winchester and another of 200 marks out of the abbey lands of St Albans. But all to no avail. The 'night crow' as he called her in private to Cavendish, 'the continual serpentine enemy about the King', refused to be mollified. And

she made it quite clear at Court that anyone ill-advised enough
to speak on Wolsey's behalf would earn her grave displeasure.
So angry was she with Sir John Russell, Knight of the Body,
who presumed to plead with the King in Wolsey's favour, that
she cut him dead for nearly a month at Court.

In January, disheartened by Anne's inplacable hostility, the
Cardinal fell ill of the dropsy and of despair. The King was
alarmed that he might die and sent Dr Butts to Esher to report
on his condition. On returning to Court, Butts was ushered
into the presence of Henry and Anne when there ensued,
according to George Cavendish, a curious scene.

'How doth yonder man . . . how do you like him?' demanded
the King.

'Forsooth, Sir,' roundly replied Dr Butts, 'I warrant your
grace he will be dead within these four days, if he receive no
comfort from you shortly, and Mistress Anne.'

'Marry,' said the King, 'I would not lose him for twenty
thousand pounds . . . Good sweetheart - ' he turned to Anne -
'I pray you at this my instance, as ye love us, to send the
Cardinal a token with comfortable words; and in so doing ye
shall do us a loving pleasure.'

Then, says Cavendish, 'she being not minded to disobey the
King's earnest request, whatsoever she intended in her heart
towards the Cardinal, took incontinent her tablet of gold
hanging at her girdle, and delivered it to Master Butts, with
very gentle and comfortable words and commendations to the
Cardinal.'

Cavendish's estimate of Anne's motives is echoed by one of
Eustache Chapuis's despatches to the Emperor. There was at
this time a rumour afloat that Wolsey merely feigned illness to
secure an interview with the King, a rumour Anne took
seriously enough to send one of her own minions to visit him,
in order, states Chapuis, to check the truth for herself. The
justification of her fears was soon apparent, for though Wolsey
did not achieve the interview Anne dreaded, his illness secured
an immediate improvement in his lot. He was allowed to
remove from Esher, an abode he had hated ever since the
removal of his beloved gallery, to a small house in Richmond
Park.

On February 6 Wolsey received his pardon - as well as tapestry for five rooms, two services of plate and a pension of 3000 angels on top of the 10,000 the King had already sent him.

Anne vented her fury on her uncle. For some devious reason of his own the cold, arrogant Norfolk, who was increasingly to become the butt of Anne's wrath, had acquiesced in the pardon; perhaps he thought Wolsey's yoke less onerous than the prospect of domination by his niece. The expectation at Court was that Wolsey would now return to his former power. Instead, doubtless yielding to Anne's pleas, the King banished him to York, his archbishopric.

Walking in his garden in the cool of a spring evening, Wolsey came upon Cavendish admiring the carving of one of the King's heraldic beasts. It was a dun cow, waiting in a corner by the wall to be put up on the King's palace, and it reminded Wolsey of an old prophecy. 'There is a saying,' he remarked thoughtfully to Cavendish:

> *When this cow rideth the bull,*
> *Then priest beware thy skull.'*

The bull was part of the Boleyn arms.

On 5 April 1530 Wolsey rode north and Anne could enjoy York Place in the secure and triumphant knowledge that its former owner would not return to oust her from the one residence where she could indeed live like a Queen.


With the spring sun came a general lightening and brightening of Anne's horizon. From the Pope Henry received overtures indicating that his threats had not been entirely wasted, that Clement was in no hurry to pronounce final sentence and push England into the waiting arms of the Lutherans. In a letter written on March 26 Clement offered to put off the trial at Rome until September if Henry would do nothing about the 'divorce' in the meantime, and Henry accepted. So Anne had at least breathing space in which to encourage him to find some alternative scheme for obtaining the 'divorce'.

That he was still determined to marry her the King proved defiantly to his gaping subjects eight weeks later. From now on, whenever Anne rode out from the Court she would do so in state. Henry presented her with a harness of black velvet for her horses, fringed with silk and gold with buttons pear fashion, tassels of silk and gold, with one great tuft of silk and gold upon the crupper. Her saddle was 'of the French fashion with a pillow of down, covered with black velvet, fringed with silk and gold, the head of copper and gilt, graven with antique works.' Even to mount this splendidly caparisoned horse Anne was provided with a footstool 'covered with black velvet fringed with silk and gold'.

Should she prefer to travel by litter, this was carried by two mules with saddles of black leather garnished with white nails, headstalls and reins of black leather. Yet a third means of transport was provided by the ever-loving King, a means that would bring them close together. He ordered for his Anne the softest of pillions 'of white fustian, stuffed with fine down with leathers and buckles to the same; one pillion cloth of velvet fringed with black silk and lined with black buckram . . . one harness to the same pillion, of black velvet fringed with black silk with buckles and pendants of copper and gilt; two white girths of twine of the double fashion . . .'

On this magnificent seat the black-haired girl rode behind the King on his great chargers. The sight of their sovereign with his beautiful 'mistress' shocked and horrified his subjects; Henry dealt summarily with their criticism. Late one May evening he arrived in London from Windsor with Anne up behind him. Two men heard merely to comment on this remarkable sight were flung into prison.

The extravagant richness of Anne's riding equipment was a flamboyant announcement to the world that the King would marry her whatever the obstacles, a declaration which must have been gratifying to Anne. But as she cantered in black and gold through the spring countryside, the constant, never-silent question haunted her: If the Pope would not give the King his 'divorce', who could? She knew her only chance of ever becoming Queen lay in persuading the King to break away from the domination of Rome. And this she now set out to do.

# Chapter 14

# PLOTS AND THREATS

As Anne rode on her gorgeously caparisoned horses past the glowering English people as though she were already their Queen, throughout the universities of Europe the King's 'divorce' had become the subject of urgent controversy. Since the autumn of 1529, stone cloisters and sun-washed courtyards had rung with debate and arguments between long-gowned theologians. Did the passage in Deuteronomy which stated that if a man's brother died, he should marry the widow, contradict the passage in Leviticus on which Henry originally based his case? Were the forbidden relationships in Leviticus part of the natural law, which should not be altered? Or were they based on no more than man-made law and custom, in which case they could be changed? Above all, if the papacy was a divine institution, could the Pope's power of dispensation be questioned?

The general opinion among European theologians was unfavourable to the 'divorce', but in the midst of these penniless scholars were the agents of the King of England jingling fat purses of gold to help them change their minds.

The immediate cause of the presence of the King's agents at Angers, Bourges, Toulouse, Orleans, Padua, Pavia, Ferrara and Bologna, was a newcomer to Anne's party, Thomas Cranmer. A man with a fluent tongue, an agile brain and soft tentative hands, who was to alter the course of Anne's destiny.

Master Thomas Cranmer had entered Anne's life the previous autumn when, on the King's recommendation, he had come to live for two months in the marble-pillared grandeur of Durham House in the Strand, to write a 'book' in favour of the 'divorce', and to act as chaplain to the Boleyn family. Earlier Cranmer had been a humble doctor of divinity from Cambridge who accidentally found himself in the King's path.

On progress with the Court in August 1529, Stephen Gardiner and Edward Fox had stayed at a house in Waltham where Cranmer was tutor. Over supper that night, discussing the 'divorce', he had remarked that although he had not studied the subject, it seemed to him they were going the wrong way about it; there was but one truth in the matter, and if the King could get the theologians to decide what this was he would not have to bother with the complications and delays of the ecclesiastical courts.

These cool words were carried to the King who, according to the martyrologist John Foxe, commented eagerly, 'He hath the sow by the right ear.' Cranmer had suggested a possible solution to Henry's problem. With his usual enthusiastic vigour the King set his servants to implement it. So began the exodus of English agents to the universities.

Did the Pope have power to dispense from the impediment of affinity in Catherine's marriage to Henry? This was the key question the university theologians were to be asked. The King's agents were instructed to get the answer No by any means in their power.

The embassy to France and to the university of Paris was headed by Anne's brother, Lord Rochford, who left England with a princely train in October 1529. His experience illustrates the degree of unscrupulousness Henry was prepared to employ to get a favourable verdict.

George Boleyn did not anticipate much difficulty in obtaining the required decision in Paris; King Francis for political reasons was in favour of the 'divorce', and he made his pleasure clear to the Sorbonne. When, incredibly, the theologians flouted his wishes and compiled a long list of signatures against the 'divorce', George Boleyn rode furiously to Francis and persuaded him to write a letter to the President of the Parliament of Paris. In this Francis expressed amazement at behaviour so contrary to the interests of his good brother and ally King Henry; and he instructed the President to dissuade any theologians from disobeying or displeasing him further by threatening them with punishment 'that would be an example to all others'. By the end of July 1530 the required verdict had been produced.

Through similarly fraudulent methods, during the course of the year 1530, other favourable verdicts trickled in. By the middle of the year King Henry already had them from eight universities in France, Italy and England, although there had been fighting at Cambridge and, at Oxford, the royal agents had been stoned by mobs of hostile women. It was a potentially useful haul. He at last had something that could pass as proof of the justice of his case. The question was: what actual use could he make of these verdicts? Henry could think of no better answer than to go back to the Pope.

A group of nobles and clergy were summoned to appear before him with their seals. On Sunday, June 12, they gathered in the King's Privy Chamber to be presented with a joint petition to the Pope which they were asked to sign. In view of the theologians' opinions as well as the danger of a disputed succession, this exhorted the Pope to declare illegal the marriage between the King and Queen; and threatened that if Clement would not grant their just and reasonable request the King and his people would have to seek some other form of redress.

The lords refused to sign the letter without discussion – they hoped to put off the matter for as long as possible – but after the meeting had adjourned Henry sent commissioners to each man's house in turn. Thus confronted, realizing they had no option if they did not wish to forfeit the King's favour, one by one the nobles and bishops of England attached their seals to the parchment, and a bearer galloped off with their supplication, dripping impressively with armorial ensigns, to Rome. There it entirely failed to impress the Pope, who did not even trouble to reply until September.

Anne cannot have been too disappointed – she had ceased to count on Clement. On the strength of the theologians' decision she urged Henry to marry her immediately. And for once, her attitude was logical. There was surely no need to wait for a formal pronouncement of 'divorce' if, as the theologians said, he had never been legally married to Catherine anyway. One of the obstacles, Anne knew, that would prevent the King following her advice was fear of the Emperor, since Henry had neither a standing army nor money to pay the forces he might need to defend his shores. So she attempted to reassure him.

Charles had not the power to invade England, she pointed out forcefully; he was too busy coping with the menace of Lutherans within his borders and Turks outside. And even if he did invade, her own family, she boasted, would provide 10,000 men for the King's service for a year at their own expense (an indication of the enormous power and wealth of the Boleyns by this date). At the thought of the ill-favoured Charles and his threat there rose inside Anne a hot wave of indignation; her mind did one of its characteristic grasshopper leaps. To think that he dared to criticize Henry on moral grounds too!

'Having married his own first cousin, he is in no position to complain,' she burst out passionately. 'He cannot decently ask others to be more scrupulous in the matter.'

Doubtless Anne pointed out also that if Henry went ahead with his remarriage he would be sure of French support. From her own point of view alone and that of her family she was probably right in urging the King to marry her at once, for delay would give Catherine's friends time to act and might rob her of the King's love. There was, however, a larger issue, ignored by Anne as she always ignored larger issues, but which prevented Henry from taking her advice. Should he do as Anne asked and then have the male heir he craved, the child's legitimacy would be in question, the succession to the throne even less safe than before; without the consent of some authority whose verdict would be accepted in England he dared not marry her.

But the anti-papal books and ideas with which Anne had fed him since 1528 were beginning to bear fruit; in his *Ecclesiastical Memorials* John Strype, who lived in the late seventeenth and early eighteenth centuries and had access to a great deal of original material, some of it since destroyed, states that she gave the King Simon Fish's *A Supplication for the Beggars*, a bitter satirical attack against the clergy. He cast around eagerly for some alternative to the Pope. Could he persuade his Privy Council or Parliament to approve the marriage?

On that same Sunday of June 12, when the lords temporal and spiritual had assembled with their seals to sign the document to the Pope, he put to them a tentative proposal. Since so many learned theologians believed his cause to be just, why should he not marry at once, without waiting for any further approval? The King looked hopefully round the ring of dour, silent faces. Suddenly one of the company threw himself down on his knees. Would the King, he implored, consider how unpopular the match would be at present with the people?

But if his Grace was determined to go ahead without waiting for the judgement of the Church, would he wait, the man begged, at least until winter, when the unrest might have subsided?

History, alas, has preserved neither the name of this daring gentleman nor the King's reply. But the effect of his words went deep. He spoke for the majority and Henry knew better than to defy the wishes of his nobles and bishops as well as of his people.

This was indeed a bad reversal for Anne. It was not just that six months is a long time in the course of a man's infatuation for a woman, especially when that infatuation has already lasted four years. It was also the fact that those very lords, who had now dissuaded the King from marrying, included men she had believed to be devoted to her cause; men who, it suddenly became disconcertingly clear, had merely joined her party because it gave them a chance to get rid of Wolsey and for whom, since the Cardinal's fall, she had lost her usefulness.

Anne had experienced the most disturbing of these betrayals a few weeks earlier when Charles Brandon, Duke of Suffolk, whom she had believed to be one of her most loyal supporters, had actually tried to influence the King against her. He had gone to Henry with some newly furbished scandal about Anne and Wyatt, who had been Marshal of Calais since 1528. Love made the King deaf to Suffolk's allegations; he banished the Duke from Court. But Suffolk was one of the King's oldest and best friends, his favourite jousting companion, his brother-in-law. Such a man's banishment could only be temporary - he was, in fact, back at Court by September 1530. The Duke's betrayal was serious for Anne.

As spring turned to summer and the leaves of the deer parks darkened in the sun, she was surrounded by a spreading cancer of unpopularity. For common people and nobles alike she was a figure of doom, a threat to everything they knew, their marriages, Church, prosperity, their very lives – and when a prophet, one of those strange half-crazed descendants of Merlin who still wandered England in the sixteenth century, looked into the future and muttered, 'A lady will destroy the kingdom,' he voiced the fear everyone felt. Even among men in the King's innermost confidence, at the heart of his 'great matter', hidden hostility lurked. The King's agent at Rome, William Benet, and his ambassadors to the Emperor, Sir Nicholas Carew and Dr Richard Sampson, had all become secret sympathizers with Catherine.

Anne's life at Court became haunted by intrigues to topple her from power. These were as yet only petty plots, not very well organized, but still disturbing enough, as we learn from George Wyatt's account of one of them. (The story might seem apocryphal were it not substantiated in one of Chapuis's reports to the Emperor.) An attempt was made to frighten her. As though by accident a book of 'old prophecies' appeared in her apartments. Curiously, Anne opened it, to be confronted by the figures of three people, helpfully labelled H, A and K. Anne never lacked courage. For a moment she stared at the offensive thing, then called gaily to her maid and namesake, Anne Gainsford: 'Come hither, Nan, see here a book of prophecy. This, he saith, is the King, this the Queen, mourning, weeping and wringing her hands, and this is myself, with my head off.'

Her maid, with the credulousness of her day, breathed in awe, 'If I thought it true, though he were an emperor, I would not myself marry him . . .'

Anne was made of different stuff. 'I think the book a bauble,' she said, shrugging, and, herself not lacking in superstition, nevertheless added with a spurt of passionate defiance, 'Yet I am resolved to have him, whatsoever might become of me.' For all her brave words, the incident cannot have eased the strain on nerves that were already too taut.

It was Anne's misfortune that her manner increased her unpopularity. In her position as rival to their beloved Queen, threat to the accepted heir to the throne, as well as to the peace

and welfare of the country, Anne could never have been loved.
But had her nature been less brash, arrogant and disrespectful
she might have been less hated. Her curious disregard for the
dignity of anyone else's rank shocked and offended people who
might otherwise have been her allies. No man was too eminent
for Anne to scold like a scullion in public, no name too illustrious for its owner to escape her highly articulate wrath.
Court decorum was outraged. In February she had berated the
Duke of Norfolk, the most powerful man in England after the
King. Norfolk had listened in grim silence, only remarking
later to Chapuis that he wished both the Queen and his niece
were dead, then the King could have peace. In June, in public,
Anne so far defied royal convention as to vent her anger
against the King himself - a scene which Eustache Chapuis,
devoted adherent of Catherine, reported to the Emperor as
proof of Anne's viciousness.

Henry, Anne had discovered, had sent some material to
Catherine with the request that she should have it made up
into shirts for him. Was this a straw in the wind? A sign that
Henry was tiring of her? About to abandon the difficulties and
frustrations of their relationship, to slip back into the old
decorous life with Catherine? The Queen constantly nagged at
him to return to her. And, dangerous link, there was their
daughter, fourteen-year-old Mary.

Anne, however, was confident of her power to dominate the
King. She would stop such backsliding. She sent for the gentleman who had taken the material to Catherine, and although
Henry was present when he arrived, Anne immediately began
to scold him.

The King interposed majestically: 'It was by our orders that
the material was sent.' Anne went on as though he had not
spoken. While Henry stood mute with astonishment, she
threatened to have the messenger, a gentleman of his own
household, severely punished.

Anne's public rows with Henry were to become a salient
feature of their relationship, a result of the terrible uncertainty
of her position and perhaps also of sexual frustration. Henry
too must have felt this; for although he could easily have
assuaged himself elsewhere, no hint of his doing so creeps into

the despatches of the watchful Chapuis who had informants in the King's intimate circle as well as among the Queen's ladies.

A few days after the episode of the shirts, Anne again urged Henry to marry her at once. She reminded him that he had already kept her waiting a long time. On this occasion Henry rounded on her with a sudden spurt of anger. Instead of flinging accusations, he said, she should be grateful for what he'd done for her. For her sake he was offending everyone, 'making enemies everywhere'.

'The wrath of the King is death,' was a constantly reiterated saying at Court. Henry's courtiers knew better than to risk it. But fear of the King's wrath did not silence Anne. She retorted she was willing to face much worse than mere unpopularity *for his sake*. 'It is foretold that at this time a Queen shall be burnt; but even if I were to suffer a thousand deaths my love for you will not abate one jot.'

By such passionate reassertions of her love Anne took the sting out of the rancour Henry might otherwise have felt at her outbursts of temper, and challenged him in his turn to prove his love by achieving the 'divorce'.

Her alternate sunshine and shadow made their relationship far from monotonous and reconciliations doubly sweet. 'As usual in such cases,' wrote Micer Mai, the Emperor's ambassador in Rome, commenting drily on one of her quarrels with Henry, 'their mutual love will be greater than before.'

Such episodes, reported in the Holy City, did nothing to raise Anne's credit with Pope Clement VII. Eventually, this patient and cynical priest believed she would sleep with Henry – if she had not already done so – and in time Henry would tire of her. Time would cure all. So Wolsey had predicted to Campeggio, and it was only logical; indeed, what Catherine herself still believed. There was no call to offend anyone by making any decision whatsoever, Clement felt; no need to do anything but continue to follow his natural inclination and procrastinate.

Not even the vigorous intervention of the French on Anne's behalf could alter the papal attitude.

In October 1530, King Francis sent Cardinal Gabriel de

Grammont, Bishop of Tarbes, to beg the Pope to grant the King of England's demands. Would Clement allow the cause to be tried again in England; on this occasion by the Bishops of London and Lincoln and the Archbishop of Canterbury? Clement replied he could only consent to the cause being tried in England if the Queen consented. When de Grammont urged that the Pope must satisfy the King in something, or he would see a greater ruin in Christendom than he had seen hitherto, the Pope replied roundly that he would be most sorry to see it, he would try to prevent it; but if any such ruin should follow he would rather it should follow for doing his duty than for lack of doing it. And he was utterly determined, he insisted, to proceed in this matter according to law and justice.

Although at the same time the Pope made no move to hurry on preparations for the 'divorce' trial in Rome, his constant refusal to accede to Henry's demands persuaded all Christendom to believe in 1530 that Anne would never succeed in marrying him, that other arrangements would have to be made for 'the King's sweetheart' or 'the lady' as they termed her in the Imperial despatches. Ever since the previous autumn rumours had been spreading through Europe of a kind guaranteed to disconcert and frighten Anne. The King had decided to cut his losses and pension her off: he would marry her to the Earl of Surrey (Norfolk's son); to the son of the Duke of Buckingham; he was giving her money or property instead of marriage.

The summer months dragged on with no promise of a solution. Henry had no new policy which would put an end to the disturbing rumours, the frustrating stalemate. The best he could do in September 1530 was practically a repetition of his efforts in June. Henry called his Privy Council together to consider a proposal by the French ambassador, Jean du Bellay. The French wanted him to go ahead immediately with his marriage. The deed done, du Bellay said, King Francis would undertake to obtain the necessary papal dispensations. Except for Wiltshire and Norfolk, the Council were unanimously against the proposal; loudest in opposition was Anne's former ally now turned foe, the Duke of Suffolk.

Having failed to persuade his Councillors, Henry tried again, summoning a group of clergy and lawyers to Hampton Court.

Would Parliament, he put it to them, be prepared to enact that the cause of the 'divorce' be decided by the Archbishop of Canterbury? They answered bluntly: it could not be done. The King, who had entertained great hopes of Parliament, angrily prorogued it until February.

The belief that time would cure the King's infatuation, that Anne could never now become Queen with power to harm them, encouraged Anne's enemies to show their hostility openly. By the autumn of 1530 Anne was engaged in an undignified running battle with the violent-tempered, outspoken Duchess of Norfolk. In an attempt to impress, Anne, like many others at Court, had persuaded the heralds to invent for her a pedigree rather grander than reality. According to this document the Boleyn line, instead of emerging from oblivion less than a century ago with the wool merchant Geoffrey Boleyn, now stretched back venerably to a Norman lord who had come to England in the twelfth century.

The Duchess of Norfolk, her own family tree beyond reproach, rudely told Anne what she thought of this invention. Indeed, this ardent supporter of Catherine missed no opportunity to attack Anne, who retaliated vigorously. Learning that her antagonist had set her heart on a marriage between her daughter and the King's bastard son by Elizabeth Blount, the Duke of Richmond, Anne did her best to stop the match - and in October used 'such high words' to her that everyone thought she would persuade Henry to have her banished from Court.

The autumn of 1530 was a disheartening time for Anne. At the end of October, after enduring the torment of seeing her hopes see-saw from victory to defeat and back again time after time, she was gripped by still another anxiety. Wolsey was making a bid for power again. His popularity was snowballing. So went the rumour from the north. On Monday, November 7, he was to be enthroned as Archbishop in York Minster, the ceremony to be preceded by a magnificent procession of all the most notable members of the diocese; after the enthronement he would hold an assembly. It was a situation of potential danger for Anne. What sort of assembly? It revived all her fears of her ancient enemy. Especially when Henry showed signs of relenting towards him.

Around the end of October or beginning of November the King, complaining to his Council of something that was not done according to his liking, said in a rage that the Cardinal was a better man than any of them for managing matters; repeating this twice, he left the room. When Anne heard of the King's words she was terrified. Should Wolsey be reinstated, she was done for. Seeking out the King she burst into fits of hysterical weeping, complained of her lost time and honour, threatening the King that she would leave him. And though the King prayed her most affectionately, tears in his eyes, that she would not speak of leaving him, she would not be comforted or agree to stay unless he would arrest the Cardinal.

Meanwhile, Norfolk, concerned for his own sake to prevent Wolsey's return to power, bribed his physician Agostini into a damning confession: Wolsey had asked the Pope to excommunicate the King and lay an interdict on the kingdom unless he dismissed Anne from Court. By which means he hoped to create a rising in the country, and in the middle of the confusion seize again the reins of government. Anne may or may not have known that the last part of the charge against Wolsey was almost certainly false, but there was enough truth in the first part to justify her extreme concern. There is no proof that Wolsey had asked the Pope actually to excommunicate Henry, but we know from a letter of Micer Mai to Charles V written on July 18 that he had been in constant communication with Chapuis and had gone so far as to approve the suggestion that the King should be admonished to separate from Anne. Either she or Wolsey must finally be removed from the scene, and Anne was determined she should not be the one. Her arguments, reinforced by the Agostini confession, prevailed over Henry.

On Friday, November 4, the blow fell. Wolsey was arrested towards the end of dinner, as he reached his fruit course, by the Earl of Northumberland. Was Anne, one wonders, responsible for giving her old admirer this opportunity to take his full revenge on the enemy who had broken up their youthful romance? If so, he was unable to enjoy it. Awed at the thought of arresting the great man who had humiliated and persecuted him for most of his life under the guise of kindness, he could not make himself utter the words – until Wolsey had conducted him like an old friend into the privacy of his Bed-Chamber. There Cavendish, who kept the door, heard Northumberland say trembling, with a very faint and soft voice, laying his hand upon the Cardinal's arm: 'My lord, I arrest you of high treason.'

They were the last words in a drama that began eight years before, when the then all-powerful prince of the church berated a young nobleman for his foolish love of little Mistress Anne Boleyn.

Wolsey was finally doomed. The Tower and the block undoubtedly awaited him, but he died on November 29 of dysentery, thus cheating his enemies of their final revenge.

Anne's oldest enemy was no more, and it was no doubt a great relief, but by the end of 1530 she was aware of new ones everywhere. Fear was oppressing her. She could trust nobody, neither among the ladies of her own chamber, nor the King's agents abroad. Not even the King himself. In November she spied on an audience Henry gave the Imperial ambassador, Chapuis, who has left us an account of this very revealing scene. Talking to him in the palace gallery, Henry suddenly became unwontedly insistent and passionate on the subject of the 'divorce', and abusive about the Emperor. Chapuis looked up and saw Anne peeping through a small round window in the King's Privy Chamber. When Henry and Chapuis had walked on out of earshot, the King's manner changed, becoming once more reasonable and diplomatic.

Tortured by suspicions, Anne had also increasingly to contend with rudeness from Catherine's ladies. Earlier in the year she had got the King to dismiss three of them. She could not make him banish them all, and knowing this, they baited her. By the end of 1530 she was as easy to anger as a trapped animal. When they goaded her she flew into a temper, became 'fiercer than a lion' and plunged into wildly indiscreet remarks. She rounded on one of her tormentors to exclaim passionately, 'I wish all Spaniards were at the bottom of the sea.'

'You should not for the sake of the Queen's honour express such sentiments,' said the lady-in-waiting with sly intention.

'I care nothing for Catherine or for her ladies,' Anne uttered wildly. 'I had rather see her hanged than confess she is my mistress.'

Harassed, hated, at bay, she had her defiance embroidered in large letters on the blue and purple liveries of her servants: '*Ainsi sera, groigne qui groigne*' (What will be, will be, grumble who may). It was a declaration of war against her horde of enemies, at Court and in the country. Against the ladies who plotted against her in the palaces, against the people who glared at her as she passed on the roads or on the river, against Catherine. It was her way of telling them all that she was still determined to win.

Already burrowing his way secretly into the King's confidence was the man who would help her to do so.

# Chapter 15

# REACHING FOR THE CROWN

IN the autumn of 1530 Thomas Cromwell was an apparently unimportant member of the King's Privy Council and, seemingly, he had no other function at Court. Possessed of an easy, pleasant manner that tempted people to confide in him, he was a rather ridiculous figure. Short and stout, dressed in black, he bustled with clumsy rolling gait among the peacock silks and satins of the courtiers – a man with small eyes, pointed nose and tiny mouth set in a square face above a double chin.

This unhandsome appearance, however, hid some exceptional gifts: an extraordinary talent for ferreting out and using other people's weak points to make them do what he wished; and a powerful mind; a mind as keen, cold and inexorable as the executioner's knife. A clever lawyer who had entered Wolsey's service and risen to be his chief assistant, Cromwell had previously been both a mercenary soldier in Italy and a merchant in Antwerp. He had ingratiated himself with the Boleyn party in 1530 by persuading his fallen master to give them lavish gifts of money in an attempt to buy their favour.

Cromwell was a layman and the son of a Putney brewer. He depended for his livelihood entirely on the King. His manual of morals was Machiavelli's *Prince*, and his avowed intention at Court, 'to make or to mar', was strangely allied with a genuine concern for the peace and prosperity of England which, he believed, lay in an all-powerful monarchy. He joined the Lutheran Anne's party, not through any particular religious sympathy, but because she represented a means of achieving all his ambitions both for himself and his country. Such was the man Anne now found on her side just when her fortunes seemed darkest, when the crown seemed to have receded for ever from her eager grasp.

For a man of Cromwell's vision and vigorous ability nothing

was impossible. Not even the 'divorce'. But the scheme Cromwell laid before the King would push it through in the teeth of opposition from the Emperor and the Pope and despite the rebellious discontent of his own subjects. Cromwell's plan, avidly seized on by Henry, would have been impossible had not Anne already prepared the ground.

Anne had been far from supine during the last two years. She had been working on Henry, trying by subtle degrees to interest him in Lutheran arguments for schism with the Pope. She did not attempt to set before him Lutheran arguments on religious observance – these she knew would only infuriate the orthodox Henry. They could come later. First she must secure her marriage. When in 1528 Wolsey took Anne's copy of William Tyndale's heretical work, *Obedience of a Christian Man*, to the King, he had merely forestalled her own action. All along – so claims George Wyatt in his biography of her – she had intended to show it to him and had already marked certain passages with her fingernail for his attention. Pleading her cause before him on her knees, she had used her opportunity to beseech him 'most tenderly' to read the offending work for himself. Henry, on indulging her whim, discovered that Tyndale's central argument, that a King should be responsible for the souls as well as the bodies of his subjects, opened golden vistas: freedom from the tyranny of the Pope, the humiliating threat of papal excommunication and interdict. He remarked with enthusiasm, 'This is a book for me and for all Kings to read.'

Anne's brilliant move began a revolutionary change in Henry's thinking. It led him in the course of the next year, by devious paths of scripture and historic myth, to the belief: the English King was of ancient right absolute Emperor and Pope in his kingdom; the Pope had unlawfully usurped his authority. It was a platform from which Henry could argue convincingly that he was entitled to have the matter of his 'divorce' decided within his own kingdom.

Cromwell's cool brain now translated this transformation in Henry's thinking into action. Cromwell's plan was typical of him, breathtakingly bold, ruthless, and based on the carefully calculated weakness of his human tools. His weapon was terror.

The clergy should be terrified into recognizing the King as supreme head of the Church in England. Then Henry could get his own Archbishop of Canterbury to grant the 'divorce' and snap his fingers at the Pope. In December 1530, working on the anticlerical feeling among the lords, Cromwell persuaded the Privy Council to trump up a fantastic charge against the entire clergy of England.

They exercised the jurisdiction of the ecclesiastical courts; the ultimate authority of these courts was invested in the Pope; therefore, Cromwell claimed, this was a flagrant case of praemunire, setting the authority of a foreign power in England above that of the King. To accuse a whole profession of implementing long-established laws was a monstrous, incredible charge. But Cromwell knew his men. Mindful of Wolsey's recent fate, in January 1531 the clergy gathered in convocation in London to discuss nervously how much money they must pay to buy their pardon from King Henry. The nature of the price he intended to demand was not yet revealed to them.

In the dark cold days of January, while the King and Cromwell communicated by clandestine means - Cromwell had a room at Greenwich Palace to which Henry had secret access - Anne was tortured by mingled excitement and anxiety; because at that moment when victory seemed so close there was alarming news from Rome, news that made her pace her chamber at night unable to sleep. It looked as though Clement was at last about to make a positive move. Urged by the Queen and the Imperial agents, in December 1530, the Pope had agreed to issue a much stronger brief to Henry - nothing less than a demand that he should separate from Anne. The brief would impose a time limit for the separation, after which the papal censures of excommunication and an interdict on the kingdom would take effect. Should Henry ignore such a brief before Cromwell had created in England the legal framework that would enable him to marry her despite the Pope, Henry would risk rebellion and invasion. Should he submit and send her from Court, Anne was terrified that out of her watchful sight he might slip back into Catherine's clutches or listen to the lies of her enemies. Waiting for the brief that might force him to separate from his sweetheart, the King could not sleep either.

Some of Anne's and Henry's actions around this date can only be ascribed to a deliberate attempt on their part to throw dust in Clement's eyes. When Henry told some of his familiars that he should never have sought a divorce had he not been assured that the papal approbation might be easily obtained, he was probably telling the truth. When he added that, since that assurance had proved false, he would now abandon the attempt for ever, he was almost certainly taking advantage of the grapevine that led from his Privy Chamber through Chapuis to the Pope.

By the end of December Anne had commanded her servants to remove her new device 'Ainsi sera, groigne qui groigne'* from their doublets. Catherine once more presided over a 'solemn Christmas' with Henry at Greenwich, and an extraordinary piece of information reached the Pope in Rome: that the father of the lady and her party were wavering and were now content to follow the ordinary course of justice.

Fortunately for Anne and Henry, the Pope had not lost his vacillating character. Clement was eager to believe rumours suggesting that nothing of a final nature was happening, that there was no need to take action that might result in England leaving the Catholic fold. He resolved on a much milder message.

On 6 February 1531, instead of the dreaded demand that he should separate from Anne, Henry received a letter from the Pope in which Clement merely defended his own conduct in the 'divorce'. It was an answer to the angry, indignant letter Henry had sent in December. Clement had also issued a brief on January 5 which, compared with what Anne had been expecting, was an innocuous document. It forbade the King to remarry until decision had been taken in the case, declaring that if he did so all his children would be illegitimate and forbidding anyone in England under pain of excommunication, whether ecclesiastical or secular, to make any decision in the affair. This brief was not, however, delivered to the King, only sent to the

* Chapuis in his report of 31 December 1530, suggests the reason she abandoned the device was because it was too close to that of the house of Burgundy, 'Groigne qui groigne et vive Bourgoigne'.

papal nuncio in England to be used in case of need. At this unexpected if temporary reprieve Anne took a deep breath of relief. And at the Shrovetide feast, to which the public were admitted, Henry celebrated by dining with her at his side, not just before an exclusive group of courtiers, but in front of a random crowd of his subjects.

Meanwhile the clergy in convocation in London had come to a decision. In exchange for their pardon they offered the King the lavish gift of £100,000. Back came the shattering reply, designed by Cromwell: the King refused to accept unless the grant accompanying the gift described him as 'protector and supreme head of the Church and clergy in England'. The clergy were appalled, outraged and unwilling, but Parliament pressed, the King was threateningly insistent, and the clergy realized they were helpless. On 11 February 1531 they accorded the required title, adding 'as far as the law of Christ allows', a qualification that would prove meaningless.

Aware that this was the first definite step in a series that would lead her to the crown, Anne made no secret of her delight. At the news, wrote Chapuis, the King's lady made such demonstrations of joy as if she had actually gained Paradise.

From now on Anne was certain she would soon be Queen. She was encouraged in her belief by a shower of fabulous jewels from the King, diamonds and pearls and rubies set in a riot of Tudor roses and symbolic hearts, a glittering promise of Henry's enduring passion and her approaching coronation. Henry's account with his goldsmith, Cornelius Hayes, between the end of December 1530 and the end of March 1531 reads like a paean of love:

nineteen diamonds for her head . . . two bracelets for her set with ten diamonds and eight pearls . . . nineteen diamonds set in trueloves of crown gold, 31 Jan . . . twenty-one rubies set in roses of crown gold. A borasse [fan-shaped palm tree] flower of diamonds for her. Two borders of gold for her sleeves, set with ten diamonds and eight pearls . . . Two buttons of crown gold, set with ten diamonds and forty

pearls; four ditto, 5 Feb. Two diamonds on two hearts, for
her head, 9 Feb . . . twenty-one diamonds and twenty-one
rubies set upon roses and hearts, for Mistress Anne, 21
March . . .

These sparkling tributes from her lover were far from being
Anne's only proof of the King's intentions. Whenever she rode
through a town in that wet spring of 1531, Anne saw tacked up
on the church doors Henry's proclamation about the divorce.
Its imperious words shouted through the rain: the sole reason
the King wished for a divorce was his uneasy conscience.
Learned divines and the universities of Europe agreed that the
Pope could not dispense in the King's marriage to Catherine of
Aragon. These facts were made public to avoid scandal.

From the primitive printing presses of England poured
tracts in support of the divorce, written by Nicholas Hawkins,
Archdeacon of Ely, who for his Protestant beliefs had been both
imprisoned and forced to walk in procession with a faggot on
his shoulder. Had it not been for his willingness to help the
King's cause, Hawkins, like Bilney burnt later that year, would
soon have been made into a bonfire for an audience of fascinated
and horrified people.

Many Protestant tenets remained anathema to Henry. But by
1531 Anne had so prevailed on the King that he was prepared
to save from the fire any man who might further the royal
cause, as Chapuis learned to his shocked astonishment in
March. Dr Crome, most vigorous Lutheran preacher in
England, about to be condemned to the stake by William
Warham, Archbishop of Canterbury, appealed to the King.
The King sent for the list of articles of heresy brought against
him, saw that they included a declaration that the Pope was
not head of the church, and promptly ordered Crome's release.
To such an extent had Anne succeeded in softening Henry's
attitude to the Protestants that in January 1531 he even invited
the arch heretic William Tyndale to return to England (an
invitation that was substituted by an order of arrest after
Henry had read his latest manuscript).

In the face of such evidence, how could Anne doubt that she
would soon be Queen? It was only a question of keeping her

enemies at bay a little longer. And the weapon Anne used against them now was Cromwell's weapon of terror. She who had begun her life of intrigue at Court by resorting only to bribery had been taught by the harshness of events to rely mainly on punishment and the lash of her tongue. Fiercely and with no attempt at tact, she laid about her, attacking both real and supposed enemies. In May she persuaded the King to banish the great Duchess of Norfolk herself, and a few weeks later, the King's childhood playmate, the Marquis of Exeter. Suspecting Stephen Gardiner of duplicity – he was, in fact, though opposed to Lutheranism, to prove one of her staunchest allies in the divorce – Anne openly proclaimed her dislike.

Suffolk was too firmly entrenched in the King's favour for Anne to succeed in having him banished again. But for his attempt to link her in a scandal involving Thomas Wyatt the previous year, she had her revenge. She accused him of having an affair with his ward, the heiress Catherine d'Eresby, who was betrothed to his son – an accusation probably founded on truth since after his own wife's death in 1536 Suffolk married the girl.

In June she peremptorily summoned the Controller of the King's Household, Sir Henry Guildford, to her presence. Guildford had been one of a deputation, composed of peers, bishops and Court dignitaries, which Henry had just sent to Catherine; their mission to try and persuade her to support her husband's plea to the Pope for the 'divorce' trial to take place either in England again or on the 'neutral' soil of France. Henry believed in hedging his bets. But Catherine refused their request, neatly rebutting the formal arguments presented by the deputation, to the secret joy of most of its members. As they withdrew from the Queen's apartments the portly, conservative Sir Henry Guildford could not contain his feelings. It would be the best deed in the world, he exploded, to tie all the doctors of canon law who had invented and supported this affair in a cart; then send them off to Rome to maintain their opinion, or meet with the confusion they deserved.

News of this outburst inevitably reached Anne. Sir Henry Guildford answered her angry summons, his lanky bobbed hair in its usual slight disarray round his thick neck. When she became Queen, Anne threatened, she would deprive him of his office.

But Anne had misjudged her opponent. The froglike eyes stared back at her undaunted. Guildford was not to be frightened into submission by this ill-mannered young upstart. Pride and tradition meant more to him than the grandest place at Court.

'I will save you the trouble, madam,' he replied with dignity, 'by resigning of my own accord.' And he promptly went to the King and yielded up his baton of office.

The King, embarrassed by Anne's behaviour, attempted to shrug the affair off as being of no importance. Lady Anne was but a woman. He should not trouble himself with what women said. But Guildford refused to be mollified and Henry had to find a new Controller. Though he knew he could not afford to lose good servants like this, he dared not remonstrate with Anne.

For her temper was the weapon she had now learned to use with calculated effect against Henry. The sharpness of her taunts wounded his vanity and brought tears to his eyes, causing him to complain repeatedly to the Duke of Norfolk that Anne 'was not like the Queen, who had never in her life used cruel words to him'. The Duke of Norfolk, mindful that 'the wrath of the King is death' and trembling for his own skin, told his wife he feared Anne would be 'the ruin of all her family'; the Duchess of Norfolk passed the information on to Chapuis. But Norfolk's gloomy prognostication proved wrong.

Anne continued to reign triumphantly over Henry's heart. And the skilful use of her weapon gave her an important victory over an enemy who could have sabotaged all her plans.


During Anne's long years of waiting for the 'divorce', Henry's daughter Mary had been growing up. Now fifteen, with a mind of her own, she was fiercely loyal to her mother and to her Church. Dead though Henry's love was for Catherine, the years of shared affection expunged from his memory as though they had never existed, for his own flesh and blood a strong paternal love yet lingered. Chapuis noticed that when he spoke of her his voice rang with enthusiasm and tears gathered in his eyes. Henry's affection, Anne realized, would allow Mary to exercise a dangerous influence over him when they were together. She devised a method of keeping them apart. According to custom, the Princess lived away from her parents with her own household but frequently exchanged visits with them. Anne stopped these, by flying into a frenzy whenever the King mentioned his daughter, by declaiming against her stubborn championship of Catherine and lack of obedience to the King, and by insisting, simply, that she would not live in the same palace with her. Rather than face these terrible tirades and the even more terrible possibility that Anne might leave him, Henry preferred to sacrifice the company of his daughter. In April 1531 Mary fell ill. She wrote to her father saying that no medicine would do her so much good as to see him and the Queen, and she begged his permission to come to Greenwich. Anne had the satisfaction of hearing Henry refuse it.

By such tactics would Anne continue to keep Henry from the dangerous pleadings of his daughter. And she could revenge herself in part on Catherine; Catherine who alone stood between her and the crown she had been promised four years before; Catherine who had written to the Pope for a brief that would drive her from the Court.

No middle way was ever possible for Anne. She was a creature of wild extremes of feeling, passionate affection or violent hatred, lavish generosity or limitless revenge. Vengefulness was a trait well marked in her family. In January 1531 her father had entertained the French ambassador to a banquet followed by a farce of Cardinal Wolsey going down to hell, an attractive little piece which the Duke of Norfolk afterwards had printed.

With this tasteless farce Anne herself may have had little to do, but in February an event had occurred for which it is not so easy to exculpate her. An attempt was made to murder John Fisher, Bishop of Rochester, who had been a tireless opponent of the divorce ever since he had spoken against it at the legates' trial at Blackfriars in 1529. Anne was terrified of this skinny, aged man with burning eyes in an already skull-like face. In 1531 he had been responsible for the clause that qualified the clergy's recognition of the King's supremacy. He had written pamphlets in answer to every tract for the divorce he could lay his hands on, smuggling his writings out of England to have them printed in Spain; and he turned up remorselessly at every sitting of Parliament, where his learning commanded enormous respect, ready to put a spoke in the wheel of any move made against Catherine or the Church.

In February 1531 a white powder was mysteriously added to Fisher's soup. It killed two men of his household (besides some beggars who drank the left-overs) and prostrated others in writhing agony. Fisher himself escaped. For this crime the cook was hanged in chains in a pot of boiling oil at Smithfield. Rumour, however, pointed the finger at Anne and her father. Whether or not she was guilty can, of course, never be proved. That she was quite capable of it, though, is strongly suggested by a message she sent to Fisher in October 1531. She advised him meaningfully not to attend Parliament in case he should have a repetition of the sickness he had previously suffered. In the year 1531 Anne was prepared to go to any lengths to achieve the crown that she once more believed was almost within her grasp.

As the wet English spring gave way to a wet English summer Henry's agents in Rome cleverly held up the trial machinery in the Rota with a succession of legal quibbles. Anne's enemies at Court, the Duke of Suffolk and the Treasurer of the King's Household, Sir William Fitzwilliam, urged their fellow-courtiers 'to dissuade the King from his folly'. And Anne went out hunting with Henry.

Always before on these long summer hunting expeditions, the King had taken Catherine. While it was Anne whose company he preferred in the privacy of the greenwood, it was Catherine who rode by his side through the villages and down the dusty roads lined with onlookers, Catherine who received the loyal greeting of the lords and governors of the districts he traversed.

In June 1531, for the first time in their marriage Henry began to leave Catherine behind. Beside the King, magnificent in his black satin cap and short riding gown, the onlookers saw, instead of the dumpy ornate figure of their beloved Queen, Anne's hated elegance.

Henry began, in the second week of June, by hunting in his parks near the capital, leaving Catherine at Hampton Court and then at Windsor. The expeditions were shockingly unconventional. Anne, never at ease with her own sex, took with her no female attendants at all. Her only chaperones were Nicholas Carew, the Grand Esquire and Master of the Horse who pretended to be one of her friends, and two other gentlemen. With this unusually small party Anne and the King went hunting nearly every day, sometimes spending the night in some convenient house before returning to Catherine and the rest of the Court. 'The King and my lady Anne rode yesterday to Windsor, and are looked for again tonight at Hampton Court,' wrote Cranmer to her father on 13 June 1531. 'God be their guide.'

Did Henry hope that, far from the listening ears and watchful eyes of the courtiers, Anne would finally yield to him and fulfil the promise she must have made to him many times, only to withdraw it as the prospect of marriage receded yet again? The answer to such questions is hidden in the mists of history; but Anne almost certainly preserved her technical virginity. And she gained from Henry in mid-July a longed-for assurance. They would be married, he told her, in three or four months' time. She could begin to decide on the officers she wanted in her royal household. She might begin by appointing an almoner.

In the intervals between these hunting expeditions, so suddenly filled with delights, Anne had the deeply satisfying task of appointing Edward Lee, writer of tracts for the divorce, to distribute her charities when she should be Queen. A further great joy was in store for her. Henry had finally decided to end the intolerable *ménage à trois*. Catherine was about to be banished from Court.

# Chapter 16

# FIRST LADY

ON the morning of 17 July 1531 the massive stonework still glimmered insubstantially in the dawn light as a large party of horse clattered out of the gateway of Windsor Castle. Anne and the King were bound on a progress; first stop Woodstock. For the Queen, who had not been warned of their departure, Henry left a curt message: she was not to follow. Riding beside him as the leafy countryside round them emerged from the shadows, Anne must have felt an exhilarating sense of freedom and anticipation.

Despite the uneasiness of their relationship, Henry and Catherine still kept up the hollow courtesy of exchanging regular visits or, failing these, messages enclosing a jewel as a token every few days. On July 25 came the expected letter. Catherine asked politely after Henry's health, complained that he had not even said goodbye to her and added, with a sigh of pained long-suffering, that she would, however, continue to have patience and obey him.

Henry's reply was all that Anne in her most extravagant dreams could have wished. It was an explosion of anger. He cared not for her adieus, Henry thundered, he had no wish to afford her the consolation of which she spoke, or any other. She had, he accused, caused him much annoyance and sorrow and had tried to humiliate him by having him personally cited to appear at Rome. The Emperor might be on her side but God was on his - and in future she could refrain from sending him messages.

But it was hard to silence this voluble Spanish princess. The daughter of Queen Isabella was not so easily vanquished. Back galloped her messenger. Whatever she had done, Catherine insisted, with what must have seemed to Anne irritating smugness, had been undertaken as much for the King's honour as for hers. Before sending a reply the King consulted for three days with Anne and his Privy Council. The outcome was a re-statement of his case against the Queen, ending on a note of exasperated feminine spite which may well have been Anne's contribution. In future Catherine had better spend her time attending to her defence instead of talking about the divorce to whoever would listen to her. The letter carried no address. Henry had decided to deprive the Queen of her title but had not yet decided on an alternative.

A fortnight later Anne had further cause to rejoice. Henry sent another message, this time ordering Catherine to with-draw from Windsor Castle. He was returning there to hunt, he informed her, so she must leave and go to Wolsey's old house, The More. Catherine had no choice but to comply.

At last after two and a half years the *ménage à trois* was at an end. No longer would Anne have to hear the trumpets blaring as Catherine went to Mass, her train carried by one of a long line of ladies signifying her royal estate. No longer would she need to keep herself hidden on feast days when Catherine rode out with Henry or dined with him in public; nor wonder what latest plea to drive her from the Court Catherine was writing in her apartments; what messages she was secretly smuggling out of the palace through Chapuis to the Pope. Now Catherine herself was driven from Court. Anne returned to Windsor and moved into the Queen's apartments in August. Catherine was summarily told that she must choose a permanent house of retirement.

Dazzled by her victory, it is unlikely that Anne considered the conscienceless ease with which Henry could rid himself of his victims. The cool way he had evicted Catherine without the unpleasantness of a personal confrontation should have reminded her of his treatment of Wolsey and the extraordinary callousness he had shown towards her sister Mary. But Anne, in her triumph, was not given to such second thoughts. It was one of her attractions for Henry that she could lose herself completely in the moment. We can imagine with what joy Anne moved into her vanquished rival's rooms and then pro-ceeded to lavish rewards on her supporters.

Her almoner, Edward Lee, became Archbishop of York in

September. Stephen Gardiner, with whom she seems to have had a rapprochement, became Bishop of Winchester.

The gradual filling of bishoprics with Anne's supporters was part of Cromwell's plan. It would give him the power he needed in Parliament to force Anne as Queen on a hostile nation. At the same time as Lee and Gardiner were promoted, Dr Edward Fox, now one of the King's ambassadors in France, became Anne's almoner and the recipient of several fat benefices. It was the first time Anne had known the power of patronage and it considerably strengthened her hand. But she could not bribe the people.

As summer drew towards autumn, as the corn was cut and carted, news that the Queen had been evicted from Court spread through the country. Not only at Windsor, but when Henry moved to his other palaces as well, Anne now occupied the Queen's quarters. England seethed with indignation, and especially the women. The involved arguments in Henry's proclamation of January were forgotten. The facts spoke for themselves. That 'goggle-eyed whore' Anne Boleyn had bewitched the King's affections and driven the good Queen away. So strongly did the women of London feel about it that they decided to avenge her.

One afternoon at the beginning of October Anne was supping alone without the King at a house on the river. Suddenly she received news that a mob of seven or eight thousand women was approaching armed with sticks and stones; they planned to surprise and kill her there. Anne stepped hastily into a boat and escaped to the other side of the Thames. The women were told she had gone and the affair was hushed up in an attempt to conceal Anne's unpopularity. News of this dramatic event, curiously, did not even find its way into Eustache Chapuis's despatches and our only knowledge of it comes from a report sent from France to the French ambassador in Venice.

Anne had nerve enough to shrug off this inauspicious and almost fatal incident; she had more important things to think about than a mob of angry women. For months now French ambassadors had been shuttling to and fro across the Channel. Anne herself was helping to negotiate a treaty of mutual defence with France. That settled, the King could marry her without fear of invasion by the Emperor. The afternoon of Sunday, October 23 saw Anne presiding over a banquet, sitting at a high table laid for three, with du Bellay and the King; looking down on her uncle, the Duke of Norfolk, and her own father, the Earl of Wiltshire. As well as the proud satisfaction of being treated as first lady in the land, Anne doubtless enjoyed an agreeable and unwonted sense of security. To be herself at the centre of political negotiations was the only way she could be sure no one was double-crossing her. And Anne had faith in France, the country that had made her. So long as that country remained on her side, she knew her position was relatively safe, despite the ever-increasing hostility of both the common people of England and the great nobles.

At Court her situation was still not an easy one, but she had found a way to insulate herself from the hatred of Catherine's supporters. She had by now her own lively circle of admirers, men with whom she flirted, gambled and danced, gentlemen of the King's Privy Chamber who, as intimate companions of the monarch, had also become those of his favourite. There was the middle-aged, gentle Sir Henry Norris, who rejoiced in the influential office of groom of the stole (royal lavatory attendant) and an income from lands and offices of £1,327; William Brereton, about whom we know nothing except that he had an annual income of £1,236 and had been brought up at Court; the dashing, charming, athletic Sir Francis Weston, who had also been brought up at Court, promoted from page to groom to gentleman of the Privy Chamber, and who was now the King's favourite tennis partner; and Sir Thomas Cheyney over whom she had quarrelled with Wolsey. There was also her brother Lord Rochford. With this inner group of favourites she could listen to the sallies of Henry's fools or the lute-playing of his talented and beautiful groom of the chamber, Marc Smeton, and lose herself in pleasure.

In friends of her own sex Anne was not so fortunate. The records for this period of her life mention, revealingly, only one. Lady Wingfield, widow of Sir Richard Wingfield, now wife to Sir Nicolas Harvey, recently ambassador to the Emperor. Anne was not the type of woman either to want or to attract many female friends. But a letter that survives from Anne to Lady Wingfield shows that with the few she trusted Anne was capable of warm disinterested feeling. Since her virtues were deliberately obscured by Catherine's ardent partisan, Eustache Chapuis, on whose venomously prejudiced reports we have to rely mostly for our information about her, this letter, which is among the few proofs of Anne's humanity, is worth quoting in full. It is a message of comfort and apology – had Anne's hasty temper run away with her? – and though the circumstances are vague a genuine feeling of concern for the recipient shines through.

Madam,

I pray you, as you love me, to give credence to my servant this bearer, touching your removing and any thing else that he shall tell you of my behalf; for I will desire you to do nothing but that shall be for your wealth [well-being]. And, madam, though at all times I have not shewed the love that I bear you as much as it was indeed, yet now I trust that you shall well prove that I loved you a great deal more than I made feign for; and assuredly, next mine own mother, I know no woman alive that I love better: and at length, with God's grace, you shall prove that it is unfeigned. And I trust you do know me for such a one that I will write nothing to comfort you in your trouble but I will abide by it as long as I live; and therefore I pray you leave your indiscreet trouble, both for displeasing of God and also for displeasing of me, that doth love you so entirely. And trusting in God that you will thus do, I make an end. With the ill hand of

Your own assured friend during my life,

Anne Rocheford

Christmas that year was again at Greenwich. For Anne it was a triumphant festival. She had displaced Catherine and the Pope had not retaliated. Rome and the Imperial Court buzzed with indignation at the usurpation of 'that diabolic woman', but Clement had not fulfilled his threats. No fearful pronouncements of excommunication and interdict had thundered over

Henry or his kingdom. He appeared to have got away with his bold action. Anne presided over the seasonal festivities, the masques, banquets and gambling, and a train of ladies nearly as numerous as the Queen's wound after her.

At the annual exchange of New Year's gifts she saw her present to the King take pride of place on the trestle tables set out for the occasion, while Catherine's, a gold cup of great value and singular workmanship, was sent back to her. It was sent late in the evening when the company had dispersed, because Henry feared Catherine's messenger might cunningly present the cup to him again, this time in public, so that pressure of opinion would force him to accept. Henry himself gave no present to his wife or to her ladies, and ordered the gentlemen of his chamber to refrain likewise.

Anne's present to the King, we learn from one of Chapuis's reports, was a curious one – 'darts, worked in the Biscayan fashion, richly ornamented', presumably hunting weapons used by the Basques. Henry gave Anne a sumptuous set of hangings to cover the walls of one room, as well as, gentle hint, a bed covered with cloth of gold and silver, crimson satin and rich embroidery. Gifts from the favoured Boleyns were well represented on the trestle tables. Wiltshire presented the King with a steel glass set in gold in a box of black velvet, Rochford with two gilt hangers [short swords] with velvet girdles. The Countess of Wiltshire, a coffer of needlework, containing six shirt collars, three in gold and three in silver, and Lady Mary Rochford, a shirt with a black collar. In exchange they received the King's customary gift to his courtiers, that prized Tudor status symbol, a piece of gilt plate to add to the collection on their already groaning cupboards.

After the King Anne was now the most powerful person in England. She could afford to ignore the grim faces of the great nobles and clergy who, in Catherine's enforced absence, found it difficult to simulate Christmas cheer. Her own family dominated the Court. They had their own splendid apartments in the crowded palaces, including a separate room for Anne's mother. Mary, for whom Anne had secured an annuity of £100, was her constant companion; George, the King's close friend. Henry lost large sums to him in wagers at shooting, hunting, playing bowls and shovelboard. He settled two years' unpaid rent for George's house at Greenwich and used him as his confidential messenger.

It was a triumphant Christmas for Anne, but one thing was wrong. Her title was still Lady Anne and not Queen. Cromwell's plans were taking a long time to work. In the coming year Anne, with characteristic impetuous desperation, would take matters into her own hands.

# Chapter 17

# DEADLOCK

THAT Anne was still not married to the King by the beginning of 1532 was not due to inactivity on Cromwell's part. His plan was to make Henry's title 'Supreme Head of the Church' a reality. After a long hard tussle lasting from January until May, the clergy agreed to make no new canon laws and to submit those already in existence to examination by a royal committee. It was a resounding victory for the King, bringing the Church in England for the first time firmly under his control. On May 16 the revered Sir Thomas More resigned his post as Chancellor in protest; although he had wished to see reform of religious abuses in England, he was totally against destroying the unity of the Catholic Church. But even the resignation of such an influential figure as Sir Thomas More must have seemed to Anne a small price to pay for a step that brought her so much closer to the realization of her ambition.

King Henry was now in a position to break with the Pope and laugh at any interdict he might impose; if indeed he dared make such a definite move against the King in the alarming new circumstances in which he suddenly found himself. For Henry and Cromwell together had in their turn forged a sword of Damocles to hang over the Pope's head. In February a bill was drawn up to deprive the papacy of a substantial part of its income in the shape of annates, the taxes paid by the English bishops to Rome. This bill, Henry menacingly informed the Pope, could, with the King's consent, become law within a year unless Clement and his Cardinals earned his friendship by the exercise of truth and justice.

It was an inspired way to frighten into inactivity the timid Pope who so far had been brave enough to make only the feeblest of protests against the Queen's eviction from the English Court. Despite this blatantly defiant act and his own previous threats of excommunication, Clement had done nothing more than issue a brief, on 25 January 1532, which expressed distress at the news, urged Henry to send Anne away and restore the Queen until sentence was pronounced, and added the indefinite threat that he hoped he would not be forced to compel the King to obey. And this feeble brief was not even presented to Henry. At the request of Catherine, who feared, rightly, that such a document would merely enrage the King without accomplishing anything, the Pope's letter was not to be delivered to him for another three months. Cromwell's plan to crown Anne Queen seemed to be making steady progress.

To keep Catherine's powerful ally the Emperor in check, another way had been found. In April negotiations with France culminated in a mutual-aid treaty against him.

By the time the palace orchards whitened into blossom that year, both the legal and the political ground had been prepared for a 'divorce' in England. Everything was ready. Everything, that is, except the man whom Henry counted on to perform the deed: his Archbishop of Canterbury.

In the spring of 1532 it must have been apparent to Anne that there had again occurred one of those maddening events that dogged the progress of the 'divorce': an apparently malleable creature suddenly became a rigid opponent.

In January 1531 the King had paid a personal visit to Warham to ask him to give judgement in his favour. William Warham had been a King's man all his life. He had spoken for the 'divorce' at the secret trial at Westminster and later at the legatine trial at Blackfriars - although it was against his conscience. For while he had originally opposed Catherine's marriage to Henry in 1509, it was one thing to try and prevent a marriage in the first place, quite another to undo one that had lasted over twenty years. But Warham was not a brave man, and when Catherine begged for his support he had merely muttered in embarrassed apology the Latin tag: 'The wrath of the King is death.' Now suddenly in his old age this man whose co-operation must have seemed a foregone conclusion to Henry found the courage to refuse his request, a request repeated over the next year and a half again and again. Not even the threat of a charge of praemunire would make Warham charge his mind; for his courage was animated by a consideration of far greater import than the rights of mere individuals. It was not Catherine whom he defended or Anne whom he opposed, but what her victory would herald: disaster to the Catholic Church, a split in Christendom, what Chapuis called the 'boiling vortex about to open here'. Warham, like More and other good men in years to come, would defend the unity of the Catholic Church with his life.

His obstinacy brought all progress in the 'divorce' to a standstill. To Anne it must have seemed even worse, as though the clock had been turned back to her most despairing hours. She was still young, but her youth was slipping away; this royal marriage was eluding her.

Checked in his course, desperate, reviled by Anne, Henry had begun to stumble through the motions of the previous year but with one significant difference: this time the opposition from the lords was more immediate and outspoken. It was gathering strength.

In February Henry commanded the Duke of Norfolk to assemble a group of leading nobles. When they had gathered, Norfolk addressed them. The King was being denied his rights and privileges by the Pope, he declared; it was the duty of them all to support these rights by insisting that the 'divorce' be decided in England by a lay tribunal – did they not agree? Lord Darcy rose to his feet. Matrimonial causes belonged to the ecclesiastical courts, he declared unequivocally. From his fellow peers came a determined rumble of assent.

To add to Anne's mounting worries in the spring of 1532 she now found her own father turning against her. Desperate to accomplish her ambition before it was too late, she had repeated her clamour for the King to marry her at once. Was he not now Supreme Head of the Church of England? Tempted to do as she wished and defy all his opponents, Henry consulted with Norfolk and Wiltshire, always previously loyal to Anne's interests. But on this critical occasion, to her amazed indignation, they advised Henry against immediate marriage. Their reasons are not hard to guess: marriage in the teeth of opposition from all the leading nobles could result only in

disaster for the country and particularly for themselves. Both
were cautious, selfish men.

Distraught at seeing her brilliant hopes eclipsed yet again,
Anne turned on her disloyal relatives with hysterical fury.
Mockingly, and at a time when Anne could have used all the
sympathy and support a father could give, Wiltshire put on an
act of frenzy to match. From this experience their relationship
was never to recover. Henceforward Wiltshire would adopt
towards her an irritating censoriousness, at which she was quick
to take offence. Their new difficult, nervy relationship is
illustrated by an incident that took place a few weeks later.
Wiltshire, who never showed mercy even to his own family,
found occasion to lecture Anne on the subject. A young priest
was about to be hanged for filing gold coins. Anne ought to
plead with the King for his life, Wiltshire told her, whereupon
Anne retorted sharply that he should not speak for a priest;
there were too many of them in the country anyway. But
despite their frequent quarrels events were to prove that Anne
to the end of her life retained her love for her father, although
he felt little for her.

Henry soothed his favourite's badly shaken confidence with
an alternative scheme for their marriage. He would take her
with him to Calais to his approaching summit meeting with
Francis, and there with the French King's connivance and
support they would marry; she could be crowned in England
later. They would tell no one about their plan, not even Wiltshire and Norfolk; negotiations would be conducted in secret
between Henry, Anne and the French ambassadors.

By June, in the light of this fresh hope, Anne had recovered
her spirits and begun to prepare her trousseau. Henry, determined that the long-awaited wedding night should live up to
expectations, paid for her to have made what must surely be
one of the most magnificent and voluminous nightdresses ever
worn. Fashioned from no less than thirteen yards of black
satin edged with velvet, it was adorned with a matching cloak
made from a further twelve yards of satin. The upper sleeves
of both garments, so Henry's privy purse expenses tell us,
were stiffened with buckram. This ravishing ensemble was
only the beginning of a whole new wardrobe of sumptuous

gowns paid for by the King and chosen by Anne in the summer of 1532.


Meantime Cromwell was busy with more sinister but equally needful preparations for the wedding: ways to muzzle her many enemies. That the King was determined to marry his favourite soon by one means or another was becoming increasingly apparent to his worried subjects. Since May 1531 the air at Westminster had been filled with the dust of falling masonry, the sound of saw, hammer and chisel and the smell of new paint. Already a whole cluster of houses at Charing Cross had been demolished to make way for the new royal park. By day and by torchlight an army of craftsmen laboured, laying green and yellow paving tiles, gilding and carving, and painting huge frescoes of the King in the new low gallery by the orchard. Wolsey's old mansion of York Place was being transformed into a palace fit for the new Queen.

Across the green fields where the Hospital of St James had stood, a spacious red brick manor was rising with Anne's initial displayed next to Henry's over the gateway in the clock tower. Most savagely ironical, workmen were embellishing the Tower of London for the important traditional part it would play in Anne's coronation ceremony. Such sights going on simultaneously with the measures against the Church betokened to the people of England fearful revolution. Against the approaching marriage, particularly in the threatened Church, they became increasingly outspoken.

Cromwell was determined to stamp out this seed of rebellion. He set up a network of spies, whose reports led to the arrest and imprisonment of accused persons. Soon it was no longer safe to criticize Anne. So good was Cromwell's spy system that individuals could be arrested for one unguarded remark, as the Abbot of Whitby had discovered to his cost. Returning weary and dispirited from a meeting of Convocation in York, he was so unwise as to give his prior the latest bad news from Court. 'The King's Grace is ruled by one common stewed whore, Anne Bullan, who makes all the spirituality to be beggared, and the temporality also,' he burst out.

The indiscreet abbot swiftly found himself in irons.

But his sentiments regarding the King's marriage and Anne Boleyn were echoed by the majority of the English clergy who from the pulpit began to launch thunderbolts of divine wrath. On Easter Sunday it happened on the King's doorstep, in the church adjoining Greenwich Palace, where the King's own daughter had been christened. Friar Peto, Provincial of the Franciscan convent there, defied the King to his face. Henry, he declaimed, was like Ahab. And as the courtiers sat dumb with astonishment at the man's daring, the friar proceeded to develop his gruesome theme in detail. The King, he said, was deprived of the truth by false councillors, the dogs would lick his blood. Henry surprisingly heard him out, then, presumably believing that reason in this instance would be stronger than force, packed him off to attend a chapter of his order in Toulouse; and in his absence attempted to undo the damage that had been done; he compelled one of his own royal chaplains, Dr Richard Curwen, to preach again in the same church, denouncing Peto's sermon. Having disposed of Peto's accusations and justified the King's conduct, Curwen rose to a crescendo of confident eloquence. He only wished, he said, that Peto were there to answer him in person so that he could demolish his arguments face to face. A sudden shout made him pause. The warden of the convent, Henry Elstowe, was on his feet: he would answer for Peto. Curwen tried to talk him down: all the universities and theologians were in favour of the 'divorce', he argued. It was a lie, Elstowe shouted. The King himself put an end to these undignified proceedings with a bellow of wrath.

When Peto on his return from Toulouse refused to obey the King's command that he should degrade Elstowe from his rank, there was no remedy but to imprison both friars and attempt to control the remainder by the use of informers in their midst. Cromwell cultivated a man called Friar John Lawrence. And, interestingly enough, Anne took time off from the feminine pleasures of collecting a trousseau to plunge with him into the arena, managing to attach to herself a lay-brother called Richard Lyst. In exchange for information, she flattered him and helped to support his old mother. It was

Anne Boleyn

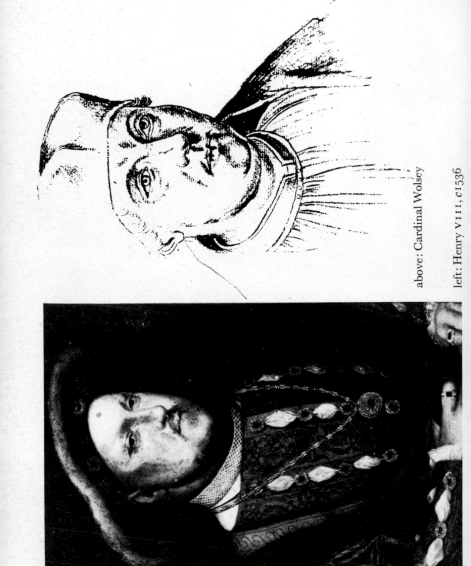

above: Cardinal Wolsey

left: Henry VIII, c1536

Hever Castle, Kent, the main country residence of the Boleyns

Thomas Wyatt

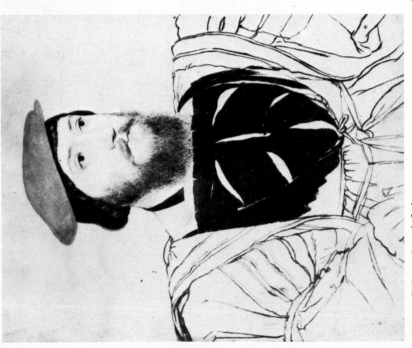

Thomas Boleyn, Anne's father

Greenwich Palace

Anne's coat-of-arms, in which the Boleyn bulls have made way for more royal quarterings

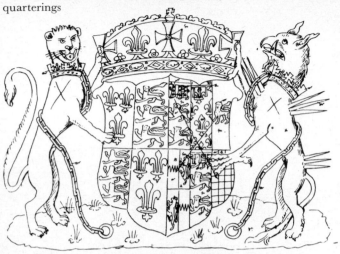

Medallion commemorating Anne's coronation, inscribed: A.R. THE MOOST HAPPI ANNO 1534. The nose has been badly damaged. This is the only surviving likeness made in her lifetime

Thomas Cranmer, Archbishop of Canterbury

Thomas Cromwell

Quenne                                    Anne

Anne's badge: the white falcon

thanks partly to Anne's astuteness in discovering the needs of the old mother that no more damagingly hostile sermons came from the friars of Greenwich.

In an age without newspapers public opinion was largely controlled from the pulpit, and in an attempt to harness this influence to Anne's cause, throughout the country priests were ordered to speak in favour of the 'divorce'. There were some who conformed willingly enough.

Anne had the support of the leading reformers in England, such outstanding speakers as Cranmer, the fiery Hugh Latimer, Nicholas Shaxton and Mathew Parker; all of whom had helped to influence the universities in her favour. And she had the support too of John Stokesley, Bishop of London, who was prepared to do anything to please the King, although, like Gardiner, he was opposed to Protestant ideology. But the sermons of such men all too often fell on the deaf ears of people who had already made up their own minds on the subject. No sooner had the preacher at St Paul's closed his mouth than a woman stood up. The King was setting an example, she screamed, that would be the destruction of the laws of matrimony. She was arrested, but opposition continued. One unfortunate priest who had followed orders and spoken in favour of the 'divorce' was contradicted, hooted, hissed and threatened with violence by his entire congregation.

On all sides the people of England loudly proclaimed their hatred of Anne. When the King took her on progress in July their route for four successive days was lined with women, screaming abuse at Anne, making catcalls at her, and urging Henry to take back Catherine. Against such demonstrations Cromwell was powerless, for it would be politically disastrous in a country whose monarch depended on the goodwill of his subjects to punish whole crowds. But Cromwell could make an example of prominent individuals.

In the summer of 1532 Anne's enemies among the great nobles were deterred from rebellion by the fate of one of them the previous year. It was no less a personage than Rice Ap Griffith, whose father and grandfather had been governors of Wales. Griffith was Anne's uncle by marriage, husband of one of her Howard aunts. He and his wife had been heard several times to criticize Anne harshly, and one of Griffith's retainers had even suggested he should join forces with the King of Scots and invade England. Of course, Griffith was too wise to accept the proposition; on the other hand, neither did he report a blatantly treasonable remark. Griffith himself was attainted for treason, imprisoned in the Tower and beheaded on 4 December 1531. In the shadow of Griffith's death his peers were terrorized, at least temporarily, into accepting the inevitable. Meanwhile fear of again becoming the victims of a trumped-up charge of praemunire kept the higher clergy silent.

Persuasion by terror was effective. It prevented Anne's enemies from gathering together, kept them isolated, expressing their hatred only in secret grumbles and confessions to Chapuis, a harmless enough occupation at the time since in public they continued to go through the motions of supporting the King's policy.

Even by those who hated Anne, Henry's instructions continued to be carried out. Benet, one of Henry's leading agents at Rome, sent a message of apology to Catherine for his actions, but continued to negotiate, as did Nicholas Carew who, against his will, was sent to France to hurry on preparations for the royal meeting.

At banquets and at public occasions where Lady Anne Rochford took the Queen's place, the nobles continued to appear; not prepared to jeopardize life and position for their beliefs. Two alone at Court dared to protest. Henry's sister Mary utterly refused to accompany Anne to the interview with King Francis at Calais. Henry indulged her. But when her husband, the Duke of Suffolk, took advantage of their long intimate friendship to remonstrate against the Calais meeting, the King sharply reprimanded him and sent him off with his fellow nobles to face the painfully unwelcome task of equipping magnificently, at his own expense, himself and his followers for the coming journey.

That summer of 1532 was a hectic one for Anne, tense with anticipation, crammed with events and secret preparation. Many of her talks with the French ambassador, du Bellay, took place in the deer parks in July. Anne gave the Bishop of

Bayonne a complete hunting outfit of gown, hat, horn and greyhound, and, with the King, they went on day-long expeditions. When they had left behind the screaming mobs of women and plunged into the shaded peace of the woods, Anne and the Bishop would wander off on their own. She would take him to a secluded spot to watch the deer running, or wait with him on one of the archery platforms to shoot the great stags as they were driven past.

When the King rejoined them they would visit one of the royal houses. Henry and Anne, like a honeymoon couple, would discuss with him the building alterations they planned. Anne was fond of the bishop, whom she kissed on greeting and leave-taking, a sign of high honour, and with whom she appears to have discussed her intimate relationship with Henry. But her pleasant July hunting days were interrupted by an intrigue that threatened the success of all her hard-fought campaign. Once again a woman was behind it.

The Duke of Norfolk handed her a letter written by the Countess of Northumberland. In it this embittered wife had written to her father, the Earl of Shrewsbury, complaining that her estranged husband, Henry Percy, had admitted to having a pre-contract of marriage with Anne. It was an eleventh-hour attempt to sabotage Anne's and the King's approaching marriage that might well have succeeded. For Anne and Percy had promised to marry; such a promise could constitute a pre-contract, and a pre-contract, according to canon law, could invalidate any future match. A pre-contract had been Richard III's basis for declaring Edward V illegitimate. The Countess of Northumberland's was thus a grave accusation. But whatever moral qualities Anne lacked, she was not short of courage. Gambling on Percy's loyalty, she took the letter straight to the King. Summon Northumberland and question him, she insisted; the story was a lie. As usual, Henry was easily persuaded to believe what he wanted to. And Northumberland, perhaps as a last ironic tribute of love, perhaps because telling the truth would gain him nothing but the King's ill will, before the Privy Council and the Archbishop of Canterbury, solemnly swore there had been no earlier betrothal. So Anne's ill-fated youthful romance fizzled out in the most cynical of ways - a denial that it had ever happened. And Anne's feeling without doubt was one of uncomplicated relief; she had learned to live in a world where her own fierce ambition had permanently displaced sentiment.

In August she began to assemble the ladies who would attend her in France. To her sister, Lady Mary Rochford, she wrote bidding her get ready for the journey to Calais where, she hinted, 'that which I have so long wished for will be accomplished'. Meanwhile, the King sent out written commands to leading peers to prepare their wives to accompany his 'dearest and most beloved cousin'. And to add to her joys, in the same month Anne's opponent, old Archbishop Warham, died, leaving the way now clear for Henry to choose an archbishop who would be willing to marry them.

One way or the other, in France or in England, by the end of the summer of 1532, Anne's marriage looked certain. The means now existed as well as the will; both Henry's ardour and his honour were engaged; he had declared publicly he would marry her.

But after five years' delay, disappointment and broken promises, Anne could not be too sure. She could not afford to lose at this stage; both the nobles and the common people of England were eager for her destruction. She dared not trust the King to keep his word. So she found a way to make quite certain of the crown.

One thing, she knew, Henry coveted even more than her body: an heir to the throne. Should she become pregnant she would put a term to delay. For the King's son must be born in wedlock.

In September 1532 Anne played her last card, the one she had been reserving all these years. In exchange for a title and a large annual income for life, at a public ceremony without precedent, she finally made a candid statement of her intentions.

# Chapter 18

# MARQUIS OF PEMBROKE

BEFORE Mass on the morning of Sunday, 1 September 1532, Anne had her ladies dress her in a narrow-sleeved gown of crimson velvet bordered with ermine, then comb her long black hair loose over her shoulders and embellish it with jewels. Escorted by the officers of arms, she was led then by Elizabeth, Countess of Rutland, and Dorothy, Countess of Sussex, into the great chamber at Windsor Castle where the King awaited her. The French ambassador, the Dukes of Norfolk and Suffolk and an assembly of nobles were in attendance.

Anne knelt before the King. Stephen Gardiner, now Bishop of Winchester, then read aloud a patent creating her Marquis - not Marchioness - of Pembroke. She was a peer in her own right - with precedence over all other marquises. With tender care, the King had put the crimson ermine-furred mantle of her rank round her shoulders, the coronet on her head. She now received the patent from him, together with another document granting her an annuity for life of a thousand pounds a year, which was the income arising from a generous grant of lands and manors in England and Wales. The trumpets sounded. She thanked him graciously and left the chamber with her attendant ladies.

But intense speculation must have begun among the bevy of nobles. For there was something unusual about Anne's patent of creation, a curious omission: two highly significant words. The patent declared that the title 'Marquis of Pembroke' was to be inherited by the male heirs of her body; but it left out the customary description 'lawfully begotten'. It was an omission the implications of which the assembled nobles could scarcely miss. Anne meant to bear the King a son. She was safeguarding

his future and her own in case she was still not married by the
time of his birth. Before the highest dignitaries in the land,
Anne had in effect made a public proclamation that she proposed now to have sexual intercourse with King Henry after six
years' fending him off. What happened after seems conclusively
to prove that this was the meaning of the Marquis of Pembroke's curiously worded patent of creation, that throughout
six years of a close relationship with King Henry, Anne had not
yet given herself to him; although he caressed her intimately,
spoke to her in the most familiar way and, since Catherine's banishment from Windsor, slept in an adjoining apartment, he had,
despite popular belief in England and at Rome, not yet proceeded to the 'ultimate conjunction'. But since, particularly in
the light of present-day permissiveness, such restraint seems
beyond belief, it is worth pausing for a moment in Anne's
history to examine the evidence for and against her having
preserved her virginity.


The most damning evidence against is the information that
reached Rome in December 1531 that she had miscarried. For
Anne to have concealed the early stages of a pregnancy would
have been quite possible in the voluminous dresses of the
period, and a miscarriage might also have been concealed in
England had her attendants been limited to her sister and a few
trusted servants, although word of it might leak out through
one of Catherine's sympathizers to Chapuis and thence to the
Emperor. Dr Ortiz, Imperial agent in Rome, who conveyed the
information to Charles V, seems to have had no doubt it was
true.
  On the other hand, it must be borne in mind that he may have
believed what he wanted to, and also what appearances after
Catherine's banishment from Court and Anne's move into her
apartments that August seemed to indicate as a likely sequel.
It must also be remembered that information reaching Rome
was by no means always reliable. Chapuis himself was prejudiced enough to twist the evidence to suit his own purposes,
and we cannot be certain that it was Chapuis who passed on
this particular story; it may have come from a much less

reliable source. The wildest of rumours had always abounded about the King of England's sweetheart.

We are fortunate in having still a letter that shows how tenuous were the grounds for some of these rumours that crossed the Channel. 'Whether she has children by the King I do not know,' observed the German scholar Simon Grynaeus, who saw her in 1531.

'She has not any acknowledged as such: they may probably be brought up in private, which, if I am not mistaken, I have heard more than once, though there are those who positively deny that the King has any intercourse with her, which in my opinion is not at all likely. But she is young, good-looking, of a rather dark complexion, and likely enough to have children.'

In such an atmosphere of speculation and gossip, the story of Anne's miscarriage remains unproven.

Of evidence for Anne's having preserved her virginity there is a considerable amount, quite apart from the nature of the King's passion for her which, inextricably mingled as it was with his desire for a son, would have been unlikely to have endured in the event of a miscarriage. No witnesses of the King's adultery had been produced, wrote the Imperial agent at Rome, Dr Ortiz, on 24 October 1531; and earlier in the year the cardinals had refused to grant the brief because, observed Micer Mai, the Imperial ambassador in Rome, on 10 January 1531; 'There is no positive proof of adultery, none having yet been produced here at Rome but, on the contrary, several letters proving the opposite.'

It was also denied by John Barlow, the Dean of Westbury, one-time chaplain of the Boleyns, in Louvain, on 22 June 1532, as well as by the King himself to Catherine on Christmas Eve 1530. In the course of a quarrel about the divorce the Queen had accused him of setting a scandalous example by associating with Anne. Henry retorted 'that there was nothing wrong in his relations with Anne, and that he kept her in his company only to learn her character, as he had made up his mind to marry her'. And 'marry her he would, whatever the Pope might say'.

Henry's Christmas Eve boast that Anne was still a virgin is supported by two remarks that Catherine herself made, one of them to Chapuis. She had always believed, so the ambassador pityingly reported to Charles V on 31 December 1529, 'that after he had pursued this course for some time, the King would . . . come back to his senses as he had always done before' - a remark which strongly suggests that, unlike Elizabeth Blount and the King's other previous loves, Anne had not allowed him intercourse, thus altering the familiar pattern of his relationship with women: hunt, capture and discard. It was a theme much on Catherine's mind according to her famous remark made when playing cards with Anne: 'You are not like the others. You will have all or none.' Wolsey too, according to Cavendish, seems to have believed that Anne's long reign over the King's heart was largely due to her refusal to sleep with him. He wished, Wolsey had told Chapuis, that the King had married Anne two years ago, then he would already have had his revenge. The meaning is clear: Henry's infatuation for Anne would die within two years of his possessing her. The pattern of the King's affairs was well known at Court and perhaps the strongest evidence of all that Anne preserved her chastity for six years is the careful instruction that would be given to her successful rival - when, eventually, it became Anne's turn to be displaced - on holding the amorous monarch at arm's length. When we consider on top of this weight of evidence the peculiar wording of Anne's patent of creation in the autumn of 1532 it seems almost certain that she had preserved her virginity until this time, but that she was now about to abandon the citadel. It was a plan - judging from a rather ambiguous letter of du Bellay's - that she had had in mind for some time and confided to him in the close companionship of their summer hunting expeditions.

The gamble Anne had decided to take was a desperate one. By yielding her embattled virginity she would clearly put her whole future at risk. There was the danger that for the King the long-anticipated moment of physical union might prove a grave disappointment. Experienced though Henry was in the art of penetrating the female body, impatience, undue self-regard, over-anxiety, could all too easily make a farce out of this romance at last about to flower. Also Anne faced the alarming possibility that she might not conceive. On the other hand, if she were fortunate enough to do so - and at her age there seemed to be no reason why she should fail - her pregnancy in the present unusually propitious circumstances would give Henry any extra incentive he needed to make her his Queen.

So, having decided the odds were in her favour, she forced herself to forget her own fear of the sex act and to let King Henry possess her. The initial outcome of her public announcement on September 1 at Windsor Castle that this was her intention must have satisfied her deepest wishes, for the King, we are told, behaved like the most besotted of bridegrooms; during the remainder of that day he could talk of nothing else but his approaching visit to Calais with the delightful new Marquis of Pembroke - the occasion when the quarry would finally be his.

'The King cannot leave her for an hour,' wrote the ever-observant Chapuis on September 15. He could not even decide on the design of the new diamond collar he would wear at Calais without calling her in to admire it. Anne, feeling all the time the need to strengthen her position, was quick to exploit this renewed ardour.

Soon after the incredible ceremony in the great room at Windsor Castle, Catherine received a peremptory demand from the King to send him her jewels. Anne had decided she would wear them on her visit to Calais; although she already possessed a fabulous collection of her own and had besides the pick of the King's jewel house, she wanted to show Catherine that she could and would step into her shoes. But in addition to the desire to score off her enemy, Anne had another reason for wanting the Queen's jewels: they would embellish her with the genuine stamp of royalty, something she much needed to rescue her from the humiliation she had so recently suffered in the negotiations for the Calais meeting.

Most of Anne's elaborate preparations had proved in vain. For no suitable royal lady in France was willing to receive her. The French Queen, sister to the Emperor, being out of the question, Francis had offered his own sister, Marguerite.

Marguerite herself, however, declared in private that she had no wish to meet the King of England's whore; and in public pleaded ill-health, an excuse that deceived no one. A rejection from this woman for whom she felt affection and admiration, one of the stars to which she had looked up in childhood, was painful indeed for Anne.

There was worse to come. The French offered the Duchess of Vendôme instead, a lady of insultingly tarnished reputation. The offer was indignantly refused and the vast train of noblewomen summoned by the King to attend on his 'dearest and most beloved cousin' countermanded. All plans for a formal meeting between Francis and Anne were perforce given up. Instead she would now have to meet him as if by accident. To grace this much humbler occasion it would be inappropriate to take more than a little group of twenty ladies, including her sister Mary and sister-in-law, Lady Rochford. Thus in this demoralizing situation Anne needed all the help appearances could give her. If she wore the Queen's jewels, even though she were not treated as a Queen, she would at least look like one.

At first, Catherine refused the King's request indignantly. Throughout the past few years, in everything that did not immediately pertain to the 'divorce', Catherine had prided herself on obeying her lord and husband. But this last request was too outrageous to be borne. She would not, she said, stain her conscience by giving up her jewels 'for such a wicked purpose as that of ornamenting a person who is the scandal of Christendom, and is bringing vituperation and infamy upon the King'.

It was the worst that this self-denying Queen had ever permitted herself to say about her rival. Though in other letters she wrote of 'the shameless life' her husband led, she described Anne in no worse terms than 'the lady companion the King takes with him', or 'the woman whom he keeps with him', her feelings finding vent only in the scornful omission of Anne's name. But her dignified self-control snapped at the thought of Anne wearing her jewels.

His wife's protest left Henry unmoved. He repeated his demand; Catherine had no choice but to obey. And triumphantly Anne added Catherine's glittering cascade of gems to the trousseau she had collected for her secret wedding which Henry had promised would take place in France in the presence of the French King.


By the time the arrangements for the interview with Francis had been perfected it was already very late in the year for the King to venture his precious person on the unpredictable autumn seas. A further hazard: plague had broken out in towns on the way to the coast. Neither fear of shipwreck nor of plague, however, would deter Anne, urged onward by her formidable will and a glittering vision of the crown soon to be hers. Her lover was not to be outdone in courage by his mistress, and on October 7 they embarked in the royal barge from Greenwich Palace on a journey that filled the kingdom with foreboding and set his subjects whispering fearfully of approaching disaster. Strange and dreadful portents had been seen:

> A few days ago, on the northern coast of this island, the sea stranded a dead fish of marvellous size, ninety feet long . . . three weeks since, there appeared here a comet, which is still visible, two hours before daybreak, to the eastward, its tail extending towards the south, five yards in length; well nigh in the form of a luminous silver beard.

Careless of these portents, Anne and Henry drifted down-river in the autumn sunshine – a leisurely trip with a honeymoon flavour, for most of the King's entourage, including the three dukes, had gone on ahead to Calais. At an island in the Thames, in the house of Anne's old favourite, Sir Thomas Cheyney, they spent a few days of delightful privacy, hours which remain Anne's and Henry's alone, since for once no spies intruded, no gossip found its way into the state papers. These do not let us glimpse the lovers again until they are at Dover, whence they embarked at five in the afternoon of October 11.

Before ten o'clock that night Anne set eyes again on the land where she had been brought up; on the vertical lines of the little town that rose from its flat surroundings in a concertina of tall narrow towers and flag-fluttering embattled walls, clearly etched by the light of flares in the darkness.

As she descended from the ship to a ceremonial welcome, did her thoughts go back to her last arrival in France, when she had stood humbly by, an unimportant little maid of honour to the future Queen of France? Now, it was she who was a future Queen, greeted on bended knee by the lesser nobility and the burgesses, riding with King Henry beneath the high round arch in the walls, going in torchlit procession to St Nicholas's Church for Mass, thence to the royal lodgings at the Exchequer. Here, Henry's great bed, shipped specially from England for the occasion, was already installed, the lock he always took with him ready on the door of his Bed Chamber.

The marriage was set for Sunday, 27 October, just over a fortnight from the day of her arrival. Henry would go alone to Boulogne to bring Francis back to Calais for the ceremony. In the ten days before his departure, Henry paraded Anne round the little walled town as though she were already his Queen, decked in the beautiful dresses she had collected at his expense, glittering with the unfortunate Catherine's jewels. He took her with him to Mass and afterwards to appraise the fortifications; for his approaching marriage to Anne had filled the King with the urge to indulge in a massive orgy of building and repairing of his possessions in France no less than in England.

For Anne those days in Calais could only have been an oasis of happiness in her long bitter fight for the crown; here she could ride or walk in public free of the mobs of catcalling women who in England lined her path and harried her. In anticipation of her wedding Anne's spirits were high; she flung herself into the sumptuous gaiety of a succession of balls and banquets, surrounded by the friends and favourites who had accompanied her.

They included Thomas Wyatt, heart-whole again and back in the royal favour, who commemorated his visit to Calais in the wake of his one-time love in a disillusioned little poem:

> *Some time I fled the fire that me brent,*
> *By sea, by land, by water and by wind,*

*And now I follow the coals that be quent*
*From Dover to Calais against my mind.*

But though the fire of his passion was quenched, he still doubtless went through the motions of flirting with and flattering Anne, for she still treated him as a special friend.

An anonymous Venetian observer has left us a revealing if uncomplimentary picture of Anne at Calais: 'Madam Anna,' he wrote, 'is not the most beautiful woman in the world, of middling height, dark complexion, long neck, big mouth and flat chest; in fact, she has nothing but the English King's great appetite, and her eyes, which are black and beautiful and have great effect on those who once served the Queen . . .'

This description of the deliberate witchery of Anne's wonderful, large, dark eyes is an interesting echo of the French poem which had depicted her at the court of King Francis: a child of less than fifteen who had nevertheless learned how to use those black eyes, 'whose power was such it had enthralled many gentlemen'. Despite the ten years that had passed and her ties with the King, Anne's flirtatious manner had not changed. All her life she would crave and get masculine admiration, the delicious drug which seems to have enabled her to forget the fear and despair that so frequently shadowed the golden light of her hopes.

At Calais in the autumn of 1532, she was about to suffer yet another setback.

On Monday, 21 October, in blazing sunshine and in the company of a large party of horsemen Henry rode off to spend four days with Francis in Boulogne. He left Anne behind, for since no one suitable had been available to meet her, this was a purely male occasion, with no high-ranking ladies present.

In public the two Kings put on a scintillating display of pageantry, feasting and present-giving: in private they negotiated like the hard-headed politicians they were. Francis told Henry he had changed his mind about the marriage; he dared not do anything at the moment to increase the Emperor's enmity - for Charles V had won a resounding victory over the

Turkish forces which had been threatening his kindgom; his armies were thus suddenly free to fight on another front.

The wildness of Anne's mood, when she first learned the wedding would not after all take place, is suggested by her treatment of Gregory Casale who, for years one of Henry's leading negotiators for the 'divorce' at Rome, was now at Calais, and was unwise enough at this disappointing moment to enter Anne's orbit. Before a crowd of courtiers, Anne railed at him, telling him sharply and unjustly that it was his fault she was not already married.

But this time her disappointment seems to have been brief. For the truth is that she did not really want to get married in France. She knew that her subjects were more likely to accept her as their Queen if she were married in the traditional way in her native country. Besides, she was still to have a talk with Francis, a meeting to which she attached much importance, since France could give her the extra help she needed at this crucial juncture to accomplish her plans. Anne had great faith in her powers both of persuasion and attraction, Francis was an old acquaintance and a susceptible man.

On Friday evening after sunset a volley of cannon shook the high walls of Calais, signal that the King of England had returned with the King of France. The cobbled streets they rode down were lined on one side with English serving men in liveries of French tawny with red caps; on the other, with soldiers in red and blue. Lady Anne did not make an appearance, but King Francis at once paid handsome tribute to her presence. He sent the Provost of Paris to her with the gift of a magnificent diamond. On Sunday, the day she was to have been married, she came into his sight for the first time, dancing to the sound of music.

The encounter was staged with all the flamboyant gaiety and drama loved by both Henry and Anne. After an afternoon spent watching bear- and bull-baiting, the two Kings had supped together at the Staple, where Francis was staying. Suddenly into the great gleaming room, decked with jewelled gold and silver hangings, with candelabra and solid gold plate, entered eight ladies masking. They wore gowns 'of strange fashion, made of cloth of gold, compassed with crimson tinsel satin . . .

with cloth of silver . . . knit with laces of gold'; they were brought into the chamber by 'four damsels apparelled in crimson satin'. Each chose an important French guest for her partner. As they danced, the King of England, in violet cloth of gold – with a collar of pearls, diamonds, rubies as big as eggs and a carbuncle the size of a goose's egg – twitched aside their visors and, behold, the lady dancing with Francis was Anne. Nothing loath to renew acquaintance with such an attractive woman and one who was so useful to his kingdom, Francis talked with her for a long time. Although the details of their conversation are unknown, it undoubtedly contributed to the very real success of the Anglo-French meeting.

The next day was spent in banqueting and watching the French wrestle against the English. On Tuesday Francis left for Paris. Anne and Henry lingered at Calais, prevented from crossing the Channel by sudden stormy weather. Not until midnight on November 13 did the seas subside sufficiently for the King to set sail. In the calm autumn night Anne turned her face to England again in a spirit of triumph and confidence.

She had reason to be content with the result of the Calais meeting. Francis had agreed to a policy that would throw dust in the Pope's eyes for just long enough to allow Anne finally to achieve her ambition. He had instructed the Cardinals of Tournon and of Grammont to visit the Pope in Bologna, where he was temporarily residing. They were to dangle before the timid ailing Clement an irresistible bribe: a peaceful solution to the whole desperately worrying, tiresome business of the 'divorce'. If the Pope would come to France and hold a 'divorce' trial there in the spring, Clement was given to understand that Henry had agreed to accept his verdict. It was just what was needed to prevent the Pope from yielding to the insistent demands from the Emperor that he should proceed now to give a definitive sentence in Catherine's favour. And while he issued a brief in November demanding that Henry should separate from Anne within one month or both would be excommunicated, he robbed the document of all force by giving it to the nuncio and telling him to present it to Henry at some appropriate occasion. It would be easy for Henry to see that no such an occasion ever arose.

Francis's intervention would give Anne's party time in which to push through the final measures needed before the 'divorce' could legally be pronounced in England.

The most vital of these measures was the appointment of the new Archbishop of Canterbury; the man who was to inherit the cope and mitre of Anne's enemy William Warham who had so conveniently died in August, and with them the role Henry had long had in mind for the primate of England.

The replacement prelate had been selected carefully and already summoned before Anne left for Calais – the choice was none other than Thomas Cranmer, who had been one of the most outspoken supporters of the 'divorce' before being sent, in January, as resident ambassador to the Imperial Court. But when news of his sudden promotion reached him in Mantua, where the Emperor had gone in pursuit of the Turk, for a moment, unknown to Anne, her fate again hung in the balance. Cranmer was in no doubt what would be expected of him should he accept the primacy, and his conscience was torn. Although he had worked for the 'divorce' since 1529, although he felt gratitude to Anne and her family, with whom he had lived in Durham House in the autumn of 1529, he had during the months of his stay abroad come to sympathize with Catherine. Out of range of the King's bullying charm and the conscience-blinding delights of high position in England, he had, like his predecessors at the Imperial Court, Sir Nicholas Carew, Dr Richard Sampson and Sir Thomas Elyot, learned to see the whole matter differently.

Cranmer, however, unlike so many of his contemporaries, was not a man who saw moral issues in simple terms. He was a Protestant; this was an exceptional opportunity to put a Protestant Queen on the throne. And he had a mediæval devotion, hard to understand today, to the King. The factor, however, that more than any other persuaded Cranmer to obey Henry was a personal one. In Germany Cranmer had defied his vow of celibacy to marry Margaret, the young niece of the leading reformer Osiander, a dangerously heretical act for which he could be made to pay with his rank, his goods, perhaps even his life.

So Cranmer really had no choice. He sold his plate to his

successor, Nicholas Hawkins, absent-mindedly cheating himself in the process. Then, travelling slowly, reluctantly, he set off along the icy roads for England. The whole business took a long time. Following in the wake of the conquering Emperor, Cranmer had not heard of his appointment for six weeks. He was not to reach England until mid-January.

As she waited for Cranmer to arrive, Anne whiled away the short days and candle-lit evenings gambling with Henry and two of her intimate friends, her cousin Sir Francis Brian, and the tennis-playing Sir Francis Weston, later to be beheaded for her sake. But with tragedy far away and unsuspected, they played a game called Pope Julius, after Julius II who had granted the dispensation for the King to marry Catherine in the first place, as well as the Spanish brief which had blocked Henry's plans for divorce in 1529. It was characteristic of Anne to make a mock of the source of her ills. Henry's privy purse expenses show that he usually lost heavily to Anne and her partners: £9 6s 8d on November 20 'to my lady Marquis, master Brian and master Weston'; £4 13s 4d on November 24 'to my lady Marquis and master Brian'; £18 13s 4d on November 26 'to my lady Marquis, master Brian and master Weston'; £11 13s 4d on November 28 'to my lady Marquis'; and £3 14s 8d on November 30 'to my lady Marquis and master Weston'. It was one way to keep his mistress content and spare himself the lash of her tongue.

In December, perhaps to quell her impatience, Henry took Anne with the French ambassador to inspect the Tower of London which was being titivated for her coronation. Before the ceremony in Westminster Abbey the sovereign traditionally spent several days and nights in the royal apartments, which surrounded pleasant gardens in the south-east corner. Labourers had been at work on them since June, adding new 'jakes', windows, roofs and flooring to the Queen's apartments, a new bridge leading into her garden and new water steps. Henry was determined nothing should be lacking for his mistress's comfort.

In the same month he presented her with plate fit to shine on a royal sideboard, gilt and parcel gilt weighing more than 326 lbs - trenchers, basins, flagons, cups, bowls, goblets, saltcellars and chandeliers - chased and ornamented with flowers, beasts and coats of arms; and including no less than three cups of assay, from which when she became Queen her wine would be tasted for poison.

But despite all these promising preparations, who knows how much longer Anne might not still have had to wait had she not already played her last card? Had that card not proved an ace? In the middle of January, Anne informed the King that she was expecting his child.

# Chapter 19

# 'THE KING'S DEAREST WIFE'

THE glad news of Anne's pregnancy forced the King's hand. Suddenly Henry could delay no longer. His son must be born legitimate; Catherine must be divorced, Anne married before the birth. Normally, Henry waited at least a year before filling a vacant bishopric; its revenue made a useful contribution to his over-strained finances. Now Henry could not afford to wait; he was in a desperate hurry.

Cranmer arrived home at about the same time as Anne discovered that she was pregnant. In the same week - at a bear-baiting, it is said - Henry appointed him Archbishop. The King's agents in Rome were instructed to procure from the Pope the bulls that would enable Cranmer to be consecrated. The King himself lent Cranmer the money for his expenses. Should Clement hesitate to issue the bulls, Henry's agents were to threaten that the King would implement the act passed the previous year permitting him to withhold annates.

For Henry and Cromwell had resolved that Clement himself should give Cranmer the authority by which Cranmer in turn would defy the Pope's orders and pronounce sentence for the 'divorce'. It would have been logical to have the 'divorce' granted first before taking a new wife, but Henry could not now afford to be logical.

At last Anne had her wish. On 25 January 1533, after nearly six years of waiting, she was married to the King.

Her wedding could not have been less like the glittering occasion Anne had witnessed as a little girl of seven in France, when Mary Tudor had married King Louis XII. Anne's wedding was hurried through in desperate secrecy in the presence of as few people as possible while most of the palace still slept. Such mystery surrounds the ceremony that none of its details, not even the identities of the priest who performed the service and

of the witnesses, are known for certain. According to the
Catholic Nicholas Harpsfield, who wrote in the reign of Queen
Mary I, Anne was married at Whitehall at dawn by the King's
chaplain, Rowland Lee, who was tricked by Henry into
believing that the Pope had given his permission; the witnesses
were Anne's train-bearer, Anne Savage, later Lady Barkley, Sir
Henry Norris and Thomas Henneage. That some kind of
trickery was, in fact, involved is shown by the Duke of Norfolk's remark the succeeding April. Anne and Henry had been
married, he said, 'in the presence of several persons without any
one of them having been summoned for that purpose'. So some
part of Harpsfield's account is correct. But according to the
story that reached Chapuis at Court at the time, they were
married by George Browne, an Augustinian friar and a
Lutheran – who subsequently became Archbishop of Dublin –
in the presence of Anne's father, mother, brother and two
intimate female friends. Yet another rumour held that Anne
had been married by the new Archbishop, a supposition fiercely
denied by Cranmer in a letter to Nicholas Hawkins.

For such secrecy to be possible, bearing in mind the attendants who teemed round Henry at even the most intimate
moments – the gentlemen who lay on pallets outside his bed-
chamber door, the footmen at the outer door, not to speak of
pages and grooms of the chamber and those constantly eager
to spy on the King's doings – the wedding must have been
most carefully planned.

Secrecy, however, was essential, since the Pope currently
believed what the French had told him: that Henry would
accept the verdict Clement would give at a court to be held in
France that year. He must not be disillusioned. News of the
marriage must not reach him until he had issued the bulls
that would enable Cranmer to become Archbishop of Canterbury and give Henry his 'divorce'. Should the news reach the
Pope before, he would almost certainly refuse to issue them
and, enraged, might even choose suddenly to give final sentence
against the King, a catalyst that could turn the hatred, discontent and fear of the English people into open revolt.

Then Anne would lose not only all hope of the crown but,
in the opinion of Chapuis, probably her life as well.

It was typical of Anne's indiscretion that at this moment, when so much was at stake and she had so nearly won, she almost ruined her chances by herself revealing the explosive secret of her marriage.

Exultant both at being married to the King and pregnant with his child, Anne was eager to tell the whole of Christendom. She could not stop herself from dropping revealing hints. For the first few weeks these consisted of statements, doubtless delivered with a secretive smile, that her marriage would take place shortly. 'I am as sure as death,' cried Anne, with characteristic exaggeration at the beginning of February, 'that the King will marry me shortly,' and she told a priest who wished to enter her service, 'You must wait a little until I have celebrated my marriage.'

On February 15, in a room full of people, she told the Duke of Norfolk, 'If I find I am not with child, I shall go on a pilgrimage immediately after Easter.' And a few days later, on February 22, coming out of her chamber into a crowded hall, she met Sir Thomas Wyatt. The news bubbled out of her.

'Three days ago,' she told him, 'I had an inestimable wild desire to eat apples. I have never liked them before. The King says it is a sign that I must be with child. I tell him no. I cannot be!' At this she laughed out loud and ran back into her chamber, leaving the assembly agog with curiosity.

Henry, almost as excited as Anne, found the secret equally hard to keep. A few days later he was at a banquet given by his new wife in her tapestry-hung apartments. So preoccupied was Henry, laughing and jesting in a low voice with Anne, who sat as usual on his right, that he scarcely said a word to her other guests; except when he suddenly addressed the Dowager Duchess of Norfolk, her step-grandmother. 'Has she not a great dowry and a rich marriage?' He gestured to the sideboard gleaming with gold plate. 'All you can see belongs to her. As well as the dishes you were served from.'

Naturally, such incidents made Chapuis suspicious of the King's intentions. Anxious to frustrate them, he wrote to Charles V warning him to try to prevent the Pope issuing the bulls to Cranmer, telling him that Henry's apparent willingness to compromise with Clement was simply a way to gain time, and adding, on February 23, the portentous news that Anne and Henry were married already. But Anne was lucky. The story reached the Emperor too late. On 21 February 1533, Clement had issued the bulls for Cranmer; they were now on their way to England.

Henry's and Cromwell's plans were succeeding brilliantly. With such a team wholeheartedly on her side, with Henry's charm and cunning, Cromwell's genius for manœuvring Parliament and people, Anne knew she could not fail. As her slim body rounded with the coming of spring, Anne could afford to relax and sink into contented idleness for the first time in years. This spring of 1533 she had no need to write frantic letters to whatever minister she felt could help her most, no need to threaten intriguing courtiers, or to fly into tantrums as the tension in her snapped.

For a few brief months, thanks to the child growing in her womb, she knew she could safely leave her cause to others.

The King and Cromwell, both steeped in Machiavellian deviousness, coupled with a certain moral crudity, had just the qualities needed to cope with the situation. Only such men could have devised the piece of chicanery about to take place, whereby Thomas Cranmer became Archbishop of Canterbury with the blessing of the Pope, yet maintained his right to act against the papal edicts.

Thomas Cranmer was to be consecrated on March 30, but before this ritual he went through another of an extraordinary kind. In a private room in front of witnesses, he read out a protestation. This declared that he did not intend to be bound by any oath he took to the Pope at his consecration if it was against the law of God, the King of England or the laws or prerogatives of the realm. At St Stephen's Church he then took the traditional oath. He swore to be faithful and obedient to Pope Clement VII and his successors, to defend the Papacy and the Church and to persecute heretics. But he added that he did this subject to the protestation already made in the chapter-house. And he again twice read the protestation aloud.

It was a solemn repudiation of papal authority in favour of

King Henry, loosely interwoven with the oath and ritual of consecration.

Henry had meanwhile been taking care of the papal nuncio, de Borgho, who held in his possession the brief requiring Henry to separate from Anne. In his interviews with de Borgho, Henry, veering between sweet reasonableness when new negotiations with Clement were suggested, and violently choleric outbursts at any mention of parting from Anne, convinced the nuncio that this was not the right time to present the brief. To encourage him in this idea, Henry flattered and probably bribed him as well, for, accused by Chapuis of being too friendly with the King of England, de Borgho retorted 'one has to live'.

Henry saw to it that he lived very well. At the beginning of February 1533, when Henry was rowed up-river in his barge to the opening of Parliament, de Borgho sat close beside him. And in Parliament Henry seated him in a rich chair on his right. Henry's object seems to have been twofold, to dazzle the nuncio into turning a blind eye to the preparations for the 'divorce', and to suggest to his subjects that he and Clement had come to some secret agreement about it. For Parliament to be amenable was vital, since it was for this session that Cromwell was preparing a Bill which would finally enable Anne to marry the King without papal consent. Henry's ruse was successful. The sight of the papal ambassador, sitting smiling benignly in his red robes beside him, helped to persuade the doubtful in a Lower House that was largely anti-clergy anyway and an Upper House that was packed, to vote for Cromwell's new measure.

The Bill, 'In Restraint of Appeals', introduced into Parliament in March, settled supreme authority in all spiritual matters on the Archbishop of Canterbury, forbade appeals to Rome, and was a measure calculated both to allow the Archbishop to pronounce sentence for the divorce and to restrain Catherine from appealing against it to the Pope. The Bill was to pass easily into law.

After Cranmer's consecration there was now no longer any need to keep the marriage secret. Preparations could begin openly for Anne's coronation. But first there was the hazardous business of making an announcement to a hostile Court and people. In mid-March Henry and Anne had attempted to prepare the courtiers from the pulpit for what was coming. Anne's and Henry's chaplains delivered identical sermons – with an astonishing theme: since the King had discovered he had been living in adultery with Catherine, it was no wonder, they proclaimed, if he wished to follow the example of Saul and David and marry a woman of low rank for the sake of her virtue and the secret merits of her person.

Spoken in front of a Court that had watched Anne being caressed in public for years, who knew that although she might not technically have been his mistress for long she had been very close to it, this was not the most convincing justification for the match.

But from Anne's point of view their sermons served a useful purpose. It told the Court that the King was in earnest; and once the King had really decided on a course of action, he was, his courtiers knew, implacable and merciless to anyone who stood in the way. The beheading of Rice Ap Griffith fresh in their memory, those nobles who, led by the Duke of Suffolk, had over the years continually tried to influence the King against Anne, now grew silent and settled down to play their traditional roles in the hierarchy. This spring there was no whisper of intrigue to gladden the heart of Chapuis and encourage Anne's enemies. In England they waited horror-struck by what they regarded as the approaching catastrophe. But before Henry made his final public announcement he needed to make sure of one important fact: that he still had an ally abroad.

In March Anne's brother was sent to France to convey news of the secret marriage to Francis, and beg him to prevent 'any impediment to it, or of the succession, which please God will follow, and which, to all appearances, is in a state of advancement already'. Francis immediately sent a letter of congratulation to Anne and promised to put further pressure on the Pope to delay sentence.

With the French alliance firmly behind him, in the second week of April Henry informed his Privy Council that he was married to Anne and that he intended to have her crowned after Easter. A delegation was sent to tell the Queen at Ampthill bluntly that she was no longer the King's wife and that she was in future to be addressed as Princess Dowager; if she would agree to this Henry would increase her revenue.

Catherine ignored the offer. She would, she declared, continue to insist on being addressed as Queen by her attendants. Neither the threat to reduce her allowance, nor to curtail her freedom – not even cruelly forbidding Mary to send her beloved mother letters or messages – stopped Catherine insisting that she was the King's rightful wife – and to prove it she ordered for her servants a whole new set of liveries embroidered all over with symbolic H's and K's.

Not unnaturally, this defiance filled the egocentric Anne with a new burst of hatred for the woman who continued to stand so exasperatingly and, it must have appeared, unreasonably and spitefully in her way. If only Catherine would accept the inevitable, so it must have seemed to Anne, she could have Mary's company and all the jewels and houses and servants she could wish; by choosing instead to become a poor, ill-treated prisoner, Catherine not only tortured herself, quite unnecessarily, but also made Anne seem vicious and unsympathetic.

Anne decided to show her enemy that she would and could replace her. Without asking the King's permission, she ordered her Chamberlain to seize Catherine's barge on the Thames, to erase Catherine's coat of arms and decorate the barge instead in Anne's heraldic colours – blue and purple – and her own red, gold, blue, silver and black coat of arms, the armorial bearings Henry had granted her as his Queen-to-be. It was a triumphant opportunity to exhibit to the world this proof of her marriage with the King.

Anne's heraldic choice is worth noting. Her coat of arms includes two quarterings sprinkled with the lions and fleur-de-lis of the royal arms, two Howard quarterings, one of which refers to her descent from King Edward I through this family, and another quartering showing the arms of the blue-blooded Butlers. But there are two revealing omissions: the Howard arms themselves do not appear – which is almost certainly a reflection of Anne's feeling against the Duke of Norfolk, who opposed her marriage; nor do the black bulls' heads of her great-grandfather, wool mercer Boleyn. Although she had agreed to let her chaplain stress her modest rank when this had seemed advantageous, at all other times she was determined to hide the humbler part of her family tree.

Anne's proud choice of armorial bearings was in line with this latest arrogant gesture in seizing the Queen's barge for her own use without the King's permission. At the sight of this defiantly decorated vessel glittering in the spring sunlight, bobbing up and down expectantly in the rippling waters at the palace steps, Chapuis protested to Henry. He complained, but one suspects not too vigorously, to Anne's Chamberlain; for he could not be very angry with the woman he believed was carrying his long-awaited son.

That glorious spring of 1533 nothing seemed impossible to Anne. Catherine's resistance was a mere fleeting shadow in sunlit days, crammed with delicious preparations; no more waiting now. The ceremonial that had been missing from her hurried secret wedding was to be more than made up for by the lavish splendour of her coronation. She was to be given the full treatment, as though she were a sovereign in her own right.

There were fittings for her gowns - cloth of gold, ermine-trimmed white 'tissue', purple velvet, with plenty of extra width allowed for the growing child; there was the new crown being specially designed for her, to replace the heavy crown of St Edward immediately after the coronation. There was her whole new rank to prepare for, no longer that of Lady Anne Rochford, the King's mistress, but of Queen Anne, the King's dearest wife. As such, she intended to have everything of the utmost magnificence around her. In an age when consumer goods were few, Anne, like so many of her contemporaries, found an intensity of pleasure that is hard to understand today in the sumptuous, tangible things of life.

She was having Greenwich Palace and her first-floor apartments there completely done over: with five new doors and new mats for her huge Bed Chamber, new mats for the passage to her dressing-room (for even in the royal apartments carpets were still used mainly on tables); new transoms for the great bay window between her Bed Chamber and Chamber of Presence; and new furniture, including a gaming-table and a breakfast-table both made of tiles of antique work. There was even to be a bright new view from her apartments which over-looked the two inner courtyards, in one of which stood the conduit. This was to be decorated with six panels painted stone colour and decorated with orbs, antique work, the King's arms and beasts in fine gold and blue, while the pillars of the conduit were to be painted 'jasper' colour.

Then there were more household officials to appoint, and extra ladies to wait at the Queen's table and act as her royal escort; and there was a new device to decide on for the blue and purple liveries of her retinue. Flamboyantly Anne chose to have the words 'La Plus Heureuse' (The Most Happy) embroid-ered across their doublets.

On April 12, Easter Saturday, Anne made her first public appearance as Queen. She went to Mass loaded with jewels, in a gown of cloth of gold frieze, its train carried by the daughter of the Duke of Norfolk. She was brought to church and back again, followed by sixty maids of honour, thirty more than Queen Catherine had in her retinue; Anne was determined to outshine the woman she had supplanted as Queen. And just in case anyone still did not comprehend, the priest in the tradi-tional prayer for the King and Queen prayed loudly for the health of Queen Anne. Afterwards Henry urged each lord in turn to kneel and pay homage to her. There is no record of any of them having had the courage to refuse. Finally Anne had beaten them.

She gloried in the state of health that made this possible, exulted openly in her pregnancy. In front not only of her own father but of the Dukes of Norfolk and Suffolk, and the Treasurer of the King's Household – all of whom had tried to prevent her marriage – she flaunted the piece of extra material she needed to have added to one of her dresses that had grown too tight. And when her father said, with his usual censorious-ness, 'You ought to remove it and thank God for the state you find yourself in', she retorted with biting truth: 'I am in a better state than you would have wished me to be.'

Henry could deal easily with Anne's opponents among the lords; the common people were more difficult. But, with his longed-for son on the way, he was not to be deterred from his purpose by mere difficulty. On Easter Sunday there occurred a demonstration of Anne's unpopularity. At St Paul's Cross the Prior of the Austin Friars was conducting a service; on hearing him substitute Anne's name for Catherine's in the prayer for the King and Queen, most of the congregation departed in disgust, without waiting for him to finish.

The King sent word to the Mayor of London, commanding him to see that such a thing did not happen again – a tall order, but one which the Mayor did his best to obey. He summoned all the guilds to meet in their various halls and ordered them to abstain from murmuring against the King's marriage, to see also that their apprentices and their wives did likewise on pain of the King's displeasure.

Not very surprisingly, this measure was ineffective, and Henry issued a proclamation: a reward was to be given for information against anyone making derogatory remarks about his marriage. As a further precaution, no one was to be allowed to preach without a licence from Bishop Stokesley of London. In the spring of 1533, to see his mistress and the prospective mother of his son safely crowned, there were no lengths to which Anne's lover was not prepared to go.

On Friday 23 May, Anne heard with feelings of triumph the news she craved. Cranmer had given judgement in the priory at Dunstable that Henry's marriage to Catherine was invalid; he forbade them to cohabit and pronounced them both free to remarry. Five days later, on May 28, 'in a high gallery' in Henry's manor of Lambeth, Cranmer gave judgement that the marriage of Henry and Anne was lawful.

The very next day the pageant of victorious Anne's coronation began.

*Chapter 20*

# 'THE MOST HAPPY'

ANNE'S vision of greatness finally came true in a dazzling burst of earthly glory. In an attempt to demonstrate to the people that she was Henry's lawful Queen, her coronation, organized by Thomas Cromwell, was scarcely less magnificent than had been Henry's own coronation in 1509. The spectacular ceremonies lasted four days.

First came a symbolic state entry into the city with a welcome and reception by the Mayor of London and the craft guilds. At about one o'clock on Thursday 29 May 1533 an extraordinary mixture of sounds floated down-river from London to Greenwich Palace, where Anne was staying – a blend of music, trumpet-blowing, cannon shot and wild cries. And soon, through the great windows of the battlemented brick palace, down the broad sunlit river, she would have seen a procession approaching. It was led by a boat with a red dragon 'continually moving and casting wild fire' surrounded by 'terrible monsters and wild men casting fire and making hideous noises'. Another boat followed close, carrying Anne's badge of a white falcon, crowned, with a sceptre in its claw, standing on a golden root from which grew red and white Tudor roses, symbol of Anne's hoped-for fruitfulness. Behind came the scarlet-clad Mayor in his own barge, then those of the craft guilds, each bedecked with arras, banners and pennons of fine gold, streaming and sparkling in the summer breeze. Every vessel carried its own little band of musicians and its own guns.

With a clamour of chain and shouted commands, the little fleet cast anchor in the harbour of Greenwich town. Then music from the vessels drifted sweetly over the water to Anne, while the state barges of the leading nobles and clergy gathered in an expectant flotilla round the palace steps. She came out at three o'clock and, dressed in cloth of gold, with her train of ladies, she stepped down into the barge that had belonged to her vanquished rival Catherine and which was now sprinkled with the gold lions and fleur-de-lis, the blue, red, silver and black of Anne's own royal coat of arms.

Surrounded by the lords and bishops in their grandly embellished craft and followed by two hundred smaller vessels bright with colour, Anne headed this memorable procession to London. Across the broad expanse of the Thames hundreds of oars dipped and glittered and dipped again. In Anne's honour the whole river, an onlooker said, seemed covered with boats. Again the water-borne music mingled with the boom of cannon, like joy threatened with tragedy, as the ships along the riverbanks fired salvoes.

One barge in particular, we learn from the contemporary chronicler Hall, Anne 'took great pleasure to behold'. It was decorated with tinkling golden bells and her coat of arms coupled over and over again with the King's, proof that this was at last really happening; that the scene most of Europe had believed to be an impossible dream had, largely through Anne's foresight and perseverance, become real.

The mighty guns of the Tower thundered a welcome. At the water-steps of the grim fortress the Constable and Lieutenant welcomed her. Then through the crowd she was escorted by the officers of arms to the postern gate. There stood the massive, beaming King.

Before everyone, Henry laid his hands lovingly on either side of the bulge that was to be his son, kissed her 'with great reverence' and led her to the Queen's apartments in the south-east corner of the citadel, apartments he had had changed specially for this occasion, adding new windows to improve the view from her dining chamber and the small chamber leading to her private garden. Installed in these palatial rooms near Henry's, Anne would have been scarcely more conscious of the prisoners awaiting death or torture in some of the narrow towers close by than she was of the menagerie and the mint also housed within those formidable moated walls. On that day at least thoughts of death must have been far from Anne's mind.

Like Henry and Catherine in 1509, Anne spent both Thursday and Friday in the Tower. On Saturday morning the traditional custom was followed. Sixty-three knights received the accolade and eighteen Knights of the Bath were created. At five in the afternoon when the sun had lost its heat, Anne took her place in yet another magnificent procession for the traditional 'conveying' of the sovereign 'through London'. The roads, strewn with gravel and railed for safety, were hung with tapestry, carpets, silks and velvets, and they were lined with the stalwart figures of the craftsmen, aldermen and constables of the city, the latter bearing great staves to keep order.

First rode twelve Frenchmen in coats of blue velvet with sleeves of yellow and blue velvet on horses caparisoned in blue 'sarcenet', powdered with white crosses. After them marched gentlemen, squires, knights, and judges in their ceremonial robes, Knights of the Bath in their purple gowns, abbots, barons, bishops, earls, and marquises in crimson velvet. Then, also all in ceremonial dress, came the Lord Chancellor of England, the archbishops, ambassadors, the Mayor of London, Garter King of Arms . . . In the middle of this procession was Anne, the traditional white and shining centre, sitting in an open litter of white cloth of gold resting on two palfreys caparisoned in white damask; above her a canopy of cloth of gold with four gold staves and four silver bells borne by four knights on foot. Her surcoat and mantle 'cut in the French fashion' were of white 'tissue' trimmed with ermine and her long dark hair hung down from a coif with a circlet of rich stones.

After the Queen rode her Chamberlain, her Master of the Horse, seven ladies in crimson velvet, followed by two chariots covered in red cloth of gold. The first of these should have borne the Duchess of Norfolk had she not flatly refused the honour. Appearances were saved by her stepmother-in-law, the Dowager Duchess, a broad-minded, realistic and tolerant lady, who agreed to grace the occasion and share the chariot with the old Marchioness of Dorset. Seven more ladies rode behind, followed by a white chariot full of ladies in crimson, then a crimson chariot full of ladies in crimson, followed by thirty gentlewomen in the silk and velvet liveries of their mistresses. The King's Guard in coats of 'goldsmith's work' brought up the rear.

Through the narrow City streets wound this dazzling procession, beneath overhanging windows crowded with ladies and gentlemen, past newly painted fountains running wine, and pageants in which allegorical figures declaimed poetry in honour both of Anne and the child she would bear.

Her pregnancy was openly acknowledged in recognition of the fact that to give birth to a prince who would ensure the peace of the country was Anne's best chance of winning acceptance by her subjects. Their present feeling towards her was all too obvious. As Anne sat in her white litter, turning her heavily jewelled head from side to side with that characteristic nervous quickness to acknowledge the expected cheers, a chilling sight met her eyes. Beyond the barriers the Londoners stood silent; no tossing off of caps, no falling on their knees to shout, 'God save the Queen!' Her subjects looked at her with sullen hatred. In vain Anne's fool tried to rectify things by shouting, 'I think you all have scurvy heads and dare not uncover.' His joke raised not a smile. And when one of her servants asked the Mayor to order the people to pay her homage, that much put-upon man replied gruffly that he could not command men's hearts. It was a cold reception indeed, and though Anne was on the crest of the wave of victory, she could hardly pretend not to notice.

Yet another unnerving sight flawed the perfection of Anne's bright day. The German merchants of the Hanseatic league, who had special trading concessions in England and whose headquarters were at the Steelyard, had erected, as they had been ordered to, a triumphal arch - the design for which by Hans Holbein can still be seen in the Staatliches Museum in Berlin. An ornate structure with no less than three archways, a profusion of baroque motifs, swags and pilasters, medallions and rambling foliage, supported a fountain spouting wine in a candle-lit arbour; here Apollo and the nine muses hymned Anne's praise with harp, lute, viol and tabor, while on either side rose the mountains of Helicon and two pillars holding up Anne's and Henry's coats of arms. A pretty sight and flattering sound, it must have seemed to Anne, until her gaze lifted to what was above.

Perched on top of the arbour, great wings threateningly outspread, was a huge Imperial eagle; a symbol that turned the whole display into an insulting gesture of hostility. It was a reminder that the most powerful ruler in Europe remained her enemy. The outspread wings of the eagle cast a forbidding shadow over the brilliant trappings of her coronation procession that Anne would not forget or forgive.

The procession had now reached the end of its journey, Westminster Hall. The Queen had been conveyed through London to the point from which on the following day the most momentous ceremony of all would start. In the middle of this huge, flag-stoned place with its gilded and painted hammer-beam roof and flying angels, between walls glowing with arras and cloth of gold, Anne finally alighted from her litter and, her white-robed figure, dwarfed in the vastness, mounted the platform to rest and take refreshment in a chair under her own cloth of estate. But the wine and 'subtleties' offered her, she sent down to her ladies, her appetite lost perhaps in her excitement. Then she thanked her attendants, slipped through a back entrance to escape the crowds, descended the water steps to her barge and floated down-river to the pleached avenues and cool quiet gardens of Whitehall where the King awaited her.

When he, according to the *Spanish Chronicle*, - which reported current London gossip - asked fondly how she had enjoyed her great day, Anne replied, 'Sir, I liked the city well enough, but I saw a great many caps on heads and heard but a few tongues.' But if this is true, she must have consoled herself with the thought that in a neighbourhood as packed with Catherine's passionate supporters as the City of London, she had been lucky to achieve her destination without some noisier, more dangerous demonstration of the people's hatred, must have consoled herself too with the thought of the morrow.

For on the following day, Sunday June 1, Anne was to be crowned.


The ceremonies established by tradition for this day were an endurance test for anyone. Most women five months pregnant might have quailed at the prospect, but Anne's egotism would not let her forgo one moment of her hard-won triumph.

Between eight and nine in the morning, in a surcoat and robe of purple velvet trimmed with ermine, she was escorted from Westminster Hall into Westminster Abbey, her train carried by the Dowager Duchess of Norfolk, the 'laps of her robe' by the Bishops of London and Winchester, Stokesley and Gardiner; and, most satisfying of sights, the crown was borne before her by the Duke of Suffolk who since Wolsey's fall had done everything in his power to prevent this event taking place. Under a canopy held by four knights of the Cinque Ports, surrounded by dignitaries, she walked slowly into the abbey and rested for a while in a 'rich' chair between the choir and high altar to gather her energies for the supreme, awe-inspiring moment.

Then she rose and walked the last few paces. The Latin words in Cranmer's voice flowed over her. He anointed her on the head and on the breast. The great weight of the crown of St Edward descended on her temples; her right hand grasped the golden sceptre; her left the rod of ivory with the dove – symbols of mercy and power, of royalty. Anne had arrived at her glittering destination. After six years of broken promises, disappointments and delays; of courtiers' intrigue, of angry mobs of women, at last, in her mid-twenties and despite the hostility of lords and people, despite the flaws in her own character which turned her few friends into enemies – she had achieved her ambition. Crowned and enthroned, she sat triumphantly on the dais in the abbey, looking down on to the great nobles who had now become her servants.

This was her hour of glory, worth all the nerve-racking agony of the years before; the beginning, so it must have seemed to Anne, of a golden, peaceful existence in which nothing surely could go wrong.

The ritual completed, she was led away, crowned, by her father and Lord Talbot to the sound of trumpets. The ceremonies, however, were far from over, and before the day was out she would need all the iron of her will. After a brief rest in a 'withdrawing room' she must preside over a coronation banquet in Westminster Hall lasting until six in the evening, while her faultless performance was adoringly observed by Henry from a closet he had had specially made in the adjoining church of St Stephen. This traditional feast had many curiously barbaric elements.

Under her cloth of estate, symbol of royalty, Anne sat at a table on the dais, Cranmer on her right, looking down at four long tables in the great body of the hall, while on either side of her chair stood the Countesses of Oxford and Worcester 'which divers times in the dinner time did hold a fine cloth before the Queen's face when she list to spit or do otherwise at her pleasure'. At her feet under the table humbly sat the customary two gentlewomen 'to serve her secretly with what she might need'. Between the Archbishop and the Countess of Oxford stood the Earl of Oxford, Lord High Chamberlain of England, with his white staff of office.

It was a noisy, splendid occasion. Countless fantastic and elaborate dishes were served with practised grace by innumerable nobles and courtiers, among whom Anne's old admirer Thomas Wyatt performed the office of carrying the ewer from which she washed her hands. The Duke of Suffolk and Lord William Howard clattered up and down the hall on horseback; trumpets and hautbois heralded each course; heralds cried largesse. At the hall door fountains flowed with free wine and 'kitchens' dispensed meat to those who could fight their way to the front of the crowd. Weary though she must have been when the banquet was finally over, Anne doubtless delighted in every aspect of the ceremony which set the seal on her triumph.

Never had there been such giddy revelling in the Queen's apartments as took place in the days succeeding Anne's coronation. Nine days afterwards her Vice-Chamberlain, Sir Edward Baynton, wrote to her brother Lord Rochford who was on embassy in France:

... as for pastime in the Queen's chamber was never more. If any of you that be now departed have any ladies that they thought favoured you and somewhat would mourn at parting of their servants, I can no whit perceive the same by their dancing and pastime they do use here.

Anne had reason for her whirl of gaiety. Catherine was divorced, she was crowned, and so far none of the prophecies of disaster had been fulfilled. France was still her ally; King Francis sent her a rich litter and three mules, a gift which pleased Anne so much she insisted on being taken a three-mile journey in it the moment it arrived. The King's sister, Marguerite, who had refused to meet her when she was Marquis of Pembroke, now that she was Queen, sent her affectionate messages. And far from launching a holy war against England, the Emperor had muted his complaints.

In her assessment of Charles V's reaction to her coronation, Anne had been right. Charles is said to have kept not only the Bible but also a copy of Machiavelli's *Prince* beside his bed. Having the Turks to contend with beyond his frontiers and the Lutherans within, he was too careful and realistic a monarch to embark on war with England as well. He did not, of course, say so in so many words. When Clement sent a message to ask what he was prepared to do about Anne's marriage, Charles replied by urging the Pope to give judgement which, he said, prevaricating, must precede recourse to the secular arm. The implication was clear enough, and it tied the Pope's hands. For unless Charles was willing to enforce a papal sentence Clement knew there was little point in passing one; King Henry would just ignore it. Far from launching a holy war against England, Charles V wrote to Chapuis commanding him to moderate his tone and 'not to threaten with war nor in any way imply that there might be a rupture in the friendship and good intelligence between the two countries'.

Anne's triumph, however, was far from complete. The dark truth burst on her in a series of alarming incidents through the summer months of her pregnancy. The threat came not through the Emperor or the Pope but through Catherine and Princess Mary. Anne had been crowned with the crown of St Edward, consecrated with the holy oil, her hands had held the orb and sceptre in the sacred precincts of Westminster Abbey. In the hearts of the common people it made no difference. To them she was the usurper: Catherine was still the rightful Queen. It was a rumpled bed Anne had made for herself. Now she had to lie in it.

The King had an edict printed and to the sound of trumpets proclaimed throughout the City. Catherine was no longer to be addressed as Queen; the punishment was death. Regardless of this terrible penalty, the order was defied. When in July Catherine, as a safety measure, was commanded to move from the manor of Ampthill in Bedfordshire to the remote house of Buckden in Huntingdonshire, the entire neighbourhood gathered to see her leave and do her honour. And as she travelled through the country villages the people gathered round, weeping, clamouring their loyalty. 'God save the Queen,' they cried. 'We are ready to die for you. How can I serve you? Confusion to your enemies!' Similar scenes had greeted Mary's move to a new house shortly before. Anne summed it up neatly and bitterly. The villagers had made as much fuss of Mary, she said, 'as though God had descended from the skies'.

Such news told Anne that though she had all the appearance of being a Queen, even now she still did not possess the reality. As her steps slowed with the growth of the coming child, the memory of those clamouring villagers robbed her victory of its flavour. She had achieved her ambition only to discover her subjects would not accept her.

Another incident that greatly troubled her that summer concerned those same Hanseatic merchants whose pageant had spoilt her coronation procession. Sailing an unusually large fleet up the Thames, they invited Chapuis to a banquet on board and fired a threatening fusillade outside Greenwich Palace where Anne was staying at the time. The country people who shouted for Catherine and the German merchants who had insulted her became part of the same haunting fear in Anne's mind. And fear in Anne's case was usually the prelude to action or at least an attempt to stir the King into action. She had tried to win the people by kindness; for the past twelve months she had distributed lavish charities. They had not responded. So, she resolved, they must be made to respect her. Was she not Queen? How dared they treat her so? Every day she nagged at Henry to punish them, reckless of the fact that no monarch without a standing army could risk alienating either large numbers of his own subjects or a powerful league of foreign merchants. That Anne, despite her quick intelligence and perception, could demand such a politically suicidal act, shows how blind she had grown to anything outside her own predicament.

Henry forgave her, soothing the irritation he must have felt at this constant carping by reminding himself she was carrying his son. Pregnant women were given to idle fancies. They must be calmed and indulged in every way feasible and sheltered from shocks. Especially the prospective mother of an heir to the throne. Since she was too far advanced in pregnancy to go with him on progress, Henry, like a male bird in the nesting season, spent the summer protectively close to her, restricting his hunting expeditions to places around London; and in August, on hearing that the Pope had taken action at last, he kept the upsetting news from her. Having secretly ordered his Privy Council and a large number of doctors of canon law to assemble at Guildford, he rode out of Windsor Castle to meet them, telling Anne he was going hunting.

But in spite of Henry's precautions it cannot have been long before Anne also learned what had happened, that on July 11 the Pope had declared Anne's marriage null and void, her issue illegitimate and Henry excommunicated, the sentence to take effect from the end of September if within that time the King had not complied with the papal requests to reinstate Catherine and separate from Anne.

Faced with this dramatic crisis, the doctors of canon law suggested an ingenious course. Henry should appeal over the head of the Pope to a general council – a move that would prevent the censures being put into effect for the time being. There was also the possibility that Francis would be able to persuade Clement to revoke or delay the sentence. None the less the situation disturbed King Henry's temper and temporarily dimmed his feeling for Anne.

In the last few weeks of Anne's pregnancy occurred an ominous event: Henry took a mistress, another woman at Court. Perhaps this was the time when he had his affair with

Nicholas Carew's wife, Elizabeth, a supposition that would fit in with the facts but cannot be proved since Chapuis's despatches on the subject of the King's new love merely say that she was 'very beautiful' and 'many nobles are assisting him in the affair', without mentioning the lady's name. By contemporary standards Henry's conduct was neither unusual nor scandalous, marital unfaithfulness being the rule rather than the exception among his fellow monarchs. Henry had now possessed Anne for eleven months, long enough to dispel the magic and realize her as a flesh-and-blood woman rather than a goddess; and besides she was heavily pregnant. Henry's unfaithfulness did not at this stage in Anne's life threaten her position. The ominous quality lay not so much in Henry's action as in Anne's violent reaction to it. Although her wisest, most dignified course would have been to count her considerable blessings and meekly accept a situation that was bound to be temporary, Anne's pride prevented her. It was not in her impetuous egotistical nature to compromise, to watch without protest while she was betrayed by the man who had vowed everlasting love, the man who had signed himself 'H seeks no other R' and 'Votre seulle H R'.

Recklessly she 'made use of certain words which he very much disliked'. The King retorted furiously: 'She must shut her eyes and endure, as those who were better than herself had done; she ought to know that he could at any time lower her as much as he had raised her.' Not surprisingly, the ungallant rejoinder did little to calm Anne. 'There has since been much coldness and grumbling between them,' reported Chapuis happily, 'so much so that the King has been two or three days without speaking to her.' But these were, he estimated, only 'lovers' quarrels'.

Though one man, William Glover, servant to Sir Henry Wyatt, the poet Thomas Wyatt's father, had had a disturbing vision, that Anne would give birth to a girl - a prognostication considered so important that two members of the Queen's household, one of her chaplains and her almoner, hurried off to interview him - everyone else, doctors, astrologers, sorcerers and sorceresses, agreed that she would give birth to a son. When that happy event occurred Henry could get Parliament at once to swear fealty to the Prince of Wales and Anne's troubles would be over; the King's also. The populace could be brought to accept a situation that would ensure stability in the country, and would finally abandon Mary.

The new baby, it was decided, should be born at Greenwich. On September Anne came by boat to the battlemented red brick palace on the river, where the traditional preparations had already been made for a royal birth. There were no less than three beds. First in her Chamber of Presence carpenters had built a great bed of state. Then for her Bed Chamber Henry had presented her two months before with a splendid bed from his treasure house, the ransom of a Duke d'Alençon.

In this room also there was a 'pallet' bed with a crimson satin canopy above embroidered with the King's and Queen's coats of arms and gold crowns. In this she would receive visitors after the event, sitting up in a mantle of crimson velvet furred with ermine; it had all been laid down by Henry VII in detailed regulations for equipping the chamber where a Queen was to be delivered. The beds were provided with sheets of fine lawn, either with a counterpane of ermine embroidered with cloth of gold or counterpanes of scarlet bordered with ermine and blue velvet.

Arrived at Greenwich, Anne went through the ceremony of 'taking her Chamber'. A group of noblemen and ladies conducted the Queen to her chapel. After taking communion here, she was served with spice and wine under a cloth of estate in her Chamber of Presence. Then when her Chamberlain had prayed aloud that God would send her a good hour, two of the noblemen led her to her chamber door, through which she was followed by the women and the women alone; from this time until after she had given birth, custom decreed that no man must set foot in the room. Nor must the Queen leave it.

A special altar and a cupboard for Anne's plate had been built there. Tapestry covered the walls, roof and all the windows except one. In this sumptuous but uncomfortably dark and airless prison lit with gleams of gold, in the summer weather Anne waited to become the mother of a prince.

For him also magnificent preparations had been made: his nursery was equipped with a piece of furniture so grandiose a new-born baby would almost disappear inside it – a 'great cradle of estate' five and a half feet long, two and a half feet wide. This enormous cot was covered in crimson cloth of gold, with four pummels of silver and gilt, engraved with the arms of the King and Queen, and had a counterpane of scarlet lined with ermine and bordered with blue velvet. It is a relief to read that for every day a humbler and cosier bed was provided, a little wooden cradle painted gold, forty-five inches long by twenty-two inches wide.

Notices were written ready to be sent out to the nobility announcing the 'deliverance and bringing forth of a prince' (with the customary space left for an 's' just in case). The King decided he was to be named Henry or Edward, and arranged for a pageant and tournament to take place in the boy's honour immediately after the birth. Anne's favourite courtiers sent to Flanders for horses.

But nature did not oblige. And when on Sunday 7 September 1533, between three and four o'clock in the afternoon, Anne gave birth to a girl, the whole foundation from which she had climbed the ladder to the throne was endangered.

# Chapter 21

# PRINCESS OF ENGLAND

ALL through the previous year Anne's luck had held. Now suddenly fortune's wheel had turned once again. So confident had Anne been of producing the longed-for son and heir to the throne that the birth of a daughter was a terrible anti-climax. With her usual lack of discretion, she made no attempt to conceal her feelings. 'The King's mistress,' reported the caustic Chapuis, showed 'great disappointment and anger.' Church bells pealed out the joyful notes of the customary *Te Deum*, but in the King's eyes the birth of a daughter rated no more. No public celebrations were ordered by Henry. That evening as she looked through the one window of her chamber not muffled in tapestry, Anne saw the purple sky unchanged. No bonfire flames reddened the night. On the morrow the horses shipped from Flanders for the joust would stand idle in their stables. Anne knew she had failed in her appointed task.

But while the infant was certainly the wrong sex, she was still a child of Anne's own body. And Anne had longed for children; as she told Henry in December 1529, they were 'the greatest consolation in the world'. In a life as perilous, fear-ridden and lonely as Anne's there was much need of such consolation. Now, as she contemplated the mite lying under velvet and ermine in the gilded, painted cradle, her first disappointment was transformed by the alchemy of motherhood into fierce protectiveness. Henceforward, Anne's fight would be for her child as well as for herself.

The birth of a daughter, while it did not have the revolutionary effect on Anne's fortunes that would have resulted had she borne a son, still considerably strengthened her position. The King had a characteristic change of heart. After his first wrathful outburst, he was delighted with his little daughter and pleased with Anne for bearing her. The child was healthy, Anne young; sons were bound to follow.

They would call her Elizabeth after the King's mother and Anne's.

Meanwhile, everything must be done to ensure that Anne's issue were accepted as legal heirs to the throne. Nothing and no one must stand in their way.

Already, as Anne lay spent after Elizabeth's birth in the great carved bed, she had heard the sweet sound of a herald's trumpet outside the palace: Catherine of Aragon's daughter was no longer to be called 'Princess of England'. It was the King's will. Mary had ceased to be heir to the throne. After seventeen years she had been deposed by her royal father to make way for the child of his new Queen.

The trumpet echoes had scarcely faded from the courtyards of Greenwich Palace before messengers were riding to Beaulieu, where Mary lived surrounded by a princely retinue of servants in gold-embroidered coats. Clattering under the massive gateway which the King had added to this former possession of the Boleyns, the messengers delivered his order. His elder daughter was henceforth to be known simply as the Lady Mary. She was to be deprived of her separate household. The Princess's badge must be removed from the gold-embroidered coats, to be replaced by King Henry's own coat of arms; and her servants were now his.

While Mary tasted this bitter fruit, Anne's hours at Greenwich Palace were filled with pleasure, her ears with the satisfying sound of saw and hammer as carpenters made furniture by day and candlelight for her daughter's nursery: tables, forms, trestles, screen and a table on which the nurse was to press the infant's clothes. Other carpenters prepared for the christening, erecting supports for the tapestry that would wall a splendid lane from the palace to the Friars' Church and building a platform there with three steps to raise the silver font above the crowd so that all could watch the ceremony to be held on the Wednesday afternoon when Elizabeth was three days old.

Elizabeth's christening was a state occasion. Barges crammed with lords, ladies, gentlemen, officers of arms, bishops and the

Mayor of London with attendant aldermen drew up at the landing stage. Two by two they marched to the sound of trumpets down the tapestry-walled lane, carpeted with fresh green rushes. The Dowager Duchess of Norfolk carried the baby Elizabeth in a mantle of purple velvet. Although Anne, according to custom, would not attend the ceremony, her family were well represented. Her brother George was one of the four lords who with slow measured pace walked beside the child, supporting the rich canopy above her; the Earl of Wiltshire carried one side of her long purple train, trimmed with ermine. Inside the church, all hung with arras, the silver font gleamed beneath the square crimson canopy, fringed with gold.

The infant princess was disrobed behind a specially built screen, by a 'pan of fire', so she would not grow cold, then carried to the font, around which stood gentlemen wearing aprons and towels around their necks, to stop any dust tainting the holy water. The moment after Anne's baby had been immersed and christened by Archbishop Cranmer, two hundred torches blazed and the voice of Garter King of Arms proclaimed: 'God of his infinite goodness send prosperous life and long to the high and mighty Princess Elizabeth.'

From church to palace, along the tapestry-lined way, Elizabeth's procession wound back, light from a forest of torches carried by attendant gentlemen glittering on the presents borne aloft before her. Up the stairs the procession moved, trumpets still playing, to the door of Queen Anne's apartments.

There this solemn procession for the three-day-old child came to an end. Elizabeth was taken away to the nursery and to the care of the wet nurse (whose food and drink were tasted for poison), while Anne, in her great state bed and crimson velvet mantle trimmed with ermine, inspected the christening gifts brought in by her ladies: from the Archbishop of Canterbury, 'a standing cup of gold'; from the Duchess of Norfolk, 'a standing cup of gold, fretted with pearl'; from the Marchioness of Dorset, 'three gilt bowls, pounced, with a cover'.

Here was tangible proof of Anne's achievement, and the lofty rank of her daughter. It was a moment of earthly glory to compare with that of her coronation, the golden dream for which Anne had risked so much. It was also one of the few moments in her relationship with Henry when her joy need not be tinged with fear or hysteria, and when her hopes for the future could have a sounder basis than wild optimism and the fighting spirit of her ancestors. The King was once more reassuringly ardent, so much so that he was overheard to say, reported Chapuis, that 'he would be reduced to begging alms from door to door rather than abandon and desert the lady, whom he loved more than ever.' Momentarily Anne's triumph seemed complete, but her brief serenity was about to be overcast by the threat of a new peril. So ran the pattern of her life.

This time the threat came from the King's elder daughter, for Elizabeth's triumph was Mary's downfall. It had turned her into an implacable enemy. As Anne's strength and looks returned she had her first intimation that Mary might prove as stubborn an adversary as her mother, that history would repeat itself and Mary stand in Elizabeth's way as Catherine had stood in Anne's.

On the morning of October 2, Mary's chamberlain came to her with a letter from the Controller of the King's household requiring her to move from palatial Beaulieu to Hertford Castle, a smaller abode befitting her new humbler rank. It was addressed simply to, The Lady Mary, the King's Daughter. Mary replied at once to the King. She could only believe, she wrote, that her father could not have known about it, and she ended on a note of pious obstinacy that was an ominous echo of her mother: 'not doubting but you take me for your lawful daughter, born in true matrimony. If I agreed to the contrary I should offend God. In all other things you shall find me an obedient daughter.'

Mary had good reason to want to frustrate the woman who had forced her mother off the throne and estranged her father - who had deprived her of both family and birthright. For of Anne's responsibility for her predicament Mary Tudor can have been in no doubt. Many incidents during the past two years must have stayed and festered in her mind. She had been with Catherine at Windsor when Henry's message had arrived banishing her from Court to The More. Mary had been sent away at the same time, to Richmond, and since then, through Anne's machinations, had not been allowed to see her mother at all and her father only very rarely. Once when she met him by accident out walking in the autumn of 1532, Anne had sent her ladies hurrying after, making him cut short the talk for fear of offending his beloved. Such treatment in the formative years of her life a girl of Mary's rigid temperament could never forgive. But both Anne and Henry underestimated her indomitable spirit. Mary was young, deceptively small, delicate. Surely she could be made to obey the King.

A deputation from the Privy Council, consisting of Dr Sampson and the Earls of Oxford, Essex and Sussex, rode off to persuade Mary that it was her duty and the will of God to submit to her father. The seventeen-year-old girl handled the situation with the craft of a mature politician. She insisted on hearing the delegation before her entire household. Only when all were gathered together, officials, secretaries, maids of honour, footmen, cooks, people who had served her from early childhood, would she listen to her father's message of disinheritance. In the emotional atmosphere that followed, the frail girl lifted her unusually deep voice.

She had no right, she declared boldly, to renounce a title that God, nature and her parents had given her; being daughter of the King and Queen, she had a right to be called Princess. Her father might do with her as he pleased, she would do nothing to prejudice her own legitimacy or her mother's cause.

When she had finished speaking the entire assembly wept, including the delegation, a sign of the loyalty to Catherine's daughter which persisted in the hearts of Englishmen of all classes.

The crux of this situation, Anne knew, was that potentially Mary was now an even more dangerous enemy than Catherine. For while Cranmer's divorce, with its appearance of legality, had more or less disposed of Catherine as a serious rival for the crown, it had done nothing to dispose of Mary's claim to be heir to the throne. For even if it was true that Catherine's marriage to Henry was void, their offspring was not necessarily illegitimate. Since the marriage had been solemnized in good faith, many canon lawyers argued, Mary was the legal heir and it was as such that she would continue to be seen abroad as well as in England, thus becoming the obvious figurehead for invasion or rebellion.

So for Anne it was essential to force her step-daughter to give up her claim and accept her new subordinate status. Mary was a perplexing problem for Anne. Her insight into character, often acute with men, was almost non-existent with women; this is the most reasonable explanation for the lack of understanding she displayed in her handling of Mary Tudor.

The first question to be solved was, where should Mary live? In a thoughtless moment before her coronation, Anne, to show her power, had boasted that she would make Mary carry her train. But now when Henry, eager to please her, arranged for Mary to come to Court, Anne realized her mistake.

At Court she would be in touch with the great nobles, most of whom were Roman Catholic and conservative, and with Chapuis, the Imperial ambassador; she would be in the best possible position to promote intrigue. Anne resolved on another solution no less harsh. And King Henry, still besotted with his apparently fruitful wife, countermanded his orders and meekly agreed.

Mary should continue to reside in the country but deprived of the company of her friends, servants and counsellors, all her own former household. Mary, she decided, should become part of the little Princess Elizabeth's household. For Mary it was an unbearable humiliation: but for Anne and her daughter it was the finishing touch to royal estate, the final defiant proof to her many enemies that she had indeed triumphed.

In an age that judged so much by appearances it was logical for Anne to be intensely anxious to make up with all the available trappings of royalty for her daughter's doubtful claim to be the heir to the throne. Thus before the birth she had demanded the christening robe Catherine had used for all her babies, a request indignantly refused by the ex-Queen and which the lords who made it had not had the heart to press. Now to the driving force of Anne's personal ambition were added unusually intense maternal feelings, according to the *Spanish Chronicle*. She 'loved this child so much,' says the anonymous author, 'that she would not let her out of her sight. Whenever the Queen came out in the royal palace where the canopy was, she had a cushion placed underneath for her child . . .' Untrustworthy though most of the chronicle is, this story which reflects credit on Anne, may well be true, told as it is by an otherwise hostile author; and it certainly tallies with what we know of her nature. If we accept this story of Anne's obsessive love for Elizabeth, it must have been painful indeed to have to part with her soon after her birth. But there was no remedy. It was the convention for the heir to the throne to have her own separate dwelling and household; already, at three months old, Elizabeth was to begin living under a different roof.

On December 13 in a velvet litter the little princess set off, escorted by the Dukes of Norfolk and Suffolk, with a large party of lords and gentlemen. So that the people could see the new heir to the throne, they rode through the cobbled streets of London before turning towards the deep gabled roofs of the fifteenth-century brick palace of Hatfield House in the flat green fields of Hertfordshire. Today we can still see one wing of the low building which in 1533 rambled round four sides of a central courtyard, a peaceful, healthy place for the little Elizabeth to grow up in.

Very different was Mary's journey from Hertford Castle the next day. Forced to travel in a humble leather litter, escorted by the stern-faced Duke of Norfolk, she had been made to leave all except two of her own household behind, including her usual long train of servants in gold-embroidered coats, the retinue which in every journey by road she had taken for as long as she could remember had signified to admiring crowds as she passed that this was the Princess of England.

On arriving tired and dusty at Hatfield, an even more humiliating experience awaited the outraged, rebellious girl. The Duke of Norfolk asked her to go and pay her respects to 'the princess'. Anne had hoped that, isolated from her friends, Mary would accept her inescapable situation. Instead Mary lost her temper. She delivered a string of insults at both Anne and her daughter. She knew, she declared, of no other princess in England but herself; the daughter of Madame de Pembroke had no right to that title but, as the King her father owned her as his own, she said sarcastically, she could call her 'Sister' as she called the Duke of Richmond 'Brother'. And she rushed to her room in tears.

In judging Anne's subsequent treatment of Mary these insults must be remembered. They were of a kind to stir a calmer nature than Anne's to vengeance; for obliquely, but clearly enough, Mary had reiterated the popular accusation that she was the King's whore, the reputation that clung to her like a nightmare miasma.

In a fury of resentment Anne retaliated. She sent a new order to her aunt, Lady Shelton (sister to the Earl of Wiltshire), in whose charge Mary had been placed: if Mary persisted in calling herself 'princess' she was to be 'slapped like the cursed bastard she was' – an order that seems callously cruel today but which was the accepted contemporary method of dealing with disobedient daughters.

Mary was deprived of her jewels, of her royal privilege of eating alone and of having her food and drink tasted for poison. The company of every one of her old servants, including her confessor, was forbidden her, as well as communication with them and with her mother.

But all Anne's efforts to break her morale and force her to admit that she was not the true heir to the throne were in vain. Throughout England the common people were loyal to Mary, and even in Elizabeth's carefully chosen household she had her secret sympathizers. As she walked along a gallery from Hatfield to the adjoining church, the country people gathered round to cheer her. Anne ordered her to be strictly confined to the house, even further church visits forbidden, but somehow messages, letters, advice from Catherine and from Chapuis still continued to reach her and steel her courage against submission.

Anne's instructions were ignored. Even her own aunt defied her. Upbraided for leniency to Mary by Lord Rochford and the Duke of Norfolk, Anne Shelton replied spiritedly that, instead of being ill-treated, Mary should be honoured for her virtues.

Deprived of her royal prerogative of eating alone, Mary would come to the public table, but not eat; she had found a friend to defy Anne's orders and bring food to her room beforehand.

In January 1534 the King himself set out to ride down to Hatfield to see if he could persuade his rebellious child to submit. But Anne had second thoughts. Henry was already on the road when in sudden terror she commanded Cromwell to gallop after him and beg him not to see his elder daughter. It is an indication of Anne's renewed sway over Henry that he unquestioningly obeyed her message, sent orders ahead that Mary was not to see him and on arrival spent his time in Elizabeth's apartments.

But even on this occasion Mary achieved a kind of victory. As the King was leaving Hatfield, Mary appeared on a terrace kneeling, with her hands together. Henry could do no less than bow and raise his cap to her, gestures which were joyfully repeated by his courtiers.

While the problem of her step-daughter can rarely have quite receded from Anne's mind in the winter of 1533-4, her new duties as Queen of England competed for her attention: she must present a magnificent spectacle in her appearance and be lavish in her generosity. For the Christmas celebrations over which she would preside at the King's side she must decide on right royal gifts. Her ladies, she presented with palfreys and saddles. For the King her choice was more esoteric: a miniature fountain in a gilt basin garnished with rubies, pearls and diamonds, with 'three naked women standing at the foot of the same fountain, water issuing from their breasts'.

When Christmas was over one of Anne's duties was to receive the many people who in their turn brought her gifts and also came to request her to use her favour with the King to obtain for them offices and perquisites; according to custom, the Queen was treated by her subjects as a kind of goddess who, if suitably appeased, could obtain almost anything for them. If she did not like their gift, on the other hand, she did not have to accept it.

One of Anne's most persistent suitors was Lady Lisle, from whom Anne accepted eighteen plovers (of which she chose six for her supper that very day, six for Monday dinner and six for Monday supper), also a length of kersey, a linnet in a cage, and a little dog, 'which the Queen liked so well', reported Sir Francis Brian, Lady Lisle's intermediary, 'that she took it from him before it had been an hour in his hands'. This dog, whom she christened Purkoy (perhaps originally *pourquoi* after his enquiring looks?), became her most cherished plaything on which she vented her frustrated maternal feelings. And he must have been some consolation in her anguish at the death in that same month of her friend and loyal supporter, Nicholas Hawkins, Ambassador to the Emperor, an event that made her weep bitterly. But Lady Lisle had struck lucky with her present, for some donors' gifts were refused, and the word went round: the Queen did not like monkeys or female dogs.

'For each gift she accepted Anne followed the royal practice of giving a reward, though not always that which the giver sought. Lady Lisle was not successful in obtaining the place in the Queen's service she coveted for her two daughters nor yet in her modest plea for 'a little vessel to have licence to carry beer over the sea and return with arras and other things'.

Apart from sitting in judgement on these suits from the public, the Queen had to supervise the administration of her own vast lands, numerous houses and large royal household; and she must attempt to preserve at least the appearance of a proper moral tone among her ladies, something Anne does not seem to have been very good at. Although in the intervals between dances she kept her ladies busy sewing tapestries and smocks for the poor, scandal still broke out. Perhaps to get her own back on the Duchess of Norfolk, Anne had chosen as one of her ladies, Bessy Holland, the Duke's mistress. Although this liaison had begun as long ago as 1525, the matter did not reach a crisis until 1533 after a quarrel in which, the Duchess claimed, her husband got his servants to sit on her until she spat blood. The Duchess left his house and refused to have anything more to do with him, thus disrupting the smooth surface of social life at Court. The King seems to have attempted unsuccessfully to patch up a quarrel which, one suspects, was brought to a head by Anne's patronage of Bessy and the gay, flirtatious atmosphere in the Queen's apartments. Anne herself if the mood took her would dance with her favourite gentlemen in her Bed Chamber, when she was not playing games of hazard with them on the little gaming-table with antique tiles that Henry had given her.

These entertainments, however, were an escape only. They never made her lose sight of the realities of her situation and the particular danger of her unpopularity, to combat which she devoted great attention to her charities, the lavishness of her gifts based also perhaps on a genuine concern for poverty as well as a desire to appear munificent. Apart from the little purse from which she used daily to scatter alms to the needy, she had – according to John Strype writing in Queen Elizabeth's reign – a remarkably well organized system. On moving to a new abode she would send her sub-almoner round neighbouring towns to draw up a list of the poor in their parish. Then she would give the towns a present of 'seven, eight, or ten pounds' to buy cattle for these poor people – a generous sum at a time when ten shillings bought a milking cow.

But Anne's efforts to court popular goodwill came too late. The majority of the people continued to regard her with superstitious horror as the cause of the imminent break with Rome, the black-eyed whore who had bewitched their King and would cut them off from their God.

That winter there were signs all around that the catastrophe they had so long feared was about to happen. In December from pulpits throughout England there thundered down among the alarmed congregations words of flagrant heresy, spoken by bishops following instructions from the Privy Council. The Pope, they preached, was merely the 'Bishop of Rome', with no more jurisdiction in this realm than any other foreign bishop. In some London churches Lutherans had already begun to desecrate images of the saints, and on every church door appeared the Act of Appeals, passed the previous spring, which settled supreme authority in all spiritual matters on the Archbishop of Canterbury. The people had no doubt who was responsible. They laid the blame on Queen Anne.

In fact, King Henry by the end of 1533 had little choice but to prepare for schism; news from Rome told him that whether he liked it or not schism was about to be thrust upon him, and that Clement was on the point of making pronouncement from which no ally could now save him. This was something even more serious than the sentence of excommunication pronounced in July, a sentence the French had persuaded Clement to defer, pending negotiations for a settlement. Now nearly seven years after the 'divorce' issue had started Clement had decided to pronounce final judgement. The verdict, he had decided, would be in favour of Catherine, and against the King. While remaining in the Church, Henry could not keep Anne and his chance of a male heir.

So to protect his people from the effects of interdict the King had to go ahead with his own plans for a separate Church in England under his own authority. It was a decision for which, with the exception of scattered handfuls of Protestants, his subjects were not grateful.

The impending schism which made Anne so unpopular with the common people also increased the hatred of the conservative Roman Catholic nobles. While prepared to accept the 'divorce' as a necessary evil, many of these felt anything was better than to be cut off from the Pope, even rebellion and invasion by the Emperor. One by one they began secretly to approach Chapuis - in the middle of a crowd of courtiers on the way back from Mass, in secret visits to his house at night - with requests for Charles V's help and pledges of support. Suspecting a conspiracy, Anne hated to see anyone talking to the Imperial ambassador at all. But she had no names and no proof. The Duke of Norfolk, whom she rated soundly for his long conversations with Chapuis, was guiltless.

Anne was fortunate indeed that between her and the hatred of her subjects the King and Cromwell still stood firm. Now, to terrorize the would-be rebels into submission, they used a half-crazed young peasant woman, a nun from Kent, in a most ingenious plot.

Elizabeth Barton was one of Anne's most notorious enemies. For seven years past she had been subject to regular fits in which she claimed to have direct communication with the saints. People of all classes flocked eagerly to hear the Holy

Maid of Kent through whose meandering revelations ran a popular theme: that God was on the side of Queen Catherine and that the King and Anne would come to a lurid end. Elizabeth was arrested and in January 1534 accused of treason. Placed on a scaffold at St Paul's, she confessed to the crowds below – she had doubtless been persuaded beforehand by the rack – that her visions were all false. The punishment was, of course, death. But her execution was postponed for some weeks while Cromwell drew up a list of her supporters among the nobility. The existence of the list was carefully made known: the names on it kept blood-chillingly secret; and since no one could be sure he or she was not included in this catalogue which could send them to suffer the halter at Tyburn or the dull chop of the axe on Tower Hill, Catherine's friends were suddenly anxious to appear loyal subjects of Queen Anne. Coolly created by the King and the ruthless Thomas Cromwell, this panic not only kept rebellion at bay and Anne safely on the throne, but also helped to spur through Parliament some revolutionary measures that were needed to strengthen the new regime in the face of the imminent pronouncement from Rome.

On March 23 Pope Clement pronounced valid Henry's marriage to Catherine. On 30 March 1534 Henry gave the royal assent to parliamentary acts abolishing the authority of the Pope in England and settling the succession on Anne's children. Finally the schism with Rome was accomplished, the momentous event that would never have happened at that precise time in the history of England had it not been for Anne Boleyn.

# Chapter 22

# SHADOWS OF FAILURE

ANNE's children were given the status of legal heirs to the throne by the Act of Succession. And Henry was determined it should be observed. Through the length and breadth of England he sent commissioners riding to administer the sacred oath. Every adult in the kingdom was to be made to kiss the Bible or a holy relic and swear to maintain the Act. As a further incentive to obedience, anyone who henceforward wrote or 'did anything' against the King's marriage or offspring would be guilty of treason. Anyone who spoke against them would be guilty of misprision of treason, an offence that carried the penalty of forfeiture of property and imprisonment; anyone hearing such words must reveal them.

While Henry thus sought to put a lid on the bubbling discontent in his kingdom, Anne did her own small best to eliminate rebellion. She decided, rather late in the day, to try whether kindness would make Mary submit.

In March 1534 she visited Hatfield and to Mary's apartments she sent a courtier with a message, gentle but firm, begging Mary to visit her and honour her as Queen. If Mary did this, she promised, Anne would see that she had everything she could wish. She would be reconciled to her father and earn Anne's gratitude. Back came Mary's proud insulting reply. She knew of no other Queen in England except her mother, but should 'the King's mistress' do her the favour she spoke of and intercede with the King her father, she would certainly be most grateful.

Anne swallowed her indignation and sent another conciliatory message, once more repulsed. Again and again Anne sent the perspiring courtier down the rambling passages of Hatfield. But however many times he came and went - though Anne tried threats as well as bribery - the reply was still the same.

Until Anne's temper snapped. She went home swearing that she would humble that unbridled Spanish blood.

A similar scene was repeated when Anne visited Eltham where Elizabeth's household moved temporarily. In the chapel Anne attended Mass at the same time as her step-daughter. Rudely Mary left the chapel first. Afterwards one of Anne's attendants, seeking to please her, told her that Mary had curtseyed to her before leaving. 'If we had seen it, we would have done as much to her,' said Anne in great excitement, and she sent a lady of honour to her step-daughter with a message of apology and an offer of love and friendship. The lady of honour found Mary at dinner and delivered the speech with which she had been charged:

> The Queen salutes your grace with much affection and craves pardon, understanding that at your parting from the oratory, you made a curtsey to her, which if she had seen she would have answered you with the like; and she desires that this may be an entrance of friendly correspondence, which your grace shall find completely to be embraced on her part.

But to this gracious and formal overture Mary made a stubborn and again insulting reply. 'It is not possible,' she answered, 'that the Queen can send me such a message; nor is it fit she should, nor can it be so sudden, her majesty being so far from this place. You would have said, the Lady Anne Boleyn, for I can acknowledge no other queen but my mother, nor esteem them my friends who are not hers. And for the reverence that I made, it was to the altar, to her maker and mine; and so they are deceived, and deceive her who tell her otherwise.' Anne was maddened by this answer, repeating that one day she would 'pull down this high spirit'.

There was no policy behind Anne's treatment of Mary. She simply did not know what to do. Her moves against the girl were impulsive, futile, desperate stabs at a problem to which there was really only one solution: death. It was the only way to dispose of a rival claim to the throne in the sixteenth century; the way the Tudors had established themselves Kings of England; Henry VII had executed the Earl of Warwick, Edward IV's nephew known as the White Rose, and Henry VIII, on a trumped-up charge of treason, had executed the Duke of Buckingham, a descendant of Edward III. But while the killing of two English lords was a domestic matter, to spill the blood of the royal house of Spain would have widespread repercussions. Unfortunately for Anne, Henry could not commit an act that would offend the whole of Europe. Although there were moments when in blind fury at her blocking of his plans he certainly wished his elder daughter dead, he dared not implement his wish without an overwhelming reason.

Catherine, though less dangerous as the potential figurehead for invasion from overseas, was a thorn in the flesh of both Anne and Henry. The King would willingly have executed her had he not been sure that such an act would bring the Emperor's forces marching into England to join Henry's own outraged subjects. Catherine he now hated. Her death was his great desire, but although he did what he could to speed it, all his attempts had been defeated. Cromwell had tried and failed to implicate mother and daughter in Elizabeth Barton's treason. Henry had arranged for Catherine to be removed from Buckden to Somersham House, which was surrounded by the unhealthy Cambridgeshire marshes. Catherine refused to go. She barricaded herself in her room and he was forced to drop the plan. The most he dared do against his wife and daughter was to make it easy for someone else to kill them by removing the safeguards on their lives and ordering that their food and drink should no longer be tasted for poison. Some poor wretch, he may have thought, would seize his chance to earn the new Queen's gratitude by ridding her of her enemies. But significantly it was an opportunity of which no one cared to take advantage.

Anne raged at her impotence. Rival queens, rival heirs to the throne, could not co-exist. It was against nature. Sooner or later one or other must be killed. By the spring of 1534 the thought had become an obsession. 'She is my death and I am hers,' she was to say repeatedly of Mary. Anne was haunted by the popular prophecies, which foretold that she would be burned alive, the penalty at this date meted out to women for treason - though in the case of those of gentle birth it was usually commuted to beheading - as well as the punishment for heretics of both sexes. In the event of a successful revolt being made against Henry, Anne might well have suffered on both counts but not, as might have happened in the second half of the century, as a witch. A horror of witchcraft, not to be made a felony until 1541, had not yet taken possession of England and the deformity of Anne's finger, the mole on her neck, did not as one might have expected in later years set people talking of a league with the Devil. The common people may have believed that Anne had bewitched the King into loving her, but her chief fault in their eyes was still her crime against morality and against their Church. For that, many of them would have been glad to see her roast.

In July of the previous year the wife of Robert Amadas, Master of the King's Jewel House, had had a brainstorm and raved against Anne and Henry. She had called the King the 'Mouldwarp', prophesied invasion by the Scots, that a religious man called 'the dead man' would hold a parliament in the Tower, and that 'the blazing star was towards the island whence the dead man would come'. She added that 'if the Queen were not burned within this half year she would be burned herself'.

So far the prophecies had not come true, Anne was to say defiantly and often throughout her reign, thus revealing how much they worried her. There was even a popular ballad on the same theme.

*When the tower is white and another place green*
*Then shall be burned two or three bishops and a queen,*
*And after all this be passed we shall have a merry world.*

So, said Anne, loudly (one can imagine the laugh with which she said it), since one Queen of England was to be burned, she would make sure it was Catherine and not herself. She would have Mary poisoned, she would put Catherine to death, she swore repeatedly – vain boasts; she knew that Henry would never consent to the one measure that would make her safe on the throne.

With Catherine and Mary dead, the political problems would vanish; there would be no need for excommunication; no fear of rebellion, for there would be no figurehead. While both

Catherine and Mary, and Anne and Elizabeth survived, there could never be peace and stability in England.

Desperately, Anne conceived a plan. Indiscreet as ever, she told everyone about it. Henry was to cross the Channel for a meeting with Francis in August; Anne expected to be regent – a dangerous task since, with the King absent, there would be real danger of revolt. She would, Anne said several times, use her authority to put the princess to death either by sword or otherwise. When her brother Lord Rochford, now living in almost royal state at Beaulieu, reminded her nervously that this would anger the King, Anne replied wildly that she did not care even if she were flayed or burned alive for it afterwards.

By the summer of 1534 Anne had a new reason for her tension, her frenzied rages when she did not get her own way, her increased fear and hatred of Mary and Catherine – a new and terrible reason. Even as the King's commissioners rode through the country forcing men to swear in priory and convent, in market-place and nobleman's halls, that they would support the Act of Succession and swear fealty to her sons, Anne was beginning to realize that there might be no sons; that, incredibly, the pattern of her pregnancies was to be as disastrous as Catherine's. For, like Catherine, she could not carry her children to term. During the first six months of 1534 she appears to have had one miscarriage after the other.

She was pregnant in January and in April. By July she had told Henry she was pregnant again. Joyfully Henry instructed Lord Rochford to put off the meeting with King Francis on the grounds that by August Anne would be so far gone with child she would not be 'mete' to be carried over 'the tumbling seas'.

The King and Queen departed on their usual summer progress; Anne travelled at a sedate pace, as befitted her supposed condition, while Henry rode furiously from one deer park to another, forgetting his political problems in the blood lust of the chase, every few days meeting Anne at some prearranged house. As she travelled the dusty roads in her royal litter, listening to the half-hearted cheers of officials and peasants, a nightmare knowledge must have obsessed her: she would soon have to tell Henry that after the miscarriages of the spring she was now not even pregnant at all; she had made a mistake - perhaps anxiety had produced the longed-for symptoms.

She could not do it, could not bring herself to confess that the schism with Rome, the Act of Succession, the new definition of treason that had stopped the mouths of rebellion in England and made Henry increasingly unpopular, were all in vain. Henry had been so convinced she would produce sons. When in the spring of 1533 Chapuis had asked how he could be sure of getting a son by Anne, Henry had rounded on him and reiterated vehemently: 'Am I not a man as other men are? Am I not a man as other men are? Am I not a man as other men are?' Now Anne had to tell him that he was not, that for all his athletic prowess, running at the ring, jousting, hunting, vaulting, shooting at the butts, for all his great size, he was unable to father healthy male children. Wherever the fault lay - and it was more probably due to a chronic anxiety state in Anne than to Henry's having syphilis, a disease modern medical authorities do not believe he ever had - the disability to father male children reflected on his image.

At the thought of her husband's reaction to this disastrous news, even Anne's reckless bravery forsook her. Instead of telling the King, she hugged her awful knowledge to herself, aware that time would soon make confession unnecessary and that she would have to meet the explosion of her husband's wrath. One can imagine the increasingly high-pitched hysterical note in Anne's famous laugh, the strained look to her face as she tried to distract Henry from suspicious glances at the betraying slenderness of her shape.

When her sister Mary, widowed in 1528, suddenly towards the end of the summer appeared pregnant, Anne rounded on her furiously: it was a scandal, a disgrace and a reflection on the Queen's honour. Mary was banished from Court. When Mary confessed that she had fallen in love with and secretly married Sir William Stafford three months before, that made her crime no less in Anne's eyes. The Queen's sister had not the right to throw herself away on a simple knight; her marriage was a political weapon, a possible means to foreign alliance, and Mary should have asked the King's permission.

So incensed was Anne that Mary did not dare to write directly to ask her sister's forgiveness, but instead begged Cromwell to plead her cause. The fault was indeed great, but what Anne must have found hardest to forgive Mary was a fruitfulness that had been denied to herself, Mary's chance of producing the son Anne so badly needed and which Henry mistakenly believed to be growing in her womb.

The truth seems to have dawned slowly on Henry. For Anne left him to guess. Of the scene when he finally did, some time around the beginning of September, we have unfortunately no record. But we know the effect: Henry's feelings for Anne changed abruptly and radically. In September 1534 Henry renewed his attentions to 'a very handsome young lady of this court', the nameless mistress with whom he had solaced himself before the birth of Elizabeth the year before. Angrily, Anne commanded her to leave Court. Henry countermanded her orders and, carefully avoiding the indignity of a quarrel, sent her a furious message. 'She had better be content with what he had done for her,' he said, 'for he would not do it now, were it to begin again. And she should consider what she came from.' Henry's warning was clear. He had counted the cost and it was too much. Finally, a year and nine months since their marriage and eight years after his infatuation began, his love for her was dead. He was telling Anne to be grateful for what she had got; that she must suffer his unfaithfulness in silence and now settle down to the role of patient, uncomplaining, discarded wife, in imitation of Catherine and Queen Claude, concentrating on religion, charities and embroidery.

The situation was one that would probably have occurred sooner or later even had Anne produced a son. For 'sporting with ladies' was to Henry a way of life, feeding his vanity and romanticism. A wife, he felt, had no right to interfere; especially not one who lacked the distinction of royal blood and who had brought him nothing but bad luck. Before their marriage Anne had herself satisfied Henry's need for extra-marital gallantry. In his demand that she should now accept the usual domestic pattern of a sixteenth-century queen's life, Henry was only, he felt, demanding his rights. And when Anne not only refused to accept her new role but also turned his affair into a public scandal that reverberated throughout Europe, he was furious and indignant. With her sister-in-law, Lady Rochford, Anne schemed to involve her unknown rival in a quarrel for which the penalty would be banishment from Court. Henry discovered the truth and, instead of his new mistress, dismissed Lady Rochford. Anne tried again. The girl, she complained in front of a bevy of courtiers, was constantly rude and disrespectful. Henry exploded into wrath: he was weary of Anne's importunity and vexatiousness. He strode hastily away from her before she could answer back and get the better of him.

Her behaviour that September was motivated by urgent need rather than hurt pride, for her predicament was much more serious than it had been in the summer of the previous year, when Henry had wooed the same lady. Then Anne had been pregnant and Henry saw in her the mother of a long line of sons. Now he saw in her but the mother of one useless daughter and the tiresome victim of a succession of miscarriages.

This time Henry's affair jeopardized her whole future. She must dislodge her rival, or be dislodged herself; for the Court beauty had become a tool of the growing opposition, and the girl's seductive whispers tipped the balance of Henry's judgement at a time when strong pressure was being put on him anyway to discard Anne.

By the winter of 1534 the nobility no less than the people saw the new Queen as the cause of terrible changes that had taken place in England. King Henry and Thomas Cromwell together had turned the kingdom into a tyranny. Cromwell could force what measures he wished through a Parliament packed with members who feared to resist and with bishops appointed for their loyalty; measures that destroyed the whole fabric of the people's lives. No longer had they freedom of speech even in their own homes. A man could no longer grumble about the regime at his own fireside. Because by an Act passed by Parliament in the winter of 1534 words as well as deeds constituted high treason.

For calling the King heretic, schismatic or tyrant; merely
for wishing to deprive the King and the Queen of their titles,
the punishment was now death: to be hanged, cut down while
still alive, disembowelled, hacked into quarters and hung up
on the most appropriate gatepost. Anyone might be accused
and many were: a hundred-year-old person, a foolish drunken
old woman, a woman in childbed who said that her midwife
was good enough for a queen, but not for Queen Anne, for she
was a whore and a harlot . . . No one was safe anywhere, for
the Act of Succession had made it illegal to conceal treasonous
words and informers abounded, motivated by fear and greed
for the reward offered in Henry's proclamation of 1533.

Now there were signs that yet another radical change was
about to take place in the lives of the people. The monasteries
and nunneries thickly scattered over England had long needed
reformation; the overfed monk and immoral nun existed in
fact as well as literature; but there were good religious houses
as well as bad. Now there were signs that all would be ruined
in the dissolution to begin the following year. In November
Henry had been named by Act of Parliament Supreme Head of
the Church with power to 'repress and extirp all errors, heresies
and other enormities'. Already in the summer he had seized
the convent at Greenwich, in whose chapel Elizabeth was
christened, and other houses of the Observant Friars – who
included many other dissidents apart from Peto and Elstowe –
and had the friars transferred to other religious houses where
they were chained, starved and tortured. In churches everywhere the priests were ordered to preach that the King was
supreme and the Pope but 'Bishop of Rome'. With a Protestant
archbishop and a Protestant queen, who knew what worse
changes might not be in store?

The upheaval of the old order was frightening and disturbing
enough, but men liked even less the increasing inroads into
their pockets. In Spain, France and Flanders, where feeling ran
high against Henry's actions, English merchants were ill-
treated and robbed of their wares. In England, at a time when
inflation and the enclosures of land for sheep-farming had
already created hardship, Henry had just imposed a new tax –
'the twentieth penny of all the goods of his subjects', foreigners

to pay double. For although by Act of Parliament he had
already seized all the Church dues traditionally belonging to
the Pope, he needed still more money to provide against the
peril of war.

For all these things the King's marriage to Anne was blamed,
as well as for smaller daily troubles. Riding home from market
in the rain, Edmond Brock, an eighty-year-old farmer, grumbled: 'It is long of the King that this weather is so troublous or
unstable, and I wene we shall never have better weather whilst
the King reigneth, and therefore it maketh no matter if he were
knocked or patted on the head.'

His treasonable sentiments were echoed silently by many.

This was fertile soil for revolution, and in the winter of 1534
the seed was already sprouting. The nobles had formed a plot.

For over a year the discontented lords and their wives had
been passing secret messages to Chapuis. Now the conspiracy
was almost complete. In September 1534 Lord Darcy and Lord
Hussey, ex-chamberlain to Princess Mary, begged Chapuis to
request the Emperor's help. If Charles would reach an understanding with the Scots and send a small force of hackbutters,
some arms, ammunition and a little money for equipment,
the lords would march under the twin banners of the Emperor
and the crucifix. Darcy declared all the lords and gentlemen of
the northern counties - with the possible exception of Anne's
old admirer, the Earl of Northumberland - would rise, and the
south would soon join them in sympathy. The lords had consulted together, had agreed that Henry must be forced to give
up both his new Queen and his new policies.

Of the details of this plot Henry was almost certainly unaware, but of the danger of revolution and the strength of its
advocates he was not. When an attempt had been made in the
summer to make an example of Lord Dacre, one of Anne's most
outspoken enemies, the lords had shown their solidarity. Dacre
had been indicted for treason, a charge that was always followed
by a verdict of guilty and the death penalty. Contrary to all
precedent, Dacre had been acquitted by his peers.

At the unexpected news Londoners had cheered and danced
in the streets. It was one of many signals that Henry's own
popularity, upon which his power ultimately rested, was in

danger, a popularity that might be saved if he sacrificed Anne. No wonder that the ruthlessly pragmatic King, encouraged by a beautiful new mistress, was tempted to treat Anne as a scapegoat, a woman whom he no longer loved and who, it seemed, could never bear him a son.

Throughout the autumn and winter of 1534 Anne saw alarming indications of Henry's new cast of mind. Not the least was the abrupt improvement in the treatment of Mary. Should Anne be sacrificed, Elizabeth logically would have to go too, and Mary be reinstated as Henry's heir. Was the King contemplating this? It certainly looked like it. In October Thomas Cromwell, who knew most of Henry's secrets, told Chapuis that the King loved Mary more than the last-born and would not be long in giving evidence of it to the world. Cromwell himself had been fiercely rebuffed by the King for saying something to Mary's disadvantage. The courtiers were quick to read the signs. In the same month some of them accompanied the Queen ostensibly on a visit to Elizabeth, who was residing at The More. On arrival, instead of cooing over the new princess, to Anne's indignation, and without bothering to ask her permission, nearly all of them suddenly swept out of the room to visit Mary.

Soon afterwards Elizabeth's household moved to Richmond. For the journey, Mary was presented with a velvet litter exactly like her sister's, in place of the lowly leather litter she had been forced to travel in since Elizabeth's birth; and instead of being made to follow her as a sign of inferior status, Mary was allowed to travel most of the way by water, while Elizabeth went by road. That evening she was permitted to escape from her usual seclusion inside the palace walls and tell her bargemen to row her down the wide dark river past Chapuis's house between London and Greenwich. There was worse to come.

When Anne rode over to Richmond to see Elizabeth settled in, she was accompanied by a more splendid escort of courtiers than usual, led by the Dukes of Norfolk and Suffolk. But it was not, she soon discovered, to do her honour. Events followed the pattern of her previous visit to The More. On arrival, most of the courtiers, led by the two dukes, deserted Anne for Mary. As though this were not humiliation enough for a reigning Queen, Anne received an insulting message from Mary herself. She would not, Mary said, leave her chamber while Anne was present; for she did not wish to see her. Anne had no redress for this treatment. Her instructions that Mary should be punished for her rudeness were immediately countermanded by the King.

For Anne that winter of 1535 was wretched. Misfortune piled on misfortune. Even as she suffered the snubs and rebuffs of Henry and his courtiers and saw the King disport himself with her rival, she learned that she had lost her old, most trusted allies. The French, on whose support she had relied through all the years of her relationship with Henry, had suddenly withdrawn it and turned hostile.

The chief reason was England's schism with Rome. Francis had wished to keep the friendship of both Henry and Clement and had tried hard for a conciliation, but now he had to choose between them. And he chose the Pope, whose help he needed in Italy. This disturbing knowledge came to Anne in the most cruel way possible just as the Court was beginning to prepare for Christmas.

On November 20 Philippe Chabot de Brion, Admiral of France, with whom Anne, according to the *Spanish Chronicle*, had been on very friendly terms during her childhood at the French Court and her visit to Calais in 1532, arrived in London as head of a special mission. Always in the past, Anne had received flattering messages of goodwill from Francis's ambassadors whom she had fêted and banqueted. But this time, arrived at Court, Admiral Chabot behaved very strangely. He failed even to ask for an audience with Anne. When Henry enquired if he would not like to pay his respects to the Queen, the Admiral merely replied ungraciously that, if it pleased the King, he would do so. Then at the audience he treated Anne with no more than cold formality. Most of the Court festivities arranged for his benefit the Admiral churlishly ignored, only twice watching the dances and the tennis not at all. Meanwhile he was discouragingly polite to Chapuis.

Anne soon learned the meaning of this unwonted behaviour.

The French had decided that even if Henry's marriage to Catherine was invalid, Mary was still legitimate; they demanded that Henry should now fulfil his promise made when Mary was aged two to marry her to the Dauphin. Should the request be refused, Chabot threatened, they could always marry the Dauphin to the Spanish princess. The Emperor had already approached Francis, according to Chabot, with the most advantageous terms for an alliance.

It was catastrophic news for Anne, coming on top of Henry's desertion. It was almost unbelievable that the two people upon whom she most depended, whom most she trusted, could both turn hostile to her at the same time. The crowned Queen of England was in more jeopardy than she had been as maid of honour. It was savagely ironic, and as always in the face of terror Anne escaped into laughter, gravely offending Admiral Chabot.

On the eve of his departure at the beginning of December, the Admiral sat next to Anne on the dais at a banquet given in his honour. During the dancing, in a sudden rare, postprandial burst of gallantry, Henry rose; he would fetch the Admiral's chief secretary, Palamedes Gontier, he said, to come and pay his respects to the Queen. Anne watched anxiously as the glittering assembly divided to let his magnificent figure stride through. Just how long would Henry's pleasant mood towards her last? Suddenly she burst into loud peals of laughter. Chabot frowned. 'What, madam? Do you mock me?' Anne stopped laughing and tried to explain. In the doorway, she told him, Henry had met his new mistress. At the sight of her everything else had gone out of his head. It was an extraordinary admission for a Queen to make to an ambassador, especially a hostile one; but Anne could not really credit this enmity. That she could be deserted by the country where she had grown up, whose fashions she still wore, whose language she spoke like a native, whose ambassadors she had confided in, she found hard indeed to believe.

As Christmas approached, however, the French hostility began to look increasingly certain. King Henry had sent word by Chabot that he would not consider the marriage of Mary to the Dauphin; Mary was illegitimate. Would Francis agree instead to a match between Elizabeth and Francis's third son, the Duke of Angoulême? Henry made it cruelly clear that Anne's fate depended upon the French King's answer. No answer came. All through December and the first three weeks of January Anne waited in anguish and in vain. Henry argued threateningly that the long delay indicated the French had deserted her and opted instead for the Imperial alliance. In which event, as Anne knew, he would discard her. Already secretly he had consulted some of his Council on how this could be done, had accumulated evidence of her pre-contract with the Earl of Northumberland to be used as grounds for an annulment of the marriage.

The royal Christmas that year was more than usually magnificent. But sitting under her cloth of estate of gold tissue, embroidered with the King's arms, surrounded by servants bearing her device *The Most Happy* on their blue and purple liveries, Anne must have presided over the revels with a hollow heart. She had all the material things and all the power she had ever wanted. As well as the revenues and extensive lands of the Marquis of Pembroke, she had acquired by Act of Parliament the Queen's jointure. She had a vast and splendid household, including – to mention only a short selection – a lord chamberlain, vice-chamberlain, master of the horse, mistress of the maidens, almoner, chaplains, physicians, cooks, secretaries, surveyors, receiver, yeomen of the wardrobe, tailor, embroiderer, and a woman fool.

Her apartments were rich with rare and costly furniture. She possessed no less than six royal chairs, 'two of timber, the one covered with cloth of gold tissue with four pommels gilt and enamelled and fringed with silk and gold; the other covered with plain cloth of gold, and likewise fringed . . . three chairs of iron: two of them covered with crimson velvet, the one fringed with silk and gold, the other with silk; and the third covered with purple velvet fringed with silk and gold.' Everywhere Anne looked there were symbols of Henry's love. In her apartments, on the gleaming plate, on the bed-hangings, were H's and A's tenderly entwined and her coat of arms lay next to Henry's.

Yet by January 1535 all Anne's rich possessions, all the

symbols of Henry's affection, were a lie. Anne was a prisoner of her position, and in desperate danger. Henry could not, his Council had advised him, discard Anne without taking back Catherine and submitting to the Pope, steps Henry would never consider. But the Council could be wrong; means might yet be found. Henry's brain was subtle. If he really wanted to get rid of her, Anne knew, somehow he would find a way. She felt terror closing in.

As she watched the Christmas jousting and masking Anne was convinced she was surrounded by spies waiting for her to commit some action that could be misconstrued into a plot against the King and give him an excuse to discard her. It is the only possible explanation of her nervousness when an answer finally came from Francis on 31 January 1535.

The ambassador this time was Palamedes Gontier, Treasurer of Brittany and Admiral Chabot's Chief Secretary. He brought with him letters for the Queen but for two days was given no opportunity to present them. When finally they met it was in a hall crowded with people, the ante-chamber of a room where a dance was about to take place. A terrified Anne seized the opportunity in a low voice to make a desperate plea. His long delay, she said, had caused her husband to doubt the French intentions. The Admiral must think of some remedy to save her from being ruined and lost. For she saw herself very near to it, and was more in grief and anguish even than before her marriage. She charged him to beg the Admiral to consider her affairs, of which she could not speak as fully as she wished, on account of her fears and, she added, glancing round nervously, the eyes which were looking at her - her husband's and the courtiers'. 'I may not write,' she added with a touch of hysteria, 'nor see you again, nor stay longer.' (Was she afraid they might accuse her of plotting with the French against the King?) She then left him abruptly; and, following the King into the next room where the dancing had now begun, Gontier noticed that Anne did not accompany him. She had sacrificed her favourite pastime to escape the hostile stares of her enemies.

Meanwhile, the Dukes of Norfolk and Suffolk called a meeting of the Council to examine the French proposals. Francis was prepared to consider a marriage between Angoulême and

Elizabeth if Henry would give up the pensions and payments France was bound by treaty to pay him, worth about 120,000 crowns a year - an exorbitant demand immediately turned down by the Council. But stiff though the French proposals were, they represented a shift in policy encouraging to Anne. At least they had opted for an English in preference to an Imperial alliance and had accepted in theory a match with Anne's daughter in place of Catherine's. Commissioners were to meet at Calais to negotiate the marriage in May. For the time being Anne was saved.

A second improvement in her situation took place the same month. It is one of the interesting facets of Anne's character that while her nerves were often stretched to breaking-point, they never snapped and she never suffered adversity passively; she took action on this occasion with excellent results. If her enemies could take advantage of Henry's ephemeral desires, it had occurred to her, so could she. Anne brought to Court her pretty first cousin, Margaret Shelton, daughter of her father's sister, Anne Shelton, guardian of Mary. Margaret proved a dutiful member of the Boleyn family; the stratagem was marvellously successful.

On February 25 Chapuis wrote to the Emperor: 'The young lady who was lately in the King's favour is so no longer.' Madge had taken her place, a gentle unselfish person, most unlike her Boleyn relatives, who did what she was told and seems to have asked nothing for herself. Now the whispers in Henry's ear were for and not against Anne, and as soon as the self-effacing Madge had completed her task of reuniting the royal husband and wife, she faded modestly from the scene.

Thanks to a shift in Christendom's kaleidoscope and a skilful bit of juggling with the King's inconstant emotions, Anne, after teetering for weeks on the brink of ruin, was precariously back in the royal favour - but for how long?

# Chapter 23

# THE LAST SUMMER

By the spring of 1535 Queen Anne felt safe once more in King Henry's affection. She recovered her bold spirit and began to override him. Instead of becoming submissive to try to avoid the behaviour he had described as 'vexatious', she veered to the opposite extreme. The winter, she was convinced, was but a passing nightmare; Henry would never desert her again. Her fear of him was forgotten and centred now on the perilous uncertainty of the French alliance and that country's mysterious new hostility towards her. But by forcing Henry to do her will and by dominating the kingdom, she seems to have felt she could survive even that.

Chapuis tells us a little about Anne's method of imposing her will: 'Where the lady wants something there is no one who dares contradict her, not even the King himself, because when he does not want to do what she wishes, she behaves like someone in a frenzy.'

She redoubled her nagging. Why did he refrain from putting Catherine and Mary to death? Not to do so showed want of prudence, it was a disgrace to the realm. They were traitors according to the statutes, the Act of Succession and the Treason Act, passed the previous year, and the cause of all Henry's troubles. She even bribed a soothsayer to prophesy that she would not conceive while the two ladies were alive, a prediction promptly disproved by her becoming pregnant in early summer. 'Her Grace has a fair belly as I have seen,' wrote Sir William Kingston, Constable of the Tower. It was something to sustain Anne against the shock of news that came from France.

On May 25 Anne's brother, Lord Rochford, burst into her apartments at Greenwich, still in his riding clothes. He had

just come from Calais, where he was one of the commissioners
for the match between the Duke of Angoulême and Princess
Elizabeth. He had not yet been to see the King. All was lost,
he confided. The French would abate none of their demands.
Since Henry and his Council would refuse such harsh terms,
no match between Anne's daughter and King Francis's son was
possible. It was obvious that the French had no real desire for
an alliance that would offend Emperor and Pope, and that they
were not prepared to help a Queen whose hold on the throne
they recognized was already shaky.

When Anne emerged from her chambers and that long dis-
tressing talk with her brother, she was finally convinced that
the country she looked on as hers had betrayed her; she had
been abandoned by her old, most trusted ally. That with King
Francis political expediency would be bound to triumph over
personal loyalty was something Anne does not seem to have
understood. It was a painful shock, since Anne's power to
maintain her position in England had always depended on
French support.

Her anguish and anxiety vented themselves in vituperation
against Francis, against all France. From now on, she knew,
no help would come to her from the rest of Europe. Henry's
attempt to gain support among the Protestant states of
Germany had failed; they did not care for his supremacy of
the Church. Her best friend henceforward abroad was the Turk,
Suleiman the Magnificent, whose fleet, ravaging the Mediter-
ranean coasts under the pirate Barbarossa, kept Charles V too
busy to interfere in England.

In her own country Anne's allies had continued to dwindle.
'All business passes through the hands of people who depend
on the new Queen,' wrote the Bishop of Faenza, papal nuncio
in France, on 22 June 1535. There were now few she could trust.
Thomas Cromwell, had supplanted Gardiner as the King's Chief
Secretary in May 1534, to become the second most powerful
man in the kingdom; he was loyal to Henry, but was he loyal
to her? With the cold, emotionless Master Secretary Anne could
not be sure. Of late he was showing increasing friendship to
Chapuis, hunting and hawking with him where no one could
hear what was said, always visiting him at his house. Now that

the French were behaving so strangely, was he contemplating an alliance for England with the Emperor? In that case she would be done for. She appealed to the only human feeling Cromwell appeared to have: fear. If he betrayed her, Anne threatened, she would have his head off his shoulders. Cromwell, about to fill Henry's empty treasure chests with the confiscated wealth of the monasteries and consequently firmly in his good graces, was unshaken by the Queen's threat. Repeating it to Chapuis, Master Secretary remarked complacently that he believed the King would protect him.

After Cromwell, the most respected and experienced minister was the Duke of Norfolk, chief of the Privy Council. Anne's relationship with him, never good, had since January been one of mutual hatred. Anne had long suspected her uncle of aiming at the crown for his own descendants through a marriage between his poet son, the Earl of Surrey, and Catherine's daughter Mary. Repeatedly and in public over the years she had lectured him, a humiliation that the proud head of the Howard family found increasingly hard to stomach, his naturally violent temper worsened by chronic neuralgia. His conservatism was outraged by everything Anne stood for: her Lutheran beliefs, her interference in the masculine province of politics, her turbulent effect on the old order he loved. But caution and personal interest had so far kept his impatience under control.

Then in January Anne went too far. She hurled 'more insults' at him 'than one would address to a dog'. Norfolk left the room. He succeeded in containing his furious indignation until he was outside the door. Then it burst forth in a vicious splutter. 'My niece,' he informed a passing courtier, 'is a great whore.' Though spoken in anger, it was a revealing remark, showing the deep disaffection that lurked at the heart of one of Anne's seemingly most solid supporters.

In the able and eloquent Stephen Gardiner, Bishop of Winchester, Anne appears to have recovered some of her trust, although he was strongly anti-Protestant. And she still relied on Edward Fox, who with Gardiner had negotiated in Rome for the divorce and campaigned successfully for a verdict in its favour in Cambridge. Ostensibly still Anne's ardent supporter,

apparently attempting to persuade Catherine to accept Elizabeth
as heir to the throne, he had been rewarded by being made her
almoner and Bishop of Hereford. She did not know that while
helping to escort Mary to Hatfield in December 1533 he had
drawn near to her litter and begged her, in a low voice, for the
love of God to stay firm, otherwise all the kingdom was in
danger of ruin and perdition; Protestant though Fox was, it
did not stop him feeling that Anne's influence on the realm
would be disastrous. As for John Wallop, resident English
ambassador at the French Court, he was in secret communication with the papal nuncio.

The only ambassadors of whose loyalty Anne could be quite
sure were her father, the Earl of Wiltshire, whose fortunes were
linked with hers though she had lost his affection, and above all
her brother Lord Rochford, on whom she increasingly depended for friendship and reassurance, a talented and graceful
courtier but an inexperienced statesman.

Such was the inadequate, unreliable team with which Anne
faced the rest of Christendom in the summer of 1535, a world
suddenly shocked into almost total hostility by a series of
gruesome executions. As the sun warmed the muddy lanes and
cobbled streets of London a number of learned and saintly men
were dragged over them on hurdles to their deaths, news of
which appalled Protestants and Catholics alike. The deaths
were an inevitable result of Henry's religious policy and probably only indirectly due to Anne and his marriage to her, but
he accorded her the blame.

Over the past year, the King's commissioners riding up and
down the country had been administering the Oath of Succession. When they came to the monasteries, however, where the
monks were gathered in their chapter-houses, the commissioners demanded something more. Monks were required not
only to swear allegiance to Anne and her children; they must
also acknowledge that the King and not the Pope was supreme
head of the Church in England. It was this clause that devout
Catholics could not stomach. Henry's supremacy, once admitted, would rend Christendom for ever; beside such an issue,
the question of who succeeded to the throne was a small
matter. And it was because of Henry's claim and not Anne's

that some of the best men in England preferred a traitor's death to swearing the oath.

On 5 May 1535 three Carthusian priors and a Brigittine monk were dragged on hurdles through London to Tyburn, where Anne's father and brother, the Earl of Wiltshire and Lord Rochford, with the Dukes of Norfolk and Richmond and most of the Court, watched as the monks were hung, cut down alive, their robes and flesh ripped and hearts and entrails thrown on the fire. Afterwards their heads were cut off and 'their quarters set up in the highways and upon the gates of London'.

It was not the monstrous brutality of the executions that shocked Christendom; executions no less horrible took place before the King and Court in France, where one unfortunate heretic was burned to death as slowly as possible. It was the status of the victims. These were no obscure, half-crazed peasants, but men with European reputations for learning and virtue. They were followed to the scaffold by two men of great eminence who, for refusing to swear the oath admitting Henry's supremacy of the Church, had been imprisoned in the Tower: John Fisher, Bishop of Rochester, and Sir Thomas More.

Fisher had been Anne's outspoken enemy since the trial at Blackfriars when he had first championed Catherine. Sir Thomas More, on the other hand, venerated at home and abroad for his learning and saintliness, had never become an open opponent of the 'divorce', his only public gesture against the King's new policies being to resign the Chancellorship in May 1532. But though More's refusal to join her party must have angered Anne, there is no proof that she was responsible for his execution, as hostile writers suggest. Henry was always good at making other people take the blame for his cruellest actions and in this case offended vanity alone would have been enough for him to wish to punish More; the King had loved and admired him, but More had refused to do the royal will. As for Fisher, although Anne had probably made an earlier attempt on his life, we know from a report of Chapuis that the King himself finally brought about the old man's death.

In June 1535 King Henry heard that the Pope had created

Fisher a cardinal. Hotly, Henry exclaimed that he would send the head to Rome for the cardinal's hat. Fisher and More were beheaded on 22 June and 6 July 1535, their heads stuck up on London Bridge. Fisher was the first and last cardinal ever to be executed in England.

An incident that took place on the day of More's execution provides a revealing glimpse into Henry's true feelings for his new Queen at the time. Henry was at the gaming-table when word of More's death was brought to him. In sudden rage, he threw the dice away and turned to Anne who was standing by his side: 'This is long of you; the honestest man of my kingdom is dead.' Beneath his appearance of restored affection for Anne, the old grudge still rankled: the price he had paid for her was too high.

Henry had flung a similar accusation at her in May. Anne had returned a devastating answer. 'You should,' she said crushingly, 'be more bound to me than man can be to woman. Have I not extricated you from a state of sin? Made you the richest prince that ever was in England? And been the cause of your reforming the Church? To your own great profit and that of all the people?'

Anne spoke truth. She had in fact done him a very good turn. The chief result of the schism for Henry, a result beside which even the birth of a son became insignificant, was the infusion into his failing treasury of the wealth of the monasteries. Henry should indeed have been grateful to Anne - had gratitude been in his nature.

Papal reaction to the executions came swiftly. Henry's old enemy, harrowed, well-meaning, devious Pope Clement VII (that 'great devil' as Cromwell called him), had died in September 1534, to be replaced by Paul III. Clement's successor was a much more resolute character. He had spent the winter and spring in attempts by peaceful means to bring Henry back into the Catholic fold, but now, shocked by news of the two venerated heads that bristled above the tower at the north end of London Bridge, he decided on a militant policy. Ambassadors were despatched to Francis and the Emperor to seek their armed assistance. Pope Paul III decided to use the ultimate weapon in the papal armoury; he would launch a holy war against Henry and deprive him of his kingdom. The Emperor could henceforward march into England with the Pope's blessing and join forces with all the enemies of Queen Anne and the new regime. His army was engaged in attacking Tunis, which the Turks had captured the previous year; but should he be victorious, England was, for the first time since Anne became Queen, in real danger of invasion.

On all sides of England the storm clouds massed. Anne's chief friend and supporter in France, Jean du Bellay, with whom she used to hunt and watch the deer running in the royal parks, changed sides. In the early months of 1534 he had endeavoured to get Clement VII to ratify the 'divorce'. Now Anne heard he had accepted a cardinal's hat from Pope Paul, but she seems to have hidden her own anxieties. If she was to remain in the King's favour, she realized, she must make the King forget his political worries and with them his grudge against her for being, as he believed, their cause. Attempting to revive her old magic, she resorted to the kind of entertainment that had brought them together years ago. In one of her London houses Anne - reminiscent of Wolsey before his fall - staged elaborate feasts and mummings to distract the King; in vain. When the music and dancing stopped, when the wine fumes cleared, there were always new problems for him to face. Not the least of these was the monstrous scandal spreading over the country about Henry's incestuous relationship with the Boleyns. 'The King's grace had meddling with the Queen's mother...' 'Master Carey... was our sovereign Lord the King's son by our sovereign Lady the Queen's sister...' News of Henry's former affair with Mary Carey had unfortunately leaked out and this titbit of gossip was rendered still more spicy by the report that now also became current that the King had slept with Anne's mother. Such gossip helped to undermine still more Anne's already perilous position in the realm.

Even fear of a traitor's death could not stop people retailing so titillating a story. Nowhere outside Protestant circles was there any respect for the Queen, not even at Court. One of the King's fools called Anne a whore and Elizabeth a bastard. Hearing of it, the King, feeling royal dignity was at stake, went in search of him, swearing to kill him with his own hand;

the fool was hidden until Henry's wrath was past by Nicholas Carew, who with two other favoured courtiers had been chosen to accompany Anne and Henry on their unchaperoned hunting expeditions in the summer of 1531, although since 1530 he had secretly sympathized with Catherine. Now he dared openly to side against Anne, as did another of her friends, her cousin, the one-eyed Sir Francis Brian, Carew's brother-in-law. Even Anne's former suitor, the Earl of Northumberland, had seemingly lost all friendship for her; he was offended by her arrogant treatment of his fellow peer, the Duke of Norfolk, and by depredations the King had made on his lands, so Chapuis reports.

In the face of dwindling support at home and abroad, from where, apart from her inner source of desperate courage and pride, did the Queen draw her strength? She was cocooned to a certain extent against harsh reality by the affection and flattery of her women and favourite courtiers and by the ceaseless stream of suits for her favour from people who did not know her true situation.

The chief source of moral strength for Queen Anne, however, as for so many of her contemporaries, was her religion, the reformed religion that in England was still in the melting-pot, so that it was possible for Anne still to observe the Catholic sacraments of Mass and confession while being regarded by English Protestants as their patron. Their dependence on her and gratitude for her help was also something for her to hold on to. Her chaplain, Mathew Parker, whom she started on the road to power by creating Dean of Stoke in 1535, referred to her years later, when he was Queen Elizabeth's Archbishop of Canterbury, with affection and admiration; he it was who kept and bequeathed Anne's childhood letter to Corpus Christi College, Cambridge. The reformer, Sir John Cheke, later tutor to Edward VI, wrote to 'the most noble and magnificent Queen' to beg for funds to support William Bill, future Dean of Westminster, at Cambridge; Anne, he said, was famous for her liberality to the student protégés of her chaplains. On hearing that a merchant of Antwerp had lost his licence to trade with

England as a result of his part in the printing of Tyndale's New Testament, she commanded Thomas Cromwell to rectify the matter. As tangible proof of the Lutherans' regard for her the author of the translation himself presented her in 1534 with a fine illuminated black leather copy, still to be seen in the British Museum today. ANNA REGINA ANGLIÆ, the words in large red letters on the gilding of the leaves, have faded; but on the second title page inside, beyond the purple silk lining, gold angels still blow their trumpets above Anne's gilded coat of arms.

Anne was responsible for creating a string of Protestant bishops: Cranmer, Archbishop of Canterbury; Hugh Latimer, Bishop of Worcester; Nicholas Shaxton, Bishop of Salisbury; William Barlow, Bishop of St Asaph; and Edward Fox, Bishop of Hereford. To Cranmer, Latimer and Shaxton, Anne also lent money. 'My bishops', she referred to them with loving pride. She counted on them to vote for Thomas Cromwell's measures in Parliament. Deep down she counted on them to come to her own personal aid if ever the need arose. In the end she was to be utterly disillusioned.

But in the long summer days of 1535 the end was still mercifully hidden; Henry still seemed to be under her sway.


It was the 'grese season' when the pleasures of the hunt usually occupied the forefront of the King's mind. At the end of July Anne rode off triumphantly on progress with him, the sun glinting on the gold bosses of her harness, shining richly on black leather and black velvet, as in the days before her marriage. But the feelings of her companion about their relationship had changed. A man with a dominating mistress was the gallant hero of courtly romance; a husband with a dominating wife was ridiculous, and against the natural order that in the sixteenth century was believed in so rigidly.

This domestic situation, which would have irked any of his subjects, was intolerable to a King such as Henry had become. At forty-four, he was greatly altered from the man who had first wooed Anne in 1526; not only in outward appearance - his increased girth, the shrinking of his eyes to points of cun-

ning in the fullness of his face, the cruel set of the small thin
lips – but also in character. From the crucible of events, the
long years of argument with the Pope and the solution his
desires had thrust upon him, he had emerged a megalomaniac,
believing himself to be as Acts of Parliament had decreed him:
'the only supreme head on earth of the Church in England';
and a 'King having the dignity and estate of the Imperial
Crown'. The mythical origins of this last claim, based on a tale
that the Emperor Constantine had granted special privileges
to King Arthur, went unquestioned by Henry, who accepted
this concept of himself as Pope, Emperor and demi-god as his
due. Only one thing marred this pleasing and proper image in
the summer of 1535: his infuriating wife.

She seemed bent on making him appear a fool. She contradicted him in public, laughed at his clothes, his poems, sometimes appeared to be bored with him. The more pompous
Henry grew, the less, it seems, Anne could resist mocking him,
and such behaviour in the new Cæsar's eyes was unforgivable.
Her scornful laughter lodged in the tenderest part of Henry –
his vanity. It was not even as though Anne had kept her
looks; she was thin and worn, and worst of all barren; her last
pregnancy had ended in miscarriage like every other one
except the first. So unattractive had Anne become to him that
the demi-god had become incapable. Anne confided in Lady
Rochford that the King was impotent. It was something else
the King would not easily forgive when he learned of it, but
as usual the build-up of malevolence was hidden behind his
affable smile.

Hunting along the borders of Wales and into Wiltshire,
taking time off to inspect a few monasteries ripe for pillage,
Henry longed to replace his thin, nagging wife; he began to
look at other women again. In September the Court came to
lodge for a few days in Wolf Hall, where one of the daughters
of the house, a modest little woman of just over twenty-five,
had been maid of honour to Catherine, but was too pale and
quiet to have drawn royal notice among the vivacious beauties
at Court. Even here in the country, Henry's small blue eyes
would probably have glanced away quickly enough had not
something happened to fix her picture in his mind.

In the second week of September 1535 came a report that the Emperor had taken Tunis, crippling the sea power of the Ottoman Empire, securing the Imperial frontiers against the Turkish menace and freeing the Emperor's forces to fight, if he so wished, against England. To Henry, Anne and Cromwell, the news was a terrible shock. On hearing of it, Chapuis reported to his master, they appeared like 'dogs falling out of a window'. The King looked round for something to cheer him up, and saw the shy, demure face of a woman who was the complete opposite of the one who had caused him all this trouble. Her name was Jane Seymour. And she brought to King Henry visions of a relationship in which peace and tranquillity would reign in place of the turbulence and problems he had known with Anne.

# Chapter 24

# THE RIVAL

JANE SEYMOUR was one of the least remarkable women ever to play a part in history. Not as shy as first appeared, her more usual manner was a quiet, prim composure, and she had a certain shrewdness beneath the apparent humility. Of medium height, with pale hair and skin, eyes neither blue nor grey, a pointed chin with a roll of flesh beneath it, she was not pretty. Nor was she witty and, at twenty-five, by contemporary standards, not even very young. It is unlikely that Queen Anne worried much when she saw the King flirting with her at Wolf Hall. Or when her cousin, Sir Francis Brian, suggested that on Anne's return from progress, Jane should come to Court as one of her ladies.

Throughout the next two months, October and November, Anne lived in a fool's paradise. For the immediate effect of Henry's meeting with Jane at Wolf Hall was an upsurge of spirits and a renewal of vitality in his relationship with Anne; the new attraction had oddly enough given a last, dying kick to the old one. 'The King and Queen is merry and hawks daily and likes Winchester and that quarter and praises it much,' wrote Sir Richard Grenville to Lord Lisle on October 2; and on October 9 Sir Anthony Windsor said in a letter to him, 'The King and Queen were very merry in Hampshire.' From Friday, October 15 until October 19 they stayed together for four days in Lord Sandes's house, The Vine, and on October 26 moved back to Windsor. Henry kept Anne constantly with him. When on October 28 Lord Leonard Grey, before departing to quell rebellion in Ireland, where he was Chief Marshal of the army, came for a farewell audience with the King, Anne stood at the King's side. And when Henry gave Lord Leonard five hundred marks, land worth a hundred pounds and a ship,

Anne, not to be outdone in generosity, impulsively tore off a gold chain worth a hundred marks from around her waist and gave it to the Chief Marshal with a purse containing twenty sovereigns.

Much though Henry resented it, he could not avoid Anne dominating him when she was in his company; and Anne had made good use of her power, which caused some courtiers to believe that he was once more infatuated with her. Autumn had brought a disastrously poor harvest; the common people were heard to grumble that it was God's judgement on the King's marriage and the influence of the new Lutheran sect. Henry immediately ordered the preachers to pronounce that, on the contrary, God had sent the bad weather to punish those very grumblers. And at the beginning of November Henry's councillors were horrified to hear him threaten the lives of both his first wife and daughter. 'I will no longer remain in the trouble, fear and suspense I have so long endured on account of the Dowager Queen and the Lady Mary,' he stormed. 'You shall see, the coming Parliament will release me therefrom. I will wait no longer.

'Tears and wry faces are of no avail,' he went on, staring defiantly at the shocked expressions of his councillors, 'for even if I lose my crown I will not forbear to carry my purpose into effect.'

It began to look as though Anne, after two and a half years of browbeating Henry, was about to succeed in forcing him to have Catherine and Mary executed. Just as she saw herself at last sitting securely on the throne, Jane Seymour arrived at Court and the vision was snatched away.


Jane seems almost at once to have recaptured Henry's attention. Now Anne, in her turn, suffered the humiliation of seeing her maid of honour wear the King's gifts as, long ago, Catherine had suffered when Anne herself - less discreet than Jane - had flaunted her young beauty in the King's satins and velvets, his diamonds flashing round her neck. Fortune's wheel had come full circle.

By herself Jane Seymour would have been no match for

Anne. But Jane was loyal to her first mistress, Catherine, and
to the Catholic interest, which made her the tool of the Imperialist party - and this included at that date her able, ambitious brother, Edward. The Imperialist party was determined
not to allow Jane to repeat the mistake made by the previous
object of Henry's desires, the nameless beauty who had become
his mistress in the summer of 1533 and the winter of 1534.
Five years older than his sister, Edward was in a peculiarly
favourable position to coach her in the art of keeping the King's
fickle affections. As Esquire to the Body from September 1530,
Edward Seymour had been one of the King's most intimate
attendants and friends in the years when Henry's passion for
Anne was at its height.

Sharing Henry's leisure hours, often in Anne's company,
Seymour had observed her technique: how she kept the King's
passion simmering by flirting heavily but never sleeping with
him. Now with the help of Sir Francis Brian and Nicholas
Carew, who had also been members of that little group of
favourites, he passed on the rules of the game to his sister. And
Jane, who, within the limits of her loyalties was malleable, did
exactly as she was told. King Henry quickly became besotted
with her.

Entering a room one day, Queen Anne discovered Jane
Seymour, her maid of honour, sitting on her husband's lap.
Anne had still not learned to shrug off such occurrences;
besides, by this time she probably realized the use to which
Jane was being put by her enemies. Fear as usual found vent
in fury. Forgetting the dignity and restraint proper to her
high rank, she resorted not merely to words but to violence,
violence that according to a reliable source was repeated. 'There
was often much scratching and by-blows between the Queen
and her maid,' says the chronicler of the life of Jane Dormer,
Duchess of Feria.

Henry took refuge from Anne's recriminations in offended
silence and avoidance. From the beginning of December he
would, when ceremony required, appear together with her in
public; he would stand or sit beside her in Chamber of Presence
and at dining board, but he would speak to her only in mono-
syllables. That Anne had conceived a child in the happy hunting

days of October made no difference; Henry knew now what to expect from Anne's pregnancies.

His affection for her was further eroded by fear of invasion. It was Anne's great misfortune that Henry's infatuation for Jane Seymour coincided with a crisis in his relations with the two main European powers at a time when the militant Pope Paul III was bent on his destruction. Threateningly the Pope ranted: 'God has placed me above Emperors, Kings and Princes. I will not spare them.'

Paul's threats had seemed to Henry little more than bombast in the summer and autumn when, it appeared, he had no one to execute them. The panic which he had experienced briefly on hearing in September of the Emperor's victory over the Turks had been dispelled a few weeks later by a most opportune political event: on October 24 the Duke of Milan, ruler of that Italian state which had long been a bone of contention between France and Spain, had died, thus bringing these two great powers to the brink of conflict. French forces marched into territory belonging to the Duke of Savoy; the next move would be over the Alps into Italy. With a full-scale war imminent between these two powers, Henry believed that not only would his shores be immune from invasion, but also that an alliance with England would be eagerly sought again by France.

Confidently Henry waited for the French to come begging for help. To his astonishment, no such request reached the eager ears of his ambassadors. Instead, the French explained with an embarrassed attempt at tact that although they valued English friendship, an alliance with the Pope, in view of their Italian interests, was still more essential. By Christmas 1535 England seemed isolated indeed and her future bleak. The consistory of cardinals in Rome on December 10 had passed Pope Paul's bull declaring Henry deprived of his kingdom, a sentence to be published as soon as the Pope found a monarch willing and able to implement it.

Against all expectation and despite the confrontation with France, the Emperor Charles now seriously contemplated launching a holy war against England. Should he do so, King Francis had secretly promised the Pope he would fight under the holy banner. Distracted by the kingdom's desperate situation, King Henry, who never blamed himself for anything, found anger and frustration mounting inside him against Anne, who was, he felt, responsible for the whole disastrous situation. Anne and Catherine – his two wives. Neither had been any use to him.

England would be at the invader's mercy, since she now had no friends. But it was not only the French alliance that was in ruins. In November King Henry had had to abandon a cherished vision of another alliance that would have made him independent of both Francis and Charles: a great northern Protestant confederacy based on Lübeck, most powerful of the Hanseatic towns in Germany. Secretly, King Henry had subsidized the army of Lübeck when it marched into Denmark to enforce an ancient right to nominate that country's King; for Denmark and Lübeck together were to form the nucleus of Henry's new ally.

It was, we can see today, an unrealistic dream, but his belief in it had for the two years of Anne's reign helped to make him feel he could keep her as his Queen without bringing disaster on the kingdom.

When in the summer of 1535 Lübeck's forces were flung out of Denmark and the party he had befriended, led by Burgomaster Jürgen Wullenwever, lost power in Lübeck's council, King Henry had refused to give up hope. But when in November Wullenwever himself was captured and imprisoned by his enemies, the King was rudely awakened to the truth: there was no alternative to a French or an Imperial alliance. But because of his present Queen both were now impossible. Somehow his marriage must be terminated. By January 1536 Anne was fearfully aware that the King waited only for the right opportunity to discard her.

On January 7 came an event that at first appeared to Anne to be her salvation. For some weeks there had been reports that Catherine of Aragon – who for two years, rather than suffer the indignity of being addressed as Princess Dowager instead of

Queen, had refused to set foot outside her Bed Chamber - was ill. Her disease, according to modern medical opinion, was cancer of the heart, but contemporary gossip would point to poison. Now she was dying.

Early in the morning of 7 January 1536 she dictated a final letter to Henry. Alluding to his disastrous love for Anne, she begged him to remember 'the health and safeguard of your soul which you ought to prefer . . . before the care and pampering of your body for the which you have cast me into many calamities and yourself into many troubles'. She ended: 'Lastly I make this vow that mine eyes desire you above all things. Farewell.' And, obdurate to the end, she signed herself firmly, 'Katherine, Queen of England.'

At two o'clock on Friday afternoon died the woman who more than anyone else had robbed Anne of the fruits of her triumph. With excited joy Anne received the news that she had achieved what she had schemed and plotted for during the past two and a half years: at last she was the only Queen in England. She gave the messenger a rich reward. But later, in her room, she wept. She realized that Catherine's death had come too late to save her, that it actually put her in greater danger than ever. The sole reason Henry had not divorced her before was that he would have had to take back Catherine in order to get on good terms with the Emperor, but now, should he divorce her, he would be free to marry the woman of his choice.

Were he to marry Jane Seymour, what would be Anne's fate?

Anne was beginning to understand what her predecessor had suffered. She had begun to follow in Catherine's footsteps. Already, she had known the pain and humiliation of being ousted from the King's favour by one of her own ladies. How much more of Catherine's sad path would she have to tread? Would she be deprived of her daughter's company? Moved to ever more distant and dismal houses in the hope that she would die? 'I am afraid,' Anne prophetically told her ladies, 'they may do with me as with the Dowager Princess.'

In public, however, she matched Henry's gaiety; Anne could always put on a brave show. She appeared in a gown of bright yellow to match Henry's own gay mourning clothes which, save for the flaunting white feather in his cap, were all in the same brilliant hue.

Henry's delight at his first Queen's death was uncomplicated and exuberant. 'God be praised,' he exclaimed, 'that we are free from all suspicion of war!' On Sunday afternoon he entered the room where the ladies danced, and joined in the sport, leaping and capering 'like one transported with joy'. Then he called for little Elizabeth, who was staying temporarily at the Court and, carrying her about in his arms, presented her for the admiration of each courtier in turn.

Henry's display of affection for Elizabeth must have raised a glimmer of hope in Anne who had known so many vicissitudes. If she could at last bear the son she was sure she carried in her womb! Already she was nearly three months pregnant. More than anything in the world she wanted a son. Should she succeed in bearing one this time, she was supremely confident of regaining the King's favour.

She could only wait, but meantime there just might be another way to recapture it: she could try again to rid him of one of his most irksome problems, that of his daughter Mary's defiance.

Anne would still have preferred to have Mary killed; as recently as October she had urged the King 'to treat her as the Bishop of Rochester has been treated'. But Jane Seymour and the altered balance of power in Europe had softened Henry's feelings, so at present, Anne realized, that was no longer a possible solution. She resorted therefore to her alternative tactic of bribery. Forcing herself to ignore all Mary's previous insolent rebuffs, Anne sent a message through Lady Shelton in the hope that Catherine's death would have made Mary more amenable. Anne offered to be a second mother to Mary, to obtain for Mary anything she wanted, if only she would submit and come to Court; she would not even make her carry her train. Mary's reply, was as rude and intransigent as ever, ignoring Anne's very existence. She would, she told her governess pointedly, do anything her 'father' commanded except what was against her honour and conscience. On receipt of this message Anne must have had to struggle to control her wrath and remember that more important matters than her pride were at stake. She tried again, this time sending a letter to Lady Shelton and asking her to leave it as though by mistake in Mary's private oratory. Patently transparent in its cunning, the missive shows what desperate and unlikely measures Anne was reduced to taking.

Mrs Shelton, my pleasure is that you do not further move the Lady Mary to be towards the King's grace otherwise than it pleases herself [she wrote]. What I have done has been more for charity than for anything the King or I care what road she takes, or whether she will change her purpose, for if I have a son, as I hope shortly, I know what will happen to her; and therefore, considering the Word of God, to do good to one's enemy, I wished to warn her beforehand, because I have daily experience that the King's wisdom is such as not to esteem her repentance of her rudeness and unnatural obstinacy when she has no choice. By the law of God and of the King, she ought clearly to acknowledge her error and evil conscience if her blind affection had not so blinded her eyes that she will see nothing but what pleases herself. Mrs Shelton, I beg you not to think to do me any pleasure by turning her from any of her wilful courses, because she could not do me [good] or evil; and do your duty about her according to the King's command, as I am assured you do . . .

Of course, the trick was ineffective. Mary gave no sign at all of having read the letter. In fact, she made a copy to send to Chapuis before putting it back where she found it. Her mother's death had not altered Mary's determination never to make friends with Catherine's supplanter.

Anne's sole hope now lay in the son she was sure she carried. Even Henry had begun to feel that this time the pattern of miscarriages might be broken and the pregnancy reach term; his hopes had recently been sharpened by a reminder of his own mortality.

In his joy at Catherine's death the King had organized a joust for January 24, the Eve of St Paul's, in which he himself took part, arriving on the field as usual on these occasions, preceded by a magnificent procession. First came the Marshal of the Jousts,

> on horseback, dressed in cloth of gold, and surrounded by thirty footmen in liveries of yellow and blue. Then . . . drummers and trumpeters, all dressed in white damask; next forty knights and lords in pairs . . . then 'some twenty young knights on very fine horses, all dressed in white, with doublets of cloth of silver and white velvet, and chains of unusual size, and their horses barded with silver chainwork, and a number of pendent bells'.
>
> Next came their pages, on horseback, their trappings, half of gold embroidery, and half of purple velvet, embroidered with stars; and then the jousters, armed, with their squires and footmen. Last of all came his Majesty, 'armed cap-a-pie, with a surcoat of silver bawdakin, surrounded by some thirty gentlemen on foot, dressed in velvet and white satin'.

Twice round the lists they went, then the jousting began; the sun flashed from the King's armour as he thundered towards an opponent. Suddenly, in place of the usual cheers as his lance struck home, came shouts of dismay. For it was the King who lay there, so still that people feared he was dead. When two hours later he came round from this apparently severe concussion, he was unharmed. But this accident which could easily have been fatal must have underlined for him the importance of having an undisputed heir to the throne.

On January 29, the day Catherine was to be buried with no more than the ceremony appropriate to a princess dowager, Anne was three and a half months pregnant. By an extraordinarily cruel coincidence, as Catherine's lead coffin was interred in Peterborough Abbey, Anne lay in premature childbed at Greenwich. The news was brought to Henry. The Queen had miscarried of his child, the long-awaited son. Henry was overwhelmed by grief and anger.

Making his way through her apartments to the ill-ventilated chamber where she still lay in pain, he glowered down at her.

'I see clearly that God does not wish to give me male children . . .' His words were an ominous echo. To Anne, who had heard the King utter similar thoughts when he first considered divorcing Catherine, his meaning must have been plain: God does not wish to give me sons by you; He might by another Queen.

She roused herself to protest. It was not God's doing, she said. There was good cause for her miscarriage: she had been alarmed at news of the King's fall; the Duke of Norfolk had broken it too roughly. And she had been upset by the King's unfaithfulness. 'Because the love I bear you is much greater and more fervent than Catherine's,' she pleaded passionately, 'my heart broke when I saw that you loved others.'

Once such a declaration would have filled Henry with romantic ecstasy, now it simply annoyed him. This wretched woman had not only miscarried of his son, she also had the temerity to suggest that the miscarriage was his fault. 'I will speak to you when you are recovered,' he said threateningly, and strode from the room.

The silence Henry left behind in Anne's chamber was broken by the wails of her women. Anne rallied from her own despair to comfort them: 'It is all for the best, I shall be the sooner with child again, and the son I bear will not be doubtful like this one, which was conceived during the life of the Princess Dowager.' Her words were a brave lie; the King had slept with her for the last time.

She may already have heard what he had confided to one of his councillors: 'I was seduced into this marriage by sorcery, therefore I believe it to be null. God has shown this to be so because He will not permit me to have sons. I believe I could take another wife . . .' It was a bit of gossip to make Anne shudder.

Although Henry's superstitions were not grounds enough for divorce, even in the credulous sixteenth century, it was only a matter of time before he found a more valid reason. Now that he had made his wish so clear some ambitious adviser would find a means to accomplish it.

From then on Anne lived in dread. She could not know what her fate would be - that of Catherine, or something worse. Or whence the blow would come. But the prophecies she had laughed at must have rung in her head.

*When the tower is white and another place green*
*Then shall be burned two or three bishops and a queen.*
*And after all this be passed we shall have a merry world.*

'They have not burned me yet,' Anne had often repeated defiantly since her coronation. But there was still time for the prophecy to be fulfilled.

# Chapter 25

# MASTER SECRETARY'S PLOT

THE month of February 1536 was for Anne the lull before the coming storm. For the Shrove Tuesday celebrations Henry rode off to London without her. She was left behind at Greenwich Palace to speculate on her fate. What scheme for her destruction was even now working itself out behind the King's small cunning eyes? She knew how brutally he could use those he once loved. A procession of his victims must have passed and re-passed through her mind: More, Wolsey, Catherine, his own elder daughter, Mary . . .

As she moved about the great rooms of the Queen's suite at Greenwich Palace, stared out over the courtyard with the conduit that had been painted jasper, gold and blue for her coronation, Anne must have known that her days there were numbered, that soon another queen would walk beneath her gilded ceilings, sit in her velvet-covered chairs, lie on the bed that had belonged to a Duke of Alençon.

Indiscreet as ever, Anne did not hide her fear. 'The King will marry again,' she declared often, 'he will do with me as with the dead Queen,' and her shrill terror found its way into Chapuis's despatches. But in the sixteenth century there was a haven for the troubled spirit, if not the body. Anne took her fears to her chaplains.

She began to arm herself in an ecstasy of faith against anything that could happen to her, an effort in which she doubtless was supported by her brother, an increasingly ardent disciple of the Lutheran faith. Now, it seems, Anne really began to appreciate the true meaning of religion independent of its trappings. And of her new concern with virtue there is one revealing sign. During Henry's suppression of the religious houses, she tried to persuade him to spare the priory of Catesby A request peremptorily refused by the King, its interest lies in the character of the prioress – no Eleanor Carey this time, with a questionable past, but a woman renowned for her goodness. Had Anne lived to reach mature years instead of dying at the age of twenty-eight, had she succeeded in establishing her position so as to be at last free of perpetual desperate anxiety, she might yet have become a responsible Queen.

Another of Anne's preoccupations which helped her to survive this grim winter of waiting is revealed by a list of her personal expenses. By now her positive emotions had few outlets left. Most of her friends had deserted her. That winter she had also lost little Purkoy, on whom she had so doted that, when the dog died of a fall, no one dared tell her; until the King himself undertook the task. Now her love centred on her daughter, as we can tell from the money and care she lavished on Elizabeth's clothes.

On January 18, so her expenses record, she had hired a boat to take a messenger from Greenwich Palace to London, where the Princess was staying, to have her small head measured for caps and to fetch her purple satin cap 'to mend it'. Did Anne intend to do the work herself rather than leave it to less careful hands? If so, the garment must have been past mending, for on February 19 Anne paid for a replacement purple cap, 'laid with a rich caul of gold, the work being roundels of damask gold'. It was followed on March 10 by a crimson fringe for the Princess's cradle head; and on March 20 by a white satin cap 'laid with a rich caul of gold, price £4; and another of crimson satin, £3 13s 4d'. Anne's motherhood was one possession the King could not take away from her.

She had need now to cling to her religion and the thought of her daughter; for she was almost in Catherine's situation of eight years ago. When, in February, Henry left Anne behind at Greenwich, he left Jane there too. But ardent lover that he was, he did not leave her without news of him. It was Anne's turn to gaze anxiously from the great windows, to listen for the sound of hoofbeats or the splash of oars that meant the King's token was arriving for the woman who was supplanting her.

Jane had already accepted rich gifts from him. Suddenly in March she changed her tactics. The King, still in London, busy with Parliament and the suppression of the smaller monasteries, sent Jane a letter and a purse of gold sovereigns. Jane refused the gift. The story soon spread round the Court and must have filled Anne with dismay; for it was so obviously the final move in the game. After kissing the letter Jane was said to have returned it unopened. Then she fell on her knees before the messenger. She begged him 'to pray the King . . . to consider . . . that I am a gentlewoman of good and honourable parents without reproach. I have no greater riches in the world than my honour which for a thousand deaths I would not hurt. If his Grace wishes to make me a present of money I beg him to do it when God might have sent me a good marriage.' Jane had followed her instructions well. The hint was not lost on Henry. The King returned a message that he considered Jane had behaved very virtuously and, to show her that his love for her was honest, he would converse with her from now on only in the presence of her relations. Cromwell would give up his chambers to Edward Seymour and his wife; here in their company he would visit her. Henry chose Cromwell's chambers as a place to woo his new mistress not only for their magnificence but also for their secrecy of approach, for they were connected to the King's apartments by private galleries, which would enable him to visit his beloved unseen.

So when Henry returned to Greenwich Anne was spared the mortification of discovering her maid of honour again on her husband's lap in one of her own rooms. Instead, she had the certainty that behind Sir Edward Seymour's closed doors her enemies were filling the King's ears with lies.

Their plan was a simple one. Eager though he was to get rid of Anne, the King was hesitating. He needed to be convinced that it would be a popular move. No one, it seemed, had yet dared to tell him this, mindful that to speak against the King's marriage was treason. The privacy of Seymour's room provided the Imperial party with their opportunity; Jane was to be their spokesman. 'Your marriage to Anne is considered an abomination by all the people, no one thinks it legitimate.'

Jane was to drop this carefully considered bombshell when the room was full of members of the Imperial party, so that when the King turned to ask for another opinion - as he usually did when a controversial statement was made – these men would be all ready to 'swear on their allegiance' that Jane spoke truth.

There is no reason to doubt that their plan, reported by Chapuis to the Emperor, was carried out.

Soon Jane and Henry were discussing their future like a King and his bride-to-be. When she became Queen, Jane said, she would like to have the King's elder daughter, Lady Mary, reinstated as heir to the throne. 'You are a fool,' Henry told her fondly. 'You ought to think of the children we shall have together . . .' Piously Jane replied, 'I was thinking about the repose and tranquillity of Your Grace as well as of the children we shall have.' These words were spoken, according to Chapuis, when Anne was still the King's legal wife; when no charge had yet been brought against her, still less proved. They testify that the plot to replace her on the throne was already a fact and that only the details needed completing.

But still more alarming in their implications for Anne than the activities behind Sir Edward Seymour's closed doors were the signs that she had been deserted by the ruthless genius who had enabled her to marry the King when no one else could, the minister who had revolutionized the English Church, no less, in order to force her as Queen on a hostile people: Thomas Cromwell, who seemingly could accomplish anything he desired. Cromwell had suddenly taken to lifting his cap when the name of the King's elder daughter, Lady Mary, was even mentioned. In March – another ominous sign of his Imperial leanings – Cromwell was actually heard to condemn the new Act of Parliament suppressing the monasteries, a measure he had himself initiated. Anne accused him to his face of plotting against her, and though no record exists of Cromwell's reply his manner must have been very different from the subservience he had practised towards her in former days; for by April it was common knowledge at Court that the Queen and Master Secretary were on bad terms.

Cromwell's reasons for turning against Anne were not personal; he admired her intelligence and courage, may even have liked her. It was simply that as Queen of England she would not fit in with the policy he had in mind and for Cromwell, true to his Machiavellian principles, individuals were always expendable for the general good. Chief minister in England throughout Anne's reign, he had long ceased to be just a shadowy figure behind the throne, automatically performing the King's will; he had emerged an independent statesman with his own views. And ever since February he had been convinced that in view of the unreliability of the French during the past year, the only viable policy for England was an alliance with the Emperor. It was the only way to insure England against the risk that she might one day find the two great powers of Europe lined up together against her. Despite the territorial rivalries between France and Spain, there had recently been disturbing signs that this could happen. Now Catherine's death had removed the main obstacle to an alliance with the Emperor, and although there were other major points of disagreement, over these, so Cromwell had promised Chapuis in February at a secret meeting in the church of the Augustine Friars, he was determined to persuade Henry to compromise. If this policy meant getting rid of Anne, Cromwell was prepared to do it.

Anne had lost her last ally. Nemesis could not delay much longer. But for the woman whose ship of fate had already suffered so many vicissitudes yet another calm was in store. A final moment of hope before the storm finally dashed her fragile bark to pieces. It came from an unexpected source.

On Easter Sunday Chapuis told Cromwell he had received new instructions from the Emperor. He requested an audience with the King, which was fixed for Tuesday, April 18. Meanwhile, Anne learned what the audience was to be about. The Emperor wished to make an alliance with England against France. He was prepared to treat not only with Henry, but also with Anne.*

The news seemed to revolutionize Anne's prospects. It plunged her and her brother, Lord Rochford, now ever more frequently in her company, into wild hope and excitement. Four years ago in 1532 Anne had declared proudly that even if Charles V should offer her the crown she would not accept it

* Chapuis had, in fact, secretly been instructed only to treat with Anne if King Henry had not already decided to take another Queen.

from such hands. Now she seized avidly on this one chance to acquire a powerful ally. She would use her irresistible charm to conquer Chapuis, and through him the Emperor.

At six o'clock on Tuesday morning Lord Rochford received Chapuis at the Palace gate when he arrived apparently to negotiate with the Queen he had described caustically in his letters to his master as 'the concubine' or 'the lady'. Rochford's charm could be as potent as his sister's. Now it flooded over Chapuis, only slightly marred by some outspoken remarks in favour of the Lutheran religion. Anne sent a message begging him to come and kiss her cheek, a courtesy reserved for the most favoured ambassadors only. In vain she waited for him to accept her invitation. To make up for her disappointment, however, she expected to have a further opportunity of winning him over.

The formal audience with the King was arranged for the afternoon. First, Chapuis was invited to go to Mass and dine at Court. On entering the chapel Anne looked for him and, on observing him behind the door, turned right round and made a low curtsey: Chapuis bowed deeply in response. During the ceremonies, doubtless at her request, he offered her two candles. A hopeful sign? Or just the respect of one enemy for another? She anticipated speaking with him in her apartments, where the King and the other ambassadors were to dine that day. But as she walked with the King from the chapel, she was dismayed to see that the favoured group crowding through the doorway leading upstairs to her suite did not include Chapuis. 'Why does he not enter, like the other ambassadors?' she asked.

'It is not without good reason,' replied her husband crushingly.

His tight little mouth closed and he resumed the habitual grim and hurtful silence that was his armour against her. She was not, after all, to have a chance to use her charm on the Imperial ambassador; he had gone at the King's command to dine with the chief courtiers in his Chamber of Presence. Over her own dinner-party Anne presided in suspense and anxiety. That Chapuis had not been asked to dine with her was a bad omen. Henry was making it clear that there was no need to consider her interests in any agreement made between himself and Charles V. Anne did the only thing she possibly could to influence Chapuis in her favour. She loudly proclaimed that she had abandoned the French and was now on the side of the Emperor.

'It is a great shame in the King of France to treat his uncle, the Duke of Savoy, as he does,' she said fervently. 'And to make war against Milan, so as to break the enterprise against the Turks. It really seems that the King of France, weary of his life on account of his illnesses, wishes by war to put an end to his days.' She knew Chapuis had spies everywhere and that her words would reach him.

After satisfying appearances by dining with his Queen, Henry left her and went to his Chamber of Presence, where Chapuis in the semi-privacy of the great bay window communicated his master's terms. Their words were inaudible, but the King's reaction was plain: the terms were impossible. He refused even to consider them and brusquely dismissed the Imperial ambassador. At least, the King had made no agreement that did not include her; Anne must have been relieved at that news, less relieved to hear the sequel.

Afterwards Cromwell had argued the issue heatedly with the King, so set on the Imperial alliance that he had braved the royal wrath. Breaking off the discussion at last with the excuse that he was too thirsty to continue, Cromwell called for wine and, puffing and snorting with frustration, went to sit on a chest out of Henry's sight. Then he had ridden home to his house crammed with rare treasures in Throgmorton Street, flung himself on his great bed and told his servants to tell the world he had a fever; he needed time to think and to plan.


Of what went on in Cromwell's active brain as he tossed restlessly beneath the silken canopy, Anne, fortunately for her peace of mind, was unaware. For we know, from Cromwell's own confession, that as he lay there he was finally, irretrievably deciding her fate, and the plot that would send her to her death.

Anne must go, he had decided; for two reasons. The first was a matter of statecraft: the Queen was still the stumbling-block in the way of the Imperial alliance. He knew that although in theory Charles V was prepared to treat with Anne, in practice any agreement while she was Queen would be impossible.

Charles V wished Mary to be recognized as legitimate. Anne would never permit it. Charles wished Henry to submit to the Pope. Henry would never agree; for he had already shored up his shaky finances with the proceeds from the sale of the lands of many of the smaller monasteries and he looked forward to making his treasury even more stable by suppressing the rest.

But he might satisfy Charles by compromising on the more extreme changes in religious observance if his Lutheran Queen no longer sat at his side. And without Anne, he might be kinder to Mary.

Cromwell's second reason for plotting against Anne was undoubtedly a personal and selfish one. By contradicting the King on the subject of the Imperial alliance he had incurred the King's wrath that was proverbially death. It would be a wise moment to prove his usefulness. What better way than to enable the King to marry Jane Seymour? That this was the King's chief desire, Cromwell had known for more than two weeks now. He had hinted as much to Chapuis in the last week of March, when the ambassador questioned him about the rumour that the King might change his wife: 'Although the King has formerly been rather fond of the ladies,' he had said, 'I believe he will henceforth live more chastely and not change again . . .' His tone was coldly ironic, and he turned his face to the window as though to hide a smile. 'The French,' he added, 'may be assured of one thing, if the King, my master, were to take another wife, he would not seek for her among them.'

Queen Anne must be disposed of, but how? Cromwell must already have discussed the question with Henry, who intended to use as an excuse the old accusation of a pre-contract with the Earl of Northumberland, proof of which he had begun to collect when Anne was in disgrace the previous year. The scheme, Cromwell recognized, was a poor one. For while the pre-contract might be true, Henry in the days of his love for Anne had managed to persuade everyone that it was not. The Earl had been examined upon oath before the Archbishops of

Canterbury and York, as well as before the Duke of Norfolk and the King's Council, and his denial of a pre-contract had been accepted.

On what other grounds could Anne be removed from her position of Queen? As Cromwell lay surrounded by his art treasures in Throgmorton Street the solution suddenly came to him: treason. There was a prophecy in Flanders of a plot against the King's life. Why should not Anne be accused of that? In truth she had cause. Anne's little group of friends in Henry's Privy Chamber could be accused at the same time. Thus no one would be left to plead for her, or pronounce her sentence unjust.

Cromwell's plan for Anne's end showed the same boldness as had his original scheme for making her Queen. It was unsentimental but tidy; it would leave no loose ends. Cromwell must have been pleased with his solution. If he spared a thought for his innocent victims it was quickly rationalized away. For pity was no part of his job and Cromwell was, above all, efficient. Cynically so. Councillors, he had remarked to Reginald Pole, should manage their prince's affairs 'in such sort as they might obtain their ends, and yet no open failure in religion or probity be observed . . . A minister should be able to reconcile the appearance of virtue, which princes are unwilling to give up, with the substantial interest of the state.' He had been prepared to sacrifice Anne for some time. What did a few more scapegoats matter?

For five days, while the world believed Cromwell to be ill, he was working out the details of his plot. On April 23 he emerged from his house. He at once drew up a secret commission, empowering Henry's leading nobles, officers of the royal household and nine judges to enquire into a long list of treasonable acts 'by whomsoever committed' and to try the offenders.

King Henry put his name to the commission the following day. It was virtually Anne's death warrant.

At the same time Cromwell set about collecting the 'evidence' that would enable him to use it. One by one, clandestinely, against a background of menace, he questioned the Queen's ladies: Lady Rochford, Anne's nervous, unstable sister-in-law;

the Countess of Worcester, Anne's closest favourite who would know anything there was to know; Nan Cobham . . . These are the only names that have come down to us, probably there were many others who, influenced by loyalty to Catherine and Mary, by jealousy, or Cromwell's threats and bribes, were eager to give him the information for which he asked. They gave him more. Cromwell's questions undammed a flood of scurrilous gossip and female slander that persuaded him to change the nature of the treason charge he would bring against Anne.

From the accusations later advanced at her trial, it is easy to reconstruct what happened. The questions Cromwell put to Anne's ladies concerned occasions when Anne had been alone in conversation with her friends, those gentlemen of the King's Privy Chamber whom she had known for years, whom she had diced and danced and flirted with long before she was married. Cromwell's informers could only twice remember Anne alone with a particular group of courtiers; but they could remember times when she had been alone with each in turn; and moments when she had exchanged presents with them and indulged in suggestive conversation.

On the basis of this information, Cromwell decided she should be accused not only of a plot against the King's life; she should also be accused of adultery.

A story later spread abroad by Anne's enemies held that her adultery came to light when a courtier, accusing his sister (who was one of Anne's ladies) of immorality, received the reply that her behaviour was nothing compared to the Queen's. This courtier then allegedly reported the conversation to the Council. That this was the origin of the treason charge against Anne is obviously untrue; it is contradicted by Cromwell's own confession to Chapuis that he was himself the author of the plot against Anne. But the lady of the Bed Chamber's comparison of her own behaviour to the Queen's may well be true, and typical of the vague insinuations that met Cromwell's ears as he questioned Anne's attendants. Insinuations that must have delighted him and filled him with new confidence in the success of his plot. For adultery was the one charge that the majority of the English people would accept. Had they not thought of her all these years as the 'great whore'? This was much more likely to stick than a charge of conspiracy.

There did indeed remain the problem of evidence. None of Anne's traducers could produce any actual proof. But given the climate of opinion against Anne even the slenderest suggestions of adultery would suffice: a suggestive word, a flirtatious look. From such insubstantial threads of evidence would he weave a web strong enough to entrap the Queen of England. The resourceful Cromwell set his omnipresent spies to watch her.

# Chapter 26

# MAY DAY

THE weather in the last week of April 1536 was hot and breathless. The sun flooded through the great windows, glittered on
the rich hangings of the Queen's apartments in Greenwich
Palace. Anne was so much filled with a foreboding of her own
end that she sought out her chaplain, Mathew Parker, and
asked, if anything should happen to her, whether he would
take special care of her daughter Elizabeth. But such thoughts
were too gloomy to dwell on. Volatile as ever, she fled from
them to the giddy triumphant delights of her youth, the
excitement and comfort of flirtation and male flattery which
had always served to fill the hollow places in her heart.

Anne had for years been on terms of friendship with the
gentlemen of Henry's Privy Chamber, well born, entertaining,
cultivated young men who shared his leisure hours and
favourite pastimes. Three of these now continued to visit her
in her Presence Chamber when wiser men had deserted it for
Jane Seymour's company. They were Sir Henry Norris, Sir
Francis Weston and Sir William Bryerton, men she had known
ever since her first arrival at the English Court. With these men
Anne had hunted and hawked, danced and gambled; in their
company she had listened to the music of the King's minstrels
and the witticisms of his fools; and, foreshadowing the habits
of her daughter, the future Queen Elizabeth, she seems also to
have encouraged them to take part in an elaborate charade of
courtly love. It was a charade which involved presents of money
and jewels on her part and pledges and trinkets on theirs - and
which had been going on with the King's approval at least
since her visit to Calais in 1532. But it amounted to nothing
more than flattery, flirtatious words and the kind of social
kisses that were conventionally acceptable at the English
Court.

Now, however, Cromwell proposed to make ruthless use of this charade. The pretence should become the reality. Soon his spies - the ladies of Anne's household he had succeeded in frightening or corrupting - had something to report.

On April 23 - the very day Cromwell emerged from his house - they saw the Queen talking, laughing and exchanging flirtatious glances with young, attractive Sir Francis Weston, the Court's star athlete and Anne's favourite partner at the card table. Anne's innocent conversation was to have terrifying repercussions. She discussed with Weston the love- life of Sir Henry Norris, another of her favourites. It was a topic frivolous and titillating enough to take her mind off her fears.

Norris, whose first wife had died, had begun negotiations to marry Madge Shelton, Anne's pretty and obliging cousin and Henry's ex-mistress, but he hesitated to take the final step. What could be the reason? Anne wondered now aloud. The most probable cause, as Weston knew, was that the Boleyns were in disgrace, consequently marriage with a member of the family might be unwise. Too smooth a courtier, however, to blurt out to the Queen this unpalatable truth, he seized on a more pleasing reason for Norris's delay. 'Norris,' he said, 'comes more into your chamber for Your Grace than he does for Madge.'

This compliment was balm to Anne's vanity, wounded by the King's desertion. But the thought of Madge, one of the prettiest of her ladies, stung her with sharp and sudden jealousy. At twenty-eight, Anne was visibly ageing, thin and worn from anxiety and continuous miscarriages. Less attractive now than Madge? Unbearable thought for a woman not only vain but dependent on her sexual appeal for her status and very safety. She had to put it at once to the test. Weston himself, she reminded him archly, had said he did not love his wife. Was he then also in love with Madge?

Weston knew what was expected of him. 'I love one in your house better than them both,' said the young courtier gallantly.

'Who is that?' asked Anne, with a delicious flutter of anticipation.

'It is yourself,' replied Weston.

Anne, who had led him up to this, realized it had gone too

far. He was uttering nonsense, she told him, abruptly terminating the conversation. But it did not end there. These harmlessly frivolous words would be repeated to Cromwell, the genius who could make something treasonable of nothing; from such weak threads of evidence he would weave his web.

As, unknown to Anne, Cromwell gathered every whisper of scandal from her ladies, the sun shafted through her great windows, the continuous breathless heat giving a curious unreality to her threatened existence, making her behave in an exaggerated way to match the extraordinary weather. She became increasingly reckless. Was Norris really in love with her? Sanity lay in keeping her thoughts to that pleasant theme.

Sir Henry Norris was older than Weston and the most trusted of the King's servants. Norris, who had served Henry since his youth, was now the principal gentleman of the chamber as well as Keeper of the Privy Purse and Groom of the Stole, with the privilege of sleeping in the King's Bed Chamber. He was probably the one Anne knew best. Norris was kind and discreet and he seems to have felt a genuine concern and affection for his Queen.

Anne had a visit from Norris in her Presence Chamber a day or two after her dialogue with Weston and she questioned him provocatively. Why did he not go through with his marriage to Madge Shelton?

'I will tarry a time,' replied Norris briefly, unwilling to go into reasons that might upset the already harassed Queen.

She misinterpreted his brevity. 'Then you look for dead men's shoes,' said Anne, who had death on her mind. Recklessly she plunged on. 'If aught come to the King but good, you would look to have me.'

To wish or prophesy the King's death was treasonable. Anne's remark was perilously close to this, and Norris hastened in horror to dissociate himself. 'If I should have any such thought I would my head were off,' he protested.

At his withdrawal Anne was clearly offended. 'I could undo you if I would,' she threatened, referring in her reckless way to what Weston had hinted about Norris's feelings for her.

A man of discretion who had survived many years and

amassed great wealth at the English Court, Norris recognized danger when he saw it and tried to bring her back to her senses. She should be more careful, there were ominous rumours about, he warned. People said she had been unfaithful to the King.

In her alarm at such news, Anne forgot her offended vanity. Norris, she begged, must contradict these terrible rumours. And the kind Sir Henry, taking pity on her, promised he would.

Part of this conversation was overheard by Cromwell's spies and carried to their master. On Sunday, April 30, they brought him a further juicy titbit of gossip. True to his word, Norris had on that day told Anne's almoner that he believed the Queen to be 'a good woman'. Norris's anxiety to defend the Queen could be used, Master Secretary Cromwell realized, to 'prove' that Anne was the opposite of a good woman and that Norris was himself one of her lovers.

Cromwell's web was almost complete.

Meanwhile Anne had allowed herself further dangerous indiscretions. On April 29 she had seen Marc Smeton, musician and groom of the King's Chamber, standing in the 'round window' of her state apartments with a lovelorn expression on his exceptionally handsome face. This gentle and sensitive young man who had grown up at Court and probably mooned after Anne for years, still - like Norris, Weston and Bryerton - loyally preferred Anne's company to the more fashionable society of Jane Seymour.

Unlike the others, however, the musician was the son of a mere carpenter and, to a man of his humble origin, Anne's rank must have enhanced her natural attractions to fairy-tale proportions.

Anne had summoned him at least once to her rooms to play the virginals. His adoration was just what the Queen needed to distract her at this time. As he stood in the round window she came up to him.

'Master Smeton,' she began, 'why are you so sad [serious]?'
'It is no matter,' he sighed.

'You may not look to have me speak to you as I would do to a nobleman; because you are an inferior person,' said Anne, queenly condescension edged with flirtatiousness.

But at the suggestion that he had presumed, Smeton hastened fearfully to apologize and retreat. 'No, no, a look sufficeth me; and thus fare you well.'

The words were just what Cromwell needed. A different construction could, without too much difficulty, be put on them. To his biased ears their very formality, with playful undertones, was characteristic of the circumspect dialogue that might be adopted in public by a man and woman who in private were most intimate. Smeton's physical beauty, his access to the Queen through the interest in poetry he shared with her brother and Thomas Wyatt, made him an ideal suspect; and his sensitive nature, his humble birth, meant he was malleable. Smeton's pathetic exchange with the Queen was the last strand in Master Secretary's web. By April 30 Cromwell was ready to pounce.

Anne must have felt imminent danger in the air. A visitor to Greenwich Palace on that day, the Scottish reformer, Alexander Aless, saw King Henry staring down from one of the great windows into the courtyard below. He saw Queen Anne approach him, Princess Elizabeth in her arms. Although their words were inaudible he got the impression that Anne pleaded with him, only to have her plea furiously rejected.

That afternoon Anne spent in the lush springtime setting of Greenwich Park casually watching a staged dog-fight. While she was engaged in what was doubtless a fashionable enough pastime in the sixteenth century, on a level with bear-baiting and cock-fighting, Cromwell invited Marc Smeton to have supper with him at his house in London; they would ride back to Greenwich afterwards. The humble groom of the chamber, flattered at the attention of the great Master Secretary himself, gladly accepted.

An unpleasant surprise awaited him. No sooner had he arrived than he was seized by Cromwell's men and the questions began. Where had his rich clothes come from? Had not the Queen given him the money for them? She had often given him money – for what services had she paid him? What were his relations with her? He had been alone with her in her chamber, had he not? He had been inflamed by desire for her? Had plotted the King's death? Such we know from the indictments later used in his trial was the nature of the remorseless interrogation Smeton faced.

Cromwell had him racked, or according to the *Spanish Chronicle*, tortured by 'two stout young fellows', who alternately tightened and loosened a knotted rope around his eyes and head. Unhappy Smeton had no rich patrons to protest at his treatment, no one to sue the King's favour for him. Cromwell may have added to his torture by holding out hope of pardon in exchange for co-operation or promised him a quick death by the axe, the form of execution reserved for gentlemen, instead of the lingering agony meted out to a man of humbler birth who was convicted of treason. Smeton was not heroic. By nightfall Cromwell had the confession he wanted.

Smeton had admitted to carnal knowledge of the Queen.

Anne was dancing at a Court ball when she received a message from one of her friends: Smeton, under cover of darkness, had been bundled out of Cromwell's house into a boat and lodged in the Tower. To judge by her subsequent behaviour, she was probably not told the reason for his arrest but the implications must have made her uneasy. Smeton was one of her protégés, one of the few members of the King's Privy Chamber who still paid court to her. Her end was beginning, at last.


The first of May was always a time of celebration at Greenwich Palace. In the afternoon Anne, with the King, watched jousting in the tiltyard from a gallery hung with the usual tapestries and gold-and-silver embroideries; the heralds blew their trumpets; on every side there were gorgeously dressed ladies and courtiers. Glittering in their polished armour, followed by retinues of liveried servants, her favourites were all taking part: her brother Lord Rochford; Sir Henry Norris; Sir William Bryerton; Sir Thomas Wyatt . . . There is a tradition that Anne infuriated the King when, after a particularly violent clash of arms, she dropped a handkerchief at the feet of one of her favourites so that he could mop the sweat from his brow.

Whether or not this incident really happened, the King certainly hid his true feelings that afternoon under a smiling mask of affability. He was especially kind to both Rochford and Norris; he even lent Norris his own horse.

It seemed a happy, lulling occasion. But no sooner were the jousts ended, the ladies dispersed from the richly hung stands and galleries, the men out of their armour, than Anne heard disturbing news. Without a word to her, the King with Sir Henry Norris, five other gentlemen and his yeomen of the guard, had suddenly clattered away from the palace on the road for London, leaving her to ask bewilderedly and aloud what his abrupt departure could mean. No worse answer than the truth could have been dreamed up in her wildest imaginings.

Norris rode in the little party of horsemen led by his royal master through the tranquil flowering meadows towards London. Suddenly the King rounded on him, accused him of committing adultery with the Queen. Grouped staunchly behind the King were his red-coated guard, each one a giant of a man, trained in the expert use of both bow and halberd.

While Norris was still getting his breath after this accusation the King changed his tack. Anne was known to have committed adultery with others. Norris must know their identities. If Norris would name and give evidence against them he could go free. Norris denied knowledge. For the rest of the long ride to Whitehall, according to Norris's servant George Constantine, later examined by Cromwell, the King persevered in his attempt to persuade him to give information against Anne and her 'lovers'.

The Queen was innocent, Norris insisted stubbornly. He offered to prove her innocence with his body. Trial by duel, however, was the last thing Henry had in mind. He needed Anne proved guilty. Norris was taken to the Tower early on the following morning.

A few hours later, at Greenwich Palace, Anne's fearful suspense ended abruptly.

She received an alarming message that a deputation of the Privy Council demanded an audience with her. Led by her uncle the Duke of Norfolk, and Thomas Cromwell, the coun-

cillors filed solemnly into her Privy Chamber. As Norfolk
began to speak, her unknown doom took on the shape and
certainty of a nightmare. Its name was treason.

She had committed adultery, the Duke of Norfolk told her
bluntly, with three men. She must confess the truth. Smeton
and Norris had already confessed. They were in prison for her
sake.

Vehemently, Anne denied the accusation. It was not true.
She was clean from the touch of man and the King's true
wedded wife.

'Tut, tut, tut!' Her uncle shook his head at her in mocking
disbelief. At last their roles were reversed. At last he had his
revenge for the humiliating public scoldings she had so often
inflicted on him. Despite his dangerous family connection with
her, for Norfolk this was a sort of triumph.

At bay among men who had been her enemies for years and
who now had her at their mercy, Anne glanced frantically
from one to another, seeking sympathy, open-mindedness,
someone who would listen to the facts. Only two men seemed
to have any feeling for her, the Treasurer, Sir William Fitzwilliam, who remained silent throughout the examination,
and the Controller, Sir William Paulet, who alone treated her
with the courtesy due to her rank. The other councillors,
believing Anne to spell disaster for England, knowing their
lives and fortunes depended on pleasing the King, joined in the
harassment, interrogating her roughly and rudely.

But Anne's proud temper was equal to such treatment. She
would not be bullied. She stood firm in her denial. The charges
were without foundation. She was innocent. Unfortunately
she would not be given the chance to prove it; Cromwell's web
of conspiracy was about to tighten round her, leaving no way
of escape.

*Chapter 27*

# THE TOWER

THAT afternoon, Tuesday, 2 May 1536, those people afloat on
the sunlit river or walking by its green verges were shocked
by a dread and to them almost incredible sight. A sombre,
silent state barge was rowed swiftly up-river and in it was the
Queen, escorted by the Lord Chancellor, Sir Thomas Audeley;
by the Duke of Norfolk, Sir Thomas Cromwell, and by Sir
William Kingston, the feared Constable of the Tower. Gone was
the accustomed music, the pageantry, while four stony-faced
matrons had displaced the usual bevy of smiling, bright-eyed
ladies: Lady Kingston, the Constable's wife, the Queen's aunt,
Lady Boleyn, Mistress Coffyn and Mistress Stoner.

Thus Anne Boleyn made her final historic journey along the
Thames which had borne her to her short-lived triumph, now
in the company of four women attendants whom the King had
personally chosen for their hostility towards her. No friends
or allies would be present to solace or support her in her
approaching ordeal.

But one humiliation at least she would be spared. She was
not to enter the Tower beneath the black jagged teeth of
Traitors' Gate. Past that gloomy place the barge floated, on
towards the drawbridge that led to the Court Gate. And there,
without ceremony, this solemn party disembarked.

Hemmed in by her escort, with halting steps Anne crossed
the moat towards the massive walled fortress looming above
her. Suddenly the realization struck her that she was crossing
this dark water to her doom, that she would probably never
emerge alive. Panic seized her. Her steps faltered and stopped.
She stood still; then, still dry-eyed, dropped to her knees on the
mossy stones and bowed her head.

Fervently, she prayed: 'God help me! I am not guilty of the

accusation.' She looked up at the King's councillors. 'I beg you to beseech the King's grace to be good unto me,' she implored.

But none of those present would sue for this fallen queen. The unsmiling courtiers turned away in silence, boarded the barge, the oars dipped and they receded across the water. Queen Anne was left alone with her four female gaolers and Sir William Kingston, the Constable, through whose incorruptible hands had passed so many celebrated prisoners, though never before a discarded queen.

Without a word he led them through the stone gateway into the moated and walled fortress that Anne knew contained, as well as the spacious rooms and gardens of the royal palace, grim towers above rat-infested dungeons underground. Anne had been told nothing of where she was to be lodged. 'Mr Kingston,' she said in a carefully deliberate voice, perhaps feeling already the shackles on her wrists, the rack tearing at her bones, 'shall I go into a dungeon?'

'No, madam, you shall go into your lodging that you lay in at your coronation.'

Relief at this unexpected reprieve snapped her superb self-control. She would revisit the abode she had entered in triumph as the King's beloved wife only three years ago. 'It is too good for me,' she sobbed in irony. Sinking on her knees again she burst into a fit of hysterics. Kingston was well accustomed to weeping prisoners. He waited with practised patience for it to pass, then continued on his way.

Brought at last to the familiar spacious rooms of the Queen's apartments overlooking the garden in the south-east angle of the Tower, Anne momentarily regained precarious control over herself. Would Mr Kingston, she requested, move the King's Highness that she might have the sacrament in the closet by her chamber? That she might pray for mercy? Her grief, anxiety and despair burst forth again. 'For I am as clear from the company of man, as for sin, as I am clear from you, and am the King's true wedded wife.'

Kingston made a non-committal reply. Cromwell had given him precise orders as to what he was to say. 'Mr Kingston, do you know wherefore I am here?' she asked. 'Nay,' lied Kingston, faithful to his instructions. Anne was to be spared the rack, but a torture more refined, subtle and appropriate had been devised for her by Sir Thomas Cromwe l: silence, lack of knowledge both of her own fate and that of her friends and associates. She was to be told nothing of the preparations for her trial, nothing of the fate of her family. That her beloved brother George was to be involved in her fall she either knew or guessed, but where he was, or whether his arrest had yet taken place had been carefully hidden from her. Cromwell, that arch manipulator of people, counted on her indiscretion, her nervous compulsion to talk. And these methods succeeded.

Anne could stand firm in the face of bullying; silence she could not bear. In the next few hours she was to say a good deal; and though much of this was the hopeful chatter of a terrified woman, it would include information which Cromwell badly needed to pad out evidence which was disturbingly thin.

Having escorted Anne to her apartments, in accordance with his orders, Kingston lingered while she plied him with questions. The ladies stood by in silence.

'When saw you the King?' she asked, probably wondering fearfully what further instructions Henry had given about her.

'I saw him not since I saw him in the tiltyard,' Kingston answered shortly. Anne's thoughts flew to her family. Were they all to suffer with her?

'Mr Kingston,' she begged again, 'I pray you to tell me where my lord my father is?'

'I saw him afore dinner in the Court.'

'Oh, where is my sweet brother?'

'I left him at York Place.' Kingston's answers were uncomforting and laconic.

Rochford had, it so happened, been taken to the Tower that morning, charged with treason against the King and incest with his sister, but of these facts Anne was to be left in ignorance for some time longer. The horror of her position, its loneliness and helplessness engulfed her. Her words rushed out in wild lament. 'I hear say that I should be accused with three men; and I can say no more but nay without I should open my body.' And she flung open her gown, revealing the rich skirt beneath. She had been betrayed - the councillors had told her -

by Sir Henry Norris, a man she had always been good to, but she understood too well the physical and mental tortures that might have elicited his confession.

'Oh Norris, hast thou accused me? Thou art in the Tower with me, and thou and I will die together; and Marc, thou art here too.'

Her mind switched to those who would grieve for her.

'Oh my mother, thou wilt die with sorrow. And my Lady of Worcester . . .' Ironically Anne mentioned the very woman who, unknown to her, had been one of her chief accusers. 'Her child did not stir in her body . . .'

It was the turn of the Constable's wife, one of her four attendants. Lady Kingston had been instructed to encourage Anne to talk as much as possible in the hope that she would incriminate herself. 'What should be the cause?' Lady Kingston goaded hopefully.

'For the sorrow she took for me. Mr Kingston,' Anne demanded, returning to anxious contemplation of her fate and, as usual, addressing herself to the man rather than to the woman, 'shall I die without justice?'

'The poorest subject the King hath, hath justice,' protested the Constable. Anne laughed bitterly. She knew what justice to expect. Of all those arraigned for treason in Henry's reign, however flimsy the pretext, only Lord Dacre had ever escaped death. When finally the Constable left her presence Anne must have heard the cannon that signalled her arrival at the Tower, the portentous heavy booming that always announced to Londoners the committal of a prisoner of high rank.

Sir William Kingston had been instructed that Anne was never to be left alone and that every word she uttered was to be memorized and reported to Cromwell, who would himself visit the Tower daily. That night, Lady Boleyn and the appropriately named Mistress Coffyn rested in the Queen's Bed Chamber. They had been ordered to hold no communication whatsoever with Anne except in the presence of Lady Kingston, who slept in the outside chamber with Mistress Stoner. It was an instruction they found impossible to carry out, for Anne, who had never known when to keep silent, found it more than ever impossible now.

Through the long, sleepless hours of Tuesday night she talked and talked. While her ladies listened eagerly she searched her memory for anything she might have said or done that could be used to substantiate the charges of adultery. The conversation with Norris – perhaps it was that they were based on. In detail she described it to the attentive Mistress Coffyn. But the next morning she remembered another damning little incident: her conversation with Weston on April 23. Weston had said in effect that he loved her, while Norris had made no such admission. 'I more fear Weston,' she confessed, and unwisely recalled the light-hearted exchange aloud. Mistress Coffyn stored Anne's words carefully in her memory and related them to Kingston, who retailed them to Cromwell in one of the written messages that flowed constantly between the two conspirators when Cromwell was not actually present in the Tower. Cromwell's spies in all probability had heard only part of the conversation with Norris and Weston. Now Anne obligingly had filled in the gaps. At a time when it appeared that the accusations against Anne would be almost too meagre to use, this additional evidence was most welcome.

For Anne's enemies were in a quandary. So far, only Marc Smeton could be persuaded to confess the crime of which he was accused. Sir Henry Norris and Lord Rochford, re-examined in the Tower, had continued obstinately to deny their guilt. And Mistress Margery Horsman, one of Anne's ladies and most intimate friends, whom they had hoped to persuade to give certain damning information, proved unexpectedly unhelpful to Cromwell and loyal to Queen Anne.

If no further proof could be found 'it should much touch the King's honour', boldly wrote Sir Edward Baynton, Anne's Vice-Chamberlain, to Sir William Fitzwilliam, the Treasurer of the King's Household.

By mid-morning that Wednesday, Anne had managed with great courage to assume an exaggerated show of gaiety. 'She has been very merry,' Mistress Coffyn and Lady Kingston reported later to the Constable. But time passed for her at a tortuously slow pace. She 'made a great dinner,' they informed him, 'and yet soon after she called for her supper.'

After supper she sent for Kingston whom she had not seen since the previous evening.

'Where have you been all day?' she asked. Kingston replied he had been with prisoners. 'I thought I heard Mr Treasurer?' she prompted.

Able to elicit no information from Kingston about the comings and goings between the outside world and the Tower, Anne protested then about her treatment, the way she had been handled by the Council at Greenwich.

'I to be a Queen and cruelly handled as was never seen. But I think the King does it to prove me,' and she laughed merrily at her own bitter joke.

It has been said that Anne's disjointed speeches in the Tower are a sign that she lost her sanity, but she had always spoken thus; it was one of her curious charms. Now this natural tendency was increased by stress and sleeplessness. A rational thread of thought, however, connected her utterances, which were desperate, but not insane.

'I shall have justice?' Anne insisted.

'Have no doubt therein,' Kingston reassured.

'If any man accuse me I can say but nay. And they can bring no witness.'

A moment's reflection, however, was enough to remind Anne that at an arraignment for treason no witness need be called, no proof given. She seized on an alternative way of escape. Could she find a deputation of powerful people to sue in her favour?

'I would to God I had my bishops, for they would all go to the King for me, for I think the most part of England prays for me,' she said.

It was wild and wishful thinking, for her bishops were more interested in saving their own skins, and the people had only prayed for her when they had been ordered to do so by preachers commanded by the King. Last year, she remembered, these same preachers had told the people when the good weather came that it was God's blessing on the King's union with Anne.

That God showed his feelings by tampering with the weather was a prevalent superstition and it was to this alluded Anne now when she threatened: 'And if I die you shall see the greatest punishment for me within this seven year that ever came to England. And then I shall be in heaven, for I have done many good deeds in my days, but . . .' and she began to protest again about her treatment, 'I think much unkindness in the King to put such about me as I never loved.'

'The King took them to be honest and good women,' said Kingston censoriously.

'But I would have had of my own Privy Chamber which I favour most,' Anne insisted.

As the Wednesday evening wore on, optimism and despair alternated in her, an exaggerated swing of the mood pendulum to which she had been subject all her life. 'For one hour she is determined to die,' reported Kingston, to whom Anne was a very strange experience, 'and the next hour much contrary to that.'

On Thursday, finally, they told her the truth about the man she had come during the last years to love best, her brother George, Lord Rochford. He and four others had been arrested. The news was presented to Anne in a way calculated to shock her into further admissions.

Anne summoned Kingston. 'I hear say,' she greeted him, 'my lord my brother is here?' 'It is truth,' he replied briefly. 'I am very glad that we both be so nigh together,' said Anne in a brave attempt not to let her enemies see how much she minded.

'Sir Francis Weston, William Bryerton, Sir Thomas Wyatt and Sir Richard Page [another of Anne's favourites to whom she had given presents] are also in the Tower,' Kingston remarked, watching her face.

But the news that these wretched men also were to be involved in her fall provoked no reaction. This has been interpreted as a belated display of caution. But Anne had never been able to hide her real feelings for more than a very short time and in all the carefully kept record of her sayings in the Tower before her trial there was to be no mention of her concern for these four courtiers. The reason is simple: beside the great catastrophes that had befallen her since Tuesday, the arrest of her friends paled into insignificance. Her chief anxiety was for her own family, her brother, and her father. She still loved her father and was tortured by ignorance about his fate. Had he too been arrested? Her ladies would not tell her.

One of the worst torments now was the constant hostile presence of these four women who went through the motions of attending on her in silent disapproval. Anne quarrelled with them openly and complained of them in their presence to Sir William Kingston. 'The King wist what he did when he put such two about me as my lady Boleyn and Mistress Coffyn, for they can tell me nothing of my lord my father nor nothing else, but I defied them all,' she loudly told him.

'Such desire as you have had to such tales, has brought you to this,' protested Lady Boleyn in umbrage, presumably alluding to Anne's delight in flirtatious gossip.

And Mrs Stoner added maliciously: 'Marc is the worst cherished of any man in the house, for he wears irons.'

'That is because he is no gentleman,' Anne said, refusing to be goaded into expressing sorrow. 'But - ' again her thoughts escaped her control, winged back to her own terrible predicament - 'he was never in my chamber but at Winchester and there I sent for him to play on the virginals, for there my lodging was above the King's. For I never spoke to him since but upon Saturday before May day . . .' She retailed in detail that last light-hearted exchange with the musician, again conveniently filling in for Cromwell anything his spies may not have overheard. Too late she regained a brave pretence of composure before her gaolers. 'Does anybody make their beds?' she asked Lady Kingston gaily.

'Nay, I warrant you,' said the Constable's wife, amazed at what must have seemed to her the wildest fancy.

'They might make balettes well now,' said Anne, punning on the similarity of the word that meant lyrics to pallets, which meant beds, 'but there is none but Lord Rochford that can do it.'

'Yes, Master Wyatt,' Lady Kingston reminded her cruelly.

From the vicious stabs of her female gaolers, Anne turned for sympathy to the Constable. Stolid he might be and faithful to his duties, malicious he was not. After anxiety for her own fate, the feeling she was least well able to hide was concern for her brother. 'My lord my brother will die . . . ?'

But from the Constable of the Tower neither more definite

information nor any comfort was forthcoming. And when she asked him to take a letter from her to Sir Thomas Cromwell he refused. He would take a message by word of mouth, no more. Kingston was a loyal adherent of Mary. Before Anne's arrest, he had joined the conspiracy to revolt in Mary's favour. He would do nothing to help Anne back to power. His emotions too brutalized by the sight of terrified weeping prisoners for him to feel more than amazement at Anne's apparent gaiety, his mind was also too blunt to understand her courage, her humour or her fancies, or her characteristically disjointed speech.

There was no sympathy in the Constable's face. Only God could help her now, Anne knew. The divinity was a recurrent theme in her thoughts. Was she not innocent? Would God not make her innocence manifest? Perhaps He was already doing so, for the heatwave had not broken. 'We shall have no rain till I am delivered out of the Tower,' she said. Kingston replied, unmoved, 'I pray it may be shortly because of the fair weather.'

While the Queen, torn by alternate hope and fear, languished still untried in the Tower, outside its massive walls people behaved as though she and her friends had already been condemned. At her fall the Londoners rejoiced openly in the streets, believing that their beloved Princess Mary would be reinstated as heir to the throne and order and safety established again in the kingdom. In the palace of Whitehall at Westminster where the King stayed there was a brisk succession of suits for the 'traitors'' lands and sinecures. When Lord Lisle wrote his request from Calais on May 8 it was to be informed in a message from the King that all suitable perquisites had been given away before his letter came. The arrest of traitors was a profitable occasion for those who happened to be on the spot at the time, a fact that encouraged courtiers to accept without too many questions the guilt of a fallen comrade. Fear was another factor that discouraged protest, for no one knew when Cromwell might pounce again. Even Anne's father made no move to save her. He would be lucky, he knew, to escape with his life, his property and his offices intact. These meant more to him than a daughter who had committed the unforgivable sin in his eyes, the sin of failure.

One man dared to plead for his benefactress. On May 3, the day after Anne's arrest, from his Palace of Lambeth, Cranmer wrote a letter of consolation to Henry: 'And if it be true,' he wrote, 'that is openly reported of the Queen's Grace; if men had a right estimation of things, they should not esteem any part of your Grace's honour to be touched thereby, but her honour only to be clearly disparaged.'

Torn between gratitude to Anne and his exaggerated respect for the King, the Archbishop was genuinely at a loss what to make of the news.

And I am in such a perplexity [Cranmer wrote], that my mind is clean amazed; for I never had better opinion in woman than I had in her; which maketh me to think she should not be culpable. And again, I think that your Highness would not have gone so far, except she had surely been culpable.

Now I think that your Grace best knoweth, that next unto your Grace I was most bound unto her of all creatures living. Wherefore I most humbly beseech your Grace to suffer me in that which both God's law, nature and also her kindness, bindeth me unto; that is that I may with your Grace's favour wish and pray for her, that she may declare herself inculpable and innocent. And if she be found culpable . . . I repute him not your Grace's faithful servant and subject . . . that would not desire the offence without mercy to be punished . . .

It was a brave letter for such a timid man as Cranmer to have written, given the uncertainty of the times. But for him also there was a consideration more important than the Queen's tragic fate, much as he regretted it, and that was its effect on the future of the new religion in England. Cranmer must do everything he could to save Protestantism from falling with her.

And as I loved her not a little for the love which I judged her to bear towards God and His Gospel; so if she be proved culpable there is not one that loveth God and His Gospel that ever will favour her, but must hate her above all other; and the more they favour the Gospel, the more they will hate her; for then there was never creature in our time that so much slandered the Gospel. And though she have offended so, yet Almighty God hath . . . never offended you.

Wherefore I trust that your Grace will bear no less entire favour unto the truth of the Gospel than you did before . . .

After Cranmer had written this lengthy and confused plea for his Queen and his Church, but before he had sealed it, he received an order to come before certain lords of the Privy Council in the Star Chamber, the Lord Chancellor Sir Thomas Audeley, the Earls of Oxford and Sussex, and Lord Sandys. It was an ominous moment for Cranmer, who might well have found himself involved in Anne's fall. As the prophecy foretold: 'Then will be burned two or three bishops and a Queen.'

What happened at this interview one can only guess. The Council either convinced Cranmer of Anne's guilt or, as seems more likely in the context of the whole situation, convinced him that it would be wise to appear to believe in her guilt. All that is certain is that when Cranmer crossed the river again back to Lambeth Palace he added a nervous postscript to tell the King that the Council had seen him. 'And what communication we had together,' he continued, 'I doubt not but they will make the true report thereof unto your Grace. I am exceeding sorry that such faults can be proved by the Queen . . . But I am, and ever shall be, your faithful subject.' There would be no more trouble from Cranmer.

Meanwhile wild rumours were current in London: that Queen Anne had been found in bed with the King's organist; that Cranmer and Wiltshire were in prison with her. Imagination embroidered a colourful tale which later found its way into the *Spanish Chronicle*, written by an anonymous Spaniard, perhaps a merchant in London at the time.

According to this account, Anne had procured Smeton to be her lover through an old woman of her Chamber called

Margaret. The old woman had hidden him in a closet and when all Anne's ladies had withdrawn to bed she called the old woman and said, 'Margaret, bring me a little marmalade' (marmalade being at this date a quince preserve eaten as a sweetmeat at any time). 'The old woman went to the closet and made Marc undress and took the marmalade to the Queen, leading Marc by the hand . . .' Another rumour circulated by the Catholics held that, trying to conceive a son, the Queen had been advised by the wicked Protestants to commit adultery and incest.

But by far the most curious behaviour provoked by the Queen's arrest and accusation was that of the King. He was, he insisted, a mere spectator of the drama. Always a master of self-deception, now he excelled himself. Apparently oblivious of the fact that on April 24 he had, with his own hand, signed the commission to enquire into treason by whomsoever committed, he behaved as though the news of Anne's guilt had burst upon him, as upon his people, amazed and unsuspecting; as though he himself had had nothing at all to do with the plot; as though he had never questioned Norris on his last ride from Greenwich or offered him life in exchange for evidence.

On the evening of May 2, the day she had been brought to the Tower, Henry staged a touching scene. When his illegitimate son, the Duke of Richmond, came to say goodnight and ask his blessing, Henry began to weep.

'You and your sister,' he said poignantly, 'should thank God for having escaped the hands of that accursed whore who had determined to poison you.' For the charge that she had attempted to poison the King's two elder children was also to be brought against Anne, to swell the evidence against her. That he himself had threatened his daughter Mary's life was conveniently forgotten by the King.

In the fortnight following Anne's arrest Henry kept himself hidden from view during the daytime, staying in his Privy Chamber or his garden rather than appear in his Presence Chamber where the public waited.

The suggestion was that he was too overcome by horror and grief at his wife's betrayal to go out among people, but the warm May nights told a different story. To the sound of lute and viol and the sweet voices of his minstrels, every evening the King had himself rowed seven miles up-river to banquet with Jane Seymour in Nicholas Carew's house where she was residing. As gay and carefree as though Anne had never existed, he was confident that Cromwell could arrange the legal side of the case, and the trifling matter of lack of evidence.

Since, apart from Smeton, none of the prisoners in the Tower could be persuaded to confess, Cromwell was forced to make do with the information he had. As though to compensate for the poor quality of the evidence by its quantity, he drew up long lists of absurdly improbable charges against Anne and her brother, against Smeton, Weston, Norris and Bryerton. Against Wyatt, who was a favourite of his, and Page, who seems not to have been as friendly with Anne as the others, Cromwell decided not to proceed, although Page for some reason that has not come down to us was to be banished from the King's Court for ever.

On the 10th and 11th of May 1536, juries at Westminster and Deptford in the counties of Middlesex and Kent where, it was alleged, the crimes had been committed, studied the charges and brought indictments against the prisoners. It was the prologue to a travesty of justice.

# Chapter 28

# 'QUEEN ANNE LACK-HEAD'

IN matters of treason in the sixteenth century the law moved swiftly. Even before the Middlesex and Kent juries had brought indictments, the King had given instructions for the trial of the four commoners in Westminster Hall. On the morning of Friday, May 12, Sir Henry Norris, Sir Francis Weston, William Bryerton and Marc Smeton were marched by the yeomen of the guard through the streets of London and into the great hall where they were to be tried for treason by jury before the King's commissioners. Among them was, of all people, Anne's father, so anxious to keep the King's favour that he was ready to forswear his daughter's life and honour. Before their eyes gleamed the executioner's axe, its cutting edge turned symbolically away, as was the custom in a trial for treason before the prisoners had been condemned.

All four men were charged with conspiring the death of the King, with having carnal knowledge of the Queen, and with having committed treason against the heirs of the King and Queen and the King's peace. Smeton pleaded guilty to having 'known and violated' the Queen, but not guilty to the other charges. Norris, Weston and Bryerton denied all the charges. But inevitably the jury found against them. In the sixteenth century the accused was presumed guilty unless he could prove his innocence, and in charges of this nature that would have been next to impossible even in the unlikely case of the prisoners having been informed of the specific charges against them in time to prepare their defence; in any case no member of the jury would have risked offending the King by going against the royal will. Slowly the cutting edge of the axe turned towards them as each in turn was sentenced to the butchery of a traitor's death. They were then marched back to the Tower.

This verdict made Anne's approaching trial a mere formality. Yet, astonishingly, her spirits remained high. She still managed to cheat herself that she had hope of life. Now she learned she was to be tried on May 15 within the precincts of the Tower by twenty-six peers in the single-storey battlemented ancient King's Hall which adjoined the royal apartments. For it was not considered appropriate or safe for the Queen of England to be taken through the streets to Westminster. Her brother was to be tried there as well.

A massed assembly of the King's subjects assailed Anne's sight as Sir William Kingston brought her, attended by Lady Kingston and Lady Boleyn, into the vast hall, where carpenters had erected a platform with benches and seats for the nobles who were to decide her fate. The Duke of Norfolk, appointed for the occasion High Steward of England and the King's representative, sat under a cloth of estate, a long white staff in his hand. His poet son, the Earl of Surrey, sat at his feet, holding a golden staff that was the emblem of the Duke's office as Earl Marshal of England. Sir Thomas Audeley, Lord Chancellor of England, sat on his right hand and Anne's old enemy, the Duke of Suffolk, on his left. Of the highest ranking nobles and officials only the Earl of Wiltshire, although he had offered eagerly to take part in the condemnation of his daughter, was absent. The other lords (including the Earl of Northumberland who was suffering from an illness that would kill him the following year) were seated according to their degree. The trial was to be conducted with great pomp and ceremony, if with scant justice.

Seated behind the twenty-six peers were the Mayor, aldermen, and four members of the principal craft guilds of London in robes and vivid liveries whose colours jarred with the solemnity of the occasion. Behind them, squeezed into every spare foot of space, were the nobles, courtiers, ambassadors, gentlemen and common people, more than two thousand, Chapuis estimated – everyone who could force his way into the hall to witness this historic event: the trial for treason, adultery and incest of England's Queen.

As ever, an audience brought out Anne's histrionic gifts, while before this great assembly both pride and self-control forbade her to show the least trace of fear. She made an entry, as one observer remarked, as though she were going to a great triumph, and sat down with elegance and grace at the bar.

The trial having in the King's name been opened, the indictments found by the juries for Middlesex and Kent were read aloud. They told a tale, not of frail womanhood tempted by some young courtier and falling briefly to his blandishments, but of monstrous insatiable lust, an unnatural calculating demoniac creature who had herself selected her lovers and on each occasion planned days in advance sexual intercourse with them:

Whereas Lady Anne has been Queen of England, wife of our Lord Henry VIII . . . for more than three years . . . she not only despising the most excellent and noble marriage solemnized between the said lord our King and the lady Queen herself, but also bearing malice in her heart towards the said lord our King, led astray by devilish instigation, not having God before her eyes and following daily her fickle and carnal appetite and wishing that several familiar and daily servants of our lord the King should become her adulterers and concubines . . . contrary to the duty of their allegiance . . . she most falsely and treacherously procured them by foul talk and kisses, touchings, gifts and various other unspeakable instigations and incitements . . . in accordance as her most damnable propensity to crime drove her on: that, moreover, for the perpetration of that most wicked and treacherous crime of adultery by the queen certain servants of the said lord King, through the most vile provocation and incitement day after day by the said queen, were given over and attached to the said queen in treacherous fashion, and that from here and from other sources this is the account, as here follows of the treacherous deeds and words . . .

There followed a long statement of the dates and places of her alleged crimes:

On 6 October 1533 at the palace of Westminster . . . and on

various other days . . . before and after, by sweet words, kissings, touchings and other illicit means . . . she did procure and incite . . . Henry Norris . . . a gentleman of the Privy Chamber of our lord the King, to violate and carnally know her, by reason whereof the same Henry Norris on October 12 . . . violated, stained and carnally knew her . . .

On 2 November 1535 Anne was accused of procuring her own brother, Lord Rochford:

with the Queen's tongue in the mouth of the said George and George's tongue in the mouth of the Queen, with kisses with open mouth, with gifts and jewels . . . by reason whereof Lord George Rochford, despising all the Almighty God's precepts . . . and every law of human nature . . . on November 5 . . . violated and carnally knew . . . his own natural sister . . .

In each instance the accusations followed the same pattern, only the name of the lover and the location of the crime changing. Anne was said to have procured each man before several days later slaking her lust with him, and in each case the crime was said to have been repeated on many occasions, sometimes at her invitation and sometimes at that of the man. In all were listed no less than ten specific dated instances of adultery.

According to the indictment found at Westminster she had committed adultery on 8 December 1533 at Hampton Court with William Bryerton after she had procured him on December 3 at Westminster; on 20 May 1534 with Sir Francis Weston after she had procured him on May 8; and on 26 April 1535 with Marc Smeton after she had procured him on April 12 at Westminster. According to the indictment found at Deptford she had also committed adultery on 19 November 1533 with Henry Norris again, after she had procured him at Greenwich on November 12; on 29 December 1535 with George Boleyn again after she had procured him at Eltham on December 22; and on 27 November 1533 with William Bryerton again after she had procured him at Greenwich on November 16; on 19 May 1534 with Marc Smeton again after she had procured him on May 13 at Greenwich; and on 20 June 1534 with Sir Francis

Weston again after she had procured him at Greenwich on
June 6.

According to these charges, which Anne, sitting tensely
before the court, was forced to listen to, her sexuality had been
so uncontrollable that to satisfy it she had risked everything.
Her adultery had been ceaseless. Within a month of Elizabeth's
birth, when she was high in the King's favour, she had arranged
sexual intercourse with Henry Norris. And she had invited
miscarriage and jeopardized her chances of bearing the longed-
for son by allegedly continuing to have intercourse with her
lovers throughout her frequent brief ill-fated pregnancies.

Anne was often indiscreet, but it was the indiscretion of the
moment, born of impulsiveness; a carefully planned course of
action that set at risk everything she had struggled to achieve
for so many years was quite uncharacteristic. Fantastic accusations in treason trials were, however, the order of the day
when the prisoner had no defence counsel to question the
prosecution's charges.

In Anne's trial no witnesses were called, and the only feeble
attempt at proof was based on gifts exchanged by Anne with
her favourites. The indictments continued with yet another
string of unproven allegations: that the five gentlemen,
'kindled and inflamed with carnal love of the said Queen',
became full of 'suspicion and jealousy' of one another, vying
with each other by 'performing at night the most services,
extraordinary in number', and also gave her 'gifts and pledges';
that she in her turn so ardently desired her lovers 'that she
could scarcely bear any of them to associate with or talk to ...
any other woman'; that to reward them for their past and
future services on 27 November 1535 at Westminster and on
31 December 1535 at Eltham, and on other days before and
after, she had given them 'great gifts'. Despite the alleged
mutual suspicion and jealousy of her lovers, all five, however,
were said to have conspired together with her the death of the
King on 31 October 1535 and on 8 January 1536. The Queen, it
was alleged, had told them 'she had never wished to choose the
King in her heart' and 'had promised to marry one of them
when the King died' (an accusation that can only have sprung
from Anne's conversation with Norris just before her arrest).

The indictments made one last supremely absurd and hypocritical accusation against Anne: that the King, becoming aware of the Queen's malice and adultery and the treachery of his servants, 'had conceived in his heart such inward displeasure and sadness . . . that certain grave injuries and perils . . . had befallen his royal body'. Had the ulcer on Henry's leg already at this date begun to pain him? Or did they blame Anne for the effect of his fall at the joust?

While the indictments were read, as, one after the other, this huge edifice of monstrous accusations was piled up against her, Anne sat apparently composed. The woman who had fallen to her knees in hysterics on entering the Tower now sat listening attentively. It was her final chance. No one else would be allowed to speak for her; she could call no witnesses on her behalf.

She pleaded Not Guilty. Sir Christopher Hales, Attorney-General, assisted by Sir Thomas Cromwell, began to argue in favour of the prosecution. They brought forward many new accusations: Anne had promised to marry Sir Henry Norris after the King's death, which indicated they wished the King to die. They placed sinister interpretations on actions that had probably been quite innocent: she had given certain medallions to Norris (the 1534 portrait medal of herself?) – this indicated, according to the peculiar logic of the prosecution, that she had poisoned the Princess Dowager and plotted to do the same to Mary. In the company of her brother she had ridiculed the King, and his clothes, and in many ways demonstrated that she did not love the King, but was bored with him. She had danced with gentlemen in her Bed Chamber; she had written a letter to her brother saying she was pregnant, which indicated the child was Rochford's.

Anne defended herself soberly and well. For once she spoke little and to the point. To Sir Francis Weston, as to many young men, she had, she confessed, given money, but the accusations of adultery she denied. She called upon God to witness her innocence. For the first time since she entered the public eye Anne had the people on her side. It was not only that a Queen on trial for her life offended their sense of order and deep conservatism. Nor was it merely the tragic appeal of youth face to face with death. The public reaction was the result also of the suspicious lack of proof and Anne's own apparently guiltless bearing. It was something that outraged their sense of justice.

Had the verdict been left to the onlookers in the hall, Queen Anne would have gone free. They remembered the gay music that had floated from the King's barge these past nights as he was rowed down-river towards Jane Seymour's abode. That the King had a new love was common knowledge. Lines from the current ballad on the subject must have rung in the heads of the Londoners, while the ambassadors and those close to the Court knew that the day before the trial, anticipating the verdict, the impatient King had sent Nicholas Carew to bring Jane to a house within a mile of Whitehall; and that here in her new residence she already dressed and dined like a queen, served by the King's own cook and other officers of his household. Anne's enemy, the ambassador Chapuis, after watching the trial, reported to the Emperor that, except in the case of Smeton who had 'confessed', the charges were based on 'presumption and certain indications, without proof or valid confession'.

The verdict, however, did not lie with the public. It lay with the twenty-six peers, including the Earl of Northumberland. When they had conferred together the Duke of Norfolk turned and demanded their decision. One by one, beginning with the lowest in rank and including Northumberland, they gave the answer they knew was required of them, the answer that would banish the fear of invasion and rebellion and enable England to be secure once more in alliance with the Emperor. 'Guilty . . . Guilty . . . Guilty . . .' Twenty-six times the word echoed mercilessly through the great hall. Then the last voice fell silent.

Anne's uncle, the Duke of Norfolk, pronounced sentence with tears in his eyes. Much as he disliked his niece, even this flint-hearted man was moved by the terrible words he must utter.

Because thou hast offended our sovereign, the King's grace, in committing treason against his person, and here attainted of the same, the law of the realm is this, that thou hast deserved death, and thy judgement is this: That thou shalt be burnt here within the Tower of London on the Green, else to have thy head smitten off as the King's pleasure shall be further known.

For a moment Anne joined her hands in prayer: 'Oh God, Thou knowest if I have merited this death.' Then, with a faint echo of her wonted sharpness, she turned to her peers. The substance of her speech is preserved in the poem written by an anonymous Frenchman who witnessed her trial, largely substantiated by Chapuis.

'I think you know well,' she said, according to this source, 'the reason why you have condemned me to be other than that which has led you to this judgement. My only sin against the King's great goodness has been my jealousy and lack of humility. But I have prepared myself to die. What I regret most deeply is that men who were innocent and loyal to the King must lose their lives because of me.' She asked to be given a little time in which to dispose her conscience. Then finally she begged the people to pray for her. She rose and was escorted from the hall.

Anne had behaved with true royal dignity. She had lost her case but won many hearts. Overcome by emotion and his debilitating illness, the Earl of Northumberland collapsed.

Kingston led Anne and her two ladies back to her apartments, where she was put under guard again. Lord Rochford then took her place at the bar. He was accused of having plotted against the life of the King and with having had carnal knowledge of Anne – an assumption based largely, according to Chapuis, on the length of time he had spent on one occasion alone with her. These charges he denied; two new ones were added. The first alleged that he had used expressions that cast doubt on the paternity of Elizabeth. To this he did not reply, thus tacitly admitting the truth of what must have been meant as a light-hearted jest, suggesting in Rochford a depth of indiscretion unrivalled even by his sister's.

The other charge was written down and handed to him on a piece of paper: his wife, Lady Rochford, had told him that the Queen had said the King was impotent. Rochford was expressly forbidden to read this out aloud. But the temptation was too great; he defied the order. And it may be, as Chapuis's report of his trial suggests, that this last mock at authority cost him his life.

Slender indeed was the evidence against him. Among the public in the hall there was heavy betting that he would go free. But Rochford's arrogance had provoked the jealous hostility of other nobles. His peers pronounced him guilty, and his uncle sentenced him to death:

> To be drawn from the . . . Tower of London through the city of London to the place of execution called Tyburn, and there to be hanged, being alive cut down . . . his members cut off, and his bowels taken out of his body and burnt before him, and then his head cut off and his body to be divided in quarter pieces, and his head and body to be set at such places as the King should assign.

As part of the punishment for them both Anne was denied a final meeting with her brother whom, she had unwisely let it be seen, she loved.


Even after her own and her brother's condemnation Anne continued to cheat herself every now and then that the King would relent. 'I shall go to a nunnery,' she told her ladies the next day. Although she knew that she would die, there was a part of her that could not believe that the passion Henry had felt for her for seven years had left no embers of tenderness, that the man who had signed a letter to her 'votre seulle HR' could now be so altered in his feelings as cruelly to order her to die in the flames.

Even when the King had tired of her, Anne could always dominate him when allowed to see him. It must have been hard for her to realize how ruthlessly implacable he could be in her absence, for while she grappled well in these last days of her life with the task of maintaining her dignity and her composure, the King was adding to the slanders about her. 'The King has said,' reported Chapuis to Monseigneur de Granville, of the Emperor's Council, 'that he thinks and

believes more than a hundred have had intercourse with her.'
Chapuis continued: 'You never saw prince or other man who
displayed his horns more or wore them more gladly. I leave
you to guess the cause.'

In the morning before Anne's trial King Henry had promised
Jane Seymour she should hear of Anne's condemnation by
three o'clock. True to his word, by the appointed hour he had
sent the welcome news by Anne's own cousin, Sir Francis
Brian. At supper with the Bishop of Carlisle at this time, Henry
showed extravagant joy, and remarked, 'I have long expected
this turn of events. And I had, therefore, before composed a
tragedy on the subject, which I have with me.' He then drew
from his doublet a little book in his own handwriting which,
unfortunately for posterity, the Bishop was too horrified and
embarrassed to read.

One last thing Henry required of Anne before sending her
to her death. In order to make way for Jane's children, or
perhaps, in the event of Jane's failing to produce a male heir,
for his own illegitimate son, the Duke of Richmond, Henry
desired the two-year-old Princess Elizabeth to be declared
illegitimate. This meant that his marriage to Anne must be
declared null. The King, as usual, wanted the best of both
worlds. Though condemned for adultery, Anne was now to be
proclaimed never to have been the King's legal wife. On May
13 a messenger had been despatched to the Earl of Northumberland to try to persuade him to admit to a pre-contract with
Anne; but the Earl denied it vigorously. So Anne instead, the
King decided, should be made to produce the evidence that
would make her own daughter a bastard.

To Archbishop Thomas Cranmer was allotted the unhappy
task of extorting this evidence from her.

Her plea that the Archbishop should come to hear her confession had so far been carefully disregarded. Now in the afternoon of May 16 Cromwell at last sent Cranmer to the Tower
with orders to extract from her the proof he so much needed.
What happened at this last melancholy interview between the
condemned Queen and her one-time protégé is a mystery. One
theory holds that she was required to contradict Northumberland's evidence and admit to a pre-contract with him; another

that she was ordered to inform Cranmer about the King's affair with her sister Mary, which made Henry and Anne related within the forbidden affinities and their marriage consequently illegal. Either excuse would have served. There are no relevant documents to help us, suggesting that the proof Henry sought was not of a nature to add to his credit. What persuasion did Cranmer use to compel Anne to give the necessary information? Did he promise her her life? Did he subtly withhold absolution until she had spoken the words he wished to hear? Or did he simply suggest what in her vulnerable overwrought state of mind would have been enough, that it was God's wish that she should obey? That by giving the King what he required she would die in charity?

To such questions there are no final answers. All we know is that when Cranmer left the Tower he carried with him the proof he needed to pronounce her marriage null and that he did so at nine o'clock the following morning at Lambeth, in the palace where three years ago he had pronounced the same marriage valid.

Meanwhile the King had exercised his prerogative of mercy. Instead of the drawn-out butchery of the death to which they had been condemned, the five men, including the humbly-born Smeton, were to suffer death by simple beheading. But what of Anne? Over the death of the woman he had loved so passionately and so long, the King, it must be said, had gone to considerable trouble and expense. She was neither to be burnt at the stake nor beheaded with an axe. Henry who regarded himself as a clement as well as gallant prince had provided a swifter death for her. He had sent all the way across the Channel for the headsman of Calais so that Anne could die as she had lived in the French way, beheaded by a sword. The executioner was to receive no less than £23 6s 8d for his fee and apparel. What more could Henry do for her? The King's conscience was clear, impressed doubtless by his own generosity. It was a gruesomely appropriate conclusion to a relationship that had begun with love-letters in elegant French.

The careful choice of executioner was in accordance with

Anne's lavish and unusual treatment in the Tower. By the King's express command every luxury was bestowed on her: she took with her into prison gowns and jewels worth £100, £20 was given her to distribute in alms before her death, and £25 4s 6d was allowed for her food. Anne was not to experience the humiliating deprivations and discomforts customarily suffered by prisoners, even of the highest rank.

But other torments were inflicted upon her.

On the afternoon of May 17, the same day that Archbishop Cranmer had pronounced her marriage null, she was conducted to a window that looked across the moat to Tower Hill and forced to witness the executions of her brother and his four fellow prisoners. So that as many as possible of the King's loyal subjects could see what happened to traitors, a scaffold had been built high above the heads of the crowd.

One by one Anne saw them mount the steps, speak for a few moments to the upturned faces, then kneel and place their necks in the rough semi-circle of the block. Five times she saw the quick heavy flash of the axe, saw the bloody trunk of a man with whom she had danced and laughed and been friendly slump to the platform. Five times she saw the masked executioner stoop, seize and hold aloft a grimacing head by its hair.

The victims' last words, however, which would have so much bearing on her future reputation, she was too far away to hear. Their speeches were brief and cryptic. They were typical of those made at the time by prisoners on the scaffold, who dared not deny their guilt strongly in case the King should refuse to pay their debts out of their confiscated property; and their families' suffering be increased. They were the speeches also of men who had been instructed by their confessors to die charitably. Anne's 'lovers' did not admit guilt of the crimes alleged, but confessed to having lived generally sinful lives.

Lord Rochford used the opportunity to proselytize at great length for the reformed religion, begging the people not to be discouraged from following Protestantism by his fall. He ended, 'For if I had lived according to the gospel as I loved it, and spake of it, I had never come to this.'

Sir Henry Norris either would not or could not say anything. Perhaps he did not wish to take part in what he felt to be a farce or maybe he felt that Rochford had said it all for him, for Norris was probably a Protestant also.

Sir Francis Weston said, 'I had thought to have lived in abomination yet this twenty or thirty years and then to have made amends. I thought little it would have come to this,' and he warned the crowd not to follow his example.

Marc Smeton said simply, 'Masters, I pray you all pray for me, for I have deserved the death.'

Anne seems to have felt that only Smeton's words would tarnish her reputation, for he alone among the condemned prisoners had testified against her at his trial. When his pathetic last sentence was reported to her she was dismayed to hear that Smeton had not withdrawn his testimony before execution. But she was too near her own end to be uncharitable. 'I fear,' she remarked, 'his soul will suffer for it.' The incident is particularly interesting since it is described in the otherwise largely hostile anonymous French poem written after her death.

Anne was told she was to die the following morning on Tower Green, within the walls of the fortress. From two o'clock that night she prayed continually with her almoner. By Thursday morning she felt prepared to face her death as bravely as pride and rank demanded. But her preparations were in vain. Still another torture was in store for her. Her execution, she was told, almost at the last moment, had been put off until the afternoon.

Bitterly she complained to the Constable of the Tower. 'Mr Kingston, I hear say I shall not die afore noon, and I am very sorry therefore, for I thought to be dead by this time and past my pain.'

Kingston in his heavy way tried to comfort her, 'It is no pain, it is so subtle.'

'I heard say the executioner is very good,' said Anne, 'and I have a little neck.' She put her hand about it, laughing loudly, and so successfully that Kingston reported afterwards in amazement to Cromwell, 'This lady has much joy and pleasure in death.'

Anne was afraid the delay would weaken her resolution to die well. In fact, the next eighteen hours or so were to illuminate her quite exceptional courage.

She had summoned Kingston, before she heard news of the postponement, to witness a last attempt to clear her name of the infamous stain upon it. In his presence and that of her ladies, she now knelt before her almoner to receive communion. 'I am innocent,' she swore before the bread touched her lips, and after she had eaten, swore again, 'I am innocent!'

Such an oath at such a sacred moment from a woman about to die was impressive. Conveyed to Chapuis by Mistress Coffyn, who spied for him as well as for Cromwell, her words strengthened the Imperial ambassador in his conviction that English justice had miscarried.

The afternoon came and, with it, news of still further delay. But this was prompted by statecraft rather than sadism, for the popular reaction in her favour had made Cromwell nervous. Should Anne declare her innocence before dying in front of a large and sympathetic audience, trouble could follow. Already, in the hope of witnessing this unprecedented event, the beheading of their Queen, excited crowds had pushed through the gates of the Tower. The execution must as usual be public, but there was a way round this awkward requirement.

Cromwell hoped that if he postponed the execution to some indefinite date and time, the people would become discouraged and go home. He particularly wished no foreigners to see Anne's death. On Cromwell's orders Kingston forced those of them who had already settled down to wait in the courtyard to leave. Reports of Anne's execution, unflattering to the King, must not cross the sea to Europe.

Anne's last afternoon wore on. Her mind moved restlessly as ever, searching for the causes that had brought her here in a reversal of fate fantastic as a dream. On first entering the Tower she had flung out a wild accusation against Chapuis. Ever since that Easter Day at Court, she had said, the King had looked on her with an evil eye, a vindictive remark which, when later reported to Chapuis, made him change his mind about her innocence. But now that her death approached she was beyond blaming other people. Now, true child of her religious times, she looked for the causes in her own conduct, examining the state of her soul which she believed was so soon to meet its maker. Could this, she wondered, be a divine judgement upon her? But her conscience was clear, she told her ladies, except for one grave sin – her ill-treatment of Princess Mary and the fact that she had plotted her death.

That night she once more put on a brave display of gaiety. 'The people,' she jested, 'will have no difficulty in finding a nickname for me, I shall be Queen Anne Lack-Head.' But the thought of Mary returned to haunt her the next morning, May 19, when a little before nine Kingston came to her for the last time.

Attended by her four ladies, she was led from the royal palace to Tower Green – where despite all Cromwell's precautions a large crowd had gathered. Waiting there also to see her die were Cromwell himself, the Dukes of Richmond and Suffolk, and most of the King's Council, with the Mayor of London, aldermen, sheriffs and representatives of the craft guilds.

Waiting too was the French headsman, with a newly sharpened two-handed sword. Anne approached him unassisted. She had lost everything. She had been deprived of both rank and reputation. Now she was about to lose her life as well. Her husband had condemned her. Her daughter was declared a bastard. Her father had turned against her. She had watched her brother and friends die for her sake. In this her last public appearance Anne's superb will and strong religious faith alone sustained her.

Smiling, though exhausted by horrifying suspense, by sleepless nights and the long wait, still determined to act this last scene of her life to perfection, Anne mounted the few steps to the scaffold. Sir Thomas Cromwell had ordered it to be built, contrary to custom, especially low so that only the people in front could see her. She wore a nightgown of grey damask, lined with fur, which left her neck bare, and beneath her

French head-dress her long black hair was folded into a net so that it would not dull the keen stroke of the sword.

Her voice at first was too feeble to be heard. Gradually it gained strength and carried boldly into the crowd:

Good Christian people, I am come hither to die, for according to the law and by the law I am judged to die, and therefore I will speak nothing against it. I am come hither to accuse no man, nor to speak anything of that whereof I am accused and condemned to die.

As Anne spoke her black eyes, ever restless, kept glancing behind her. Did she hope even at this late hour for a reprieve from the King, the lover who had sworn he would never change towards her, but who was now sending her to her death?

Always a creature of extremes, Anne was as exaggerated now in her charity towards her new enemy, Henry, as ever she had been in cruelty towards her old ones. Without a tremor her voice continued:

But I pray God save the King and send him long to reign over you. For a gentler nor a more merciful prince was there never: and to me he was ever a good, a gentle and sovereign lord. And if any person will meddle of my cause I require them to judge the best. And thus I take my leave of the world and of you all, and I heartily desire you all to pray for me.

Before the ladies she hated could come forward to help her, Anne herself lifted off her headdress, then knelt before the scaffold. One of her ladies tied the customary piece of linen about her eyes. Anne bowed her head, gave the signal to the executioner.

'To Christ I commend my soul, Jesu receive my soul, to Christ - '

The sun flashed on the great sword. The murmur ceased. Queen Anne's head rolled beyond the scaffold.

Tradition said her eyes and lips went on moving for a while, but at last this woman who could never rest in life was still. She had gambled and won gloriously, and finally she had lost. She had paid the price she had known she might have to pay since the day she gave her adoring royal lover the symbolic jewel of a lady in a storm-tossed ship. Throughout the years of her relationship with Henry, Anne had been surrounded by such impossible hazards that she had only the slenderest chance of survival. Now she had met the doom she had been lucky to avoid for so long.

One of her ladies picked up the head, the others the body. They wrapped both in a winding sheet and laid them in the waiting coffin, then with assistance carried them into the plain little chapel of St Peter ad Vincula by Tower Green. Here, in the choir, she was buried.

It was three years, all but twelve days, since she had been crowned Queen.

On receiving the welcome news of his wife's death, King Henry dressed himself in white for mourning, took his barge and went to spend the day in her house on the river with Jane Seymour.

# EPILOGUE

As Queen Anne's truncated body lay in the humble coffin in the bare little chapel her infamy was blazoned across Europe, a process deliberately furthered by Cromwell. To the English ambassadors in France, Sir John Wallop and Stephen Gardiner, he wrote informing them of the 'Queen's abomination both in incontinent living and other offences towards the King's Highness . . . so rank and common,' he insisted, that the ladies of her chamber 'could not contain it in their breasts' and informed the Privy Council. The small matter of lack of proof he hid in a convenient smokescreen of moral indignation. 'I write no particularities, the things be so abominable that I think the like was never heard.' He followed this suspiciously brief and imprecise reference to Anne's alleged crimes with a request that it should be given out as the official story. 'And therefore,' he proceeded, 'I doubt not but this shall be sufficient for your instruction to declare the truth if ye have occasion so to do.' Sir John Wallop, he added, would be remembered in the reallocation of the traitors' goods and Gardiner would receive £200 of the yearly pension of £300 paid out to them from the revenues of his own bishopric of Winchester; a financial reward that, while it seemed inadequate to Gardiner who believed he ought to have the lot, must surely in the context of this letter be regarded as a bribe.

What Cromwell's policy began, anti-Protestant writers continued, so that in Italy, Spain and Portugal her name became a term of opprobrium. Even today it is still in use in Spain and Portugal where an *Ana-bolena* means an evil, designing woman. In Sicily up at least until the 1850s the heretical Queen was believed to be confined beneath Mount Etna as punishment for her sins.

In England it was a different story. Here in the course of the

century Anne Boleyn's fame after death was to suffer vicissitudes as extreme as she had suffered in her brief life.

Immediately after her execution King Henry did his best to
erase the fact of her existence. In the Queen's palace apartments
her heraldic badges, coats of arms and her initials, linked in
true lovers' knots with Henry's, were replaced by those of
Jane Seymour, to whom Henry was betrothed the morning
after Anne's execution and married on May 30. To make way
for the children of the King's new love, Anne's daughter was
known simply as Lady Elizabeth.

Fortune's wheel, however, turned rapidly in the sixteenth
century. On some of her principal enemies Anne soon had her
revenge. Jane Seymour died on 24 October 1537 of puerperal
fever; Nicholas Carew was executed in 1539; Thomas Cromwell
in 1540. The Duke of Norfolk was only saved from the block
by the King's own death.

Twenty-two years after her execution, Queen Anne's name
was exonerated at the coronation of Elizabeth. Jane Seymour's
son was dead, as was Catherine of Aragon's daughter Mary.
Elizabeth, Queen Mary had said often throughout her reign,
was no sister of hers; she resembled Marc Smeton. But King
Henry himself, significantly, had never questioned her paternity. And now as Elizabeth rode in her shining litter through
London, carried past the cheering citizens, her mother's image
smiled down from a pageant at Gracechurch. The pageant was
built in three tiers: Queen Elizabeth at the top; Henry VII and
his Queen at the bottom; and, restored to her place next Henry
VIII in the middle, Anne Boleyn.

Throughout her long life Elizabeth is said never once to
have referred to her mother. But that is no proof of Anne's
guilt, since Elizabeth could not speak kindly of her mother
without casting blame on the father whose royalty she had
inherited. Elizabeth used, as her favourite badge, Anne's white
falcon, crowned and sceptred, standing on a root sprouting
red and white roses. And, though she made no reply, she was
known not to be averse to hearing and reading her mother's
praise, as illustrated in a letter to her from the Scottish
reformer, Alexander Aless.

Aless had been in London in the days before Anne's execution but, having kept to his house, had heard nothing of her impending fate. At sunrise between two and three o'clock, so he wrote to inform Elizabeth, on the morning of 19 May 1536, he had woken in terror, having seen in a dream or a vision the Queen's severed head with all its veins, arteries and nerves. Immediately he got up, crossed the Thames and went to Lambeth, where he found Cranmer walking in the garden and told him what he had seen. For a moment Cranmer remained silent in wonder, then he asked, 'Do not you know what is to happen today?' On Aless asserting that he did not, the Archbishop looked up at the sky. 'She who has been the Queen of England upon earth will today become a Queen in heaven,' he said, and burst into tears. It is an odd postscript to Anne's curious story – but one that in an age that believed in visions and prophecies may well be true.

To believe in the innocence of the woman who catapulted England into the Reformation became part of the Protestant credo. Was she innocent? I believe she was. But proof, of course, there is none. The evidence remains circumstantial. In the end we are left with Anne's own cryptic plea to posterity as she stood on the scaffold: 'If any man will meddle with my cause, I pray you to judge the best.'

# SELECTIVE BIBLIOGRAPHY

PRINTED BOOKS
(Manuscripts are included in Notes and Sources)

*Ballads & Instrumental Pieces Composed by King Henry VIII* . . . ed.
Lady Mary Trefusis, 1912
BAPST, EDMOND : *Deux Gentilhommes Poètes de la Cour de Henry VIII*,
1891
BAYLEY, J. : *History and Antiquities of the Tower* . . . vol. I, 1821
BENGER, I. O. : *Memoirs of the Life of Anne Boleyn, Queen of Henry
VIII*, 1827
BOWLE, JOHN : *Henry VIII*, 1964
BRANTÔME (PIERRE DE BOURDEILLE, SEIGNEUR DE) : *Lives of
Gallant Ladies*, trans. Robert Gibbings, 1924; *Famous Women*, A. L.
Humphreys, 1908
BREWER, J. S. : *The Reign of Henry VIII*, 2 vols., 1884
BURNET, G. : *History of the Reformation of the Church of England*, ed.
Nicholas Pocock, 7 vols., 1865

*Calendar of Ormond Deeds* 1172–1603, ed. E. Curtis, 1942–3, vols. III &
IV
*Cal. For. Pap. Eliz. Calendar of State Papers, Foreign Series of the Reign
of Elizabeth* . . . ed. J. Stevenson & A. J. Crosby, 1863–80, vol. I
CARTE, THOMAS : *History of the Life of James Duke of Ormond*, 1851
CAVENDISH, GEORGE : *The Life of Cardinal Wolsey*, ed. S. W.
Singer, 1827; *Metrical Visions*, incorporated in 1825 edition of
above
CHILDE PEMBERTON, W. S. : *Elizabeth Blount and Henry VIII*, 1913
*Chronicle of Calais in the Reigns of Henry VII and Henry VIII to the
year 1540*, ed. J. G. Nichols. Camden Society, 1846
CLIFFORD, HENRY, ed. J. Stevenson: *Life of Jane Dormer, Duchess
of Feria*, 1887
COCKAYNE, G. E. C. : *Complete Peerage*, 1913

DOLMETSCH, MABEL : *Dances of England and France 1450–1600*,
1949
DUNLOP, IAN : *Palaces and Progresses of Elizabeth I*, 1962

ELLIS, HENRY: *Original Letters Illustrative of English History*, series I, vol. 2, 1824; series II, vol. 3, 1827

'*Epistre contenant le procès criminel fait a lencontre de la Royne Boullant d'Angleterre*', printed in *Lettres de Henri VIII*, G. A. Crapelet, 1826

*Essex Review*, 17, 1908

FONBLANQUE (EDWARD B. DE): *Annals of the House of Percy*, vol. 1, 1887

FOXE, J.: *Acts and Monuments*, ed. S. R. Cattley, vol. V, 1838

FRIEDMANN, PAUL: *Anne Boleyn, a Chapter of English History 1527–36*, 2 vols., 1884

FURNIVALL, F. J.: *Early English Poems and Treatises on Manners and Meals in Olden Time*, 1868

GAIRDNER, JAMES: 'Mary and Anne Boleyn' in *English Historical Review*, vol. 8, 1893

GIUSTINIAN, SEBASTIAN: *Four Years at the Court of Henry VIII* . . . trans. L. Rawdon Brown, 2 vols., 1854

HALL, EDWARD: *The triumphant reigne of Kyng Henry VIII*, ed. Charles Whibley, 2 vols., 1904

HARPSFIELD, NICHOLAS: *A Treatise on the Pretended Divorce between Henry VIII and Catherine of Aragon*, ed. Nicholas Pocock, Camden Society, 1878

HAWKINS, EDWARD: *Medallic Illustrations of English History*, vol. 1, 1885

HERBERT (LORD EDWARD OF CHERBURY): *The Life and Reign of Henry VIII*, 1649

*Household Ordinances. A Collection of Ordinances and Regulations for the Government of the Royal Household*, Society of Antiquaries, 1790

KIRBY, J.: 'Building Work at Placentia 1532–3 and 1543–4' in *Transactions of the Greenwich and Lewisham Antiquarian Society*, vols. V and VI, 1954

LAW, ERNEST: *History of Hampton Court Palace*, 1885–91, vol. 1

LE GRAND, JOACHIM: *Preuves de L'Histoire du Divorce de Henry VIII et de Catherine D'Arragon* . . . vol. III, 1688

LETI, GREGOIRE: *La Vie D'Elizabeth Reine D'Angleterre, traduite de l'Italien*, 1684

*Letters and Papers, Foreign and Domestic, of the Reign of Henry VIII*, ed. Brewer, Gairdner and Brodie, 1862–1932

LINGARD, JOHN: *History of England*, vol. 4, 1849

*Love Letters. The Love Letters of Henry VIII*, ed. Henry Savage, 1949

MATTINGLY, GARRETT: *Catherine of Aragon*, 1961; *Further Supplement to Letters, Despatches and State Papers relating to the negotiations between England and Spain* . . . *1513–42*, 1947
*Memorial from George Constantyne to Thomas Lord Cromwell*. Printed in *Archaeologia of Miscellaneous Tracts Relating to Antiquity*, Society of Antiquaries vol. 23, 1831
MERRIMAN, ROGER: *Life and Letters of Thomas Cromwell*, 2 vols., 1968
METEREN (EMANUEL VAN): *L'Histoire des Pays-Bas*, 1618

NEALE, J. E.: *Queen Elizabeth*, 1934
NICHOLS, JOHN GOUGH: 'Memoir of Henry Fitzroy Duke of Richmond.' Printed in the *Camden Miscellany*, Camden Society, 1855
*Notes and Queries*. 2nd series VI, 1858; 3rd series IV, 1863

*Parker Correspondence 1535–75*, ed. J. Bruce & T. T. Perowne, Parker Society, 1853
PARKER, K. T.: *The Drawings of Holbein at Windsor Castle*, 1945
PARKER, T. M.: *The English Reformation to 1558*, 1966
PARMITER, G. DE C.: *The King's Great Matter*, 1967
PARSONS, W. L. E.: 'Some Notes on the Boleyn Family.' *Norfolk Archaeology* . . . XXV, 1935. Norfolk and Norwich Archaeological Society
POCOCK, NICHOLAS: *Records of the Reformation, the Divorce 1527–33*, 2 vols., 1870
POLLARD, A. F.: *Henry VIII*, 1966; *Wolsey*, 1965
PRESCOTT, H. F. M.: *Mary Tudor*, 1958
*Privy Purse Expenses of Henry VIII*, ed. Nicholas Harris, 1827

READ, CONYERS: *Bibliography of British History 1485–1603*, 1903
REED, L.: *Lutheran Liturgy*, 1947
RIDLEY, JASPER: *Thomas Cranmer*, 1962
ROUND, J. H.: *The Early Life of Anne Boleyn*, printed in Pamphlets, 1886
RUSSELL, J. GLEDHILL: *The Field of Cloth of Gold*, 1969

SAINT-MAUR, H.: *Annals of the Seymours*, 1902
SALTER, E. GURNEY: *Tudor England through Venetian Eyes*, 1837

SANDERS, NICOLAS: *Rise and Growth of the Anglican Schism*, trans. David Lewis, 1877

SCARISBRICK, J. J.: *Henry VIII*, 1968

SERGEANT, PHILIP W.: *The Life of Anne Boleyn*, 1923

SHREWSBURY, J. F. D.: *A History of Bubonic Plague in the British Isles*, 1970

SMITH, LACEY BALDWIN: *A Tudor Tragedy. The Life and Times of Catherine Howard*, 1961

*Span. Cal. Calendar of Letters, Despatches and State Papers Relating to the Negotiations between England and Spain* . . . ed. G. A. Bergenroth and Pascual de Gayangos, 1862–86

*Spanish Chronicle. Chronicle of King Henry VIII of England*, trans. Martin Sharp Hume, 1889

*State Papers of Henry VIII*, 1830–52

STOW, JOHN: *A Survey of London*, 1908

STRICKLAND, AGNES: *Lives of the Queens of England*, vol. 4, 1844

STRONG, ROY: *Holbein and Henry VIII*, 1967; *National Portrait Gallery Tudor and Jacobean Portraits*, 1969

STRYPE, JOHN: *Ecclesiastical Memorials* . . . 1820–40; *Life of Sir John Cheke*, 1821

THOMSON, PATRICIA: *Sir Thomas Wyatt and his Background*, 1964

TYTLER, PATRICK FRASER: *Life of King Henry VIII*, 1837

*Ven. Cal. Calendar of State Papers and Manuscripts relating to English Affairs preserved in the Archives of Venice* . . . ed. L. Rawdon Brwon, 1864–84

WILLEMENT, THOMAS: *Banners, Standards and Badges* . . . 1904

WILLIAMS, NEVILLE: *The Royal Residences of Great Britain*, 1960

WILLIAMS, PENRY: *Life in Tudor England*, 1964

WOOD, ANTHONY À: *Athenae Oxonienses*, 1813

WOOD, M. A. E.: *Letters of Royal and Illustrious Ladies* . . . 1846

WRIOTHESLEY, CHARLES: *A Chronicle of England during the Reigns of the Tudors from 1485–1559*, ed. William Douglas Hamilton, vol. 1, 1875

WYATT, GEORGE: 'Memoir of Queen Anne Boleyn.' Printed in George Cavendish, *Life of Wolsey*, ed. Singer, 1527

# NOTES AND SOURCES

*So dramatic was Anne Boleyn's short life that it has inspired a great quantity of colourful apocrypha, founded on nothing more substantial than the imaginations of our predecessors. Such is the pretty story of Anne's first meeting with King Henry in the rose-garden at Hever, popularized by Leti, who in the seventeenth century visited England, collected all the picturesque gossip he could find and inserted it – doubtless with additions of his own – in his* Life of Elizabeth I *Such also is the account of Anne's alleged words when Henry first propositioned her, words based on nothing older than a seventeenth-century manuscript. Such also, almost certainly, is the poignant last letter supposedly written by Anne to Henry from the Tower. None of these has found a place in this biography, which is based on the most reliable – mainly printed – sources available: a rich store. In an attempt to unravel the truth from the fiction that has crept into books purporting to be history, I have felt it necessary to give these sources in detail. And where the truth, as in many aspects of Anne's life, still remains controversial, I have given the evidence for my conclusions.*

### ABBREVIATIONS

| | |
|---|---|
| B.M. | British Museum |
| P.R.O. | Public Record Office |
| *L & P* | *Letters and Papers of the Reign of Henry VIII* |

*In the case of 'L & P', 'State Papers' and 'Ven. Cal.' I have referred to documents by number except in one or two instances where a page reference is more helpful.*

### CHAPTER I: THE YOUNGEST BOLEYN

For Anne's appearance see George Wyatt, *Memoir* in Cavendish, *Wolsey*, p. 42, and Sanders, p. 25. For her date of birth, see Gairdner, *Eng. Hist. Rev.*; Clifford, *Jane Dormer*, p. 80; and D. C. Bell, *Notices of Historic Persons Buried in the Tower*, quoted in Sergeant, p. 297. If Anne was born in 1507 as these sources suggest, it follows that she

was probably born at Hever, by that date her father's chief residence.
Hever Castle's history is described in the 1968 guide.

On the vexed question: Was Mary Boleyn older than Anne? I have
followed Gairdner's convincing argument in *Eng. Hist. Rev.* About
George's age, I agree with Sergeant's argument, p. 304. My deduction
as to Mary's age is based on both these, and Thomas Boleyn's statement, 'She brought me every year a child,' in *L & P* XI, p. 13.

Details of the Ormond possessions are to be found in Carte, intro. l
xxxlv. Anne Boleyn's ancestry is discussed by Parsons in *Norfolk
Archaeology*.

The duties of an Esquire to the Body are listed in *Household
Ordinances*.

Sergeant, Appendix C, conclusively disproved the theory that
Lady Elizabeth Boleyn was Anne's stepmother; for the scandal regarding her relations with Henry VIII, see *L & P* IV, p. cccxxlx.

For Thomas Boleyn's avarice, see Brewer II, p. 168.

Details of the upbringing of children and of sixteenth-century
etiquette are to be found in Furnivall; methods of hunting are
described in Le Grand III, pp. 556, 557.

The correspondence between Thomas Boleyn and Margaret of
Austria is quoted in Sergeant, pp. 12, 13, 309.

My conclusions as to the date of Anne's arrival in France and
duration of her stay there are based on: Gairdner, *Eng. Hist. Rev.*;
*Spanish Chronicle*; Meteren Fol. 20–21; *Journal 5 de May MSS de
Brienne* fol. 80 quoted by Lingard, p. 486; *Epistre*, p. 168; Cavendish,
*Wolsey*, p. 120.

The description of Henry by Pasqualigo can be found in Salter,
pp. 80, 81. Mary Tudor's arrival in France and marriage to King
Louis comes from Hall I, pp. 123, 124.

The lists of attendants accompanying Mary out of England and
allowed by Louis to remain with her in France can be found in
*Chronicle of Calais*, pp. 76, 77.

Anne's letter to her father is printed in *L & P* IV, 1. The translation 'five o'clock' is suggested by Gairdner in *Eng. Hist. Rev.*

### CHAPTER 2: A FRENCH EDUCATION

The Brantôme quote comes from *Lives of Gallant Ladies*, pp. 78, 79,
as does the story of the ribald joke (p. 75) and that of the Cardinal's
sexual interests, pp. 79, 80.

Sanders believed it was Anne who had the bad reputation, but
this is disproved by Gairdner in *Eng. Hist. Rev.*, who quotes Francis's
reference to Mary, whom he had known in France, he said, as '*una*

*grandissima ribalda'* (*L & P* X, 450). Admittedly Francis also remarks 'how little virtuously Anne had always lived' (*L & P* VIII, p. 390), but this can be taken to refer to her pre-marital relationship with Henry.

Hostility on the part of Thomas and Elizabeth Boleyn towards Mary is indicated in *Love Letters*, no.9, and in Mary's letter to Cromwell: Wood, *Letters* II, p. 194.

Anne's exceptional attractions when still very young are described on p. 169 of *Epistre*, the long French poem written by an anonymous contemporary and dated London, June 2, 1536.

The strength of Anne's feelings for Marguerite, sister of the French King, is indicated in *L & P* VIII, 378. Marguerite is described as the 'greatest heretic' in Brantôme, *Famous Women*. That Anne was never her attendant, however, but a maid of honour to Queen Claude is proved beyond doubt by both *Epistre* and Mattingly, *Supplement*, p. 30.

My account of the Field of Cloth of Gold derives from J. Gledhill Russell's excellent book on the subject as well as from Hall. Giustinian's description of the English King comes from *Four Years at the Court of Henry VIII*, p. 312.

The Ormond-Boleyn dispute is summarized in Cockayne; the drinking-horn bequest is mentioned by Carte, and the Ormond claims appear in detail in *Calendar of Ormond Deeds*. For the Boleyn-St Leger protest to the King, see *L & P* II, 1230; for Sir Piers's refusal to attend the hearing, see *L & P* II, 1269; for the Lord Deputy's order, see *L & P* II, 1230. The correspondence on the subject between Norfolk, the King and Wolsey can be found in Round *Pamphlets*, with a discussion on relative dates.

For King Francis's letter mentioning Anne Boleyn, see *L & P* III, 1994.

## CHAPTER 3: AT COURT

Mattingly, *Supplement*, p. 30, gives the date of Anne's return to England. For domestic details of Court life, see *Household Ordinances*. There is a good description of Greenwich Palace in Neville Williams, *Royal Residences*, and Ian Dunlop, *Palaces and Progresses of Elizabeth I*; added details in Kirkby, *Transactions of the Greenwich & Lewisham Antiquarian Society*.

James Butler's youth is mentioned in *L & P* IV, 4847. For his upbringing and residence at the English Court, see *L & P* XII, 963; *L & P* III, 1011; *L & P* IV, 81. And for his reluctance to return to Ireland, see *L & P* IV, 1279.

For Thomas Boleyn's control of his mother's property, see *L & P* XV, 611; Round *Pamphlets*, p. 11. For Henry's purchase of Newhall (Beaulieu), see *L & P* II, 1470; for its description, see *Essex Review*, no. 17.

The palace kitchens and the duties of the Controller are described in Williams, *Royal Residences*, p. 7.

Edward Boleyn is mentioned in *L & P* III, 3214. Catherine of Aragon's habits of self-denial are described in Clifford, *Jane Dormer*, p. 74. The particulars of Thomas Wyatt's life I have taken mainly from Patricia Thomson's biography. George Wyatt's description of Anne is in his *Memoir* included in Cavendish, *Wolsey*, p. 424. The hostile description of her is in Sanders, p. 25. For an account of the Anne Boleyn portraits, see Strong, *Tudor and Jacobean Portraits*, according to which neither the double-chinned lady at Windsor Castle nor the sly-eyed, commonplace girl in the Earl of Bradford's collection is an authentic likeness.

The account of the shepherd revel comes from Cavendish, *Wolsey*, pp. 112, 113. The revel in which Anne appeared with the King is described in *L & P* III, pp. 1557–9, and Hall, pp. 238–40.

Elizabeth Blount's age is discussed on p. 50 of her biography by Childe Pemberton; her revel with the King and her son's birth on p. 88. For her marriage, see *L & P* III, 2356, and for Wolsey's hand in this, *L & P* IV, p. 2558.

Thomas Boleyn's correspondence with Wolsey about the Treasureship of the Royal Household is in *L & P* III, 223, 447. See also *L & P* III, 2213 (24) for the date at which he at last realized his ambition.

For the King's immediate attraction to Anne, see Cavendish, *Wolsey*, pp. 119, 120, and in the same volume George Wyatt, *Memoir*, pp. 423, 424.

### CHAPTER 4: FIRST LOVE

For Percy's character, see Fonblanque, p. 391, and *L & P* IV, 3967. His relationship with Anne is described in Cavendish, *Wolsey*. For his Sunday morning meetings with Anne, see pp. 107, 121. On p. 100 there is a description of Wolsey's dining habits; on pp. 105, 106 an account of his magnificent processions to Westminster Hall; and on p. 108 a description of his trips down-river and reception at Greenwich Palace. His dalliance with Anne and their falling in love is described on p. 121.

The ambassador's report of the banquet is in *Ven. Cal.* III, p. 19. For Northumberland's promise of his son in marriage to Shrewsbury's daughter, see *L & P* II, 1935; Fonblanque, p. 346; *L & P* III, 1523, 3321. For his reluctance to send Percy to Court before he was 'better learned', see *L & P* II, 1935. See Cavendish, *Wolsey*, pp. 121, 122, for Percy's scolding by the Cardinal and the King's reaction to the romance. See p. 126 for Northumberland's greeting and p. 129 for Anne's banishment to Hever.

CHAPTER 5 : EXILE

Henry VIII's temporary generosity to his mistresses is indicated in *L & P* XIV, p. 18, and also by Mary Carey's letter to Cromwell. For Mary's long relationship with the King, see Lingard, p. 475, quoting Reginald Pole's letter to Henry in 1535.

For the King's grants to William Carey, see *L & P* III, 317, 1114, 2074, 2297, 2994. The ceremony when Thomas Boleyn was made a peer is described in Nichols, *Memoir of Henry Fitzroy*.

For the grant to George Boleyn, see *L & P* IV, 546, and for his alleged studying at Oxford, see Wood, *Athenae Oxonienses*. In one of his own letters (*L & P* IV, 6539), George states he can understand but not write Latin or Italian. His attractions and seductions are described in Cavendish, *Metrical Visions*; see also Bapst, p. 139. A book of French poetry belonging to George Boleyn with Thomas Wyatt's signature on it (Royal MS 20 B XXI) is in the B.M.; *L & P* X, 877.

The suggested date for Anne's return to Court is based on 'more than a year struck with the dart . . .' in *Love Letters*, no. 4

Thomson's biography of Thomas Wyatt has a useful discussion on Anne's relationship with him and the poems that specifically refer to her. The Earl of Surrey's epitaph (in Tottel's *Miscellany*) describes Wyatt's delightful character and appearance. The poem on which Anne is alleged to have scrawled a message is in the Devonshire MS Add. 17492 fol. 67 in the B.M.

Sources for the description of Henry VIII are Giustinian II, p. 312; Hall I, p. 19; Salter, p. 82.

The rivalry between Thomas Wyatt and the King and the final flare-up over a game of bowls is described by George Wyatt in his *Memoir* in Cavendish, *Wolsey*, pp. 426, 427. The tablet was probably something like the little book of devotions described on p. 442. George Wyatt's version of how his grandfather came by this love-token rings false and was, I believe, the version Anne gave the King to exculpate herself.

For the King's contribution to Anne's sister-in-law's dowry, see Ellis, *Letters*, series I, vol. 2, pp. 67, 68; Bapst, p. 21.

## CHAPTER 6: A ROYAL PROMISE

'*Nunquam . . . regem in corde suo deligere volebat,*' Anne's alleged statement in the indictments at her trial (Wriothesley, p. 222), is translated in *L & P* X, 876, as 'would never love the King in her heart'.
The true meaning, it seems to me, is rather 'never wished to choose',
which sheds a softer light on Anne's original intentions.

Photographs of all the King's surviving letters to Anne, with
transcriptions, can be seen in *Love Letters*. Anne's apocryphal letter
to Henry is in Wood, *Letters* II, pp. 15, 16, quoting Leti, *La Vie
d'Elizabeth*, p. 50.

For Reginald Pole's claim that Anne first suggested the divorce
to Henry through her chaplains, see Lingard, p. 480. George Boleyn's
book with the signatures of Thomas Wyatt and Marc Smeton is
again Royal MS 20 B XXI in the B.M.

For the banquet at which Henry led out Anne as his partner, see
Lingard, p. 486, quoting *Journal 5 de Mai MSS de Brienne*; *L & P* IV,
pp. 1413, 1414; and Prescott, *Mary Tudor*, p. 30.

## CHAPTER 7: THE KING'S SECRET MATTER

For Mendoza's letter, see *Span. Cal.* III (ii), pp. 193, 194. Henry's
announcement to Catherine is described in *Span. Cal.* III (ii), p. 276.

Cavendish, *Wolsey*, describes the designs of Anne and her party
against the Cardinal on p. 147, and his great procession through
London on pp. 149, 150.

G. de C. Parmiter, on whom I have relied extensively for details
of 'divorce' negotiations, gives an account of Wolsey's troubling
message from the King on p. 16.

On 16 August 1527 Mendoza reported to Charles V that Henry
would marry Anne – *Span. Cal.* III (ii), p. 327. Wolsey probably
realized this when he heard that Thomas Boleyn had been chosen
to sup with the King at Beaulieu in July (*L & P* IV, 3318). Wolsey's
terrified letter to Henry is in *State Papers* I, 267; *L & P* IV, 3382.

Cavendish, *Wolsey*, p. 130, describes Anne as appearing 'haughty
and stout [proud] having all manner of jewels and rich apparel'.
See Sanders, p. 25, for the quote on Anne's fashionable dress.

For an account of the dispensation for bigamy, see Parmiter, p. 21,
and for the dispensation to marry Anne, pp. 26, 27.

Anne's confrontation with Wolsey was reported by Mendoza,
*Span. Cal.* III (ii), p. 432.

That Anne was in daily attendance on Queen Catherine is stated on p. 131 of Cavendish, *Wolsey*. See *ibid* for the Queen's patient treatment of her rival, and p. 428 of this volume (Wyatt, *Memoir*) for Catherine's words to Anne as they played cards.

For Knight's first letter, see *L & P* IV, 3638. For the Pope's shabby dwelling at Orvieto, see *ibid*, 4090. For Knight's report that Clement had granted the dispensation, see *ibid*, 3749, 3750, 3751, 3851; Burnet IV, 34, 37; State Papers VII, 36. For Knight's enforced stay in France when Henry discovered the reworded dispensation was useless, see Pocock I, p. 160; *L & P* IV, 4185.

## CHAPTER 8: A TRIANGLE OF FRIENDSHIP

For Henry's attempt to persuade Clement of the excellence of Anne's character and the purity of his own motives for seeking a 'divorce', see *L & P* IV, 3913. This includes the list of her alleged virtues.

For membership of the anti-Wolsey party in October 1527, see *Span. Cal.* III (ii), pp. 432, 433. For Wolsey's secret hostility to and fear of Anne, see *ibid*, pp. 432, 790.

A photograph of the King's letter, this time in English, entrusted to Fox and Gardiner is in *Love Letters*, p. 108.

Details of Wolsey's settlement of the Boleyn-Butler feud are to be found in *Ormond Deeds*, IV, p. 117. Anne's grateful letter to Wolsey is in Cavendish, *Wolsey*, pp. 467, 468. '. . . prepared great banquets . . . realm': *ibid*, p. 134. 'Mistress Anne thinketh long till she speak with you . . .' is from Henneage's letter in *State Papers* I, 289. 'There is none here . . . evening' is from Ellis, *Letters*, series II, vol. 3, p. 131. For Anne's message thanking the Cardinal for his kind letter and gently indicating her displeasure at his treatment of Cheyney, see *L & P* IV, 4081.

The plight of Gardiner and Fox on arrival in Orvieto is described in *L & P* IV, 4090. For the optimistic tone of Gardiner's first report to Wolsey, see Pocock I, p. 120; *L & P* IV, 4167.

Fox's report of his interview with Anne is in Pocock I, p. 141, and Strype, *Ecc. Mem.* I (ii) p. 26.

Henry's tennis gear is described in Law, *Hampton Court*, p. 139.

Du Bellay's descriptions of the 'sweat' are in Le Grand III, pp. 129, 143; *L & P* IV, pp. 1924, 1925, 1941. Brian Tuke would not ride far or go out in the sun for fear of the 'sweat', see *L & P* IV, p. 1932.

For the Court's plan to move to Waltham, see *L & P* IV, 4356, and *State Papers* I, 289.

For Anne's despatch to Hever on the morning of the move, see Le Grand III, p. 137.

For the date Anne contracted the 'sweat', see *L & P* IV, 4408.

CHAPTER 9: THE COMING OF THE LEGATE

The King's letter – originally in French – may possibly have been written at the time of Anne's earlier indisposition. The King's remedies, with others no less intriguing, can be found in Brewer I, p. 611. The progress of symptoms comes from Penry, *Life in Tudor England*, pp. 103, 104, quoting John Caius's sixteenth-century *Book Against the Sweating Sickness*.

Anne's danger from the 'turning in of the sweat' is mentioned in *L & P* IV, p. 1932, which also says that Henry sent her for her consolation a letter of support from King Francis. That George Boleyn had contracted the 'sweat' is stated in *Love Letters*, pp. 30, 31. For the date at which Thomas Boleyn caught the 'sweat', see *L & P* IV, 4408; and for Carey's death, see *L & P* IV, 4408, 4413. For those of the King's companions who contracted the disease, see *Love Letters*, pp. 44, 45; *L & P* IV, 4440; and Le Grand III, pp. 144, 145. For the King's terrified flight, see *ibid*; also *L & P* IV, 4409.

*L & P* IV, 4413, lists Carey's offices for which suit was immediately made after his death. For the King's grant to Anne of the wardship of Henry Carey and the custody of his father's lands, see *L & P* V, 11.

Before Anne's and Henry's joint letter (see pp. 103, 104) was damaged by fire it had been copied by Burnet in *History of the Reformation* I, pp. 103, 104.

For Wolsey's appointment of Isabel Jordan, see *State Papers* I, 313, 315. For the King's messages to Wolsey on this subject, see *L & P* IV, 4488, 4497; for the King's letter to Wolsey, see *ibid*, 4507, and for the King's acceptance of Wolsey's submission, see 4509.

For Anne's visit to Court at the end of July, see *L & P* IV, 4538.

My description of Durham House comes from Strickland, *Lives of the Queens of England*, p. 192, which quotes *Norden's Survey* written in the reign of Queen Elizabeth.

For the mysterious interception of Anne's and Henry's letters, see *L & P* IV, p. 2021, Le Grand III, p. 164.

For the King's infatuated behaviour when Anne returned to Court in August, see Le Grand III, p. 164; *L & P* IV, p. 2021. Mendoza's report in *Span. Cal.* III (ii), p. 789, describes how Henry was persuaded to send Anne from Court yet again. Anne and her mother were in Kent by the time Campeggio arrived, according to *L & P*, IV, appendix 206. For Henry's and Anne's plans for their wedding, see *Span. Cal.* III (ii), p. 789.

### CHAPTER 10: THE SPANISH BRIEF

Campeggio's former visit to London is described in Hall I, pp. 166, 167; Brewer I, pp. 280, 282; *L & P* II, 4348. For Campeggio's arrival at Bridewell in the rain, see Hall II, p. 144; *Ven. Cal.* IV, pp. 177, 178.

Brewer II has a useful account of Campeggio's activities in England as well as some translations of his correspondence with Rome. For 'if an angel descended from heaven . . . contrary', see Brewer II, pp. 298, 299; *L & P* IV, p. 2101. For the legates' first attempt to persuade Catherine to enter a nunnery, and for Campeggio's interview with Fisher, see Brewer II, pp. 300–2. For Catherine's insistence that she would rather be torn apart than give up the state of matrimony, see Brewer II, pp. 303, 304.

For the Pope's change of mind about the 'divorce' and fresh instructions to Campeggio, see Brewer II, pp. 304, 489, 490. For Sanga's letter, see *L & P* IV, 4737. For Campeggio's letter to Rome begging the Pope to 'take some resolution', see *L & P* IV, 4875.

Mendoza's report in July 1527 declaring that news of the 'divorce' had already leaked out is in *Span. Cal* III. (ii), p. 276.

The indignation of the Londoners and how they cheered Catherine of Aragon is described in *Span. Cal.* III (ii), pp. 845, 846. Henry's speech to the Mayor and aldermen is described in Brewer II, p. 307; Hall II, pp. 146, 147; *L & P* IV, p. 2145; Le Grand III, pp. 217, 218.

Henry's decision to join his beloved in the country and her insistence that he should return to London is described in *Span. Cal.* III (ii), p. 846. For Catherine's surprising cheerfulness, see Le Grand III, p. 170; *L & P* IV, p. 2096. The significance of the Spanish brief is discussed by Parmiter, pp. 77, 78. For the burning of the decretal commission, see *ibid*, pp. 70, 71, and Scarisbrick, p. 215.

Du Bellay's account of Anne's triumphant return to London is in Le Grand III, p. 231; *L & P* IV, p. 2177.

### CHAPTER 11: ANNE AND WOLSEY

Anne's lodging at Greenwich is described in Le Grand III, p. 200; *L & P* IV, 5063. 'Greater court . . . time' comes from Le Grand III, p. 231; *L & P* IV, p. 2177.

For George Boleyn's career, see Bapst.

Christmas 1528 is described in Hall II, p. 149, and the reception of the Venetian embassy in *Ven. Cal.* IV, p. 184. The apparent harmony in which Henry and Catherine lived is mentioned in *Ven. Cal.* IV, 584, p. 271.

Sources for Henry and Catherine sharing not only the same table but also the same bed are: Le Grand III, p. 170; *L & P* IV, p. 2096; *Span. Cal.* III (ii), p. 861. The King had, however, told Campeggio he had not had intercourse with her for two years, see Brewer II, p. 299; *L & P* IV, p. 2101. See also letter 7 in *Love Letters*, which strongly suggests the King was not at that date having intercourse with anyone. The quotation 'caresses her openly . . . desire' comes from Brewer II, p. 486. For Henry's diminishing potency, see *L & P* XI, 285.

For the delegation sent to threaten Catherine and its message to her, see *L & P* IV, p. 2163; Pocock I, p. 212; *Span. Cal.* III (ii), pp. 844, 845, 861.

Chapuis called Anne 'more Lutheran than the Lutheran's' in *Span. Cal.* IV (ii), p. 71, and 'the cause and principal nurse of heresy', see Friedmann I, p. 235.

For Anne's letter to Wolsey about Dr Farman, see *L & P* IV, appendix 197. For Farman's harbouring of Lutheran books and part in their dissemination, see *L & P* IV, 4004; Ellis, *Letters*, series II, vol. 3, p. 77; *L & P* IV, 4017, 4030; Strype, *Ecc. Mem.* I (ii), p. 63; *L & P* IV, 4175.

For Cranmer's attitude to Lutheranism at this date, see Ridley, p. 21.

Wolsey's attempt to undermine Anne by taking her copy of Tyndale to the King is related by George Wyatt and Strype, both in Cavendish, *Wolsey*, pp. 438–41. That Anne's hostility to Wolsey was suddenly renewed after many months of abeyance is indicated by *Span. Cal.* III (ii), pp. 885, 886. Du Bellay described Anne's public tirade against the Cardinal: Le Grand III, p. 296; *L & P* IV, p. 2296.

For Henry's bracing letter to his envoys in Rome, see *L & P* IV, 5427; Burnet IV, p. 115. Anne's letter to Gardiner is in the P.R.O. and is printed in Burnet V, p. 444.

Henry's attempted ruse to reword the pollicitation is described by Parmiter, p. 90 (*L & P* IV, 5523). For Brian's and Gardiner's gloomy letters to the King in May, see *L & P* IV, 5518, 5519; *State Papers* VII, 169.

## CHAPTER 12: QUEEN OR CONCUBINE

Campeggio in his letter of June 4 (*L & P* IV, 5636) refers to the cold weather. For the seating of the legates at the trial, see Hall II, p. 150.

For the King's stay at Durham House, see Le Grand III, p. 325; *L & P* IV, 5679, 5681. For Catherine's letter begging Clement to revoke the cause, see *L & P* IV, 5685; *Span. Cal.* IV (i), p. 133.

Catherine's speech is taken from Cavendish, *Wolsey*, pp. 214–17. For the mob of women who waited outside Blackfriars, see *L & P* IV, 5702. For the depositions of Lord Rochford and the Dowager Duchess of Norfolk, see *L & P* IV, p. 2581; 5778 (ii).

'God knows . . . danger' comes from Brewer II, p. 353; *L & P* IV, 2581. Wolsey's prophetic outburst against Rochford and his party is a quotation from Cavendish, *Wolsey*, pp. 225, 226; Campeggio's speech comes from the same work, p. 230.

Suffolk's angry words at the end of the trial were so reported by Hall II, p. 153; a slightly different version is given in Cavendish, *Wolsey*, p. 231.

For Clement's complaint that he was between the hammer and the anvil, see *L & P* IV, p. 2566.

Wolsey prevented Boleyn becoming Treasurer of the royal household according to *L & P* III, 223.

Wolsey's banishment from Court is mentioned in *Span. Cal.* IV (i), pp. 214, 235; the King's fury at his defeat in the trial, on p. 133. *L & P* IV, 5965, lists the places stayed at by the King in his summer progress of 1529.

The Spanish ambassador (*Span. Cal.* IV (i), p. 235) reported the humble manner of Wolsey's arrival at Grafton; his further humiliations there and Anne's triumph over him are described in Cavendish, *Wolsey*, pp. 237–45.

For King Francis's suggestion, according to Suffolk, that Wolsey was too friendly with Campeggio and the Pope, see Brewer II, p. 363.

Cavendish, *Wolsey*, pp. 248–51, describes how Wolsey set out his surrendered treasures in York Place and his final departure. Anne's and Henry's secret journey to inspect the loot was reported by Chapuis, *L & P* IV, p. 2683; *Span. Cal.* IV (i), pp. 303, 304.

## CHAPTER 13: ANNE'S VENGEANCE

York Place became Anne's favourite residence: *Span. Cal.* IV (ii), p. 154; *L & P* V, p. 110. See *Span. Cal.* IV (ii), p. 222, and *L & P* V, p. 167, for Henry's regular visits and messages to Catherine.

Henry's January 1529 boast that he would throw off his allegiance to Rome is in Le Grand III, p. 295; *L & P* IV, 5210. The King's quarrels with both his wife and sweetheart on the same day are described in *Span. Cal.* IV (i), p. 352.

Anne and Mary Boleyn are referred to respectively as Lady Anne Rochford and Lady Mary Rochford in *Privy Purse Expenses*. The banquet where the new Lady Anne took the Queen's place was reported by Chapuis: *Span. Cal.* IV (i), p. 366. For Henry's presents to Anne, see *Privy Purse Expenses.*

Chapuis's descriptions of the King's infatuation are in *Span. Cal.* IV (i), pp. 361, 366.

Henry's reason for sending Anne's father to Bologna is given in Le Grand III, pp. 408, 409. His ambassador's allowance is recorded in *Privy Purse Expenses*, p. 19. For the disastrous result of Wiltshire's mission, see Le Grand III, pp. 401, 454; Friedmann I, p. 107; *L & P* IV, 6290, 6293.

The contents of the papal brief are in *L & P* IV, 6256.

Clement's suggestion that the King should commit bigamy comes from Parmiter, pp. 39, 40; *L & P* IV, 3802.

For Wolsey's intention to revenge himself on Anne if he had the power, see *Span. Cal.* IV (i), p. 368. 'It will cost me a good 20,000 crowns . . .' is in *Span. Cal.* IV (i), p. 366. The promise Anne extracted from the King never to give Wolsey a hearing was reported by du Bellay, Le Grand III, p. 375; *L & P* IV, p. 2676.

Cavendish, *Wolsey*, gives a vivid account of his fall. The story of Norris and the King's ring is on pp. 253–5. Esher's lack of eating utensils, etc. is on p. 258 and the spiteful removal of the tall yeomen on p. 286. The luxurious beds once owned by the Cardinal were described by du Bellay, quoted in Tytler, p. 235.

'If the displeasure of my Lady Anne . . . favour': *L & P* IV, p. 2730. For Wolsey's letter to Anne herself, see *L & P* IV, p. 2715. And for his presents to George Boleyn, see *L & P* IV, 6115. Anne's anger with Sir John Russell is mentioned in *Span. Cal.* IV (i), p. 449; *L & P* IV, p. 2781.

Cavendish, *Wolsey*, p. 287, describes the King's request to Anne to send Wolsey some comforting message in his illness. For Anne's despatch of a servant to make sure he really was ill, see *Span. Cal.* IV (i), p. 450; *L & P* IV, p. 2781.

Anne's anger with Norfolk for helping to obtain Wolsey's pardon is mentioned in *Span. Cal.* IV (i), p. 449; *L & P* IV, p. 2781. For Wolsey's heraldic prophecy, see Cavendish, *Wolsey*, pp. 299–301.

Details of the marvellous harness the King gave his sweetheart in May 1530 are in *L & P* IV, p. 3187. *Span. Cal.* IV (i), p. 536, reports the imprisonment of the men who commented when she rode pillion behind him.

CHAPTER 14: PLOTS AND THREATS

An account of George Boleyn's attempt to gain the support of the theologians of the Sorbonne for the 'divorce' is given in Bapst, p. 34.

See also *L & P* IV, 6459. For the verdicts of the universities, see Parmiter, p. 124. The way Henry persuaded the lords to sign a petition to the Pope is described in *Span. Cal.* IV (i), pp. 598, 599, 616.

For Anne's passionate argument that the King should marry her at once without waiting for anyone's permission, see *Span. Cal.* IV (i), p. 634.

Anne gave the King Simon Fish's *A Supplication for the Beggars*: see Scarisbrick, p. 248. Henry's instructions to Wiltshire (*L & P* IV, 6111) indicate the King's increasingly cynical attitude to the papacy.

The story of the gentleman who flung himself on his knees begging Henry not to marry Anne at least until the autumn is in *Span. Cal.* IV (i), p. 599. Suffolk's attempt to discredit Anne is described on p. 535, and her increasing unpopularity in the country on p. 585 of the same volume. For the prophecy that a lady would destroy the kingdom, see *Span. Cal.* IV (i), pp. 852, 854.

For Benet's, Carew's and Sampson's secret sympathy with the Queen, see Friedmann I, p. 151; *L & P* V, 614, 696. George Wyatt (Cavendish, *Wolsey*, pp. 429, 430) describes the atmosphere of intrigue against Anne, including the incident of the book of prophecies.

Anne's tirade against Norfolk is reported in *Span. Cal.* IV (i), p. 449; his privately expressed wish to Chapuis that both the Queen and his niece were dead is in *Span. Cal.* IV (i), p. 627.

For Anne's scolding of the gentleman who had asked Catherine to have some shirts made up for the King, see *Span. Cal.* IV (i), p. 600.

'It is foretold that at this time a Queen shall be burnt . . . jot': *Span. Cal.* IV (i), p. 634.

'As usual in such cases their mutual love will be greater than before': *L & P* V, 61.

Wolsey told Campeggio that time would cure the King of his love for Anne – see Campeggio's letter in Brewer II, pp. 486, 487.

For the Pope's reply to Cardinal Gabriel de Grammont, see Pocock I, p. 453 (*L & P* IV, 6705). The rumours that the King, despairing of marriage to Anne, considered making other arrangements for her are reported in *Span. Cal.* IV (i), pp. 325, 580, 590.

The King's attempt to persuade lawyers and clergy that Parliament could give a legal decision is described in *Span. Cal.* IV (i), p. 758.

For Anne's new pedigree and the Duchess of Norfolk's comments, see Friedmann I, pp. 37, 38, 130. For Anne's high words against the Duchess in October, see *Span. Cal.* IV (i), p. 762. Anne later changed her mind about the marriage of the Duchess's daughter to the Duke of Richmond and paid the dowry, according to Wood, *Letters* II, p. 363.

Rumours from the north about the banished Cardinal are described in Pollard, *Wolsey*, p. 293. For Anne's threat to leave the King unless he arrested Wolsey, and for the bribing of Agostini, see *Span. Cal.* IV (i), p. 819; *L & P* IV, p. 3035. For indications that Wolsey was plotting with Chapuis against Anne, see Pollard, *Wolsey*, p. 289; *Span. Cal.* IV (i), pp. 647, 804, 805. Wolsey's arrest by Northumberland is described by Cavendish, *Wolsey*, pp. 347, 348.

Anne's eavesdropping on the King and Spanish ambassador is reported by Chapuis, *Span. Cal.* IV (i), p. 803. Her dismissal of the ladies who had offended her is reported in *Span. Cal.* IV (i), p. 600. The description of Anne as 'fiercer than a lion' is in *Span. Cal.* IV (ii), p. 3, and her defiant motto is in *Span. Cal.* IV (i), p. 852. See also Friedmann I, p. 128.

For Anne's livery colours, see Thomas Willement's *Banners, Standards and Badges*.

## CHAPTER 15: REACHING FOR THE CROWN

Cromwell's responsibility for the policies that finally enabled Henry to marry Anne is based on his own admission: *Span. Cal.* V (ii), p. 82; *L & P* X, p. 244. George Wyatt's story of how Anne made the King read Tyndale is in Cavendish, *Wolsey*, p. 438.

Scarisbrick gives an illuminating account of Henry's conversion to Cæsaropapism. For Anne's influence on him, see also *Span. Cal.* IV (ii), pp. 71, 445; *L & P* V, p. 50. Secret access to Cromwell's room at Greenwich is mentioned in *Span. Cal.* V (ii), p. 85, and *L & P* X, p. 245.

The Pope agreed to a brief ordering Henry to separate from Anne: *Span. Cal.* IV (i), p. 832, and IV (ii), p. 70; *L & P* IV, 6772, 6757. Anne and Henry were unable to sleep: *Span. Cal.* IV (ii), p. 28; *L & P* V, 45.

Cardinal Pole in his *Apologia Carolum Quintum* quoted by Lingard, p. 555, stated that Henry was discouraged enough to consider abandoning his attempt to marry Anne.

Anne had her defiant motto removed from her servants' doublets: Friedmann I, p. 128. Christmas 1530 at Greenwich Palace is described in Hall II, p. 171.

The information that Anne's party were suddenly content to follow the ordinary course of justice is in *L & P* IV, 6780. For Clement's mild letter to Henry and his reception of it, see *L & P* V, 31 and p. 46; *Span. Cal.* IV (ii), pp. 61, 62. For Clement's brief issued on January 5 forbidding the King to remarry until a decision had

been made in the case, see *L & P* V, 27. For Anne's and Henry's relief
and his public dining with her at Shrovetide, see *Span. Cal.* IV (ii),
pp. 70, 78; *L & P* V, p. 49.

'The King's lady made such demonstrations of joy . . . paradise':
*Span. Cal.* IV (ii), p. 63.

The jewels the King showered on Anne are listed in *L & P* V, 276.
Chapuis commented on the incessant rain, *L & P* V, p. 83. For the
King's proclamation, see *Span. Cal.* IV (ii), p. 35.

An account of Dr Crome's rescue from death is in *Span. Cal.* IV
(ii), p. 96; *L & P* V, p. 69. Henry's order for Tyndale's arrest is
described in Merriman I, p. 101.

For the banishment from Court of the Duchess of Norfolk and
Marquis of Exeter, see Friedmann I, p. 146; *Span. Cal.* IV (ii), pp.
154, 214; *L & P* V, pp. 110, 111, 161. Anne's criticism of Stephen
Gardiner is mentioned in *Span. Cal.* IV (ii), p. 175, and *L & P* V, p.
137. Chapuis reported Anne's accusation that Suffolk had had
criminal intercourse with his own 'daughter', an obvious confusion
with his ward whom he afterwards married: *Span. Cal.* IV (ii), p. 214;
*L & P* V, p. 161.

Guildford's outburst is described in *Span. Cal.* IV (ii), p. 176;
*L & P* V, p. 138. A drawing of him by Holbein is at Windsor Castle.
Anne's threat to Guildford and its sequel are in *Span. Cal.* IV (ii),
p. 177.

The story about the King pleading with Anne's relations to patch
up his quarrel with her is in *Span. Cal.* IV (ii), pp. 33, 35; *L & P* V,
61, 64. For Norfolk's fear that Anne would be the ruin of all her
family, see Friedmann I, p. 134.

Anne's campaign to alienate Henry from his daughter is described
in *L & P* V, p. 101; *Span. Cal.* IV (ii), p. 256. See *Span. Cal.* IV (ii),
p. 40, and *L & P* V, 62, for the farce of Wolsey going to Hell.

Her fear of Fisher and threatening request that he should not
come to Parliament in case he should 'catch any sickness as he did
last year', is reported in *L & P* V, 472; *Span. Cal.* IV (ii), p. 261.
'Previous year' refers to the regnal year computed from April 22.

The plot to dissuade the King from his folly is mentioned in
*Span. Cal.* IV (ii), p. 177; *L & P* V, p. 138.

The unconventional way in which Anne went hunting with
Henry in June 1531 is described in *Span. Cal.* IV (ii), p. 212; *L & P* V,
p. 161. See *ibid* for her boast that she would be married in three or
four months' time and for her appointment of an almoner.

### CHAPTER 16: FIRST LADY

For Henry's abandonment of Catherine at Windsor, see *Span. Cal.* IV (ii), pp. 212, 291; *L & P* V, p. 161; Hall II, p. 197. For the Queen's message to Henry and his reply, see *Span. Cal.* IV (ii), p. 222; *L & P* V, 361. Catherine was ordered to leave Windsor before Henry returned there according to *Span. Cal.* IV (ii), pp. 228, 239; *L & P* V, 375, 416.

Fox became Anne's almoner: *Span. Cal.* IV (ii), p. 796; *L & P* V, 432. Anne occupied the Queen's apartments: *Span. Cal.* IV (ii), p. 354. The story of the women who marched out of London to kill Anne is in *Ven. Cal.* IV, 701. The feast where she presided alone at the high table with the King and du Bellay is reported in *L & P* V, 488.

The incomes of Norris and Brereton are given in *L & P* X, 878. Norris's position at Court is described in *Household Ordinances*; *L & P* X, 865. For Brereton's career, see *L & P* IV, p. 1430. For Weston's, see *Privy Purse Expenses* and *Epistre*, p. 195. Smeton is described as very handsome in Clifford, *Jane Dormer*, and as a groom of the Privy Chamber in Wriothesley, appendix. Further details of the lives of all four men are given in Cavendish, *Metrical Visions*. These were probably the inner group of favourites referred to in *Ven. Cal.* IV, p. 365, and *Span. Cal.* IV (ii), p. 630.

Anne's letter to Lady Wingfield is in Wood, *Letters* II, pp. 74, 75.

'That diabolic woman': *L & P* V, 744. Anne's first Christmas and New Year without Catherine at Greenwich Palace and the King's rejection of his wife's present are described in *Span. Cal.* IV (ii), pp. 353, 354; *L & P* V, 696. The King's presents to and from other members of the triumphant Boleyn family are listed in *L & P* V, pp. 327, 328. For the Countess of Wiltshire's separate room at York Place, see *L & P* V, p. 448. For Mary's annuity, see *L & P* V, p. 306. For the King's lavish treatment of Anne's brother, see *Privy Purse Expenses*.

### CHAPTER 17: DEADLOCK

For Clement's indefinite threat, see Pocock II, p. 166.

'Boiling vortex': *Span. Cal.* IV (i), p. 854.

The lords' refusal to allow the 'divorce' to be decided in England by a lay tribunal is described in *Span. Cal.* IV (ii), p. 384; *L & P* V, 805. Wiltshire and Norfolk quarrelled with Anne when she wanted to marry the King regardless: Friedmann I, p. 157; *Span. Cal.* IV (ii), p. 699. More sharp words between Anne and her father, over the hanging of a priest, are reported in *Span. Cal.* IV (ii), p. 481; *L & P* V, 1165.

Secret negotiations between Anne, Henry and the French ambassador are mentioned in *Span. Cal.* IV (ii), pp. 488, 509. For Anne's trousseau nightgown, see *Privy Purse Expenses*, and for her new sumptuous dresses, *Span. Cal.* IV (ii), pp. 253, 254, 524; *L & P* V, p. 591. (The first *Span. Cal.* report is wrongly dated 1531 instead of 1532.)

*L & P* V, 952, gives a list of payments for the transformation of York Place into great Whitehall. See also *L & P* V, 260, and *Span. Cal.* IV (ii), p. 154. Bayley, *History of the Tower*, appendix pp. xix–xxi, gives details of alterations to the royal apartments in the Tower of London preparatory to Anne's coronation; their location is shown on the 1597 plan, plate II in the same work.

The Abbot of Whitby incident is in *L & P* V, 907. For the Peto incident, see *L & P* V, 941, 989. For Anne's correspondence with Lyst, see *L & P* V, 1525; *L & P* VI, 115, 116, 168, 512, 1264. The incident with the woman at St Paul's is described in *Ven. Cal.* IV, 768. For the priest who was threatened by his congregation, see *Span. Cal.* IV (ii), p. 412. The mob of women who insulted Anne is mentioned in *Span. Cal.* IV (ii), p. 487; *L & P* V, 1202.

For Rice Ap Griffith's arrest and execution, see *L & P* V, 432, 563; *Span. Cal.* IV (ii), pp. 248, 323. For Benet's letter to Catherine, see *L & P* V, p. 335; *Span. Cal.* IV (ii), p. 352.

Although it is stated in *Ven. Cal.* IV, 802, that the Duchess of Suffolk was to accompany Anne to Calais, we know from the same source that she had stoutly refused to go; and since there is no mention of her at Calais she presumably got her own way. For the King's reprimand of the Duke of Suffolk, see *Span. Cal.* IV (ii), pp. 509, 512.

The hunts shared by Anne, du Bellay and the King are described in Le Grand III, pp. 556, 557; *L & P* V, 1187. Her confiding in him is suggested by Le Grand III, p. 555.

For the Countess of Northumberland's allegation, see Friedmann I, pp. 159–61; Burnet VI, p. 167; *L & P* X, 864. For Anne's proposed long train of attendants, as well as for her letter to Mary, see *Span. Cal.* IV (ii), pp. 494, 495.

For Henry's description of Anne as his 'dearest and most beloved cousin', see *Span. Cal.* IV (ii), p. 511.

## CHAPTER 18: MARQUIS OF PEMBROKE

The creation of the new Marquis of Pembroke with an annual income of £1000 is described in *Ven. Cal.* IV, 802; *Span. Cal.* IV (ii), p. 508; *L & P* V, pp. 552, 563, 585.

For the familiar and scandalous conversation between Henry and Anne, see *Span. Cal.* IV (ii), p. 227; *L & P* V, p. 169. For her alleged miscarriage, see *Span. Cal.* IV (ii), pp. 335, 343; *L & P* V, 594, 615. Simon Grynaeus's letter to Martin Bucer is quoted by Sergeant, pp. 130, 131.

No witnesses of the King's adultery had been produced: *L & P* V, 492. 'There is no positive proof of adultery . . . opposite': *Span. Cal.* IV (ii), p. 8. The Dean of Westbury's testimony is in *L & P* V, 1114. Catherine reported to the Pope Henry's claim that there was nothing wrong in his relations with Anne: Friedmann I, p. 130. 'She had always believed . . . before': *Span. Cal.* IV (i), p. 386.

Wolsey's prophecy that Henry's infatuation would die within two years of marriage to Anne is in *Span. Cal.* IV (i), p. 533. Jane Seymour was warned not to give in to the King until he had married her, according to *Span. Cal.* V (ii), p. 85.

'The King cannot leave her for an hour': *Span. Cal.* IV (ii), p. 512; *L & P* V, p. 571. For the King's eagerness to consult Anne on his new diamond collar, see *L & P* V, 1298, 1299.

Anne's request for Catherine's jewels and Catherine's refusal are described in *Span. Cal.* IV (ii), pp. 254, 524, 525; *L & P* V, p. 591. For Marguerite's refusal to meet Anne at Calais, see *Span. Cal.* IV (ii), p. 528; Mattingly, *Catherine of Aragon*, p. 253. 'The Queen said that her greatest wish next to having a son was to see you again,' wrote an anonymous Frenchman to Marguerite in a letter dated 15 September 1535: *L & P* IX, 378.

The Duchess of Vendôme's tarnished reputation is mentioned in *Span. Cal.* IV (ii), p. 528; *L & P* V, p. 529. For the train of ladies originally ordered to accompany Anne to Calais, see *L & P* V, p. 545. For the ladies she finally took with her, see *Ven. Cal.* IV, 822; *L & P* V, 1484.

'The lady companion the King takes with him'; 'the woman whom he keeps with him': *Span. Cal.* IV (ii), p. 510; *L & P* V, 176. Anne was the chief instigator of the trip to Calais, according to *Span. Cal.* IV (ii), p. 534. For the portents that attended Anne's departure, see *Ven. Cal.* IV, 816. The greater part of the Court crossed the Channel before the King: *Ven. Cal.* IV, 811.

Particulars of Anne's journey from Greenwich to Calais are in *L & P* V, 1484; Hall II, p. 213; *Span. Cal.* IV (ii), p. 524. For the King's lodging at Calais, see Hall II, p. 213. Henry's marriage plans are described in *Ven. Cal.* IV, pp. 363, 368; *Span. Cal.* IV (ii), p. 562. Henry took her with him to Mass and to appraise the fortifications: *Ven. Cal.* IV, p. 365; Hall II, p. 214. For the succession of balls and banquets, see *Ven. Cal.* IV, p. 368.

That Wyatt was a favoured friend is indicated by her outburst to him in 1533 on discovering she was pregnant. For the Venetian's description of Anne at Calais, see *Ven. Cal.* IV, 365. Fine weather when the King went to Boulogne is mentioned in *Span. Cal.* IV (ii), p. 560; *L & P* V, p. 662.

Anne's tirade against Gregory Casale is reported in *L & P* V, 1538. That Anne did not really want to get married in France but in England like other Queens is stated in *Span. Cal.* IV (ii), p. 527; *L & P* V, p. 592. For King Francis's arrival at Calais, see *Ven. Cal.* IV, 823; *L & P* V, p. 625. The description of Anne's meeting with him is in Hall II, p. 220. Their long conversation is mentioned in *L & P* V, 1546, and Henry's clothes are described in *L & P* V, p. 625.

King Francis's message to the Pope regarding the 'divorce' is in *L & P* V, 1541. For Clement's November brief, see *L & P* V, 1545.

For Cranmer's secret sympathy with Catherine, see Friedmann I, p. 179; Ridley, p. 43. For Anne's visit to the Tower, see *Span. Cal.* IV (ii), p. 566; *L & P* V, p. 679. For Henry's lavish gift of plate, see *L & P* V, 1685.

## CHAPTER 19: 'THE KING'S DEAREST WIFE'

For Anne's marriage, see Friedmann I, p. 183, and II, pp. 338, 339; *Span. Cal.* IV (ii), pp. 609, 642, 674; *L & P* VI, p. 167, 180, 661; Ellis, *Letters*, series I, vol. 2, p. 39. Harpsfield's version is quoted on p. 94 of Sanders. For the danger to Anne's life in the event of a popular revolt, see *Span. Cal.* IV (ii), p. 597.

Her boast that the King would marry her shortly is in *Span. Cal.* IV (ii), p. 602; *L & P* VI, p. 74. Her remark to the priest who wished to enter her service is in *Span. Cal.* IV (ii), p. 600; *L & P* VI, p. 66. See Friedmann I, p. 190, for her remark about her craving for apples and for her declaration that if she were not pregnant she would go on a pilgrimage. The King's boast about her dowry is in *Span. Cal.* IV (ii), p. 617; *L & P* VI, p. 97.

Chapuis's report to Charles V that Anne and Henry were married: *Span. Cal.* IV (ii), p. 609; *L & P* VI, p. 82. For Cranmer's protestation, see Ridley, pp. 55, 56.

For the identical sermon given by Anne's and Henry's chaplains, see *Span. Cal.* IV (ii), p. 618; *L & P* VI, p. 107. Rochford's departure for France is mentioned in *L & P* VI, p. 107, and *Span. Cal.* IV (ii), p. 619. For King Francis's letter to Anne, see *Span. Cal.* IV (ii), p. 645;

*L & P* VI, 242. For Henry's letter to Francis hinting an heir was on the way, see *State Papers* VII, 427; *L & P* VI, 230.

Henry told his Privy Council Anne was to be crowned after Easter: *Span. Cal.* IV (ii), p. 628; *L & P* V, p. 150. Catherine was informed and refused to co-operate: *Span. Cal.* IV (ii), pp. 629, 642, 643, 646; *L & P* VI, pp. 150, 167, 179. The new livery covered with H's and K's that she ordered for her retinue is described in *Ven. Cal.* IV, 923.

The story of Anne's seizing Catherine's barge is in *Span. Cal.* IV (ii), p. 693; *L & P* VI, pp. 240, 241. Anne's coat of arms is described by Willement.

Anne's coronation dresses and specially made crown are described in *L & P* VI, 396, pp. 277, 278.

For alterations to Greenwich Palace, see Kirby, *Transactions of the Greenwich & Lewisham Antiquarian Society*. For Anne's household officials, see *Ven. Cal.* IV, 872, 886. For Anne's device 'The Most Happy', see her coronation medal, also *Span. Cal.* V (ii), p. 157; *L & P* X, p. 450.

Anne went to Mass as Queen: *Span. Cal.* IV (ii), p. 643; *L & P* VI, pp. 167, 168. For her retinue compared with Catherine's, see *Ven. Cal.* IV, p. 287.

'You ought to remove it and thank God for the state you find yourself in': *Span. Cal.* IV (ii), p. 699; *L & P* VI, p. 243. The demonstration of Anne's unpopularity and the King's order to the Mayor are mentioned in *Span. Cal.* IV (ii), p. 646; *L & P* VI, p. 179.

For the King's proclamation and his refusal to allow anyone to preach without a licence, see *Span. Cal.* IV (ii), p. 688; *L & P* VI, p. 235. For Cranmer's sentence of 'divorce', see *L & P* VI, 528, and for his judgement that Anne's and Henry's marriage was lawful, see *L & P* VI, 737 (vii).

CHAPTER 20: 'THE MOST HAPPY'

Anne's coronation ceremonies are described in *L & P* VI, in Hall II, and in Wriothesley. 'One o'clock': *L & P* VI, p. 276. The boat with a red dragon comes from Hall II, p. 230. The dragon was a Tudor emblem.

The whole river seemed covered with boats: *L & P* VI, p. 264. For Henry's reception of her at the Tower, see *L & P* VI, pp. 250, 276. The description of her procession through the City comes from Hall II, pp. 232–6. For Anne's clothes, see Ellis, *Letters*, series I, vol. 2, p. 37; *L & P* VI, 265, 277.

The Duchess of Norfolk's refusal to join the procession is in *L & P*

VI, 585. 'I think you all have scurvy heads . . .' is in *L & P* VI, 585. For the Hanseatic triumphal arch, see Hall II, p. 234; *Span. Cal.* IV (ii), p. 740; *L & P* VI, p. 356. The night after this procession Anne spent at Whitehall, according to Hall II, p. 236; Ellis, *Letters*, series I, vol. 2, p. 38. The *Spanish Chronicle* quote is on p. 14.

For the bearers of 'the laps of her robe' and for her rest in a 'rich' chair, see *L & P* VI, p. 277. The coronation banquet lasted until six in the evening, according to Hall II, p. 242. For the closet Henry had specially built, see Hall II, p. 241; Harleian MS 41, fol. 12 in the B.M.; *L & P* VI, p. 278. The two gentlewomen who sat at the Queen's feet are mentioned in *L & P* VI, pp. 265, 278. The meat handed out at the hall door is mentioned in *L & P* VI, p. 266.

For 'pastime in the Queen's chamber', see *L & P* VI, 613. For King Francis's litter, see *Span. Cal.* IV (ii), p. 721; *L & P* VI, p. 318. For Marguerite's affectionate messages, see *L & P* VI, 692.

The gist of Clement's message to Charles V is in *Span. Cal.* IV (ii), p. 662. For the Emperor's letter to Chapuis, see *Span. Cal.* IV (ii), p. 687; *L & P* VI, pp. 234, 235. The King's proclamation making anyone who called Catherine Queen liable to the death penalty is mentioned in *Span. Cal.* IV (ii), p. 754; *L & P* VI, pp. 356, 397.

The cheers of the country people for Catherine are reported in *Span. Cal.* IV (ii), p. 754; *L & P* VI, pp. 396, 397. 'As though God had descended from the skies' is in *Span. Cal.* IV (ii), p. 740. A description of Anne's nagging at Henry is in *Span. Cal.* IV (ii), pp. 740, 755; *L & P* VI, pp. 356, 397. For Anne's charities and attempt to court popularity, see *Span. Cal.* IV (ii), p. 675; *L & P* VI, p. 211; Foxe, *Acts and Monuments*, pp. 62, 63.

Henry's lie to Anne that he was going hunting is in *Span. Cal.* IV (ii), p. 755; *L & P* VI, p. 397. For the Pope's declaration that Anne's marriage was null and void, see *L & P* VI, 807. For the King's unfaithfulness and Anne's reaction, see *Span. Cal.* IV (ii), pp. 777, 788; *L & P* VI, 1054, pp. 436, 453. For Glover's vision, see *L & P* VI, 1599.

For the date on which Anne took her chamber, see *L & P* VI, 890, 948, 1004. Her three beds are described in Kirby *Transactions of the Greenwich & Lewisham Antiquarian Society*, p. 49; *Span. Cal.* IV (ii), p. 788; *L & P* VI, p. 453; *Household Ordinances*. The ceremony when a Queen took her chamber is described in Julius B XII fol. 56 in the B.M. For the Queen's bedding, cradle and furnishing of her room, see *Household Ordinances*.

The prince to be named Henry or Edward: *L & P* VI, p. 453. Anne's favourites sent to Flanders for horses: *Span. Cal.* IV (ii), p.

788; *L & P* VI, p. 453. For Elizabeth's birth, see *Span. Cal.* IV (ii), p. 789; *L & P* VI, 1112; Hall II, p. 242.

### CHAPTER 21 : PRINCESS OF ENGLAND

Anne's disappointment and anger at giving birth to a daughter are reported in *Span. Cal.* IV (ii), p. 789; *L & P* VI, 1112. There were no celebration bonfires, according to *Span. Cal.* IV (ii), p. 795; *L & P* VI, p. 470. 'The greatest consolation in the world': *Span. Cal.* IV (i), p. 352.

Elizabeth proclaimed 'Princess of England': *Span. Cal.* IV (ii), p. 795; *L & P* VI, p. 470. The preparations for her christening are in Kirby, *Transactions of the Greenwich & Lewisham Antiquarian Society*, p. 50. A description of the christening ceremony is in Hall II, pp. 242, 243. Additional details from *Household Ordinances*. Elizabeth's gifts are in Hall II, p. 244.

The King's ardent declaration that 'he would be reduced to begging alms from door to door rather than abandon' Anne is from *Span. Cal.* IV (ii), p. 842; *L & P* VI, p. 557.

The story of Mary's interrupted meeting with Henry in the fields is in *Span. Cal.* IV (ii), p. 256; *L & P* V, p. 592. The King even refused to see her when she was ill: *L & P* V, p. 101. For her speech before her assembled household, see *Span. Cal.* IV(ii) pp. 819, 820, 830; *L & P* VI, 1249, 1296. For Henry's decision not after all to bring Mary to Court, see *L & P* VII, p. 48; *Span. Cal.* V (i), p. 27.

Anne's request for Catherine's christening robe is in *Span. Cal.* IV (ii), p. 756; *L & P* VI, p. 397. The *Spanish Chronicle* quote is on p. 42.

Elizabeth's and Mary's contrasting journeys to Hatfield and Mary's outburst against her stepmother are described in *Span. Cal.* IV (ii), pp. 877, 894; *L & P* VI, pp. 611, 617, 629. Anne's order that Mary should be 'slapped like the cursed bastard she was' is in *L & P* VII, p. 69. All her old servants were removed and the assay was no more to be given, according to *Span. Cal.* IV (ii), p. 898; *L & P* VI, p. 633. Lady Shelton's defence of Mary and the description of the country people cheering her as she walked in a gallery are in *Span. Cal.* V (i), p. 57; *L & P* VII, p. 85. The incident where Mary knelt on a terrace before the King is in *Span. Cal.* V (i), pp. 11, 12; *L & P* VII, pp. 31, 32.

For Anne's New Year present to her ladies, see *L & P* VI, 1589. The fountain for Henry is described in *L & P* VII, p. 4. For Lady Lisle's gifts to the Queen, see *L & P* VII, 92, 654; VIII, 232, 1084; IX, 402 (wrongly dated; see *L & P* VIII, 919), 991, 1004; Wood,

*Letters* II, pp. 311, 312. For 'tapestries and smocks', see Wyatt, *Memoir*, in Cavendish, *Wolsey*, p. 443; Foxe, *Acts and Monuments*, p. 63.

Details of the quarrel between the Duke and Duchess of Norfolk are given in *L & P* VI, p. 487; *Span. Cal.* IV (ii), p. 814; Wood, *Letters* II, pp. 365-72.

Anne danced with gentlemen in her Bed Chamber according to *Cal. For. Pap. Eliz.* I, 1303.

Lutherans had begun to desecrate images: *L & P* VI, 1311. For secret pledges of support, see *Span. Cal.* IV (ii), p. 814; *L & P* VI, p. 487; Friedmann I, p. 234.

Norfolk scolded by the Queen: *Span. Cal.* IV (ii), p. 794; *L & P* VI, p. 469.

## CHAPTER 22: SHADOWS OF FAILURE

Anne's attempt to win Mary over at Hatfield is described in *Span. Cal.* V (i), p. 72; *L & P* VII, p. 127. A similar attempt at Eltham is described in Clifford, *Jane Dormer*, pp. 81, 82. Henry's moments of wishing Mary dead are reported in *Span. Cal.* V (i), pp. 570, 572; *L & P* IX, pp. 288, 290. 'She is my death . . .': *L & P* IX, p. 294; *Span. Cal.* V (i), p. 573. Mrs Amadas's prophecy is in *L & P* VI, 923. For the ballad prophecy that Anne would burn, see *L & P* VI, appendix 10. Anne's boast that she was crowned and not yet burnt is in *Span. Cal.* V (ii), p. 122; *L & P* X, p. 381.

'Since one Queen of England was to be burned . . .': *Span. Cal.* V (i), p. 172; *L & P* VII, p. 282. For Anne's other threats against the lives of Mary and Catherine, see *Span. Cal.* V (i), pp. 33, 198; *L & P* VII, pp. 68, 323.

For Anne's pregnancies and miscarriages in 1534, see *L & P* VII, pp. 37, 44, 94, 221; *Span. Cal.* V (i), pp. 19, 21, 67; *State Papers* VII, 565. 'Am I not a man as other men are?': *Span. Cal.* IV (ii), p. 638; *L & P* VI, p. 164.

For Mary Boleyn's banishment and pleading letter to Cromwell, see *L & P* VII, 1554; *Span. Cal.* V (i), p. 344; Wood, *Letters* II, pp. 194-7. Details of Henry's new love-affair and arguments with Anne about it are in *Span. Cal.* V (i), pp. 260, 264, 293, 344; *L & P* VII, 1174, 1279, 1554; pp. 463, 485. Henry's new mistress a tool of the opposition: *Span. Cal.* V (i), pp. 280, 300; *L & P* VII, pp. 485, 498.

For the midwife, the hundred-year-old parson and the drunken old woman, see *L & P* VII, 840, 1330; *L & P* VIII, 844. For the King's 'pilling and polling', see *L & P* VII, 1609, and *L & P* VIII, 838. Edmond Brock's words are in *L & P* IX, 74.

A detailed account of the nobles' plot is given by Mattingly, *Catherine of Aragon*, p. 287. Dacre's acquittal is in *Span. Cal.* V (i), p. 225; *L & P* VII, p. 389. Cromwell rebuffed by the King: *Span. Cal.* V (i), p. 295; *L & P* VII, p. 495. Mary's journey in a velvet litter and her visit from the courtiers at The More and Richmond are described in Friedmann II, p. 37; *Span. Cal.* V (i), pp. 299, 300; *L & P* VII, p. 497.

The French demand that Mary should marry the Dauphin is in *Span. Cal.* V (i), p. 331; *L & P* VII, p. 551. Admiral Chabot's offhand treatment of the Queen is described in *Span. Cal.* V (i), pp. 331, 376; *L & P* VII, p. 551; *L & P* VIII, p. 15. An earlier, more intimate relationship between them is suggested on p. 32 of the *Spanish Chronicle*. Henry consulted the Council on getting rid of Anne: Friedmann II, p. 55; *Span. Cal.* V (ii), pp. 107, 108; *L & P* X, p. 330.

Anne's royal chairs and cloth-of-estate are described in *L & P* VI, 602. For her jointure, see *L & P* VII, 1204. For H's and A's entwined, see Law, *Hampton Court*, pp. 164, 179. There is a list of Anne's plate in *L & P* VIII, 44. Anne's hysterical plea to Gontier is in *L & P* VIII, p. 61. 'The young lady who was lately in the King's favour is so no longer': *ibid*, p. 104.

'She behaves like someone in a frenzy': Friedmann I, p. 285. Anne upbraided Henry for not putting Catherine and Mary to death: *Span. Cal.* V (i), p. 454; *L & P* VIII, p. 251. For the story about the soothsayer, see *Span. Cal.* V (i), p. 433; *L & P* VIII, p. 169. And for Anne's new pregnancy, see Kingston's letter, *L & P* VIII, 919.

Rochford's long session with Anne and her consequent vituperation of all things French are described in *Span. Cal.* V (i), p. 476; *L & P* VIII, p. 312. 'All business passes through the hands of people who depend on the new Queen': *L & P* VIII, 909. Anne's threat to have Cromwell's head off his shoulders is in *L & P* VIII, p. 317.

For Anne's suspicion that Norfolk was aiming at the crown, see *L & P* VIII, p. 390. For Norfolk's description of her as a 'great whore', see *Span. Cal.* V (i), p. 355; *L & P* VIII, p. 1. Fox's whispered plea to Mary to stay firm is in Prescott, p. 48. Wallop's hostility to Anne is mentioned in Friedmann I, p. 298. For the executions watched by Anne's father and brother, see *Span. Cal.* V (i), pp. 453, 474; *L & P* VIII, pp. 251, 294; Clifford, *Jane Dormer*, p. 40.

Henry would send Fisher's head to Rome for the Cardinal's hat: *Span. Cal.* V (i), p. 492; *L & P* VIII, p. 345. Henry blamed More's death on Anne, according to Clifford, *Jane Dormer*, p. 79. *Epistre*, pp. 174, 175, also claims that Anne was responsible for his death. 'You should be more bound to me than man can be to woman': *Span. Cal.* V (i), p. 454; *L & P* VIII, p. 251. Ambassadors despatched by the Pope to seek armed assistance: Friedmann II, p. 135. The feasts Anne staged to distract the King are reported in *Span. Cal.* V (i), p. 493; *L & P* VIII, p. 346.

Details of the scandals about the King and Anne's sister and mother are given in *L & P* VIII, 565, 567; *L & P* IV, p. cccxxlx. Anne was called a whore by one of the King's fools, according to Chapuis quoted in Friedmann II, p. 194. Even Northumberland had turned away from her: *Span. Cal.* V (i), pp. 354, 355; *L & P* VIII, p. 1.

Sir John Cheke's letter is in *Parker Correspondence*, pp. 2, 3. Anne's letter regarding the Merchant of Antwerp is in Ellis, *Letters*, series I, vol. 2, p. 46. The reference to 'my bishops' is in Cavendish, *Wolsey*, p. 457; *L & P* X, 797. Anne laughed at Henry's clothes and poems and declared he was impotent: *Span. Cal.* V (ii), pp. 126–8; *L & P* X, p. 378.

'Like dogs falling out of a window': *L & P* X, 357.

### CHAPTER 24: THE RIVAL

Jane Seymour's appearance and character are described in *Span. Cal*, V (ii), p. 158; *L & P* X, pp. 374, 450. Clifford, *Jane Dormer*, p. 40. states that Brian was responsible for her coming to Court. Anne is described as 'merry' in *L & P* IX, 525, 571. Her stay with Lord Sandes is mentioned in *L & P* IX, 639. For her generosity to Lord Grey, see *ibid*, p. 700.

God had sent the bad harvest to punish those who grumbled against the King's marriage: *L & P* IX, p. 251. 'I will no longer remain in the trouble, fear and suspense . . .': *L & P* IX, 776, 861; *Span. Cal.* V (i), 570.

Seymour had been Esquire to the Body in 1530: *Annals of the Seymours*. For Jane's tuition by the Imperial party, see *Span. Cal.* V (ii), pp. 85, 106; *L & P* X, pp. 245, 315. The story of Anne's finding her on the King's lap comes from Sanders, p. 132; see Clifford, *Jane Dormer*, pp. 41, 79.

Henry's avoidance of conversation with Anne is noted in Friedmann II, p. 199; *Span. Cal.* V (ii), p. 59; *L & P* X, p. 134. Friedmann II gives a detailed description of the political background to Anne's last months: the Pope Paul III quote is on p. 205; Francis's agreement to join the papal forces on p. 135. Friedmann also gives a full account of Henry's relations with Lübeck.

Catherine's refusal to step outside her Bed Chamber is in *Span. Cal.*

V (i), p. 590; *L & P* IX, 983. Anne's reaction to the news of Catherine's death and fear that Henry would discard her are reported in *Span. Cal.* V (ii), p. 28; *L & P* X, pp. 69, 172. For the gowns of yellow worn by Henry and Anne, see *Span. Cal.* V (ii), p. 19; *L & P* X, p. 51; Hall II, p. 266.

Anne urged the King to have Mary killed: *Span. Cal.* V (i), p. 573; *L & P* IX, p. 293. For Anne's messages and letters to Mary and her rude reply, see *Span. Cal.* V (ii), pp. 12, 27, 44; *L & P* X, pp. 48, 69, 117, 118. For Henry's and Anne's belief that this time she would bear a son, see *Span. Cal.* V (ii), p. 40; *L & P* X, p. 117.

The description of the joust procession is in Law, *Hampton Court*, p. 137, quoting Giustinian II, p. 101. For the King's fall, see *L & P* X, pp. 71, 172; *Span. Cal.* V (ii), p. 67. The King's words on Anne's miscarriage come from Friedmann II, p. 193. But compare *Span. Cal.* V (ii), p. 59; *L & P* X, p. 134; Sanders, p. 132; Clifford, *Jane Dormer*, p. 79; Wyatt, *Memoir*, in Cavendish, *Wolsey*, p. 444.

Anne's boast that she would soon conceive again is in *L & P* X, 352. The King's remark that he had been seduced into marriage by sorcery comes from Friedmann II, p. 203. The tragedy Henry had written is mentioned in *Span. Cal.* V (ii), p. 127; *L & P* X, p. 378. Anne's boast that they had not burned her yet is in *L & P* X, p. 381; *Span. Cal.* V (ii), p. 122.

## CHAPTER 25: MASTER SECRETARY'S PLOT

Henry left Anne at Greenwich: *Span. Cal.* V (ii), p. 59; *L & P* X, p. 134. 'The King will marry again' comes from *Span. Cal.* V (ii), p. 39; *L & P* X, p. 103. For Anne's religious ecstasy, see *Epistre*, pp. 202, 203; *Span. Cal.* V (ii), p. 127; *L & P* X, p. 378. For Rochford's religious fervour, see *Span. Cal.* V (ii), p. 91; *L & P* X, p. 290. For Anne and the Prioress of Catesby, see *L & P* X, 383, 858; Wood, *Letters* II, p. 185. Little Purkoy's death is reported in *L & P* IX, 991. A list of Princess Elizabeth's new caps is in the P.R.O., *L & P* X, 913.

For the King's gifts to Jane Seymour, see *Span. Cal.* V (ii), pp. 39, 40; *L & P* X, p. 103. Her words on refusing the purse are in Friedmann II, pp. 221, 222; *Span. Cal.* V (ii), pp. 84, 85; *L & P* X, p. 245. The little speech she was told to make to the King about Anne is in Friedmann II, p. 233; *Span. Cal.* V (ii), p. 85; *L & P* X, p. 245.

Jane's and Henry's discussion of the children they would have is in Friedmann II, p. 213; *Span. Cal.* V (ii), p. 124; *L & P* X, p. 377. Hints of Cromwell's defection are noted in Friedmann II, pp. 213, 225; *Span. Cal.* V (ii), p. 81; *L & P* X, pp. 243, 244. Cromwell's meeting with Chapuis is recorded in Friedmann II, p. 212; *Span. Cal.* V (ii), p. 54; *L & P* X, 351.

The ambassador's visit to Greenwich and Cromwell's angry exchange with the King are reported in Friedmann II, pp. 231–3; *Span. Cal.* V (ii), pp. 93, 95; *L & P* X, pp. 291, 292. Cromwell was author of the plot against Anne: *Span. Cal.* V (ii), p. 137; *L & P* X, p. 441.

'Although the King has formerly been rather fond of the ladies . . .': Friedmann II, p. 227. For Henry's plan to use the pre-contract with Northumberland as an excuse to dispose of Anne and for Northumberland's denial, see *L & P* X, 864; p. 330; *Span. Cal.* V (ii), pp. 107, 108. For the commission to inquire into treason by whomsoever committed, see Wriothesley, appendix, pp. 189–91. For the Countess of Worcester and Nan Cobham, see *L & P* X, 953.

For different versions of how Anne's alleged adultery came to light, see Merriman II, p. 12; Pocock II, p. 575; *Epistre*, pp. 179, 180.

## CHAPTER 26: MAY DAY

For the hot dry weather in April and May, see *L & P* X, 338; Cavendish, *Wolsey*, p. 454. As with all the Kingston letters regarding Anne's imprisonment, this should be compared with Strype, *Ecc. Mem.* I (i), chapter XXXVI, since Strype studied these manuscripts before they were damaged. For Anne's words to Parker about Elizabeth, see *Parker Correspondence*, p. 59; see also pp. 70, 178, 391. Anne's bestowal of trinkets on her favourites is reported in Wriothesley, appendix; *Span. Cal.* V (ii), pp. 125, 126; *L & P* X, pp. 377, 378. For her flirtatious behaviour with them as early as 1532, see *Ven. Cal.* IV, p. 365.

Anne's ageing appearance is noted in *Span. Cal.* V (ii), p. 127; *L & P* X, p. 378. Her conversation with Smeton is in *L & P* X, 798; Cavendish, *Wolsey*, pp. 454, 455. Her conversations with both Weston and Norris are in *L & P* X, 793; Cavendish, *Wolsey*, p. 452. For her conversation with Norris, see also *L & P* X, 799. Anne's argument at the window is described in *Cal. For. Pap. Eliz.* I, 1303.

For the staged dog-fight, see *Epistre*, p. 184. Smeton's arrest is described in *Memorial from George Constantyne* and in *Spanish Chronicle*, pp. 60, 61. Anne received the news that same night, according to *L & P* X, 797; Cavendish, *Wolsey*, p. 457. For a description of the May Day joust, see *Epistre*; Wriothesley, p. 35; Sanders, p. 133. For Anne's fearful wondering at Henry's sudden departure, see Hall II, p. 268. For Norris's arrest and refusal to testify, see *Memorial from George Constantyne*; *Epistre*; *L & P* X, 782, 799; *Span. Cal.* V(ii) p. 107.

For Anne's examination by members of the Privy Council, see *L & P* X, 793, 797; Cavendish, *Wolsey*, pp. 451, 452, 456.

## CHAPTER 27: THE TOWER

The names of those escorting Anne to the Tower are given in *Span. Cal.* V (ii), p. 107; *L & P* X, p. 330; Wriothesley, p. 36. There is no mention of Margaret Wyatt. Anne's entry through the Court Gate and outburst on arriving there are described by Wriothesley, p. 36, and Cavendish, *Wolsey*, p. 444.

'Mr Kingston, do you know wherefore I am here?': *L & P* X, 793; Cavendish, *Wolsey*, p. 451. Rochford's arrest is described in *Span. Cal.* V (ii), p. 107; *L & P* X, p. 330. The councillors had told Anne that Norris and Smeton had testified against her: *L & P* X, 793; Cavendish, *Wolsey*, pp. 451, 452. 'Shall I die without justice?': *ibid.* Cannon signalled the committal of a prisoner of high rank, according to *Cal. For. Pap. Eliz.* I, 1303.

For Anne's indiscreet chattering through Tuesday night, see *L & P* X, 793; Cavendish, *Wolsey*, pp. 452, 453. Only Smeton would confess: *L & P* X, 799; Ellis, *Letters*, series I, vol. 2, p. 61. 'I would have had of my own Privy Chamber which I favour most': *L & P* X, 797; Cavendish, *Wolsey*, p. 457. 'My lord my brother will die?': *L & P* X, 798; Cavendish, *Wolsey*, p. 455. For Kingston's decision to revolt in Mary's favour, see Mattingly, *Catherine of Aragon*, p. 295. The letter to Lisle refusing his request for the 'traitors' lands and offices is in *L & P* X, 952.

Cranmer's letter to Henry is in Burnet I, pp. 320–2. The story that Anne had been found in bed with her organist is in *L & P* X, 888. The *Spanish Chronicle* version of this is on p. 57. For the theory that the Protestants had instigated Anne's adultery, see *Span. Cal.* V (ii), p. 122. For the touching scene between Henry, the Duke of Richmond and Mary, see Friedmann II, p. 176. Henry stayed in his Privy Chamber or his garden: *L & P* X, 919. For his evening trips up-river to visit Jane, see *Span. Cal.* V (ii), pp. 125, 127; *L & P* X, pp. 377, 378, 385. For the fate of Page and Wyatt, see *L & P* X, 855. For the indictments found at Middlesex and Kent, see Wriothesley, appendix.

## CHAPTER 28: 'QUEEN ANNE LACK-HEAD'

The King's instructions are in Wriothesley, appendix. See *Epistre*, pp. 192, 193, for description of the commoners being marched to the hall and the turning of the axe. (The second line of p. 209 in *Epistre* should be the bottom line of p. 192.) Compare Hall I, p. 261.

For the conduct of the trials of the four commoners, of Anne and of Rochford, see Wriothesley, appendix.

Anne still had hope of life, according to *L & P* X, 890; Cavendish, *Wolsey*, p. 459. Anne's trial scene is described in Wriothesley, p. 39. The crowd numbered 2000, according to *Span. Cal.* V (ii), p. 125; *L & P* X, p. 377. For Anne's entry, see *Epistre*, p. 200; Wriothesley, p. 37. For her defence and guiltless bearing, see *Epistre*, p. 201; Wriothesley, pp. 37, 38; Friedmann II, p. 278; *Span. Cal.* V (ii), pp. 126, 127; *L & P* X, p. 378.

See *Love Letters* for the Jane Seymour ballad. Jane brought to a house near Whitehall: *Span. Cal.* V (ii), p. 129; *L & P* X, pp. 377, 379. The charges based on 'presumption and certain indications . . .': *Span. Cal.* V (ii), p. 125. For Norfolk's tears, see *Memorial from George Constantyne*. For his speech, see Wriothesley, p. 38. For Northumberland's collapse, see Wriothesley, appendix.

Anne and Rochford were not allowed to see each other, according to Wriothesley, appendix, p. 223; *Span. Cal.* V (ii), p. 126; *L & P* X, p. 378. See the last two sources for details of Rochford's trial; also *Memorial from George Constantyne*; *Cal. For. Pap. Eliz.* I, 1303; Wriothesley, p. 39. For Anne's hope that she might be sent to a nunnery, see Cavendish, *Wolsey*, p. 460; *L & P* X, 890.

'You never saw prince . . . who displayed his horns more . . .': *Span. Cal.* V (ii), p. 121; *L & P* X, p. 380. Jane receives news of Anne's condemnation: *Span. Cal.* V (ii), p. 129; *L & P* X, p. 379. For the tragedy written by the King, see Friedmann II, p. 268. Northumberland's denial of a pre-contract is in *L & P* X, 864. Anne's desire to be 'shriven' by Cranmer is in *L & P* X, 902 (this should precede 896). For a description of Anne's executioner, the fee and the money allowed Anne in prison, see *L & P* X, 902; XI, 381, in P.R.O.

Anne was forced to watch the executions of her 'lovers', according to *Span. Cal.* V (ii), p. 128; *L & P* X, p. 379. Their speeches are in *Memorial from George Constantyne*. Anne's alleged comment on Smeton's failure to exonerate her is in *Epistre*, p. 207. Anne prayed continually with her almoner: *L & P* X, 910. For Anne's complaint at having her execution put off, see *L & P* X, 910; *Span. Cal.* V (ii), p. 131; *L & P* X, p. 380. Anne's oath on taking the sacrament – see last two sources – convinced Chapuis she was innocent, a conviction altered apparently in anger when he heard of her remarks against him: *Span. Cal.* V (ii), pp. 120, 121; *L & P* X, p. 380.

All foreigners made to leave the Tower: *L & P* X, 910. 'Queen Anne Lack-head': *L & P* X, p. 453. For her guilty feelings about Mary and the scene at Anne's execution, see *Span. Cal.* V (ii), pp. 130, 131; *L & P* X, p. 380; Wriothesley, p. 41. The description of

Anne's garments comes from Friedmann II, pp. 294, 295. For different versions of Anne's speech, see Hall II, p. 268; Friedmann II, pp. 295, 296; Wriothesley, pp. 41, 42; *Epistre*, and *Memorial from George Constantyne*.

Anne removed her own headdress, according to Friedmann II, p. 296, and *Epistre*. Her eyes and lips went on moving: Strickland, p. 276. Wriothesley, p. 42, states she was buried in the choir. Henry dressed himself in white and went to visit Jane Seymour, according to Hall II, p. 269; *L & P* X, 926.

## EPILOGUE

Cromwell's letter is in Merriman II, p. 12. *Ana Bolena* as a term of opprobrium (see *Notes & Queries*, 2nd series, VI, p. 525, and 3rd series, IV, pp. 245, 404) is still to be found in dictionaries and encyclopedias. For the substitution of Jane's badges and initials for Anne's, see Law, *Hampton Court*. Neale, p. 68, describes the pageant at Queen Elizabeth's coronation. The Aless story is in *Cal. For. Pap. Eliz.* I, 1303.

# INDEX

# INDEX

If you have enjoyed this Pan book,
you may like to choose your next book from
the titles listed on the following pages

## Charles Edward Stuart  95p
David Daiches

The Life and Times of Bonnie Prince Charlie

'Brilliant . . . makes it possible to understand both the strengths and weaknesses of Bonnie Prince Charlie's expedition'
**Antonia Fraser, Sunday Times**

'Excellent . . . a deftly drawn historical background, and against it a nicely painted portrait of a boy who grew up with one single, stubborn purpose in his mind . . . That his adventure brought misery and disaster to the Highlands cannot be denied, but it gave them a story of infinite gallantry, of invincible loyalty, and to reread the story starts, yet again, sheer astonishment that the prince could do so much'
**Eric Linklater, Guardian**

'Splendidly told . . . The author brings to bear on the prince and on the events an historical imagination which is infused with a deep affection for the nation of Scotland'
**Scotsman**

# The Backgammon Book 95p
## Oswald Jacoby and John R. Crawford

'The Bible of the game'
**New York Post**

A complete, up-to-date, step-by-step guide on how to play Backgammon for love or money—and win.

Written by two world champions and illustrated with large, precise diagrams this essential guide ranges from the crucial opening moves to the finer points of the middle and end games.

Simple, clear instructions and authoritative analyses will entice the beginner and benefit the expert.

In addition to probability tables, etiquette and the official rules of the International Backgammon Association, there are chapters on the history of the game, how to run a tournament and how to play chouette (backgammon for more than two people) plus a useful glossary.

'Written by enthusiasts for enthusiasts . . . it will raise the standard of play'
**Economist**